MANAGEMENT, WORK AN̄ ORGANISATIONS

Series editors: **Gibson Burrell**, Warwick Business School
Mick Marchington, Manchester School of Management, UMIST
Paul Thompson, Department of Business Studies, University of Edinburgh

This series of new textbooks covers the areas of human resource management, employee relations, organisational behaviour and related business and management fields. Each text has been specially commissioned to be written by leading experts in a clear and accessible way. An important feature of the series is the international orientation. The titles will contain serious and challenging material, be analytical rather than prescriptive and be particularly suitable for use by students with no prior specialist knowledge.

The series will be relevant for a number of business and management courses, including MBA and post-experience courses, specialist masters and postgraduate diplomas, professional courses, and final-year undergraduate and related courses. The books will become essential reading at business and management schools worldwide.

Published:

Paul Blyton and Peter Turnbull   **The Dynamics of Employee Relations**
J. Martin Corbett   **Critical Cases in Organisational Behaviour**
Sue Ledwith and Fiona Colgan (eds)   **Women in Organisations**
Karen Legge   **Human Resource Management**
Michael Rowlinson   **Organisations and Institutions**
Harry Scarbrough (ed.)   **The Management of Expertise**

Forthcoming:

Helen Newell and John Purcell   **Business Strategy and the Management of Human Resources**
Helen Rainbird   **Training in the Workplace**
Harvie Ramsey   **Involvement at Work**
Adrian Wilkinson, Mick Marchington, Tom Redman and Ed Snape
    Total Quality Management

ORGANISATIONS AND INSTITUTIONS

Perspectives in Economics and Sociology

Michael Rowlinson

MACMILLAN
Business

First published 1997 by
MACMILLAN PRESS LTD
Houndmills, Basingstoke, Hampshire RG21 6XS
and London
Companies and representatives
throughout the world

ISBN 0–333–57858–9 hardcover
ISBN 0–333–57859–7 paperback

A catalogue record for this book is available
from the British Library.

This book is printed on paper suitable for recycling and made from fully managed and sustained forest sources.

10   9   8   7   6   5   4   3   2   1
06   05   04   03   02   01   00   99   98   97

Copy-edited and typeset by Povey–Edmondson
Okehampton and Rochdale, England

Printed in Great Britain by
Antony Rowe Ltd, Chippenham, Wiltshire

For Thara

Contents

List of figures

List of tables

Preface

This book has two aims. First, to introduce organisational economics to non-economists, primarily organisation theorists and sociologists. Second, to help economists understand the objections to organisational economics from organisation theorists and sociologists. The book takes an approach that is more familiar in sociology than economics in that it does not propose an all-encompassing synthesis. Instead it attempts to provide a framework in which to examine the extent of agreement and disagreement between organisational economics and sociologically informed organisation theory, and to locate diverse perspectives in relation to each other. A theme is that organisation theorists cannot have it both ways, criticising neoclassical economics for failing to offer any analysis of organisations on the one hand, and dismissing organisational economics as neoclassical on the other.

My own background is in sociology and organisation theory. More specifically, I see myself as part of the ongoing labour process debate which developed out of Marxist sociology in the wake of Harry Braverman's (1974) *Labor and Monopoly Capital*. The idea for this book first occurred to me when I read Alfred Chandler's (1962) *Strategy and Structure*, Ronald Coase's (1937/1993) 'The Nature of the Firm', followed by Oliver Williamson's (1983) *Markets and Hierarchies* and (1985) *The Economic Institutions of Capitalism*. I realised that the work of these authors represented a challenge to the view of organisations that I was familiar with from sociology and organisation theory. Unlike many other sociologists and organisation theorists, I believe that the work of Coase, Williamson and other economists cannot be dismissed out of hand. This book is my contribution towards developing a dialogue between organisation theory and organisational economics. My intention is to facilitate discussion across disciplinary boundaries rather than to close down debate. So, any organisation theorists hoping for a definitive demolition of organisational economics will be disappointed, as will economists anticipating a final admission of the futility of organisation theory from a sociologist.

MICHAEL ROWLINSON

Acknowledgements

I am grateful to Peter Clark and Stephen Procter for discussing this book with me endlessly. They have helped me to clarify my ideas on many occasions. The series editors, Gibson Burrell, Mike Marchington and Paul Thompson, have provided useful suggestions, and Stephen Rutt at Macmillan has been very patient and helpful. In addition, I would like to thank my friends and colleagues who have offered advice and encouragement. I hope I have not missed anyone from the following list: Andrew Brown, Trevor Buck, John Child, Graham Crow, Paul Dobson, John Hassard, Rachel Jones, Chris Smith, Paul Smith and Steve Thompson.

I have been a lecturer at three institutions during the time of writing this book: the Universities of Aston, Southampton and Nottingham. I would like to thank the students at each institution who have endured numerous versions of various chapters in the making. Of course, readers should blame me and none of the above for any shortcomings of this volume.

MICHAEL ROWLINSON

The authors and publishers would like to thank the following for permission to use copyright material: Routledge for Table 5.2 from R. J. Holton (1992) *Economy and Society*, table 4.2, p. 86; Sharpe (M. E.) Inc., USA, for Figure 3.1 from R. Swedberg, A. Etzioni and P. R. Lawrence (eds) (1991) *The Battle of Methods: Toward a Paradigm Shift?*, figure 3.1, p. 22. Every effort has been made to trace all the copyright-holders, but if any have been inadvertently over-looked the publishers will be pleased to make the necessary arrangement at the first opportunity.

Introduction and outline

Economists have increasingly become interested in some of the same issues as organisation theorists. Since economic theories of organisation have not been integrated into organisation theory, it is convenient to distinguish between organisation theory, which is informed by sociology, and organisational economics. Probably the single most important influence on organisational economics is Ronald Coase's seminal article, 'The Nature of the Firm' (1990 [1937]). Coase asks 'Why is there any organisation?' This is the first of series of rhetorical questions that have structured discussion in organisational economics. Other such questions are: 'Does organisation matter?' (Milgrom and Roberts, 1992, ch. 1); 'What is a firm?' (Chandler, 1992); 'Why not organise everything in one large firm?' (Williamson, 1985, p. 131); and 'Why are there bosses?' (Hess, 1983, ch. 7). These questions are concerned with the legitimacy of capitalist corporations. By and large, organisational economists are keen to endorse that legitimacy, but posing these rhetorical questions opens up the possibilities for wider debate. There is potential for dialogue concerning the legitimacy of the capitalist corporation, not only between mainstream organisational economics and organisation theory, but also radical organisation theory and Marxian political economy, all of which are given serious attention in this book.

Two issues that are central to the legitimacy of the capitalist corporation are work organisation and the relationship between ownership and control in corporations. These are taken up in Part 3 of the book. Four alternative perspectives on the need for divisions of labour and hierarchy are set out in Chapter 5. In Chapter 6, the perspectives outlined in Chapter 5 are related to the two major historical transformations in work organisation that feature most in historical discussions. These are: the origins of the factory system during the Industrial Revolution in Great Britain between 1780 and 1820, and the development of a new factory system in the United States of America between 1880 and 1920. Chapter 7 identifies four alternative viewpoints concerning ownership and control, and then Chapter 8 traces the major developments in the history of the modern corporation, starting with its origins in the United States during the nineteenth century, through the

1

emergence of the multidivisional structure in the US, and finally considering the implication of the multinational corporation.

Before discussing the disagreements between organisation theory and organisational economics in relation to the contentious issues of work organisation and ownership and control in corporations, it is worth considering their differences in more general terms. Herbert Simon believes that 'organization theory, economics (especially the theory of the firm), and cognitive psychology are all basically concerned with the same phenomena'. He has made substantial contributions in all three domains. However, he is rather optimistic, or even naïve, in suggesting that the main reason why there has been not been more dialogue is simply because they have 'developed in relative isolation from the other two' (Simon, 1982, p. xv). If the study of organisations has not drawn on economics to anything like the same extent as it has on psychology and sociology, that is at least in part because economics has not been much concerned with issues of organisation. Chapter 1 traces the origins of organisational economics in game theory and critiques of the orthodox neoclassical economic theory of the firm which highlight its neglect of organisational issues. Chapter 2 gives an overview of the major schools of thought in organisational economics, these being: transaction costs; agency; property rights; and evolution. The two chapters in Part 1 of this book provide an account of organisational economics that is intended to be accessible to non-economists, in particular organisation theorists and sociologists, as well as identifying some of the problems with organisational economics from the point of view of organisation theory.

Even though organisational economics is emerging as a coherent body of thought with its own textbooks (Milgrom and Roberts, 1992; Douma and Schreuder, 1991), sociology and psychology are still seen as the 'key disciplines' for the study of organisations (Wilson and Rosenfeld, 1990, p. 7) To some extent psychological and sociological approaches to organisations complement each other. This can be seen from the quasi-discipline of organisational behaviour, which is a mainstay of most business schools. Textbooks for organisational behaviour, (for example, Wilson and Rosenfeld, 1990), usually combine psychology and sociology; they are often written collaboratively by psychologists and sociologists. They generally follow what is thought to be a logical route through several levels of analysis: from the 'individual', through the 'group', to the 'organisation' and its 'environment'. The individual is the province of psychology; the group and the organisation are shared between social psychology and sociology, and the environment falls to sociology with contributions from economics where organisational behaviour shades into another business school quasi-discipline, strategic management (Moore, 1992).

Leading writers on organisations, such as Derek Pugh, conflate organisational behaviour and organisation theory (Pugh *et al.*, 1975, p. 1). However, to describe organisation theory as 'the body of thinking and writing which addresses itself to the problems of how to organize', as Pugh does (1990, p. ix), pre-empts the question of why organisations exist in the first place. It implies that there is a universal problem of organising. What is more, the problem of how to organise is often identified with the problems perceived by the managers of large capitalist corporations, as if the problems they face are the same as those facing all organisations. Radical organisation theorists in particular complain that all too often the organisational world is taken as given in organisational behaviour (Smircich, 1985, p. 62). Discussions of the legitimacy of organisations in general, or of specific forms of organisation, have been dominated by sociologists, especially radical sociologists, so much so that organisation theory can be taken to refer to the sociological approach to organisations (Donaldson, 1985; Hassard, 1993), as it is in this book.

While psychology and sociology may be complementary in their approaches to organisations, the development of organisational economics raises issues concerning the interaction between disciplines in the study of organisations, and the relationship between economics, sociology and psychology in general. Since organisational economics has something to say about the same aspects of organisations as both psychology and sociology, it cannot be compartmentalised neatly as another complementary viewpoint; it is more of a competing perspective on organisations. Inevitably, when dealing with interdisciplinary debate there is confusion over terminology, and disagreement about the boundaries between disciplines. Part 2 of this book provides a framework for understanding the differences between organisational economists and organisation theorists. First, Chapter 3 sets out the relationship between the disciplines of economics and sociology, using a series of cleavages which generally separate social theorists. Then Chapter 4 clarifies the contours of the disputes between economic and sociological theories of organisation, focusing on the relative importance of efficiency in explaining organisations, which is favoured by organisational economists, and power, which is preferred by radical organisation theorists.

The brief conclusion suggests ways in which interdisciplinary dialogue could be facilitated between organisational economics and organisation theory concerning the issues set out in Part 3. Organisational economists ought to be more reflexive in relation to their discourse. This might mean, for example, admitting that their characterisation of hierarchical work organisation as efficient is an expression of, rather than the basis for, their belief in the legitimacy of capitalist corporations. Organisation theorists should refrain from proclaiming the dawn of a new organisational era akin to the industrial or managerial revolutions. To indulge in such speculative futurology allows organisation theorists to sidestep serious consideration of existing theories, such as those found in organisational economics, which might give a genuine insight into the nature of organisational change.

PART 1

CHAPTER 1

Economics and organisation

Introduction

Organisational economics has been developed by economists who realise that for the most part economics has 'neglected to develop theories of organizations', thus leaving the study of organisations to psychology and sociology (Olson, 1971, p. 1, nt. 1). It may seem strange that economists have ignored issues of organisation, given that microeconomic analysis in neoclassical economics is virtually synonymous with the theory of the firm. It turns out that most economic theories of the firm are not theories of organisation at all. They are models that purport to explain the relationship between demand, costs and output. Economic theories of organisation have developed from two directions. First, the economists' realisation that they could apply economic modelling techniques to the general problem of organisation, and second, their awareness that the orthodox theory of the firm is inadequate as a theory of organisation. The mathematical modelling technique that is most commonly applied to issues of organisation is game theory, which is more than just a theory of the firm: it is an attempt to provide a universal theory of human groups and organisations. As for the critique of the neoclassical theory of the firm, two major theoretical challenges, the managerial and behavioural theories of the firm, can be considered as precursors of organisational economics.

Game theory

Game theory originated in mathematics. It was developed by John von Neumann, who felt that if it was to reach a wider audience than mathematicians, then it could be of most use to economists (Poundstone, 1993, ch. 3). Game theory provides a way to work out a strategy for situations that can be modelled as games. Initially, game theory focused on zero sum games; that is, games where only one player can win and the other loses, making co-operation impossible.

A simple example of a zero sum game is the cake division problem. An adult gives two greedy children a piece of cake. Knowing that neither child will believe that a grown up could cut the cake fairly, the adult lets one child cut the cake and the other child choose the piece s/he wants. The cutter knows that if s/he cuts the cake unevenly, the chooser will take the biggest slice and the cutter will end up with the smallest slice. So there is only one rational strategy for the cutter: that is, to cut the cake as evenly as possible and to end up with nearly half the cake. Game theory uses mathematics to crank out the rational solution to zero sum games that are more complicated than cake division and which involve any number of players.

Game theory is better known for the social dilemmas it has highlighted through non-zero sum games. By far the best known example is the 'prisoner's dilemma', which was first formulated in 1950 (Poundstone, 1993, ch. 6). The prisoner's dilemma is a story about two prisoners, most often known as Prisoner X and Prisoner Y (see Figure 1.1; Sen, 1982, pp. 62–5; Axelrod, 1990, pp. 7–12). Both are known to be guilty of a serious crime, but there is only enough evidence to convict them of a minor crime. The police separate the two prisoners and do not allow them to communicate. The prisoners are both given the opportunity to confess, and a confession from either will furnish sufficient evidence to convict the other prisoner of the more serious crime. They are both told that if only one of them confesses s/he will only go to prison for one year in exchange for co-operating with the police, and the one who does not confess will go to prison for twenty years. They are also told that if they both confess they will both go to prison for ten years, but if neither of them confesses, they will both go to prison for only two years convicted of the minor offence.

For a prisoner's dilemma it does not matter what the actual payoffs are, in this case the prison sentences, so long as they are ranked in such a way that each prisoner faces a dilemma. The dilemma is that each prisoner sees that it is definitely in his or her interest to confess, no matter what the other one does. If the other prisoner confesses, then either prisoner can avoid a twenty-year sentence by confessing. If the other prisoner does not confess, then by

		Prisoner Y	
		Confess	Not confess
Prisoner X	Confess	Y gets 10 years X gets 10 years	Y gets 20 years X gets 1 year
	Not confess	Y gets 1 year X gets 20 years	Y gets 2 years X gets 2 years

FIGURE 1.1   The prisoner's dilemma

confessing either prisoner can get off with only one year in prison. Each prisoner feels that no matter what the other one does it is always better to confess. Guided by rational self-interest each prisoner confesses and goes to prison for eight years longer than is necessary, which is the cost of making a 'rational choice' (Sen, 1982, p. 63). The peculiar twist of the prisoner's dilemma is that 'logical' players cut their own throats (Poundstone, 1993, p. 120).

The game can be played in a variety of different circumstances to demonstrate the possibility of different outcomes. Most notably, if the game is played over and over again each prisoner is less likely to confess because both prisoners know that if they confess in the first game they can be punished by the other prisoner confessing in the next game. However, if they both know that there will be a final game they might both confess in the first game, so as to get their revenge in first, in case the other prisoner decides to confess in the last game. What the game shows is that, collectively, both prisoners would prefer it if there was a rule of non-confession, which would mean that they would both be better off. But if it is not possible to make and enforce an agreement not to confess, then both prisoners are 'doomed to suffer the penalty of their own rational calculus' (Sen, 1982, p. 64).

Not to confess in a prisoner's dilemma is to 'co-operate' with the other prisoner, and to confess is to 'defect'. But co-operation only works if both prisoners co-operate. It is not possible for one person to gain from co-operation if the other person defects. Extending the prisoner's dilemma to situations with many players, rather than just two, gives rise to the 'free rider dilemma' (Poundstone, 1993, p. 126). In economics, the problem of free rider defection is used to discuss public goods.

Public goods are goods which, once they are produced, are available to everyone, including free riders who have not contributed towards the costs of producing them. Collectively everyone may desire that a public good is produced, but each individual may decide not to contribute towards the costs of production, knowing that even if s/he contributes there is no guarantee that everyone else will contribute. Individuals may therefore be tempted to make a rational decision to become a free rider, enjoying the benefits of a public good while everyone else incurs the costs of producing it. If there are too many free riders, then the public good will simply not be produced and everyone, including the free riders, will be worse off. This is a parallel to the prisoner's dilemma: the decision to become a free rider is equivalent to the prisoners deciding to confess.

According to Amartya Sen, an economist best known for his work on poverty and inequality, the prisoner's dilemma illustrates the problem that 'the interdependence between different people's welfare may make the pursuit of individual interests produce inferior results for all, *in terms of those very interests*' (Sen, 1982, p. 6). There is nothing new in the realisation that there can be 'conflict between individual and collective rationality . . . between individual and group interests' (Poundstone, 1993, pp. 123, 125). It played an important part in Thomas Hobbes's and Jean Jacques Rousseau's treatment of the state (Sen, 1982, p. 6), and other examples can be found in politics, philosophy and literature: 'The prisoner's dilemma has thus been "discovered", commented upon, and forgotten many times, usually without the realization that it is a universal problem' (Poundstone, 1993, p. 125; Ordeshook, 1990, p. 16). Game theory provides a more formal way of thinking about the conflict between individual rationality and social optimality than various proverbs (Sen, 1982, p. 83). As such, game theory holds a 'peculiar fascination for many social theorists' (Callinicos, 1989, p. 195), not just for mathematically-inclined economists.

The prisoner's dilemma is merely a story that was invented to illustrate a mathematical theory, but 'one problem with dramatizing the prisoner's dilemma in a story is that it brings in emotional factors that are irrelevant' (Poundstone, 1993, p. 119). When first presented with the prisoner's dilemma, many people will argue that they would not confess. This is because there is a certain amount of moral opprobrium attached to words such as confess and defect. Most people would prefer to be seen as co-operators rather than defectors.

It can be argued that the point of the prisoner's dilemma is missed if players choose to co-operate because they feel it is 'the right thing to do' (Poundstone, 1993, p. 120). Since the prison sentences are supposed to represent the full amount of any utility to be derived from the situation, in effect moral incentives amount to changes in the payoffs. It is possible to think of situations where co-operation between players in a prisoner's dilemma might not be socially desirable, such as price fixing by companies (Axelrod, 1990, p. 125), and of course, if the prisoners in the story of the dilemma are murderers it is not necessarily a good idea that they should be able to devise a strategy to minimise their sentences. Players in hypothetical games might respond differently if co-operation and defection were renamed respectively, say, collusion and self-determination.

On the other hand people's reluctance to confess may reflect a general non-confession rule which ensures that a person facing a prisoner's dilemmas does not suffer the penalty of his or her own rational choice calculus. Even if people facing a prisoner's dilemma only pretend to have moral scruples, so long as they do not defect they still end up better off (Sen, 1982). However, economists are so keen to appear to be rational that they are obsessed with the free rider problem. They generally assume, even if it is only for the sake of making an assumption, that everyone will act rationally and that defection will be the dominant strategy (Lutz and Lux, 1988, pp. 100–2).

Experiments with graduate students in America suggest that economists are more likely to be free riders than other students (Marwell and Ames, 1981). Further evidence indicates that economists do not learn to become free riders from studying economics, but that they are self-selecting free riders. This is possibly because 'self-interested calculation is a skill at which economists excel' (Carter and Irons, 1991, p. 175) It may be mere coincidence, but in the first ever game of the prisoner's dilemma one of the players was Armen Alchian, the economist, and he started out by 'expecting both players to defect' (Poundstone, 1993, p. 107).

This may be no more than some fun at the expense of economists, who cannot be trusted to contribute their fair share towards public goods. More seriously, if economists assume that people are rational, and that rational behaviour naturally leads people to become free riders, then economists' policy advice will carry an implicit assumption that free riding is a problem. This is not to say that free riding is not a problem, but that economists predict free riding 'as a matter of theoretical principle, and not as an empirical statement' (Lutz and Lux, 1988, p. 100). Thanks to the policy recommendations of economist, free riding may become a self-fulfilling prophecy (Weick, 1979, pp. 162–4).

The best-known application of game theory to organisational issues is Mancur Olson's book, *The Logic of Collective Action* (1971). He rejects psychological and sociological theories which assume that there is a 'universal joining tendency' or a "functional" explanation for the existence of organisations because they do not explain what incentives there are for individuals to join organisations (Olson, 1971, pp. 17, 110). Olson argues that organisations, such as trade unions and business associations, cannot rely on voluntary membership. Thus they have to resort to coercion, or the provision of selective incentives that are not available to non-members, in order to recruit and retain their membership. Similarly, the state is financed by coercion.

Olson draws on organisation theory, especially from Barnard and Simon, to show that social incentives can be treated in the same way as monetary incentives. But he avoids any discussion of the moral force of social incentives and concentrates on the material incentives for group action. In general, he argues, 'social pressure and social incentives operate only in groups of smaller size, in groups so small that the members can have face-to-face contact with one another' (Olson, 1971, pp. 61–2). So if the benefits of organisation are public goods, then in all but small groups coercion is necessary to ensure that free riders do not avoid contributing towards the costs of organising by not joining the organisation. Olson does not offer any analysis of corporations as coercive organisations. He has had more influence on political theory and the broadly-defined field of public choice (Ordeshook, 1990, p. 15) than on the theory of business organisations.

In *The Evolution of Cooperation* (1990), Robert Axelrod demonstrates that co-operation can emerge without coercion. He criticizes most experimental work on game theory which uses players who are unfamiliar with the prisoner's dilemma. Instead, he invited professional game theorists, including psychologists, economists, physicists, biologists, political scientists, mathematicians and computer scientists, to submit their favourite strategy for playing the prisoner's dilemma. He then organised two computer tournaments of a repeated prisoner's dilemma, in which each strategy was played against every other strategy, against itself, and against a program that randomly selected co-operation or defection. In the first tournament there were two hundred moves', in the second the games were of variable length. The winning strategy was also the simplest: it is called 'tit-for-tat', it was submitted by Anatol Rapoport, a psychologist. Tit-for-tat starts with a co-operative choice, and then does whatever the other player did on the previous move. So if the other player defects in the first move, tit-for-tat will defect in the second game, and so on.

Using tit-for-tat, Axelrod shows that for co-operation to evolve at least some social structure is necessary (Axelrod, 1990, p. 145). Co-operation is promoted among the members of an organisation when relationships are 'structured so that there are frequent and durable interactions among specific individuals' (p. 180). Axelrod believes, optimistically, that corporations are structured in this way:

> Hierarchy and organization are especially effective at concentrating the interactions between specific individuals. A bureaucracy is structured so that people specialize, and so that people working on related tasks are grouped together... By binding people together in a long-term, multi-level game, organizations increase the number and importance of future interactions, and thereby promote the emergence of cooperation among groups too large to interact individually. This in turn leads to the evolution of organizations for the handling of larger and more complex issues. (Axelrod, 1990, pp. 130–1)

An army of game theorists have extended, elaborated and modified the insights into the possibilities for co-operation in the prisoner's dilemma. These insights have been picked up by economists interested in organisation. Douglass North, an economic historian, uses game theory to argue that there are limited opportunities for co-operation to evolve along the lines described by Axelrod. Therefore, a coercive third party, namely the state, is necessary to sustain the sort of complex, impersonal exchange that is the hallmark of a modern, high-income society (North, 1990a). Summarised in game theoretic terms, his view is that:

> wealth maximizing individuals will usually find it worthwhile to cooperate with other players when play is repeated, when they possess complete information about the other players' past performances, and when there are small numbers of players. But turn the game upside down. Cooperation is difficult to sustain when the game is not repeated (or when there is an endgame), when information on the other players is lacking, and when there are large numbers of players. (North, 1991, p. 97)

It is the latter situation which most closely approximates modern industrial capitalist societies, where 'the essence of impersonal exchange is the antithesis of the condition for game theoretic cooperation' (North, 1990a, pp. 12–14;

Axelrod, 1990, p. 125; Demsetz, 1988, p. 5). It could be argued that this insight lies at the heart of organisational economics, whether or not it is derived explicitly from game theory.

Theories of the firm

Neoclassical theory of the firm

Before the mid-1960s economics had little to offer the study of organisations. As Edith Penrose explained in her seminal book, *The Theory of the Growth of the Firm*, the 'firm' in the so-called 'theory of the firm' that is commonly found in economics textbooks is not a 'firm' at all. It bears little relation to 'the innovating, multi-product, "flesh-and-blood" organizations that businessmen call firms' (Penrose, 1959, p. 13). Marschak's chapter, 'Economic Theories of Organization', in the valuable *Handbook of Organizations* (March, 1965), outlines the reasons for the neglect of organisations in the economic theory of the firm:

> The economists' theory of the firm has not been, at least until very recently, a theory of organization, for the theory ignored the fact that a firm is a group of individuals and dealt with the firm as if it were, in effect, a single person. A good theory of the firm, in this view (and, for that matter, a good theory of the household) is one which provides good predictions about interesting observable magnitudes – predictions, in particular, about aggregate behaviour in a market. The realism of the assumptions is of secondary importance; and of two theories providing equally good predictions, the simpler one is preferable, even if its assumptions are less realistic. Since the theory of the 'one-person', profit-maximizing firm was as simple as one could wish, and since it allegedly predicted well, little effort was made to suggest alternatives to it. (Marschak, 1965, p. 447)

It is clear from accounts of how the neoclassical, or marginalist, theory of the firm developed that an overriding orthodoxy emerged during the 1930s (O'Brien, 1984; Moss, 1984; Stephen, 1984a), an orthodoxy that still prevails in economics textbooks and teaching up to undergraduate level (Nelson and Sheffrin, 1991). After Adam Smith (1976[1776]), and, of course, Karl Marx (1976[1867]), any interest in the internal organisation of the firm was gradually displaced (McNulty, 1984; Moss, 1984). Instead economists concentrated on refining a model of the firm that would be able to predict the direction and magnitude of price changes which occur in response to events taking place outside the very narrowly-defined firm. For this purpose there is little need to know anything about the internal organisation of individual firms, only the conditions facing firms in general. Fritz Machlup expresses this succinctly in his robust defence of the marginalist theory of the firm: 'Frankly, I cannot quite see what great difference organizational matters are supposed to make in the firm's price reactions to changes in conditions' (Machlup, 1967, p. 13).

Firms are modelled merely as 'reactors' (Machlup, 1967, p. 8). The internal decision making process is irrelevant, and the firm is treated as if it is a single entity, a single brain. As every economics undergraduate learns: a firm under perfect competition continues to produce output until marginal cost is equal to marginal revenue. In the long run, if equilibrium is reached, the price equals the average cost of production and there are zero profits in an industry. If profits were positive or negative, firms would still be entering or leaving the industry and so it would not be in equilibrium. Marginalists reject the criticism that their model of the firm is inadequate because it is unrealistic. Realism is deemed to be superfluous if it adds nothing to the predictive powers of the model in terms of price changes.

Neoclassical theories have come to terms with the existence of monopolistic and oligopolistic situations where firms are more or less free to fix prices as they choose or in response to each others pricing strategies. Oligopoly has been a fruitful area for game theory. However, the theories of monopoly and oligopoly retain a view of the firm as essentially a unitary actor that maximises profits, so that the internal decision-making process can still be ignored.

Critics of the neoclassical theory of the firm concede that the internal logic of the perfectly competitive model is 'impeccable' (Latsis, 1972, p. 219; Lazonick, 1991, p. 95); it is only inconsistent with reality. In a difficult philosophical paper, Spiro Latsis suggests that all the major variants or models within neoclassical research, whether of monopoly or perfect competition, are characterised by *'situational determinism'*, which means that they concentrate on 'the *logic* of the agent's *situation'* and ignore 'the complexities of the *psychology of the agent* in that situation'. There is an impression that, given the overriding constraints of any situation, there is only ever one logical course of action. Latsis describes this as a *'single exit'* or *'straightjacket'* view of situations facing the firm (Latsis, 1972, pp. 207–11).

Neoclassical economics is usually criticised by organisational economists for treating the firm as an 'empty box' (Clapham, 1922, quoted by Ricketts, 1987, p. 151), or a 'production function' (Ricketts, 1987, p. 151; Milgrom and Roberts, 1990, pp. 58–9). Malcolm Sawyer, a radical economist, has given a concise summary of economic theories of the firm. According to Sawyer, in neoclassical theory, 'the firm is viewed as a "black box", with inputs being fed in and outputs emerging, and with the outputs being as large as is technically feasible (given the inputs and the state of knowledge)' (Sawyer, 1979, p. 9) If the standard economic analysis firms, as found in economics textbooks, treats the firm as a "black box" which transforms the factors of production into outputs', that is, a production function, then this means that economists have little to contribute to the study of management and organisation (Teece and Winter, 1984, p. 118).

The distinction between technical feasibility and the state of knowledge begs the question of just what technology is, if it is not the existing state of knowledge. The essential point is that the technological factors which determine the costs of a firm are 'considered to be entirely exogenous to the firm' (Moss, 1984, p. 313). Neoclassical economists are no more interested in the genesis of technology than they are in the internal management and organisation of real firms. They do not try to disentangle technology from the existing state of knowledge about how to run a firm; they simply take both as given. This allows them to assume that all firms in an industry face the same cost curves (Moss, 1984, p. 315).

Neoclassical economists revel in what they see as the 'fascinating paradox that the received theory of the firm, by and large, assumes that the firm does not exist' (Thorelli, 1965, quoted by Machlup, 1967, p. 10). So it turns out that neoclassical price theory does not really attempt to offer a theory of the firm at all: the firm is 'merely an interface between factor markets and product markets' (Stephen, 1984a, p. 4). The point is summarised by other organisational economists, Michael Jensen and William Meckling, who reckon the neoclassical economic 'theory of the firm' is 'actually a theory of markets in which firms are important actors. The firm is a "black box" operated so as to meet the relevant marginal conditions with respect to inputs and outputs, thereby maximizing profits' (Jensen and Meckling, 1986, p. 211).

Managerial theory of the firm

Neoclassical orthodoxy has been challenged on several fronts from within economics and from other disciplines. Major extensions of marginalism, as well as major alternatives to it, were refined by economists during the 1960s. These are the managerial and behavioural theories of the firm (Machlup, 1967). These two theoretical perspectives moved the theory of the firm in the direction of organisational economics.

Adolf Berle and Gardiner Means' book, *The Modern Corporation and Private Property* (1967 [1932]) posed a major challenge to the neoclassical orthodoxy. Their research suggested that a large proportion of industrial corporations in America were controlled by their managers, not the owners, and that the managers pursued objectives other than profit maximisation. The general thesis that there has been a 'managerial revolution' (Burnham, 1962) as a result of ownership being separated from the control of corporations is associated with the term 'managerialism' in both sociology and economics. Managerialism is one of the main issues that has fuelled debates in both organisational economics and organisation theory. It is discussed at length in Chapter 7 below.

Economists responded to the challenge posed by Berle and Means by refining the marginal theory of the firm to accommodate the utility preferences of managers. The leading proponents of managerial theories of the firm were William Baumol, Oliver Williamson, and Robin Marris (Sawyer, 1979, ch. 7). They regarded the assumption of profit maximisation as being inadequate because it does not take into account the competitive conditions in which a firm operates, which can allow managers to enjoy considerable discretion (Williamson, 1963, p. 238). Within a marginalist framework, managerial theories attempt to model the way in which managers will exercise their discretion. Baumol's theory centres on the proposition that managers will seek to maximise the sales revenue of their firms. Williamson gives managers more room to manoeuvre and sees the determinants of their behaviour as salary, status, power and prestige, and security, each of which he incorporates into a formal model. Marris emphasises managers' manipulation of the market valuation of their firms over the long term in order to avoid the threat of takeover. They do this by making sure that the firm's reported and retained profits are such that they are unlikely to attract a takeover bid (Sawyer, 1979).

Managerial theories of the firm within economics are a response to managerialism, but they do not necessarily endorse the managerialist thesis. If anything, they are an assertion that the neoclassical marginalist methodology is not rendered redundant by the realisation that the managers of firms in the real world enjoy discretion. In fact it makes very little difference whether discretion is enjoyed by the owners or managers of firms, since the utility preferences of either can be incorporated into the marginalist model.

Managerial theories of the firm can be characterised as 'managerial marginalism', on the grounds that their proponents 'never claimed to be anything but marginalists' and managerial theory has allowed behavioural goals to be incorporated within marginal analysis (Machlup, 1967, pp. 6, 29). Managerial theory departs from orthodox theory in so far as it does at least raise the issue of managerial motivation, whereas orthodox theory treats management as just another input that can be taken as given (Nelson and Winter, 1982, pp. 34–5). But the 'managerial motivation' theorists do not take issue with the orthodox assumption of maximisation, they merely argue that in managerial models, managers rationally maximise whatever it is that they seek to achieve, which may not merely be maximum profits. Managerial theory retains a view of the firm as a black box when it comes to technology. The production possibilities are taken as given – only management's choices between them are elaborated – and so technical progress is ignored (Sawyer, 1979, p. 103).

Behavioural theory of the firm

The theories of the firm examined so far have all assumed that economic actors are rational and that the firm can be treated as a unified entity for the purpose of predicting the behaviour of aggregated firms within an industry. The behavioural theory of the firm challenges the neoclassical theory on both of these issues and explicitly draws on organisation theory. The leading figures in the behavioural school are Herbert Simon, James March and Richard Cyert. Simon's *Administrative Behavior* (1976 [1945]), along with March and Simon's *Organisations* (1961 [1958]) are classics in organisation theory as much as, if not more than, they are in economics, while Cyert and March's *A Behavioral Theory of the Firm* (1963) gives the 'behavioural' school the title by which it is known in economics (Sawyer, 1979, ch. 8).

The behavioural theorists do not completely reject neoclassical theory, instead they focus on a different set of problems, specifically 'the internal allocation of resources and the process of setting prices and outputs.' (Cyert and March, 1963, p. 15). Whereas the neoclassical theories of the firm make behavioural assumptions in order to model aggregate changes in prices in an industry, behavioural theorists make assumptions in order to be able to model the decision-making process within individual firms. This means that they do not treat the firm as a unified entity with a single motivation, be it profit maximisation or managerial utility. This involves modelling the firm as an organisation with an internal decision-making process from which organisational goals emerge. Cyert and March make the point succinctly: 'People (i.e., individuals) have goals; collectivities of people do not' (1963, p. 26).

All marginalist theories, including the managerial theory of the firm, assume situational determinism, even in situations where there is not perfect competition (Latsis, 1972). When circumstances diverge from the perfectly competitive model, situational determinism still prevails, because firms are assumed at all times to be rationally maximizing whatever it is that gives them utility. If, in monopolistic situations, the management of a firm enjoys considerable discretion, the way in which that discretion will be exercised is a foregone conclusion, given the assumption of rational utility maximisation on the part of managers and all other actors. There is no more real discretion, in the sense of being able to exercise judgement, when oligopolistic or monopolistic firms are able to pursue objectives which diverge from profit maximization, than there is in perfectly competitive situations.

The behaviouralists explain why maximisation, whether of profit or managerial utility, is unattainable. For a start, there is the problem of defining the goals of the firm. The goals of a firm cannot be taken as given because they change according to who the participants in the firm are, and the process of bargaining between them. March and Simon (1961, p. 134) warn against an over-reliance on game theory and mathematical models for understanding bargaining and conflict in organisations. They advise that the sociological and psychological assumptions that are implicit in most bargaining situations need to be specified. Cyert and March maintain that 'Organizations resolve conflict among goals, in part, by attending to different goals at different times' (1963, p. 118).

The goals of organisations are to meet satisfactory rather than optimal standards (March and Simon, 1961, p. 140). Simon (1982, p. 296 [1959, p. 262]) contrasts economic and psychological theories of decision-making to argue that organisations 'satisfice' rather than maximise. In terms of business behaviour this means that firms do not maximize profits; instead, they seek to attain at least a satisfactory rate of profit, or to hold a satisfactory share of the market. The optimising behaviour that is assumed by marginalists would require an organisation to compare continuously all the alternative courses of action open to it in order to select the best one. Satisficing only requires an organisation to search for an alternative course of action that meets or exceeds the minimal acceptable standard. The illustration given by March and Simon is 'the difference between searching a haystack to find the *sharpest* needle in it and searching a haystack to find a needle sharp enough to sew with' (1961, p. 140).

Organisations are compelled to satisfice rather than optimise because optimising requires an unlimited capacity to process information in finding and evaluating alternative courses of action. Simon uses the term 'bounded rationality' to describe the limits on the human capacity to process information. Bounded rationality is at the heart of Simon's contribution to economics and it is also his point of departure from orthodox economics and his entry into organisation theory (Prescott, 1978). Bounded rationality affects the realm of human behaviour that is '*intendedly* rational, but only *limited* so'. Simon believes that 'human behaviour in organisations is, if not wholly rational, at least in good part *intendedly* so' (1976, p. xxviii).

Economics and statistical theory attribute to human beings virtually infinite information processing capabilities, what Simon calls a 'preposterously omniscient rationality' (1976, p. xxvii). March and Simon contrast this concept of rationality to 'a theory of rationality that takes account of the limits on the power, speed, and capacity of human cognitive faculties' (1961 [1958], p.172). Economists are reluctant to relinquish their attachment to this strong version of rationality, but from the behaviouralist point of view it makes organisation not only superfluous, it makes it impossible: 'If there were no boundaries to rationality, or if the boundaries varied in a rapid and unpredictable manner, there could be no stable organization structure' (March and Simon, 1961, p. 169). This is because organisations represent structured search routines for finding and assessing alternatives. If economic actors could know all the alternatives in advance, as well as their choices between the different alternatives, then there would be no need for any search routine in the form of organisations. Indeed, economic actors would hardly be likely to join collective organisations which satisfice if they could optimise for themselves.

The game of chess is often used to illustrate bounded rationality (Simon, 1982 [1972]). With '*perfectly logical players interested only in winning*' (Poundstone, 1993, pp. 44–51) chess would be a trivial game: White would make the first move and Black would resign. In game theory, a strategy is much more than just a plan. A strategy must be a complete description of how to play a game. If chess strategies were to be assessed as game theory strategies they would have to be submitted in advance and played against each other in a computer tournament in the same way that Axelrod compared strategies for the prisoner's dilemma. A true strategy for chess has not emerged because there are too many possibilities to be computed. It is simply not possible to specify in advance what should be done in all the possible situations that could arise in a game of chess. A best strategy for chess would be equivalent to the tit-for-tat strategy for the prisoner's dilemma. It is only because such a best strategy has not emerged that chess is still worth playing. (Computers can now beat all but the best human players at chess, but this has not ruined the game, because humans cannot memorise the computers' strategies.) By analogy, participation in organisational search routines is only worth while for economic actors who are unable to optimise because their bounded rationality prevents them from specifying a best strategy.

Some organisational economists, such as Jensen and Meckling, maintain that Simon's use of the term 'satisficing' is confusing, because it suggests rejection of maximising. They insist that Simon's work has been 'misrepresented as a denial of maximizing behavior . . . . rather than maximization subject to costs of information and of decision making' (1986, p. 211n). In fact, March and Simon (1961, p. 141) were sceptical about attempts to retain an optimising model by introducing cost of search considerations. The optimising model insists that actors know what they want but that they cannot compute all the alternative ways to get it. However, once bounded rationality is admitted it can no longer be assumed that the individual's goals are given, since aspirations themselves are subject to bounded rationality, and people tend to aspire to what is possible rather than what is optimal. Furthermore, even if their goals could be taken as given, optimising individuals would constantly have to assess the routines by which they were satisficing to ensure that they were optimising subject to computation costs, which is contradictory, because continuous assessment would require unbounded rationality. Jensen and Meckling's implicit assumption is that the search for information is subject to diminishing marginal returns, whereas the next piece of information that an individual acquired, had s/he continued searching, might have changed his or her whole perception of the situation. The nature of information is such that its significance cannot be known until it is acquired.

Conclusion

The behavioural theory of the firm is intended to apply to the most representative type of modern firm, 'the large, multi-product firm operating under uncertainty in an imperfect market' (Cyert and March, 1963, p. 115). It is worth remembering that, strictly speaking from the neoclassical perspective, a firm is equated with a production function, so it only corresponds to a single product. It is only after it is recognised that usually many product lines are combined in individual firms that issues of internal organisation can be explored. In fact, a single product line corresponding to a production function is an abstraction that can only be dealt with empirically in terms of aggregates for a national economy as a whole, such as the production function for capital and labour. Almost any departure from the pure model of markets mediating between separate production functions that constitutes the neoclassical theory of the firm comes up against the problem of providing an adequate definition of a firm as an organisation.

Unlike their orthodox neoclassical colleagues, organisational economists appear to accept that it is legitimate to ask the question, 'What is a firm?' (Chandler, 1992a) Of course, their answers differ widely. Not all of them set out game theory explicitly as their starting point for analysing organisations. North, the economic historian, believes that his economic approach to organisations and institutions is both compatible with, and an extension of, neoclassical economics. He also sees the parallels between his own approach and game theory in a positive light. He believes that game theory 'provides an excellent foil (very much like the pure neoclassical economic model) against which to compare actual performance' (North, 1990a, p. 12; 1991, p. 97). What he means by this is that game theory and neoclassical economics provide a useful starting point for research by posing the questions of whether economic actors are co-operating, or maximising their utility, and if not, why not (see McCloskey, 1990, p. 69; Giddens, 1984, p. 313). Some radical economists see the similarity with game theory as a reason to criticise organisational economics, since game theory is one more abstract mathematical modelling device beloved by economists which they can apply to all human interaction (Dugger, 1989, pp. 1–2).

There is disagreement among both the proponents and opponents of organisational economics as to whether the theories associated with it constitute a genuine departure from neoclassical orthodoxy. Some economists advocate an economic approach to organisation but claim to adhere to the basic tenets of neoclassical economics concerning maximisation. Essentially, they argue that maximising takes place subject to the inevitable costs of acquiring information by boundedly rational actors (North, 1990, p. 25), but the maximising orientation of neoclassical economics is 'unobjectionable, if all the relevant costs are recognized' (Williamson, 1985, p. 45). The costs of finding and assessing information provides a fundamental explanation for the existence of an organisation.

Other organisational economists take a more drastic view. They believe that the old theories of neoclassical economics are beyond repair, and 'the basic conceptual structure that orthodoxy provides for the interpretation of economic behavior' is merely 'excess baggage that will seriously encumber theoretical progress in the long run' (Nelson and Winter, 1982, p. 5). These economists totally reject models of the firm and organisation based on assumptions of maximising behaviour, even if some models take into account information, imperfections, costs and constraints. They argue that neoclassical economists try to 'figure out why a firm is doing something, or what it would do differently under different conditions, on the basis of an assessment of its objectives and its choice set'. This method has come to be known as a counterfactual argument; asking what would have happened if actors had been maximising their utility, or if they had had sufficient information to maximise their utility, and comparing it to what actually happened. In contrast, a more evolutionary economic approach to organisation recognises that regular and predictable patterns of behaviour in organisations is explained by routines rather than rational choice, albeit boundedly rational choice (Nelson and Winter, 1982, pp. 12–14).

There is a danger that, since neoclassical economics has ignored issues of organisation, organisational economics will be seen as a residual category that includes any vaguely economic perspective that takes organisation seriously. However, it can be said that organisational economics has emerged out of the critiques of neoclassical economics starting with Ronald Coase, and most organisational economists started out as neoclassically trained economists. So it is a matter of emphasis or preference whether organisational economics is identified with, or differentiated from, neoclassical economics. As often as not, organisational economics is associated with, or distanced from, neoclassical economics according to whether an author believes that such an association will have a positive or negative effect on the credibility of organisational economics. Unfortunately, organisational economists who identify with neoclassical orthodoxy in order to enhance the reputation of organisational economics with their colleagues in economics may well undermine the acceptance of organisational economics by organisation theorists.

CHAPTER 2

Organisational economics

Introduction

Nearly every organisational economist seems to feel compelled to give his or her own definition of the firm as an organisation. So any classification of economic theories of organisation is necessarily a simplification. Economists will probably object to it because they will see greater differences between themselves than an organisation theorist will see between them. Four concerns are set out in this chapter, from which the major economic approaches to, and definitions of, organisation are derived. These are: transaction costs; agency; property rights; and evolution. As theoretical camps they are by no means mutually exclusive. It could be argued, for example, that, implicitly or explicitly, game theory underpins more or less all economic theories of organisation. Nevertheless, these four concerns seem to correspond to schools of thought that are represented by different authors.

As a prelude to setting out the various schools of thought within organisational economics, the relationship between organisational economics and the revival of institutionalism in economics ought to be considered. In the minds of most organisation theorists, organisational economics and the new institutional economics are virtually synonymous. However, this means that organisation theorists may overlook the wider institutionalist literature in economics.

First of all, it is important to distinguish between the old and new versions of institutionalism in economics. The old institutionalism emerged in the USA during the early years of the twentieth century. Essentially, it consisted of a critique of orthodox economics for the failure to account for the existence of institutions and organisations, especially the capitalist corporation. The leading figures were Thorsten Veblen and John R. Commons. Veblen launched a 'frontal assault' on classical economic theory between 1898 and 1900 (Veblen, 1968), pointing out its failure to develop any theory of the evolutionary process by which institutions change over time. Veblen anticipated many contemporary of the contemporary concerns with the inadequacy of neoclassical economics (Seckler, 1975, pp. 1, 33) which have led to the emergence of organisational economics. But Veblen was not taken seriously by economists. As far as they were concerned he was a sociologist, and definitely 'not an economist' (Lerner, 1948, p. 10).

Commons, along with his colleagues and students at the University of Wisconsin, had an enormous influence on social policy and the development of the welfare state in the USA during the 1930s (Galbraith, 1987, p. 214). Commons was more of an 'activist' than a theorist. He was interested in real issues such as industrial disputes, rather than academic puzzles and text-books. As a result he has been picked up by contemporary (self-styled) 'radical institutionalists' (Dugger, 1989), but it is generally accepted that 'the modern successor' to the old institutionalists is John Kenneth Galbraith (Coase, 1984, p. 230; Seckler, 1975, p. 45) rather than the new institutional economists. Commons' style of writing partly explains why he has not been more widely read, but he is important for contemporary institutionalism because he attempted a comprehensive survey of economic thought in his book, *Institutional Economics* (1961).

While the old institutionalists mounted a telling methodological critique of neoclassical economics, even as it was becoming the orthodoxy in economics, they 'largely avoided any overall theoretical formulation' of their own (Galbraith, 1958, p. 40n). In the best overall survey of contemporary institu-tionalism, *Economic Behavior and Institutions*, Thrainn Eggertsson reckons that, 'The critical issue for institutional economics is to rise above methodological criticism' (Eggertsson, 1990, p. 10). Contemporary institutionalism in econom-ics could be thought of as the body of theory developed by neoclassically trained economists which counters the critique of economics from the old institutionalists.

Eggertsson identifies two broad strands within contemporary economic institutionalism. These he terms, somewhat confusingly, 'neoinstitutional economics' and the 'new institutional economics'. Neoinstitutional economics, which is Eggertsson's prime focus, is more closely linked to traditional microeconomics. Roughly speaking, neoinstitutional economics uses more narrowly-defined concepts to analyse a broader range of phenomena, such as the emergence of markets, property rights and the state, and the differences in economic performance between capitalist states, and between capitalist and non-capitalist institutions. These are the concerns of economic historians, most notably North (1990), who aligns himself with neoclassical economics, pre-sumably in order to differentiate his work from the atheoretical empirical research carried out by the earlier institutionalists.

What Eggertsson calls the new institutional economics rejects 'elements of the hard core of neoclassical economics, such as the rational-choice model' (1990, p. 6). This means that the implications of the behavioral theory of the firm concerning bounded rationality and satisficing are accorded more importance. The new institutional economics focuses on a narrower range of economic phenomena, primarily capitalist firms, but relaxes the assumptions of neoclassical economic theory to a greater extent than neoinstitutional economics. Although there is not a clear-cut distinction between neoinstitutional economics and the new institutional economics, it could be said that neoinstitutional economics is more concerned with the emergence of societal institutions within which organisations operate, whereas the new institutional economics focuses on the forms that organisations take within given societal institutions. The new institutional economics, as defined by Eggertsson, is more akin to what is termed in this book, organisational economics. However, the broader neoinstitutionalist literature needs to be referred to, especially since one of the criticisms of organisational economics is that it fails to give adequate attention to the institutional context within which specific forms of organisation exist.

Transaction costs

The neoclassical view of firms is that they are single production functions corresponding to separate activities which are co-ordinated by market exchanges. But the single product firm is a theoretical fiction, because virtually all firms in the real world carry out more than one activity. A genuine single-product firm would consist of only one activity, which would mean that it would be comprised of only one production function. The interface between each production function would be a market exchange between separate firms. If this were the case there would be no organisation within firms. In fact, much of the co-ordination between separate activities takes place within firms, and it is this co-ordination that is a defining characteristic of firms as they really exist. This is the starting point for transaction cost economics, which seeks to explain why some interfaces between separate activities occur within firms while others take place across market exchanges.

It was Commons who first suggested that the ultimate unit of economic investigation should be the transaction. Commons' typically opaque term for a transaction is 'a unit of transfer of legal control' (1961, p. 4; 1951). According to Commons, a 'going concern' is constituted to carry out collective action when the ownership of individual units is transferred through 'bargaining transactions' between willing buyers and sellers (1961, p. 59). Following a bargaining transaction there is a 'managerial transaction', when the physical control of a unit is actually transferred.

Coase was probably unaware of American institutionalism when (in 1932) he was formulating the ideas for his famous article, 'The Nature of the Firm' (1993a, p. 34). Even though the term 'transaction costs' does not appear in Coase's original paper (Coase, 1990b; Hodgson, 1988, p. 299n), transaction cost economics owes more to Coase than to Commons. Although some organisational economists, notably Williamson (1983, 1993), generously and consistently cite Commons' institutional economics as an antecedent of organisational economics, it might be fairer to say that Commons has been rediscovered in the light of new institutional economics, by both its adherents and its critics. He anticipated the focus of the new institutionalists, in particular the transaction as the unit of analysis, but not their methodology.

Coase realised that if production really was regulated by the price mechanism, firms would not exist and production could be carried out without any organisation whatsoever. This led him to pose the question, 'Why is there any organisation?' He rejects the view that firms are analogous to state planning which is imposed on industry because firms arise voluntarily. Coase assumes that 'the distinguishing mark of the firm is the supersession of the price mechanism' (1990b, p. 36) He argues that there must be a cost of using the price mechanism for co-ordination, so that it can be profitable to carry out co-ordination within a firm.

The costs of using the price mechanism include discovering the relevant prices of products as well as 'The costs of negotiating and concluding a separate contract for each exchange transaction which takes place in a market'. A firm is created when the owners of the factors of production make a contract whereby they 'agree to obey the instructions of an entrepreneur *within certain limits'*, instead of having to make a series of contracts with each other. According to Coase a firm is more likely to arise when a long-term contract is both possible and desirable (1990b, pp. 38–40).

In Coase's view, it must be possible to analyse the determinants of the size of the firm. Having established that firms exist because they can reduce or eliminate the costs of making transactions in the market, Coase asks, 'Why . . . are there any market transactions at all? Why is not all production carried out by one big firm?' (1990b, p. 43). In answering this question, Coase invokes the neoclassical concepts of marginalism and equilibrium. He maintains that firms will experience 'diminishing returns to management', so that 'a point must be reached where the costs of organizing an extra transaction within the firm are equal to the costs involved in carrying out the transaction in the open market, or, to the costs of organizing by another entrepreneur' (1990b, pp. 44–5).

Given the diversity of transactions, the sizes of firms will vary throughout the economy. The sizes of firms will be limited by factors such as the spatial distribution and dissimilarities between transactions, and the probability of price changes for factors of production. Coase briefly discusses the effect of technological change such as the telephone. On the one hand, the telephone could increase the size of the firm by improving managerial technique, but on the other it could reduce the size of the firm by lessening the costs of market transactions.

As Coase himself has noted, up to the 1970s 'The Nature of the Firm' 'had little or no influence'; it was 'much cited and little used' (1993b, p. 61). Coase accepts that one reason why his article was not more widely used before the 1970s was because he had failed to make the issues 'operational'. That is,

Coase did not specify the circumstances under which transactions were most likely to be economised by firms or markets. Subsequently, transaction costs have been operationalised within at least three fairly separate camps. First there is Williamson's 'markets and hierarchies' perspective (1983, 1985), which has become almost synonymous with the new institutional economics, or organisational economics, especially in the eyes of organisation theorists and sociologists (Francis *et al.*, 1983). Second, there is the approach originated by Steven Cheung (1974, 1983), corresponding to Eggertsson's neoinstitutional economics (1990, pp. 6–8), which emanates from the University of Washington (North, 1990a, p. 27). Finally there is the transaction cost explanation for the existence of the multinational enterprise (Hennart, 1991).

Williamson's markets and hierarchies perspective started with a consideration of vertical integration of production and the question of whether firms should make or buy their inputs (1986b, ch. 6). From the outset, Williamson was suspicious of explanations for vertical integration that rely on 'technological interdependency' or monopoly. He believes there are very few activities that are so technologically inseparable that they have to be joined together within the same firm. On the other hand, this does not mean that the only reason for vertical integration within firms is to reap monopoly profits. Williamson goes on to develop a framework within which vertical integration can be explained without invoking technological or monopoly factors.

Essentially, what Williamson has done is to combine the behavioural assumptions from Simon's behavioural theory with Coase's insights to explain the causes of transaction costs and why transactions occur within markets or firms. The behavioural assumptions are bounded rationality and opportunism. Like Simon, Williamson believes that rationality is a common theme throughout social science, but that economists are the only social scientists who assume 'hyperrationality' (Williamson and Ouchi, 1981, p. 350). Williamson contends that his assumptions are closer to 'human nature as we know it' (1983, p. ix; 1985, p. xiii). He never explains how it is possible for boundedly rational actors to know for sure what constitutes their own nature. It would appear to be inherent in the human condition that human beings cannot know what their own nature is. Of course, economists, such as Williamson, are by no means the only social theorists who are impertinent enough to claim omniscience when it comes to human nature.

What Williamson means by 'opportunism' goes beyond the assumption of self-seeking which prevails in conventional microeconomics (1983, p. 7). Opportunism allows for '*strategic* behavior' involving 'self-interest seeking with guile' (Williamson, 1983, p. 26). It 'includes, but is scarcely limited to more blatant forms, such as lying, stealing, and cheating. Opportunism more often involves subtle forms of deceit. . . . More generally, opportunism refers to the incomplete or distorted disclosure of information, especially to calculated efforts to mislead, distort, disguise, obfuscate, or otherwise confuse' (Williamson, 1985, p. 47). Without opportunism, 'all behavior could be rule governed', because any unanticipated events could be dealt with by general rules. The problem of enforcing contracts would be overcome if every contract contained a clause which said:

> I agree candidly to disclose all relevant information and thereafter to propose and cooperate in joint profit maximization courses of action during the contract execution interval, the benefits of which gains will be divided without dispute according to the sharing ratio herein provided. (Williamson, 1985, p. 48)

The problem of opportunism means that parties to an agreement need to give and receive 'credible commitments'. These are commitments which are at once both believable and binding, and therefore not entered into lightly.

Williamson's apparently jaundiced view of human actors as inherently prone to lie, cheat, steal, embezzle or shirk is distasteful to many sociologists, and especially radical sociologists who object to Williamson's obsession with portraying workers as having such tendencies. Unfortunately this detracts from the insights to be gained from the assumption of opportunism, namely the difficulty of making and keeping to commitments. People making commitments they cannot meet may be deceiving themselves as much as others. In some instances, unforeseen altruism rather than opportunism may just as well result in an unexpected outcome.

If bounded rationality and opportunism are assumed, then transaction costs will be affected by environmental factors; Williamson (1985, p. 52) categorises these as asset specificity, uncertainty and frequency. Asset specificity occurs when an investment is made for a specific rather than a general purpose. Once an investment is made for a specific purpose, that is, in relation to a particular transaction, then the asset cannot easily be used for another purpose, that is, for another transaction. Examples of asset specificity are the location of assets and the skills acquired to carry out particular activities. The decision as to whether to make specific or general-purpose investments does not only depend on the prospective cost savings that might follow from a transaction-specific investment, there is also the issue of the contractual and organisational safeguards available for investments that are asset specific. If there are no safeguards then it is unlikely that any investments will be made for specific purposes. One form of safeguard may be internal organisation, so that transactions involving asset-specific investments take place within one firm.

Not being able to know in advance what people will do in different situations is the most important source of uncertainty, and it results in part from bounded rationality and opportunism. Behavioural uncertainty is more important than the uncertainty that arises from random acts of nature because it is people's reactions to unforeseen events that is not only unpredictable but also likely to be significant. People make strategic plans about how they will react to other people in various circumstances, but they either cannot or will not disclose all their possible reactions to future situations. As Williamson says, 'The capacity for novelty in the human mind is rich beyond imagination' (1985, p. 58).

When there is certainty, transactions are relatively uninteresting and it is does not really matter whether they take place in markets or firms (Williamson, 1986b, p. 117). But as uncertainty increases, the framework within which transactions take place can become crucial if asset-specific investments are at stake. The problem facing contracting parties is whether they can find a way to govern their transactions so as to reduce uncertainty. If the transactions between two parties are only occasional, then they may devise some sort of procedure for arbitration should any problems arise. These are the contracts which are drawn up for transactions in the market. As the frequency of transactions increases it becomes more likely that the parties will unify and that they will become vertically integrated within a single firm. Of course, if uncertainty subsequently decreases (for example, as an industry matures) then the disintegration of a firm may ensue. To some extent it is this expectation that under certain circumstances firms will decompose of their own accord that distinguishes transaction cost economics from much of organisation theory and neoclassical economics, because if organisation and integration only ever resulted from the pursuit of power or monopoly profits, voluntary disintegration on the part of firms would be most unlikely to occur.

Even economists complain that 'if you can't understand it, it must be transactions costs' (Winship and Rosen, 1988a, p. 8), and critics allege that 'Williamson has failed to provide an adequate definition of transaction costs' (Hodgson, 1988, p. 200; Kay, 1993, p. 245; Niemark and Tinker, 1987, p. 668; Perrow, 1981, p. 375). Williamson uses a mechanical metaphor to define transaction costs:

> A transaction occurs when a good or service is transferred across a technologically separable interface. One stage of activity terminates and another begins. With a well-working interface, as with a well-working machine, these transfers occur smoothly. In mechanical systems we look for frictions: do the gears mesh, are the parts lubricated, is there needless slippage or other loss of energy? The economic counterpart of friction is transaction cost: do the parties to the exchange operate harmoniously, or are there frequent breakdowns, and other malfunctions? (1981, p. 552)

According to Williamson, transactions take place in markets or in firms according to which causes least friction.

While Williamson clearly rejects technological determinism in terms of technological inseparability determining the size of firms (1985, pp. 86–90), his definition of a transaction is problematic because he takes technologically separable interfaces as given (Dietrich, 1993, p. 166). However, it is important to recognise that technological separability is the outcome of social processes, especially when it comes to work organisation (Neimark and Tinker, 1987, pp. 668–9). The only technologically separable interface that can be said to be given is between corporeal human beings. But not all transactions are synonymous with transfers between people. A transaction may occur when one person transfers from one activity to another, depending on whether the two activities are seen as separable. They are more likely to be seen as separable activities if in other circumstances the two activities have been separated and carried out by different people.

In a detailed critique, Neil Kay (1993) argues that Williamson conflates two definitions of a transaction. The first is a 'contractual or exchange based' version of transaction costs that is consistent with Commons, which is quite a different interpretation from the second definition of a transaction as a transfer across a technologically separable interface (Kay, 1993, p. 245). It is difficult to see how in the second version transaction costs can be differentiated from the physical delivery costs incurred in transfers between one activity and another (Hodgson, 1993, p. 82). Since physical delivery produces 'place' and 'time' utility (Commons, 1951, p. 84), it is difficult to distinguish these transaction costs from any other costs of production.

Other institutional economists – those described by Eggertsson as neoinstitutional – admit that, 'a clear cut definition of transaction costs does not exist'. However, Eggertsson goes on to say that, 'In general terms transaction costs are the costs that arise when individuals exchange ownership rights to economic assets and enforce their exclusive rights' (1990, p. 14). Using this definition, North makes a distinction within the total costs of production between transformation costs, consisting of 'the resource inputs of land, labor and capital involved . . . in transforming the physical attributes of a good (size, weight, location, chemical composition and so forth)', and the costs of transacting, which include 'defining, protecting, and enforcing the property rights to goods (the right to use, the right to derive income from the use of, the right to exclude, and the right to exchange)' (1990, p. 28).

It is clear that in the neoinstitutional approach (Cheung, 1983; North, 1990) transaction costs increase with complexity and the division of labour. But this does not entail technological determinism as long as it is acknowledged that transaction costs, transformation costs, and the institutional framework are interdependent (North, 1990, p. 65). For example, the choice of technique and the technological separation of activities is affected by the institutional framework and transaction costs. This leads the neoinstitutionalists into a historical analysis of institutions, whereas Williamson tends to take technology and the institutional framework as given in order to focus on the effects of transaction costs on the size and organisational form of capitalist firms.

Agency

Agency relationships exist in any situation where one actor, the principal, depends on the action of another actor, the agent. If potential readers can be thought of as principals, with authors as their agents, then John Pratt and Richard Zeckhauser fulfil their role as agents for their readers by providing a good overview of agency theory (1985, p. 2). The agency problem arises when the principal tries to ensure that the agent behaves in ways that are consistent with the principal's interests (Putterman, 1986a, p. 3). The terminology has been borrowed from law, although typically lawyers tend to have a tighter definition of the terms 'principal' and 'agent' (Clark, 1985) than is found in the economic literature on agency (Arrow, 1985, p. 37).

It must be obvious that the agency relationship is all-pervasive – it is not confined to economic life but is found in practically all human interactions. A useful starting point for understanding the agency problem is the saying, 'If you want a job done properly, then do it yourself' (Sappington, 1991, p. 45; Ricketts, 1987, p. 116). An agent is unlikely to carry out any activity on behalf of the principal in exactly the same way that the principal would have carried out the activity for him- or herself. This is because the interests of principals and agents are rarely identical. This means that in all sorts of principal–agent relationships:

> Parties cannot always count on getting precisely what they bargained for, be they employer–employee, franchisor–franchisee, steel producer–fabricator, or even husband–wife. Indeed it *always* pays for a party not to perform its part of an agreement if that non-performance does not decrease the probability that the other parties will fulfil their obligations and if it suffers no loss. (Goldberg, 1980, p. 253)

Agency theorists (Pratt and Zeckhauser, 1985) argue that conventional microeconomic price theory is predicated on an unstated assumption that agents always fulfil the agreements they make with principals. This limits the applicability of price theory because it ignores the ubiquitous agency loss, or agency costs, that arise from having to ensure that agents do, in fact, act in the interests of principals. According to agency theorists, organisation arises as one way of ensuring that agents act in the interests of principals. But if every agent understands and agrees to carry out precisely everything s/he agrees to do for a principal there would not be an agency problem, and there would be no need for any arrangements such as organisation to minimise agency costs.

Before turning to agency in relation to organisation it is worth elaborating on the agency problem and its relation to game theory and transaction costs. The most obvious way to overcome the agency problem is to secure a strong alignment of the principal's and agent's objectives (Pratt and Zeckhauser, 1985, pp. 14–15). This is most likely to happen when principals and agents perceive their interests to be more or less identical, and would mean that an agent could be relied upon to act in the principal's interests without any instructions from the principal. Ideally, this would come about if an agent could ask him/herself what s/he would expect from an agent were s/he in the position of the principal, and then act accordingly. Were this possible, it would reinforce the centrality that 'the norm of reciprocity' enjoys in both transaction cost economics (Williamson, 1985, p. 152) and game theory.

Ethical injunctions to reciprocate from religion and philosophy are a favourite source of illustration for writers trying to make game theory accessible (Poundstone, 1993, p. 123). Avinash Dixit and Barry Nalebuff liken the tit-for-tat strategy for the prisoner's dilemma to the 'eye for an eye' rule of behaviour. They go on to argue that if everyone followed the golden rule from the New Testament, 'Do unto others as you would have them do unto you', instead of the Old Testament tit-for-tat strategy of 'Do unto others as they have done unto you', then 'there would be no prisoner's dilemma' because everyone would co-operate unquestioningly (Dixit and Nalebuff, 1991, p. 106n). But in one of the lectures collected in Kenneth Arrow's influential little book, *The Limits of Organization*, he notes that 'the incommensurability and incomplete communicability of human wants and values' (Arrow, 1974, p. 24) makes absolute reciprocation impossible. He quotes George Bernard Shaw to reinforce the point: 'Do not do unto others as you would have that they do unto you. They may have different tastes.' This means that unlike the prisoner's dilemma, where it is assumed that both prisoners have full information, so that they both know precisely what the possible payoffs are for themselves and the other prisoner, the agency problem does not disappear even if everyone reciprocates.

While the agency problem does not disappear even where there is an alignment of principals' and agents' perceived interests, agency theorists are more interested in situations where the principal and agent have divergent interests, and where the agency problem is exacerbated by other factors (Pratt and Zeckhauser, 1985). Apart from the alignment of objectives, agency structures have two major devices for overcoming the agency problem: monitoring and incentives. Obviously there is a relationship and a potential for trade-offs between the two. A principal who does not offer any incentives to an agent may have to rely on excessive monitoring to ensure that the agent acts in the principal's best interests.

The design of agency structures using incentives and monitoring is problematic because it is rarely the prerogative of an individual principal or agent to design such structures. In analysing agency relationships it is often difficult to decide which party is the principal and which the agent, and in all but the most simple market transactions it is likely that both parties will be both principal and agent with regard to different interests and activities. Furthermore, there are likely to be multiple principals and agents in many agency relationships, each with heterogeneous interests.

James Coleman, the leading mathematical sociologist, suggests that:

> A natural person encompasses two selves, object self and acting self, or principal and agent, in one physical corpus. A minimal corporate actor is created when principal and agent are two different persons. With this same minimal structure, the principal

may be a corporate actor, or the agent may be a corporate actor, or both may be corporate actors (as when a corporation owns another corporation). The most extensively developed corporate actor is one with multiple principals, constituting the object self, and multiple agents, constituting the acting self. This is the way a publicly owned corporation is conceived of in modern society. (1990, p. 421)

Principals have the problem of articulating their interests and constructing the agency structure so as to take account of the different types of agent. Agents have the problem of identifying their principals and reconciling the often contradictory interests of multiple principals.

Perhaps the best example of the difficulties of identifying and satisfying multiple, heterogeneous principals and agents is the relationship between the electorate and an elected government (Pratt and Zeckhauser, 1985, pp. 22–4; North, 1990b, p. 190). Similarly, as agents, corporate managers have difficulty in identifying their principals, and the principals' interests are certainly weighted differently. Pride of place is given to the shareholders in most analyses by agency theorists, but arguably this only reflects the effectiveness of the agency structures constructed to safeguard shareholders' interests, which make shareholders appear as the most salient principals to their agents. Ultimately, the agency problem must be all-encompassing, with everyone who is interconnected in any way being simultaneously both principal and agent with respect to everyone else who is, was, or might be affected by their actions.

As with transaction costs, the neoinstitutional approach to the agency problem is more restrictive and relates agency to property rights. Eggertsson notes that although agency theory does apply to all forms of exchange, it is most commonly used to analyse hierarchical relationships where: 'An *agency relationship* is established when a principal delegates some rights – for example, user rights over a resource – to an agent who is bound by a (formal or informal) contract to represent the principal's interests in return for payment of some kind' (1990, pp. 40–1).

A predominant concern of agency theorists is therefore finance and the firm (Fama, 1986; Jensen and Meckling, 1986; Grossman and Hart, 1983), because the separation of ownership from control of corporations gives rise to an agency relationship between the owners and managers of corporations that is susceptible to analysis by agency theory. But within a hierarchical structure, where 'rights are transferred down the organizational ladder', individuals at all levels are simultaneously both principals and agents in relation to other members of the hierarchy (Eggertsson, 1990, p. 41). This means that the employment relationship is also amenable to analysis by agency theory (Ricketts, 1987, pp. 137–43). The relationship between monitoring and incentives is of vital interest to both managers and managed within hierarchical firms since it will affect the relationship between the number of managers required for monitoring and the effort expended by workers.

Michael Jensen has concentrated on the relationship between agency theory and accounting, and the importance of accounting practices for the form that organisations take. He notes that there are two, almost entirely separate, agency literatures: 'the principal–agent literature is generally mathematical and non-empirically oriented, while the positive agency literature [in which Jensen locates his own work] is generally non-mathematical and empirically oriented' (1983, p. 334). The principal–agent literature represents a return to neoclassicism. It concentrates on refining predictive models of optimal incentives which only take account of a few variables, while the positive agency literature incorporates 'richer specifications' in order to gain a closer understanding of observed phenomena (Jensen, 1983, p. 335). While it is quite possible to contribute to both literatures (Pratt and Zeckhauser, 1985, p. 215, n. 5), it is the positive agency literature that is closest to an institutional perspective (Eggertsson, 1990, p. 42; Jensen, 1983, p. 334n; see Kreps, 1990, p. 91) that is the subject of this book.

Property rights

Property rights can be defined as 'the rights of individuals to use resources' (Eggertsson, 1990, p. 33). As with the terms 'principal' and 'agency', the meaning of property rights in the economic literature is much wider than legal concepts; for one thing, it includes social norms. The modern approach to property rights in economics owes most to Ronald Coase and a series of articles by Harold Demsetz on what he calls 'the economics of ownership' (1988, p. 12). The theme of 'The Problem of Social Cost', Coase's second seminal article, is that 'problems of law and economics are interrelated' (Coase, 1990d, [1960] p. 147), and the study of property rights is also known as the subject of 'law and economics'. Coase was the editor of the *Journal of Law and Economics* for nineteen years until 1983.

Coase uses the issue of the benefits and harms resulting from various activities, specifically the nuisance caused by neighbours, to illustrate the difficulty of delimiting legal rights. If one party is a nuisance to another party: say, if one occupant of an office makes so much noise when working that s/he interferes with the other occupant's work, then ideally the two occupants of the office should be able to reach an agreement. They may agree to build a partition, so long as the extra work they are both able to do once it is built more than covers the cost of building it; or the noisy occupant may compensate the other occupant for the work that s/he prevents him or her doing; or else the other occupant may pay the noisy occupant to stop working. Whatever they decide to do will depend on how much it is worth to either of them to be able to carry on working. Assuming that such an agreement can be reached easily, neither party need be blamed for making the noise or for not putting up with it, because if the office space is to be used efficiently, then it is 'desirable that both parties should take the harmful effect (the nuisance) into account in deciding on their course of action' (Coase, 1990a, p. 112).

To assume that parties can easily reach an agreement in the market (say, that one occupant will pay for a partition to be built and the other occupant will contribute towards the cost) would mean that the situation is unaffected by the 'initial delimitation of rights' – that is, whose office it was in the first place. Of course, as Coase says, and as must be obvious to anyone who has ever shared an office, this is 'a very unrealistic assumption' (1990d, p. 114), but it is an assumption that is implicit in orthodox neoclassical economics. So whether or not a partition will be built does not only depend on the relative prices of building the partition and the output of the two occupants of the office, it will also be affected by the cost of reaching an agreement to build the partition, and this in turn is affected by the initial assignment of rights: that is, who the office belongs to. Thus the costs of assigning and reassigning the right to use the office, which is a transfer of the property rights to the office, are affected by the costs of reaching and enforcing any agreement over the use of the office – these are the transaction costs.

Coase (1990d) cites numerous examples where it would be difficult to reach an agreement in the market to reassign the rights to use a resource. He then uses these as the basis for a critique of mainstream economics on two fronts. First, he argues that it is a mistake to think that the problems associated with the assignment of property rights are limited to the benefits and harms of very specific activities, for example, so-called public goods, where it is allegedly intrinsic to the goods themselves that it is difficult to restrict access to the benefits, or where it is difficult to identify the causes of a nuisance, or to make those whose decision caused the nuisance pay for the harmful effects. Within mainstream economics these are seen as instances of market failure that call for government regulation of some sort. Coase is generally wary of government regulation of any kind. He argues that government regulation also incurs costs: for example, the costs incurred in collecting taxes to pay for public goods or in monitoring the harmful effects caused by particular uses of resources. Furthermore, government regulation is liable to distortion from 'political pressures' (1990d, p. 118).

Coase's point about public goods is illuminated by his article, 'The Lighthouse in Economics' (1990e). Economists, he says, regularly 'use the lighthouse as an example of a service which could only be provided by the government'. But this is not based on any historical studies of the provision of lighthouses. Coase gives a brief history of lighthouse provision in Britain and shows that in the seventeenth century lighthouses were 'built, operated, financed, and owned by private individuals'. They were paid for by tolls levied on ships calling at nearby ports, which were presumed to have benefited from the lighthouse. Private individuals were able to do this by being granted authority to do so by the Crown, which is an assignment of property rights. Later the provision of lighthouses was taken over by the government and entrusted to Trinity House, 'a private organization with public duties, but the service continued to be financed by tolls levied on ships' (Coase, 1990e, pp. 212–13). According to Coase, this shows that a diversity of arrangements is possible for the provision of all goods and that the alternative selected is likely to depend on the assignment of property rights, in this case the right to collect a toll.

Lest it be thought that Coase is simply an apologist for *laissez-faire* economic policies, as he is sometimes portrayed (Lutz and Lux, 1988, pp. 183–5), it is important to bring in the second part of his critique of mainstream economics. In a state of *laissez-faire* there would be no need for a monetary, legal or political system, because factors of production would naturally flow to 'the places where the value of the product yielded was greatest without any use of the pricing system' (Coase, 1990d, p. 150). This means that it is a contradiction to speak of prices in a situation that is akin to perfect competition. Prices arise as one way to facilitate making agreements about the best use of resources. When a resource is exchanged in a market, a price is paid in order to acquire the rights to use that resource for particular purposes, to be able to create certain harmful effects with impunity, and to enjoy the exclusive benefits from using the resource. But these rights are necessarily constrained as soon as they are defined.

Commons (1961) argued that classical and neoclassical economics effectively eliminates issues of ownership by identifying ownership with materials and ignoring the problem of ensuring that transactions which transfer of ownership are matched by transfers of control. One reason why the importance of ownership and property rights has been overlooked by mainstream economists is that, according to Coase, factors of production are usually thought of as physical entities, instead of rights to perform certain (physical) actions: 'If factors of production are thought of as rights, it becomes easier to understand that the right to do something which has a harmful effect (such as the creation of smoke, noise, smells, etc.) is also a factor of production' (Coase, 1990d, p. 155).

Unfortunately, the tendency for economists to think of factors of production as physical entities rather than '*bundles of rights*' (Eggertsson, 1990, p. 103) is so strong that even those who are sympathetic to Coase have misunderstood his argument (Coase, 1990f, p. 159). The best illustration of this is the formulation of the so-called 'Coase theorem' by George Stigler. Instead of taking on board the problem of defining property rights, Stigler formulated the 'Coase theorem' to show that, in the absence of transaction costs, the initial assignment of property rights does not matter because resources will always find their way to the most efficient use, and the distribution of wealth will bear no relation to ownership. The law would merely identify the person with whom it would be necessary to make a contract in order to use a resource, and since there would be no costs involved in making a contract with that person it would not matter who it was that 'owned' the resource in the first place.

Coase's point was that such a situation is so unrealistic there is not much point in discussing it: 'A better approach would be to start our analysis with a situation approximating that which generally exists' (1990d, p. 154). The extent of the misunderstanding of Coase is such that, as he says himself, 'The world of zero transaction costs has often been described as a Coasian world. Nothing could be further from the truth. It is the world of modern economic theory, one which I was hoping to persuade economists to leave' (1990f, p. 174).

Whereas most of the debate within economics has been concerned with refining a model without transaction costs, the misleadingly named Coase theorem, Demsetz has tried to elaborate on the importance of property rights. He maintains that 'the essence of effective regulation is to truncate the bundle of rights that defines ownership' (Demsetz, 1988, p. 12). Possibly the most important truncation of the bundle of ownership rights occurs in order that they can be reassigned over time. This is because, if ownership is to be transferred, it needs to be defined. The less well defined ownership rights are, the more difficult it will be to set a price for them and to transfer ownership. Ownership rights are necessarily restricted by being defined. That is, they specify the person or persons entitled to exercise ownership rights, and they are likely to restrict the uses to which those persons can put the resources which they own. Demsetz believes that, since ownership always exists in one form or another, it is worthwhile examining 'the sources of change in the bundle of rights that define ownership' (1988, p. 20); that is, to endogenise ownership rather than take it as exogenously determined, as is done in mainstream economics.

Although the basis of the bundle of rights that define ownership is determined by a broad 'set of considerations related to the history, religion, and culture of societies', Demsetz believes that the direction of change is determined by the costs and benefits of change (1988, p. 23). Specifically, as the competing uses to which a resource can be put increase, the more productive it becomes to specify full ownership rights; or, to put it another way, 'Other things being equal, property rights tend to be made more precise as resource values rise' (Libecap, 1986, p. 231). This conveniently allows any questions of the relationship between property rights and the wider society to be sidestepped.

The specification of property rights allows particular individuals to decide, within certain limits, how resources will be used. By determining how the benefits and harms will be allocated between the decision maker and other individuals, property rights allow individuals to develop expectations about the effects of their dealings with other individuals. Furthermore, the specification of property rights means that 'different individuals concurrently may hold different rights to the use of a particular resource' (De Alessi, 1980, p. 3). For example, a variety of legal agreements can be made between apartment landlords and tenants. The landlord retains certain rights, such as the right to transfer ownership, while the tenant enjoys the benefit of occupying the property for specified periods at a price that is set according to an agreed procedure. Of course, these legal agreements are beset with expectations on both sides that are bound up with social norms. These play their part in the specification of property rights and are often the source of confusion.

Both Coase (1990d; 1990f) and Demsetz (1988) recognise that property rights are a prerequisite for markets. Demsetz makes the point that property rights are only worth exchanging if they can be enforced. For example, there would be little point in an individual reaching an agreement with a landlord to become a tenant if squatting in a property was a relatively costless alternative. Therefore the value of the bundles of rights that are traded depends crucially on the enforcement of those rights, which allows for a market valuation of rights. This implies that markets are most effective when the institution of property is most private. But if, for a particular good, the costs of production fall drastically, because of new production techniques, say, or if the costs of enforcing private property rights become prohibitively high, then it may not be worthwhile to provide a market. In such cases, some form of common ownership may emerge which dispenses with the market as a means of transferring a resource from one use to another.

Demsetz (1988) makes the point that where there are positive transaction costs, the distribution of wealth will be affected by the assignment of property rights. This in turn will affect the demand for resources. Therefore the study of property rights brings aspects of demand into the purview of economic analysis, whereas mainstream economist usually take demand as being determined exogenously by subjective preferences. The consideration of property rights allows for a broader approach to institutions that is appealing to economic historians concerned with periods within which property rights change significantly.

Gary Libecap has surveyed the property rights research in economic history. The starting point for economic historians is the recognition that 'Property rights exist as a continuum'. They range from open access with vague definitions of rights at one extreme, to specific, well-defined exclusive private property rights at the other (Libecap, 1986, p. 235). The terms 'public' and 'private' ownership generally refer to different specifications of ownership by the state, ranging from greater to lesser truncations of ownership rights for the private users of resources. Communal ownership, or open access, on the other hand, ultimately refers to a stateless society (Demsetz, 1988, pp. 19, 110). This means that the development of property rights is bound up with the emergence of the state (Eggertsson, 1990, ch. 9).

Economic historians are concerned with the interaction between 'property rights, transaction costs, and economic and political forces'. Since 'private property rights formally and visibly designate a particular wealth distribution' they can become the focus for 'distributional conflicts'. The 'importance of relative political power in property rights outcomes' is at the forefront of debate over the causes and effects of the forcible enclosure of common fields in England during the eighteenth century (Libecap, 1986, pp. 228–35, 240–1).

While most contemporary research on property rights derives from the work of Coase (1990d) and Demsetz (1988), it is acknowledged that both Marx and Commons appreciated the importance of property rights. It is a matter of conjecture whether Marx was 'the first social scientist to have a theory of property rights' (Pejovich, 1982). Marx believed that 'the forcible expropriation of the people' in England between the fifteenth and eighteenth centuries, culminating in the enclosures, laid the basis for the development of capitalism in the nineteenth century. Not only did the enclosures conquer the common lands for capitalist agriculture, they also created a proletariat, a class of workers free from any property 'in the soil', and therefore compelled to seek work in the factories (Marx, 1976, ch. 27). Not surprisingly, this explanation for the disappearance of feudal communal property is contested by contemporary property rights theorists (Demsetz, 1988, pp. 110; Pejovich, 1982) and institutional economic historians, who conspicuously fail to mention issues such as 'class structure, class conflict and exploitative social relations' (Gustafsson, 1991a, p. 36).

Commons emphasised the inseparability of sovereignty and private property, since: 'It is the sanctions of sovereignty that make property what it is for the time being in any country, because physical force, or violence, is the last and final appeal when the other sanctions are deemed inadequate to control individuals' (1951, p. 41). The 'historical separation of property from sovereignty', the physical force of the state, has allowed for the exchange of property rights to develop without the threat that hereditary sovereigns would intervene to transfer property rights arbitrarily. Thus *laissez-faire* does not really mean leave property rights alone. Since property rights are 'artificial' and have to be enforced, ultimately, by sovereignty, *laissez-faire* is really an appeal to the state to uphold the existing property rights against any interference (Commons, 1951, ch. 5).

Commons' view that sovereignty, primarily in the form of the state, is a prerequisite for private property rights and markets, is at odds with the positions of Coase and Demsetz. Coase counterpoises the state to markets and firms, seeing each as alternative, rather than interdependent, institutional arrangements for transferring property rights (1990c, p. 10; 1990d, pp. 114–19). Demsetz sees the state simply as an agent for principals who have delegated to it the enforcement of truncated property rights (1988, p. 18).

Both Coase and Demsetz have difficulty in reconciling their hostility to government regulation with the role of the state in enforcing property rights. They are wary of government regulation because the state is 'subject to political pressures', and because it operates without any of the competitive checks which, they allege, constrain markets and firms (Coase, 1990d, p. 118; Demsetz, 1988, p. 19). To concede that the existence of the state is essential for the enforcement of private property rights would be to risk having to admit that the allocation of wealth and property rights within and between firms and markets necessarily owes something to political pressures on the state to enforce certain property rights rather than others.

Evolution

A major criticism of orthodox economics is that it fails to account for change. In the theory of the firm the effects of external changes, such as changes in consumer demand and technology, are accounted for in terms of price changes, but there is no attempt to try to explain the causes of such external changes. What is more, external changes are considered in terms of how an equilibrium will be restored after their effects have been felt, rather than how there will be a process of ongoing change. Economics in general treats the sources of change as exogenous. Endogenising issues such as changes in demand, technology and organisation means trying to explain the sources of change and the processes by which it takes place. Economists concerned with issues of organisation in particular have addressed change through an evolutionary approach.

Evolutionary theories are almost too diverse to be considered together. A common theme is their use of analogies with biological theories of natural selection. There is a long history of interaction between economics and biology. Economists feel that they are entitled to borrow from biology, since Adam Smith and Thomas Malthus provided the stimulus for Charles Darwin's formulation of natural selection (Gould, 1992, pp. 328, 353). Many economists can be claimed as the forerunners of contemporary evolutionary economics, including Karl Marx, Thorsten Veblen, and Joseph Schumpeter (Hodgson, 1992). Kenneth Boulding is an outstanding, if idiosyncratic, economist. His book, *Evolutionary Economics* (Boulding, 1981) does not focus on organisational issues, nor does he draw on developments in organisational economics. Nevertheless he provides a valuable insight into an evolutionary model and the similarities and differences between biological evolution, and social and economic evolution.

Boulding's definition of evolution emphasises constant change and the ongoing interaction between populations of species of all kinds. He believes that all processes of production, whether of biological species, economic or social organisations, or material 'things',

> originate in some kind of information structure or 'know-how'. In the biological individual this is the genetic information as it exists in its origin in the fertilized egg or divided cell. In social systems the genetic material consists of knowledge in the heads of persons, or in the blueprints, plans, libraries, or computers of organizations, including one-person organizations in the form of single craftsmen. (Boulding, 1981, p. 25)

The major differences between processes of production in biological and social species are that biological artefacts are the product of information from only one parent, or two at the most in sexual reproduction, whereas social and economic artefacts are multiparental, which allows for much greater variety in the information used in their production. Biological artefacts also contain all the information for their production within themselves, while the genetic instructions for producing social and economic artefacts are contained in separate artefacts. This 'contributes to the great rapidity of evolution in social artifacts, because the artifacts which contain the genetic instructions have become specialized and hence particularly subject to change' (Boulding, 1981, p. 26).

Probably the most comprehensive recent statement of an evolutionary position, especially concerning issues of organisation, is Richard Nelson and Sidney Winter's book, *An Evolutionary Theory of Economic Change* (1982). Nelson and Winter borrow the basic idea of natural selection from biology, but they eschew the use of biological analogies for the sake of it. They are quite prepared to modify biological theories in order to achieve a better economic theory – for example, by allowing for the inheritance of acquired characteristics – which makes theirs a Lamarckian rather than a Darwinian version of natural selection. On the other hand, they reject the orthodox economic assumptions of rationality and maximisation. Their views are similar to the behaviouralists, who stress bounded rationality and satisficing. In Nelson and Winter's version of 'organisational genetics' and evolution, 'routines play the role that genes play in biological evolutionary theory'. The general term 'routine' covers *all* decision-making within firms, and it is the existence of routines that accounts for the regular and predictable behaviour patterns of firms. Routines include 'decision rules' and production 'techniques'.

The word 'routine' is not intended to suggest that they are only interested in the mundane; in fact, routines can include the strategic heuristics that shape a firm's approach to distinctly non-routine problems. For example, it may be routine for an organisation to call an emergency meeting at times of crisis. Such a meeting constitutes one of the routines that are in place in the organisation to deal with phenomena that are hard to predict. So the existence of routines does not preclude choice, but it suggests that choices are made within routines which influence the choices that are made. Routines are not only involved in 'doing' things but also in 'choosing' what to do and how to do it. Routine therefore guides the process of change. For an organisation the routines for changing its processes, its 'search' routines, are likely to be a crucial determinant of its ability to adapt to changes in its environment (Nelson and Winter, 1982, pp. 14–18). Winter makes a 'case for "routines" as a fundamental unit of analysis in the evolutionary approach to organizations' but recognises the dangers of going too far and obscuring the distinction between heuristics and routines, since the latter are associated with repetitiveness (Winter, 1990, pp. 271, 276).

Nelson and Winter believe that they diverge from behavioural theory because they are more interested in developing a theory of industry behaviour rather than individual firm behaviour (Nelson and Winter, 1982, p. 36). Nevertheless their analyses of 'Skill' (ch. 4), and 'Organizational Capabilities and Behavior' (ch. 5) elaborate their concept of routines in relation to human performance, innovation and strategy within organisations. They argue that there is a trade-off between developing capabilities to carry out repeated activities (that is, acquiring skill) and exercising choice between activities. They define skill as the capability of making choices without deliberation, a capacity which is limited by bounded rationality. Innovation represents a change of routine, even though, as Schumpeter recognised, within modern corporations innovative activity itself can be routinised. Changing routines clearly limits the extent to which skills can be acquired and stored within the organisational memory, which is why innovations in organisational routines often consist of different configurations of existing routines. As for the routine aspect of strategy, this is expressed in the most fundamental heuristic imperative for top management, which is to *have* a strategy (Nelson and Winter, 1982, pp. 132–3).

A distinction can be drawn between 'organisational evolution and organi-sational ecology', although the latter is 'possibly a subset of the former'. Evolutionary perspectives emphasize 'change within organisations' whereas ecology is more concerned with the 'turnover in organisational populations' (Meyer, 1990a, p. 298; Winter, 1990, p. 285). Economists have tended to ignore the internal aspects of evolution, treating the firm as a black box and concentrating on analysing the selection environments facing firms in parti-cular market sectors – that is, industries (Nelson and Winter, 1982, pp. 268–72). Organisational economists have paid more attention to the internal organisation of firms than have mainstream economists, and in the case of Nelson and Winter this has prompted an explicit recognition of the need for an evolutionary approach making use of biological analogies.

The 'population ecology', or 'organisational ecology' school was founded by Michael Hannan and John Freeman (Hannan and Freeman, 1977). Although they are sociologists, their approach complements Nelson and Winter, and it is similar enough to economic approaches to organisation to be considered as part of the family of organisational economics (Douma and Schreuder, 1991). Hannan and Freeman maintain that organisation theorists and sociologists have tended to concentrate on the internal evolution of organisations and have neglected the selection environment. Against this they argue that change within populations of organisations 'is more Darwinian than Lamarckian', since 'inertial pressures prevent most organizations from radically changing strategies and structures' (Hannan and Freeman, 1989, p. 22).

Narrowly defined, population ecology focuses on 'organizational birthrates and death rates' (Winter, 1990, p. 270). This is one aspect of organisational ecology, which is 'the investigation of how social environments shape rates of creation and death of organizational forms, rates of organizational founding and mortality, and rates of change in organizational forms.' (Singh, 1990, p. 11). Apart from the explicit use of analogies with biological population ecology, organisational ecology differs from economics in that it does not restrict its analysis of competition in selection environments to business organisations; Freeman, for example, has studied trade union mergers (Freeman and Brittain, 1977). Furthermore, when analysing business organisations, organisational ecologists take a wider view of the selection environment than economists generally do, paying special attention to technology and legitimacy rather than just profitability.

The criticisms of organisational ecology echo the long-standing scepticism of social theorists (Callinicos, 1989, p. 60; Giddens, 1986, p. 360) and biologists (Gould, 1992, pp. 63–6) towards the use of biological analogies in economics, and in social science generally. Boulding believes that this can be put down to the early influence of social Darwinism, which 'gave evolutionary theory a bad name, especially in sociology' (Boulding, 1981, p. 18). But this obscures the more substantive objections that social scientists have against the import of biological theories into social science (Benton, 1991).

Marshall Meyer is an institutional organisation theorist who wishes to retain and develop an evolutionary approach to organisations, but he objects to the primacy that ecology attributes to environments in shaping organisations because it detracts from the 'learning, adaptation, and change' that takes place within organisations (Meyer, 1990, pp. 299–301). In a sustained critique of Hannan and Freeman, Ruth Young alleges that 'they do not think that organizations change and adapt; they consider that a new organization has been founded each time there is a significant change' (Young, 1988, p. 2). This relates to the more general problems of determining the appropriate units of analysis in terms of deciding when an organisation has come into existence and when it has ceased to exist, and developing a taxonomy of organisations in order to be able to identify distinct populations.

The 'difficulty with the definition of organisational death' is a major problem:

> since fluctuations, births, and deaths of species are the main facts to be explained by population–ecology theory, there should be no ambiguity at all about what constitutes a birth and what constitutes a death; otherwise, the entire theoretical exercise has become purposeless. In fact, if a corporation has died and a new one has been born every time a company adds or subtracts a product or market; moves, opens, or closes a plant; merges; changes stockholders or ownership; reorganizes some division, deaths and births are almost infinite in number. (Young, 1988, pp. 7–8)

Freeman tries to sidestep the problem semantically by using the terms '*entries and exits* . . . rather than *births* and *deaths*' (Freeman, 1990, p. 60).

Edith Penrose, in her critical article, 'Biological Analogies in the Theory of the Firm' (1952, p. 808), hit upon the fundamental reason why the births and deaths of firms are problematic. It is that birth, youth, maturity, old age and death are characteristic only of biological organisms that reproduce sexually. Organisms whose reproductive processes are primarily asexual follow a different path of development in which death plays no part. If a biological organism divides asexually into two separate organisms it is difficult to say that the original organism has died, and unless the two separate organisms are both destroyed the original organism can be said to have continued in existence. The life-cycle that is inherent in the evolution of sexually reproduced biological organisms is absent in economic and social organisations. In her later work, Penrose argues that:

> rudimentary biological theories of the growth of firms break down over merger: life-cycle analogies make no provision for abrupt discontinuities and changed identity in individual development; ecological analogies have trouble with sudden unpredictable changes in the very nature of individual organisms and the consequent changes in their relation to their environment. (1959, p. 154)

Winter remarks upon the absence of death when businesses merge, which is analogous, by inversion, to the reproduction of asexual organisms whereby one organism separates into two, neither of which necessarily dies:

> the proposition that a business has 'disappeared' through acquisition by another has – in the absence of other information – virtually no useful meaning for the purposes of evolutionary theory. . . . Death by acquisition is . . . likely to be followed by some sort of reincarnation as a different but recognizable entity, and even ultimate resurrection as a free-standing firm is a common outcome. (1990, p. 280)

Similarly, Meyer notes that the 'stable long-lived organisation, which never changes yet never dies' departs from both ecological and evolutionary models of organisations (1990a, pp. 298–9).

The most obvious way in which sexually reproducing species of biological organism can be differentiated is by their capacity for interbreeding. If two types of organism are incapable of interbreeding this constitutes one of the criteria for identifying them as separate species. With organisms that reproduce asexually, taxonomy is much more difficult, having to resort to structural homology or the occupation of a similar niche, in the absence of a genetic compatibility demonstrated by successful sexual intercourse. As Young points out, taxonomies of organisations, such as those offered by organisational ecologists, are 'vague in comparison with biology's rule on interbreeding', and 'defining a species in terms of its niche' is tautological (Young, 1988, pp. 3, 5).

One way round the problems that arise because populations of organisations are almost impossible to specify is to revert to some sort of genetic reductionism. In defending an evolutionary position, Geoff Hodgson notes that some biologists 'argue that the gene, not the individual, is the unit of selection', while many other 'biologists and philosophers argue that several different levels of selection, including group selection, are viable' (Hodgson, 1993, p. 86). Winter implies that if there is disagreement among biologists about the unit of analysis, this excuses the lack of agreement among committed cultural evolutionists about exactly what it is that is transmitted through time. This is a prelude to a reiteration of Nelson and Winter's preference for the biological analogy that is 'evoked by the phrase *routines as genes'* (Winter, 1990, pp. 269, 274). Since organisations are composed of combinations of routines, making routines the unit of analysis avoids the problem of specifying a typology of organisations.

Meyer believes that although the notion of routine is conceptually appealing, 'operationally, bounding and measuring routines may prove controversial, and, probably, elusive' (Meyer, 1990a, p. 311). Part of the difficulty is that routines correspond to actual traits, whereas genes are the mechanism whereby traits are inherited, and the relationship between genes and all but the simplest traits are difficult to unravel. Sexually reproducing biological organisms can afford to have a life cycle which ends in death because their traits are inherited through their genes, whereas in the absence of any mechanism of inheritance, if a social organisation dies its routines for acquiring resources disappear with its death. Winter concedes that 'the biological analogy provides little help' in dealing with 'the problem of inheritance mechanisms' (Winter, 1990, p. 275).

Given the long-standing scepticism about the use of biological analogies in social science, and the constant need to qualify and extend biological theories, it is worth asking whether an evolutionary approach to organisations is worth pursuing? Young concludes 'that the concepts of biological ecology do not lend themselves readily to organizations'. Not unreasonably she makes the point that unlike the biological ecology literature, 'Hannan and Freeman articles are difficult to read', suggesting that their application of ecological models is forced. She is not suggesting that the organisational ecology research is worthless, only that it would lose nothing and gain in clarity if the biological theory were omitted, and replaced by more explicit references to the sociological and organisation theory from which it is derived and with which it is compatible (Young, 1988, pp. 21, 15).

When Bo Gustafsson comes to assess Nelson and Winter in his review of theoretical approaches to economic history he makes a similar point to that made by Young. He notes that the basic concept of 'organizational routines' is 'clearly sociological' (Gustafsson, 1991a, p. 25). In fact it owes a lot to the behaviouralists, in particular to Simon's notion of satisficing (Nelson and Winter, 1982, pp. 35–6). Gustafsson excuses the abstract nature of Nelson and Winter's theory, but is critical of their adherence to biological analogy (Gustafsson, 1991a, p. 26). This issue of biological analogies, will be taken up in the next chapter; in the meantime, suffice it to say that, whether or not any connection with biology is insisted upon, an evolutionary approach to organisations suggests an emphasis on change that is lacking in mainstream economics.

Conclusion

Organisational economics represents a serious attempt by economists to come to terms with the existence of firms as organisations instead of treating them as black boxes containing production functions and relegating their analysis to 'business schools, or worse still, to sociologists' (Stiglitz, 1991, p. 15). This chapter has outlined four major issues in organisational economics: transaction costs; agency; property rights; and evolution. Although each of these issues corresponds to a particular perspective within organisational economics, it is largely a matter of emphasis and focus as to whether they are considered as separate theoretical camps.

Transaction cost economics and agency theory, for example, have significant features in common and each could probably be expressed in terms of the other. So these two theoretical perspectives at least are largely to be distinguished in terms of the primacy they give to particular issues. Williamson (1985, pp. 24–9) characterises agency theory as being more concerned with the incentives that are used to structure the agency relationship, whereas his version of transaction cost economics focuses on what he calls the 'governance structures' which administer transactions between parties, primarily looking at business firms as governance structures rather than the state.

Property rights are of concern to virtually all organisational economists, not only the property rights school associated with Coase (1990d) and Demsetz (1988). There is a tension between property rights and transaction costs. The impression given by Williamson (1985) is that the need for property rights arises from the transaction costs involved in making transfers between technologically separate activities, and the transaction costs determine whether those transfers take place within firms or markets. But this takes property rights for granted, in that a transfer of ownership in the market is taken as the norm from which organisations diverge. As Coase (1990c) and Demsetz (1988) recognise, markets themselves require the prior specification of property rights.

It can be argued that if property rights are not specified at all then the opportunities for transactions of any sort are severely constrained, if not absolutely impossible. From this perspective, it is the specification and enforcement of property rights that gives rise to transaction costs (North, 1990a, p. 33). Two conflicting positions can be set out: from the first position, technology determines transaction costs, and therefore influences the choice of appropriate property rights; the second position is that property rights determine the choice of technology and the extent of technological separability, and therefore influence transaction costs. The former position takes technology as being determined exogenously, notwithstanding Williamson's disavowal of technological determinism (1985, pp. 86–90), which only amounts to keeping technology constant in order to explore the organisational alternatives that are possible with the same technology. The latter position is a movement in the direction of endogenising technological change.

Technological change remains problematic for organisational economics, even if less so than for neoclassical economics. Nathan Rosenberg points out that economics has generally consigned technological phenomena to a black box, hence the title of one of his many books on the history of technical change: *Inside the Black Box* (1982). But the neoclassical position which takes technology as being generated exogenously is untenable, since process innovations, which change production techniques, are typically product innovations from the point of view of the firms producing them. Thus the course and rate of technical change is likely to be influenced by the allocation of property rights between firms making product innovations, firms imitating those innovations, and firms using those product innovations as process innovations (Nelson and Winter, 1982, p. 268). The resulting transaction costs between technologically separable activities will owe a great deal to the initial specification of property rights.

Neoclassical economics conveniently consigned all issues of organisation to a black box labelled 'the firm'. Organisational economics has opened up that black box. This raises the possibility of opening up the other black boxes that remain within economics; and not least, given the difficulties of distinguishing between technological and organisational issues, the box containing technological phenomena. Economists should not be surprised to find that other social scientists have already been looking inside the various black boxes in order to study organisation, technology, and the relationship between them. Sociologists may even resent the belated intrusion of organisational economists claiming to know in advance the contents of all the boxes before they have even looked inside.

PART 2

CHAPTER 3

Economics and sociology

Introduction

Organisation theorists tend to see the division between economic and socio-logical approaches to organisation as a manifestation of wider differences between economics and sociology. Sociologists have attempted to set out the differences between the two disciplines (Hirsch *et al.*, 1990; Swedberg, 1991). Economics is dominated by neoclassical economics, so much so that 'econom-ics' is virtually synonymous with neoclassical economics (Bartlett, 1989, p. 18). Sociologists have concentrated on developing a critique of a narrowly defined version of neoclassical microeconomic theory (Swedberg *et al.*, 1990, p. 59), especially the 'unrealistic and bizarre policy recommendations' it comes up with (Hirsch *et al.*, 1990, p. 42). Neoclassical economics is a refinement of the classical tradition of economics that developed in Britain during the nine-teenth century based on the ideas of Adam Smith, Thomas Robert Malthus and David Ricardo (Galbraith, 1987). The major difference between classical political economy and neoclassical economics is the abandonment of any theory of value and the development of marginalism.

It is beyond the scope of this chapter to attempt to define neoclassical economics. Amitai Etzioni, a leading organisation theorist and a major critic of economics, characterises neoclassical economics as 'a utilitarian, rationalist, and individualist paradigm. It sees individuals as seeking to maximize *their* utility, rationally choosing the best means to serve their goals' (Etzioni, 1988a, p. 1). Gary Becker is said to be, 'one of the most faithful adherents to the precepts of neoclassicism'. He equates neoclassical economics with 'true' economic analysis (Bartlett, 1989, p. 17). For Becker, the 'heart of the economic approach' consists of 'The combined assumptions of maximizing behavior, market equilibrium, and stable preferences, used relentlessly and unflinch-ingly' (Becker, 1979, p. 10). According to Etzioni:

> Neoclassical economics, and the paradigm that underpins it, have been criticized to perfection. No part has been left unscathed. The paradigm has been shown to be

extremely unrealistic in its assumptions, especially its notions of a rational, self-centred individual, and of the existence of a self-regulating market. It has also been shown to be tied to a particular ideology, that of laissez-faire conservatism. And it has been found to be highly deductive and rather aempirical; a kind of mathematical scholasticism. (1988b, p. vii)

Neoclassical economics takes a position of extreme methodological individualism in which the individual economic actor is treated as the primary unit of analysis, and individuals are treated as if they only interact within the market, which is taken to be a universal phenomenon. Therefore neoclassical economics pays little or no attention to institutions or organisations, in the sense of enduring practices and collectivities. Organisational economics, almost by definition, admits the existence of institutions and organisations, although the explanations for their existence vary widely.

Hirsch, Michaels and Friedman (1990, p. 43), as well as Swedberg, Himmelstrand and Brulin have set out the 'Points of divergences between the paradigms of neoclassical theory and economic sociology' (Swedberg *et al.*, 1990, p. 60) in terms of a dichotomy, listing the characteristics of economics on the one hand and sociology on the other. This offers valuable insights, but it is limited to the contrast between the relatively discrete 'ideal types' (Hirsch *et al.*, 1990), or 'paradigms', of neoclassical economics and economic sociology (Swedberg, Himmelstrand and Brulin, 1990). Organisational economics and organisation theory diverge from these narrowly defined 'paradigms'. According to Richard Swedberg (1991, pp. 20–3), a dichotomous view best characterises the relationship between mainstream economics and sociology that prevailed in the USA during the period from the 1920s to the 1960s, when the two disciplines became distorted mirror images of each other (see Figure 3.1).

A problem with this dichotomous view of the disciplines is that it identifies virtually all economists with neoclassical economics. This reinforces the tendency for organisation theorists to see economics as a monolithic discipline (Hesterly and Zenger, 1993), which makes it difficult for organisation theorists to perceive any significant differences between orthodox neoclassical economics and organisational economics. Furthermore, it often portrays sociology as a residual category into which any dissenters from the neoclassical position within economics can be dumped. This means that divergences within economics and sociology end up being portrayed as manifestations of differences between the disciplines. Instead, it would be more useful to see the differences between particular positions within economics and sociology as a manifestation of wider divisions within social theory. This would allow for the possibility that various economists and sociologists can find themselves agreeing on some issues and disagreeing over others. These divisions within social theory can be set out as a series of dichotomies or dualities (see Figure 3.2) which are used to structure the discussion in this chapter.

	Homo economicus	*Homo sociologicus*
Actor	Individual actor	Collective actor
Principle of action	Freedom of action	Constraint of social structure
Motive of action	Rational calculation	Irrational feelings, tradition, and values
Arena of action	The market	All society but the market
Steering principle	Multiple, decentralised decisions	Decisions involving social and political power
Types of concept used	Analytical and abstract	Empirical and descriptive
Goal of the analysis	Prediction as explanation	Description as explanation
Image in relation to the other social science	Self-sufficient	Self-sufficient

Source: Swedberg, 1991, p. 22.

FIGURE 3.1   **The neoclassical paradigm and the sociological paradigm as mirror images of each other (mid-twentieth century)**

Discipline		
Economics Sociological economics		Sociology Economic sociology
Methodology		
Models Action Equilibrium		Histories Structure Evolution
Subject matter		
Economy Markets		Society Organisations
Political orientation		
Mainstream		Radical

FIGURE 3.2   **Dichotomies and dualities in social theory**

Interdisciplinary dialogue is inhibited because sociologists are anxious that it is merely a pretext for economists to intrude into other disciplines. In an optimistic survey of 'The Impact of Economics on Contemporary Sociology', Baron and Hannan dwell on the question of 'Why hasn't economics influenced sociology more?' but they only mention in passing the question of 'Why hasn't sociology influenced economics very much (and could it)? (Baron and

Hannan, 1994, p. 1115). This suggests that sociologists are right to believe that the intellectual trade between the disciplines is likely to be all one way. Economists are keen to export to other disciplines under the guise of free trade in ideas, but they maintain their own barriers against imports. The trading analogy reflects the way in which economists and sociologists see the social structures of their disciplines in terms of their own theoretical rhetorics, as described by Baron and Freeman:

> Economists appear to regard their discipline as a marketplace for ideas, with the competitive success of some ideas indicating their inherent worthiness. Sociologists, in contrast, tend to attribute differences in socioeconomic outcomes to systematic inequalities and structures of reproduction, and this seems to be true for how they view sociology itself. (1994, p. 1119)

Sociological economics and economic sociology

Sociologists fear a general invasion of sociology by neoclassical economists bent on imposing their behavioural assumptions of self-interested rational actors and their methodological preference for deductive modelling (Hirsch *et al.*, 1990, pp. 46–7; Swedberg *et al.*, 1990, p. 57). Increasingly economists have tackled sociological topics by using economic concepts. Economists and their sympathisers within sociology refer to the use of 'rational choice theory in sociology' (Coleman and Farraro, 1992, p. ix) as social or 'sociological economics' (Levy-Garboua, 1979), or else 'rational choice sociology' (Swedberg and Granovetter, 1992, p. 2), but many sociologists see the introduction of neoclassical analysis into other social science disciplines as 'economic imperialism' (Swedberg, 1991, p. 23). Organisation theorists (Barney, 1990, pp. 383, 389–90; Donaldson, 1990, p. 395; 1991, p. 17; Hesterly *et al.*, 1990, p. 402), along with writers on corporate strategy (Rumelt *et al.*, 1991, p. 5), see organisational economics as part of the imperialistic expansion of economics.

There are two aspects to economic imperialism. First, there is the tendency for economic models to displace historical narratives. Second, and more prosaically, there is what Nelson and Winter call the 'defiantly autarkic stance' of economics, which means that it is cut off from other social sciences because of its self-sufficiency. For example, most economists 'have shown no interest in the findings of students of organizational behavior that have demonstrated that what is done within organizations is only loosely circumscribed by "technology"' (Nelson and Winter, 1982, p. 405).

Imperialistic economics emanates from the University of Chicago. The leading imperialists are seen to be Gary Becker, Ronald Coase, Robert Fogel, George Stigler and Richard Posner, along with their allies in sociology, such as James Coleman. Between them they have tackled a range of issues that hitherto were the province of other disciplines, such as: anthropology;

criminology; demography; economic history; ethics; law; politics; and political philosophy. Using concepts such as human capital theory, economists have analysed sociological issues such as racial discrimination; education; the family; marriage and divorce; sexual behaviour; fertility; and child production (Becker, 1976; Lutz and Lux, 1988, p. 179; McCloskey, 1986, pp. 76, 179; Stigler, 1984, p. 304; Swedberg, 1991, p. 25). If anything, compared to other areas of sociology, organisation theory has largely been spared the attention of the more outspoken economic imperialists, which seems paradoxical given its proximity to the economic theory of the firm.

Lest it be thought that the fears of sociologists are exaggerated it is worth sampling some of the imperialist pronouncements by economists. Becker's position is that 'the economic approach is a comprehensive one that is applicable to all human behavior' (1976, p. 8). In his paper 'Economics – The Imperial Science', George Stigler predicts 'that economic theory will be used extensively in sociology, particularly to study the behavior of individuals and families under the postulate that they are seeking to maximize their utility'. He concludes that economics 'is an imperial science'. His only qualm is that the 'imperialistic age' of economics did not begin sooner (Stigler, 1984, pp. 309, 311).

Another bombastic statement of economic imperialism appears in Hirschleifer's article, 'Economics from a Biological Viewpoint', which is aimed directly at organisation theory:

> The social sciences can be regarded as in a process of coalescing. As economics 'imperialistically' employs its tools of analysis over a wider range of social issues, it will *become* sociology and anthropology and political science. But correspondingly, as these other disciplines grow increasingly rigorous, they will not merely resemble but will *be* economics. (1977, pp. 3–4)

Up to now Becker has been acknowledged as the 'Kipling of the economic empire' (McCloskey, 1986, p. 76), largely in recognition of his economic *Treatise on the Family* (1981). But his place may well be taken by Richard Posner, with his 'economic theory of sexuality' (1992, p. 3). Posner rejects any notion of the social construction of sexuality in favour of a combination of sociobiology and rational choice. Not surprisingly, he anticipates the reception his work is likely to receive:

> Whenever one tries to apply functional, means–end, rational – in other words, economic – theory to nonmarket behavior (not that there are no explicit markets, notably prostitution, in the area of sex), howls of protest are heard. It is said that economics works only for the analysis of markets, that applied to other areas it misses the point, or at best simply relabels familiar insights in an impenetrable jargon; that it is dehumanizing, ideological, complacent, imperialistic, reactionary;

that it is at once obvious and obviously wrong, and immoral to boot. These charges
. . . amount to a wholesale rejection of one of the most exciting areas of social science
today. (Posner, 1992, pp. 85–6)

Posner is adamant that economic theory is not only compatible with, but that
it also 'incorporates, integrates, and transcends' philosophy, psychology,
sociology, anthropology, women's studies, history and law (1992, p. 3). Even
before he produced his economic theory of sexuality, there were warnings that
'economic imperialism, Posner-style, is the academic equivalent of AIDS'
(Lutz and Lux, 1988, p. 199). As long ago as 1934, Talcott Parsons warned
that economic imperialism could lead to the extinction of other social sciences,
and that sociologists *'must stand up and fight'* (quoted by Swedberg, 1991,
p. 23).

Partly as a response to the advance of economic imperialism, there has been
a concerted effort to revive economic sociology, both as a distinctive perspective within sociology and as a rival to economics (Martinelli and Smelser, 1990).
The 'key notion' of this 'new economic sociology' is 'that many economic
problems that by tradition belong to the economists' camp can be fruitfully
analyzed with the help of sociology' (Swedberg and Granovetter, 1992, p. 2). In
his book, *The Moral Dimension*, Etzioni characterises his own attempt to develop
a cross-disciplinary alternative to neoclassical economics as 'socio-economics'
(1988a, p. 15). The term has found favour with other sociologists (Etzioni and
Lawrence, 1991), who have vied with each other to see how far back they can
trace its origins. Richard Coughlin names Amartya Sen, a contemporary
economist and philosopher, as a 'founding father' (Coughlin, 1991, p. 5), while
Swedberg maintains that it was Max Weber who first used the term (1991, p.
18). There are other, more idiosyncratic, challenges to mainstream neoclassical
economics, such as Lutz and Lux's (1988) 'humanistic economics' based on
Abraham Maslow's psychological theory of human needs. Given this diversity
there is obviously a danger that economic sociology, like organisational
economics, could be seen as a residual category which includes any approach
to the economy that is not neoclassical and takes social factors at all seriously.
Thus Veblen is claimed as a forerunner of economic sociology (Zukin and
DiMaggio, 1990a, p. 22), which lets economists off the hook for not taking his
critique of their discipline more seriously.

As long as sociologists 'stayed away from core economic questions such as
price formation, investment decisions, and the like' (Swedberg, 1991, p. 21),
and economists were content to concentrate on these issues alone, the two
disciplines could carry on more or less independently without having to
consider what separated them. The emergence of sociological economics and
the revival of economic sociology makes it difficult to accept that economics is
simply what economists do, and sociology is what sociologists do. The
boundary between the disciplines is called into question on two fronts. First,
concerning the methodological differences between the disciplines, and sec-

ond, whether there is a distinctive subject matter that is appropriate for each discipline given their methodological approaches.

Models and histories

Sociologists are particularly critical of the unrealistic and simplistic assumptions that neoclassical economics makes about 'human nature' (Hirsch *et al.*, 1990). Sociologists have focused on the objections that can be raised to the assumption of economists' that everyone behaves selfishly. But, as economists have pointed out, 'this assumption is made for reasons of convenience, not because economists empirically assume that all persons act only out of selfishness' (Akerlof, 1984, p. 175). As sociologists, Alberto Martinelli and Neil Smelser concede that although the simplified 'view of people as instrumental, rational, maximizing materialists' excludes 'most of the rest of psychological nature, an argument might still be made for it on theoretical and methodological grounds as necessary for creating an analytical model for scientific analysis' (Martinelli and Smelser, 1990, p. 3).

A few economists, such as George Akerlof, are quite prepared to admit that the neoclassical assumption that 'all agents engage in individualistic maximizing behavior' is very restrictive (Akerlof, 1984, p. 2; Sen, 1982, p. 317). But even though he modifies his assumptions, Akerlof still considers himself to be an economist, and on reading his work all but the most pedantic would readily agree that it is economics. So the more important methodological issue is not so much the whether particular assumptions about human nature are justifiable, but the extent to which any assumptions are admissible for the purpose of constructing artificial models. Although it is worth noting the way in which economists always introduce their assumptions: 'if we assume that individuals are motivated only by . . .'; 'Absent other considerations'; 'Suppose that' (Kreps, 1990); and, of course, 'other things being equal'. They never say, 'let's pretend', even though that is what they mean, because it would sound somewhat less authoritative.

Sociologists have conjured up a picture of economists staying in their offices building nice clean abstract models, while sociologists get their hands dirty carrying out research in the real world (Hirsch *et al.*, 1990, pp. 43–6). This image is confirmed by the few economists who are prepared to reflect on what it is that they do and enjoy doing. Peter Buckley and Mark Casson have contributed to a wide range of issues in organisational economics, such as game theory and multinational firms. They admit that 'Economic theorists are by nature system-builders' (Buckley and Casson, 1993, p. 1035). Influential agency theorists, John Pratt and Richard Zeckhauser, confess that, 'A favorite pastime of economists and other students of markets is to assess market phenomena and speculate why they exist. A fundamental premise underlying most such discussions is that the participants within the markets are rational, intelligent beings' (Pratt and Zeckhauser, 1985, p. 6). In other words, a set of assumptions is worked out where something resembling the existing situation is the logical outcome.

Milton Friedman's seminal essay, 'The Methodology of Positive Economics' (1953), is an eloquent defence of unrealistic assumptions in economics. He asserts that 'the more significant the theory, the more unrealistic the assumptions', on the grounds that a hypothesis needs to provide 'valid prediction' rather than accurate description. He sees theoretical models as the logical embodiment of a half-truth: 'There is nothing new under the sun'. On the other hand, the rules for applying models need to take account of an equally significant half-truth, 'History never repeats itself' (Friedman, 1953, pp. 14, 25). If, as Friedman says, models imply generalisation and replication, then narrative histories emphasise the uniqueness of events. Economists are hell-bent on developing models they believe to be universally applicable, models which would be described as unifying theories in the natural sciences that economists seek to emulate. Model building at this level of abstraction is unlikely to be interrupted by descriptive histories of apparently unrepeatable, unquantifiable, one-off occurrences.

Akerlof has made a significant contribution to organisational economics with his treatment of the issues arising from imperfect information. In the introduction to a collection of his articles, *An Economic Theorist's Book of Tales* (1984), Akerlof defines a 'good economic theory' as any theory which poses interesting 'if . . . then . . .' propositions relevant to some economic issue, along the lines of: *if* certain assumptions are fulfilled, *then* there will be an optimal equilibrium. He is quite prepared to countenance assumptions other than 'individualistic maximizing behavior', but he still makes assumptions in order to construct formal mathematical models from which he can generate 'if . . . then . . .' propositions that can be tested against reality (Akerlof, 1984, pp. 2–3).

Nelson and Winter suspect that neoclassical orthodoxy is driven by its increasing mathematical sophistication, since it is only the mathematical devices that change, while the theoretical concepts which facilitate a mathematical approach stay the same (1982, p. 13). As an accomplished economic historian and econometrician, McCloskey is sufficiently well placed within the neoclassical camp to know what goes on there. In his criticisms of his own discipline, McCloskey reveals that:

> Economists spend a lot of time worrying whether their metaphors – they call them 'models' – meet rigorous standards of logic. They worry less whether their stories – they call them 'stylized facts', a phrase that makes tiresome trips to the library unnecessary – meet rigorous standards of fact. (1990, p. 22)

McCloskey's recent books, *The Rhetoric of Economics* (1986), and *If You're So Smart (Why Ain't You Rich?)* (1990), have been hailed as part of a powerful antipositivist postmodern critique of the 'modernist precepts' of economics (Hodgson, 1988, p. 42, 279n). Yet McCloskey does not argue that economists should abandon their discourse, only that they should be less naïve about it, by recognising that their models are merely rhetorical literary devices, like metaphors in poetry (1986, pp. 174–5; 1990, p. 1). Extending the analogy with literature, McCloskey contends that metaphors and stories correspond to models and histories in economics and other social sciences, and that 'subject to the discipline of fact and logic', they are merely alternative ways of answering a question. He believes that metaphors and stories mix well: 'The best economics combines the two, the static model and the dynamic story, the economic theory and the economic history' (McCloskey, 1990, pp. 10–11).

While there is clearly a distinction between analytical, neoclassical economic theory, and more descriptive economic sociology, it is not clear whether they should be treated as being complementary or mutually exclusive. Comparing 'Sociological and Economic Approaches to the Analysis of Social Structure', sociologists Winship and Rosen (1988a) characterise sociology as more empirical, with an inductive approach to theory which is much less rigorous than in economics, whereas in economic theory mathematical models are developed deductively in order to generate fairly precise hypotheses that can be tested.

Winship and Rosen observe that, 'economists often view sociology as being too broad and diffuse and see the behavior that sociologists examine as being too complex (at least initially) for modelling', while 'sociologists view economics as being too narrow and based on unrealistic assumptions'. But Winship and Rosen appear to endorse McCloskey's view that metaphors and stories can and should be mixed: 'Of course, all good science is a combination of inductive and deductive methods, a constant interchange between data and theory. It simply cannot be asserted that either one or the other comes "first" as a matter of principle' (Winship and Rosen, 1988, p. 5).

This dilemma over the relationship between economic theory and economic sociology is not new. Although Weber and Schumpeter are claimed as forerunners of contemporary economic sociology (Martinelli and Smelser, 1990; Zukin and DiMaggio, 1990a), they both saw economic theory and economic sociology as being complementary. Weber tried to mediate between the more empirically orientated 'German historical school', which was attempting to develop a history-led theory of economics, and the emerging marginal utility theory of economics (Shionaya, 1991, p. 197; Swedberg, 1991). In fact, he welcomed the rise of marginalist economics, which he saw as complementary to his own historical sociology (Clarke, 1982).

Yuichi Shionaya (1991) gives a good account of Schumpeter's attitude towards the debate. Schumpeter tried to stimulate theoretically informed work in history in order to save the German historical school from degenerating into endless data collection. He believed that opposition to theory on principle would lead to a scenario of never-ending, detailed, but purely descriptive, historical studies. He identified four basic methods in economics:

history; statistics; theory; and economic sociology. Economic theory takes the institutional economic framework as exogenously given, whereas economic sociology involves a theoretical analysis of the development of institutions. McCloskey's view that metaphors and stories mix well echoes Schumpeter's statement of the complementarity between economic theory and economic sociology: 'economic analysis deals with the questions how people behave at any time and what the economic effects are they produce by so behaving; economic sociology deals with the question how they came to behave as they do' (Schumpeter, 1954, quoted in Shionaya, 1991, p. 198).

Although, ideally, history should inform theory, this is not what tends to happen in practice. Marginalism eclipsed the German historical school, and more recently, with the use of econometric techniques in economic history, and the development of econometric history, otherwise known as the 'new economic history' or cliometrics (McCloskey, 1987, pp. 11–13), the trend has 'tended to be one-directional, moving from theory to history with little or no feedback' (Shionaya, 1991, p. 197). As economic history has become more economic, with 'explicit hypotheses, mathematical modelling, counterfactual arguments and statistical testing' displacing detailed narratives, so historians have either had to master the tools of economics, or be replaced by economists (Gustafsson, 1991a, p. 26; Stigler, 1984, p. 307). During their heyday in the 1960s and 1970s the cliometricians from economics revelled in their ascendancy and the demise of the old narrative economic historians' journal, *Explorations in Entrepreneurial History* (Gustafsson, 1991; McCloskey, 1990, pp. 52–3, Miller, 1979). Shionaya (1991, p. 195) alleges that something similar is taking place in institutional economics, with the institutionalist mantle passing from the old institutionalists like Veblen and Commons, who were more historically orientated, to the new institutional economists whose work is derived from neoclassical economic theory.

Neoclassical economic theory tends to displace the traditional interests of history by focusing on those areas where statistical data is available that is susceptible to sophisticated mathematical analysis (Shionaya, 1991; Stigler, 1984, pp. 306–7). But even mainstream economists have complained that 'it is no fun reading' the new economic history, which merely 'gives back to the theorist the same routine gruel that the economic theorist gives to the historian' (Solow, quoted in Gustafsson, 1991, p. 48n).

In the study of organisations there is a good example of the tendency for models to displace histories. This is the corporate culture literature. The concept of culture has been welcomed in organisational behaviour in the hope that it might induce a more 'historical perspective' (Nord, 1985, p. 191; Rowlinson and Hassard, 1993). According to Steven Ott (1989, ch. 5), the culture perspective is seen by its adherents in organisation theory as being synonymous with a qualitative, narrative approach to research. Given the runaway success of the popular business books that draw on the concept of culture, notably Tom Peters and Robert Waterman's *In Search of Excellence*

(1982), it would certainly appear that management students the world over were yearning for a more narrative, or even anecdotal approach to their subject. And yet the economists have come along with their dreary models that purport to explain the enthralling narratives. In 'Corporate culture and economic theory', David Kreps (1990) reduces culture, not surprisingly, to game theory. The paper is replete with mathematical equations and a mathematical appendix, but there is not one piece of coherent narrative. The concept of corporate culture itself is only introduced after thirty-four pages of suppositions out of a fifty-two-page paper. Another economic theorist who has turned his attention to corporate culture using game theory is Mark Casson (1991). He asks business case study writers to supply him with real life stories of corporate culture that he can use to illustrate game theory.

Given the tendency for models to displace narratives, it is understandable that, 'many contemporary sociologists probably feel that analytical abstractions are something to stay away from and that the analysis should stick close to the empirical facts from the beginning' (Swedberg *et al.*, 1990, p. 77; Winship and Rosen, 1988a, p. 5). However, the danger of abstaining from theory, either on principle, as in the German historical school, or by default, as in business history (Hannah, 1983), is that it leads to a stream of detailed but unconnected case studies (Shionaya, 1991). According to Martinelli and Smelser, 'any attempt to depict all of perceived reality simultaneously must thus be regarded as at worst an impossibility and at best as indiscriminate descriptiveness' (Martinelli and Smelser, 1990, p. 49, n2). It is also very inviting to neoclassical economists who are only too willing to fill any theoretical vacuum with their ready-made models.

An outright rejection of economic modelling cuts off sociologists and organisation theorists from the efforts being made by some economists, especially organisational economists such as Akerlof (1984), to make their models more realistic by modifying the underlying assumptions in the light of insights from sociology and psychology. Divergence from the most unrealistic assumptions made by neoclassical microeconomic theory, such as hyperrationality, raises the possibility of some convergence between sociology and economic theory. In particular, the attempt by organisational economists 'to remedy the deficiencies in the microeconomic concept of rationality' with concepts such as 'bounded rationality' opens up the possibility of 'a sustained debate about rationality' (Swedberg *et al.*, 1990, pp. 67–8). This would be facilitated if organisational economists were more prepared to 'take economic rationality as a variable feature in human institutional life, and to devote research to understanding and explaining that variation' (Martinelli and Smelser, 1990, p. 31), instead of asserting, as Williamson does, that their modified assumptions constitute 'human nature as we know it' (1983, p. ix).

So far in this chapter, economic sociology has been identified with economic and social history. In fact it is somewhat misleading to see sociology as being characterised by 'an unreflective empiricism and dogmatic rejection of analytical abstractions' (Swedberg, 1991, p. 21), in the same way that, say, business historians are 'inveterate empiricists . . . eschewing general theories' (Hannah, 1984, p. 219). The forerunners of contemporary economic sociology, notably Marx, Weber, Schumpeter, Karl Polanyi, and Talcott Parsons and Neil Smelser (Martinelli and Smelser, 1990, p. 5), can hardly be called atheoretical. When Schumpeter considered the place of economic sociology explicitly he saw it as 'a theoretical analysis of the development of institutions abstracted from history', involving 'generalization, typification, and stylization of history' (Shionaya, 1991, p. 198).

The relationship between sociology and history is not unproblematical, even if the problems that arise are different from those encountered in the interaction between economic models and economic history. It should be noted that 'Working historians sometimes complain that historical sociologists do not do original research but weave their interpretations from the studies of others' (Callinicos, 1989, p. 7). It would be difficult to name a more outstanding historian than Fernand Braudel. He confesses to being 'allergic' to Weber's 'subtle and confusing method of argument', and dismisses the Weberian view that Puritanism was responsible for the rise of capitalism as 'misleading retrospective sociology'. Braudel believes that his own way of working allows the answers to historical questions to emerge through the accumulation of historical evidence. But he reckons that it would require an 'unusual faith in history' for a sociologist to do the same (Braudel, 1985, pp. 568–9, 586).

Anthony Giddens acknowledges that narrative historians have been justifiably suspicious of sociology (1986, p. 361). Whereas economic theorists impose models on historical data, sociologists impose periodizations and typologies, and they then proceed to draw parallels between periods and identify relationships between reified types. Philip Abrams identified the challenge facing sociologists in his manifesto for historical sociology, it is to produce historical studies 'in which theory, evidence and concept really do maintain a close, fluent dialogue with no bullying' (Abrams, 1980, p. 15).

When confronting economic theory, sociologists cannot claim that sociology either is, or should be, atheoretical. To do so would be to deny sociology any separate identity from, say, purely narrative history, or even journalism. Sociological theory differs from economic theory because 'it does not consist of, and does not aim directly at establishing empirically testable hypotheses, it is merely meant to *prepare the ground* for an empirical investigation of social structures and actors' (Mouzelis, 1993, p. 676). Even if economists modify their assumptions in the light of sociological and psychological research, as organisational economists have done, they still try to incorporate their assumptions into more or less formal models from which to be able to generate specific propositions. Whereas many economists would prefer to spend their time refining their models, most sociologists would rather scrutinise the adequacy of any set of assumptions on which models are to be built. They are just as likely to do this through theoretical critiques based on epistemology and ontology as by raising empirical questions that economic models are hard put to answer.

Action and structure

In the eyes of neoclassical and rational choice economists, sociology and institutionalism subordinate individual social actors to overarching social theories in explaining social action because of their adherence to structuralism, functionalism and evolutionism. This could be interpreted in terms of sociological models, not economic models, displacing historical accounts which accord adequate significance to individual decision-making. Thus Jon Elster (1979, 1990), a Marxist rational choice theorist and a leading advocate of sociological economics, has portrayed the division between functional, evolutionary sociology and his own rational choice version of utilitarian theory as a manifestation of the 'antinomies' of 'action' and 'structure' that, according to Giddens, pervade virtually all social theory (1979, p. 49). (The term 'agency' is often used instead of action, but it will be avoided here so as to avoid any confusion with the meaning attached to agency in terms of principals and agents.)

The dualism of action and structure is captured by Marx's oft-quoted aphorism, 'Men [let us immediately say human beings] make history, but not in circumstances of their own choosing.' (Marx, 1969, quoted by Giddens, 1986, p. xxi). 'Well, so they do,' says Giddens, 'But what a diversity of complex problems of social analysis this apparently innocuous pronouncement turns out to disclose!' (Giddens, 1986, p. xxi). The concepts of action and structure relate to one of the 'classic disputes in sociology', the debate over the relationship between the 'individual and society' (Sharrock, 1987). It is generally accepted that action suggests voluntarism of the individual, while structure stresses determinism by society.

Structural analysis accords 'a priority to the object over the subject' (Giddens, 1979, p. 50) and explains individual action by reference to society, whereas individual intention is the focus for theories that explain society by reference to individual action (Dawe, 1979, p. 367). It is the goal of social theorists such as Giddens to transcend these antinomies, but they do so in the knowledge that consistently sociology has 'begun with the concept of social action and ended up with its negation, paradoxically by its repeated translation of the concept from the level of the social actor to that of the social system' (Dawe, 1979, p. 408). Socialisation is one of the most pernicious concepts, which denies the importance of intention in explaining social action. It is unfortunate that socialisation is so widely identified with sociology.

Economics is associated generally with individual voluntarism and rationality, while sociology is linked with determinism at the level of society. This is captured by an aphorism from James Duesenberry which retains widespread currency: 'economics is all about how people make choices; sociology is all about how they don't have any choices to make' (1960, quoted by Baron and Hannan, 1994, p. 1116). Elster alleges that functionalism and structuralism are derived from biological analogies. Against this he reasserts rational choice and denies the importance of structure. He illustrates, by the use of a little homily about cattle in a field that echoes Duesenberry, what he sees as the mistaken view that theorists concerned with structure and action merely have a different focus. Were they compatible, Elster says, the structuralist would study the constraints imposed on cattle by the fence around their field, whilst the action theorist would study the activity of the cattle within the limits imposed by the fence. But, he argues, the structuralist would end up asserting that 'the cattle have very little freedom of movement within the fence' (1979, p. 67). In reply, the structuralist would probably say that, in effect, rational choice theory denies the existence of any fences.

According to Elster, 'the sociologist, or some caricature thereof', ends up arguing that there 'really is no "choice" at all, but that individuals are *propelled* into certain channels by . . . norms and values. The economist, by contrast, tends to assume that individuals are *attracted* by differential rewards associated with the possible courses of action. The sociologist, that is, looks at the action as a product of its causal antecedents, the economist as motivated by future rewards: causality versus intentionality' (Elster, 1979, p. 75). Elster's argument gives the misleading impression that the only alternative to structuralism and functionalism is rational choice theory. Arthur Stinchcombe, an economic sociologist, acknowledges that any explanation must 'satisfy the requirements of methodological individualism . . . since all social action is carried out by individual human beings'. But he maintains that when 'the plea for methodological individualism is coupled with a preference for rational actor explanations: it is a concealed plea for utilitarianism. There is, however, no inherent reason why the model of individual action in a methodologically individualist account must be a rational one' (Stinchcombe, 1990, p. 108). Thus the dichotomy between rational choice and functionalism is false. It does not capture the diversity of possible explanations that stress the importance of either structure or action. More importantly, it obscures the conflicts between models and histories which arise within both individualistic and structural approaches to social action.

It is worth pointing out that for rational choice theorists to pose as the only advocates of an explanation for social action based on choice and intention is disingenuous, since their 'deterministic or mechanistic' view of human actors as merely rational reactors to external stimuli effectively denies choice in any meaningful sense (Hodgson, 1988, p. 10). The 'thoroughly methodical person' that rational choice economists assume everyone to be is ridiculed by Sen as a 'rational fool', who 'may be "rational" in the limited sense of revealing no inconsistencies in his choice behaviour', but is 'close to being a social moron' if he cannot make any moral distinctions between his preferences (Sen, 1982, p. 99). Critics from various perspectives 'have all noted the lack of real choice in, and the deterministic nature of, neoclassical theory' (Hodgson, 1988, pp. 10, 276n).

The outcome of choices made by rational individual actors with fixed preferences are, in effect, predetermined. As James Coleman concedes, rational choice theory is intended to explain the realisation of purposive action. But the purposes or preferences of individuals are simply taken as given, and rational choice theory is hard put to explain how changes in individual preferences or interests come about, 'Despite the fact that anyone knows, if only through introspection, that interests change'; thus, 'A theory based on rational action . . . has the same deficiency at the level of the individual (considered as a system) as a theory which begins with societal purposes or social norms has at the level of the social system' (Coleman, 1990, p. 292). Almost any action can be construed as the outcome of a utility maximising choice, just as it can be construed as fulfilling some functional requirement of society. Both rational choice and functional models can be invoked to avoid carrying out empirical research into individual intentions in terms of actually asking the actors themselves what intentions lay behind any action. The principle of rationality gets round the problem of the 'privacy' of beliefs and desires by inferring them from actual behaviour (Callinicos, 1989, p. 13).

Although neoclassical and rational choice economists locate themselves on the subjective side of social theory, they are peculiarly reluctant to investigate subjectivity. Economists tend to concentrate on the 'revealed preference' of actors in the market. As Sen points out, this excludes *verbal* and *written* behaviour, including responses to questionnaires that are a mainstay of other social sciences:

> Much of economic theory seems to be concerned with strong, silent men who never speak! One has to sneak in behind them to see what they are doing in the market, etc., and deduce from it what they prefer, what makes them better off, what they think is right, and so on. There is, of course, the problem of ascertaining the veracity of communication, e.g., in responses to questionnaires, but the difficulties of *strategic non-verbal* choice behaviour (departing from preference) are serious too. (1982, p. 9)

Equilibrium and evolution

Having established that the division between social theories emphasising action and structure does not correspond to the separation between models and histories, it is necessary to return to the latter dichotomy. Evolutionary organisational economists need to be located in terms of whether their versions of evolutionism promote empirical research. The tendency for models to displace narratives, or as McCloskey (1986) puts it, for stories to give way to metaphors, extends beyond the relationship between economic theory and history, there are parallels in natural science.

Stephen Jay Gould, an evolutionary biologist, protests against the condescending attitude of most scientists towards paleontology. Biologists themselves envy or feel threatened by theoretical physicists, who are the masters of elegant mathematical models which can predict the behaviour of atoms and galaxies. Gould believes that scientists generally tend to denigrate history as 'mere description' (1991, pp. 51, 97):

> The worst of human narrowness pours forth in the negative assessment of monographic work as merely descriptive. Scientific genius is equated with an oddly limited subset of intellectual activities, primarily analytical ability and quantitative skill, as though anyone could describe a fossil but only the greatest thinkers could conceive of the inverse square law. (1991, p. 100)

It is widely accepted that neoclassical economists have sought to identify themselves with the methodology of physics, which they see as an exemplar for scientific research (Hausman, 1992; Mirowski, 1988). Thus the economy has been conceptualised as a mechanical system tending towards equilibrium and governed by laws akin to the physical laws that govern the universe in Newtonian physics. This is the utilitarian tradition of economics, in which mathematical formalism was imported from nineteenth-century physics on the basis that there is a parallel between the conservation principles that apply to 'energy' in the universe and 'utility' in the economy (Gustafsson, 1991, p. 5). Abstract individuals maximising their utility under constraints are thought to behave in the same way as heavenly bodies in the universe that are subject to the forces of gravity. To mathematically inclined economists, utilitarianism appears to have immensely powerful explanatory capabilities because it is deductive and its laws are proven in mathematical theorems (Callinicos, 1989, p. 114).

Critics of utilitarian theory in general, and of neoclassical economics in particular, see the reliance on metaphors derived from Newtonian physics as anachronistic in the light of the dynamic models advanced by the 'New Physics' (Callinicos, 1989, p. 73; Capra, 1983; Nelson and Winter, 1982, p. 10). Ever since Veblen posed the question, 'Why Is Economics Not an Evolutionary Science?' (1948 [1919]), evolutionary and institutional economists have attempted to insulate themselves from the influence of mechanistic Newtonian physics (Commons, 1951, p. 190; Hamilton, 1975 [1953]; Mirowski, 1988; Nelson and Winter, 1982). Boulding, an evolutionary economist, declares that 'Economics has rested too long in an essentially Newtonian paradigm of mechanical equilibrium and mechanical dynamics'; this is because the Newtonian system in economics was mathematised so successfully that the evolutionary perspective was lost (Boulding, 1981, p. 17). Nelson and Winter believe that 'economics has never really transcended the experiences of its childhood, when Newtonian physics was the only science worth imitating and celestial mechanics its most notable achievement' (1982, p. 10).

It is difficult for institutionalists to maintain an explicitly evolutionary position in economics when, on the one hand, many other organisational and institutional economists appear to see no contradiction between mechanical and evolutionary models of the economy (North, 1990a, p. 7; Williamson, 1985, pp. 46–7), and on the other, most sociologists, who might be seen as the natural allies of institutionalist economics, are keen to exclude any 'biologistic overtones' from social theory (Callinicos, 1989, p. 60). Heavyweight social theorists in sociology, such as Giddens (1986) and Robert Nisbet (1969), have taken a clear anti-evolutionary stance. As a cautious advocate of biological analogies in social science, Ted Benton maintains that the hostility to evolutionary theory in the social sciences is best understood as a defensive reaction 'to the intellectual imperialism (and, in many cases, moral and political conservatism) of biological reductionist programmes, especially various forms of social Darwinism' (1991, p. 25). He believes that developments in evolutionary biology have tended to undermine reductionism, and this is reinforced by recent biographies of biologists such as Charles Darwin (Desmond and Moore, 1992) and Charles Doolittle Walcott (Gould, 1991), which show how reductionism in biology was often an expression of moral and political conservatism. However, if the sociologists' dispute with social evolutionism consisted of no more than an objection to social Darwinism, then it would be easy to reconcile them with evolutionary theory (Boulding, 1981, p. 18), but (as was noted in the last chapter), the objections to evolutionism are more complex.

According to Giddens, 'evolutionism' in the social sciences means:

> the explication of social change in terms of schemas which involve the following features: an irreversible series of stages through which societies move, even if it is not held that all individual societies must pass through each of them to reach the higher ones; some conceptual linkage with biological theories of evolution; and the specification of directionality through the stages indicated, in respect of a given criterion or criteria, such as increasing complexity or expansion of the forces of production. (1986, pp. xxviii–xxix)

The arguments for and against social evolutionism within sociology are carefully surveyed by Stephen Sanderson (1990), one of a minority of sociologists who advocate an evolutionary approach, although he does not cover the debate over evolutionism within contemporary economics. It is clear that for sociologists such as Giddens, evolutionism is identified with functionalism and structuralism, and a view of 'history as "subjectless" – as occurring "behind the backs" of its participants' (Sanderson, 1990, pp. 212–13). Giddens' objection to functionalism is that it denies the role of 'intentional action' on the part of human actors in shaping society; instead, 'social items or activities are

66 Organisations and Institutions

held to exist because they meet functional needs'. Consequently, he warns that, 'Evolutionism . . . can easily be an enemy of history rather than the ally it might superficially seem to be' (1986, pp. 295–7, 360, 236–43; Lenski, 1976, p. 550).

Sociologists' criticisms of evolutionism certainly seem to apply to the most important evolutionary approaches in economics. Armen Alchian's paper, 'Uncertainty, Evolution, and Economic Theory' (1950), is an influential statement of an evolutionary position; indeed, Nelson and Winter cite it as 'a direct intellectual antecedent' for their contemporary statement of an evolutionary perspective (1982, p. 41). Faced with the managerialist argument that individual firms neither can nor do maximise profits, Alchian dispenses with the assumption of 'profit maximisation' as an intention on the part of individual firms. Instead, he reverts to what he sees as 'the essentials of Darwinian evolutionary natural selection', to argue that 'the forest of impersonal market forces' operates as 'a process of economic natural selection'. This ensures that firms which realise positive profits, whatever their motivation, will survive, while those which suffer losses will disappear. Alchian does not deny the existence of purposive behaviour, but he renders it redundant as a necessary assumption for sustaining marginal analysis as the basis for 'prediction, explanation, or diagnosis' in economic theory (Alchian, 1950).

Edith Penrose's (1952) critique of Alchian anticipates sociologists' objections to evolutionism. Penrose recognises that the immediate purpose of invoking the analogy with natural selection is to get around the logical problem that 'in a world characterized by uncertainty' it cannot be assumed that firms maximise their profits because they cannot know in advance which actions will maximise profits. But she argues that: 'The characteristic use of biological analogies in economics is to suggest explanations of events that do not depend upon the conscious willed decisions of human beings'; therefore she alleges that biological reasoning 'obscures, if it does not deny, the fact that firms are institutions created by men to serve the purposes of men' (1952, pp. 808–9).

Penrose alleges that Alchian uses the natural selection analogy 'to provide an explanation of human affairs that does not depend on human motives. . . . No matter what men's motives are, the outcome is determined not by the individual participants, but by an environment beyond their control' (Penrose, 1952, pp. 809–12). Hannah (1976, p. 6), a business historian, makes a similar criticism of Alchian's view that the study of purposive behaviour in individual firms is of little value. Hannah believes that Alchian's view renders redundant the case studies of individual firms carried out by business historians. Furthermore, crude natural selection models of the economy, such as Alchian's, leave no place for the 'entrepreneur' who is seen as playing an important role in shaping the economy by other social scientists (Hannah, 1984, pp. 222–3), especially economists of the Austrian school (Ricketts, 1987, ch. 3).

Neither rational choice methodological individualism nor the functionalist version of evolutionism favoured by economists promotes the empirical study of historical processes. In economics, as in paleontology, 'Anyone can invent a plausible story after the fact' (Gould, 1991, p. 236; Ricketts, 1987, p. 266), and this is just what economists seem to do, whether it is by invoking rational choice or natural selection. This is because, as J. Hirschleifer makes explicit, the evolutionary approach favoured by economists stresses the 'processes leading to *equilibrium*', rather than the 'processes of ongoing *change*' (1977), which evolutionary biologists such as Gould are more concerned with. Economists such as Alchian, Coase and Williamson retain marginalism and equilibrium within an evolutionary framework by maintaining an almost complete separation between organisations and their environment. According to Alchian, the 'impersonal market system' is 'completely independent of the decision processes of individual units' (1950, p. 213).

Alchian's position is untenable, firstly because, as Nelson and Winter point out, the distinction between an organisation and its selection environment is rarely as clear-cut as the separation between the firm and the market as portrayed by neoclassical economics (1982, p. 269). Second, firms need to be taken seriously as economic actors (Whitley, 1987) who shape their own environments. Since the environment is composed of other organisations, this means that: '"competition" cannot be regarded as synonymous with some exogenously determined market structure unrelated to the nature of the firms of which the market is comprised' (Ricketts, 1987, p. 277).

In relation to transaction costs, an equilibrium in which the marginal costs of transactions within a firm are equal to the marginal costs of transactions in the market is unlikely to be reached following an organisational or technological innovation, because firms cannot change their transactions on a 'one-by-one basis' since 'market transactions exist in patterns' (Burt, 1983, p. 73). An additional transaction carried out within a firm may transform the whole configuration of transactions for the firm itself and for other firms in the industry, and this is all the more likely if it is the result of a radical organisational or technological innovation, which in turn will affect the relative costs of transactions in the market and induce further innovations.

Williamson does not allow for the interaction between organisations and their environments, either in the sense of organisational innovations constantly changing the whole configuration of transactions, or, more importantly from the point of view of sociology, in terms of behavioural characteristics changing in response to environmental change. In this sense he has not broken from the situational and technological determinism of neoclassical theory (Friedman, 1984, pp. 176–8). Williamson excludes the possibility that organisational change can alter the whole environment within which organisations subsequently operate. Effectively, he denies the role of contingency in history, and forces the historical evidence concerning work organisation and corporate structure into his evolutionary schemas.

The difficulty of defending history against models is illustrated, inadvertently, by Geoff Hodgson, a radical institutionalist who advocates 'painstaking historical research, rather than bold evolutionary generalizations based on dubious "biological laws" '; this statement is belied by his own exposition of 'evolutionary theory' which, typically for an economist, involves an illustrative 'hypothetical example' underpinned by game theory that assumes 'two types of firm, type A and type B' (Hodgson, 1993, pp. 90–3). This is hardly the product of in-depth research in an archive, something that Hodgson himself seems not to have done. The same goes for his colleague, Christos Pitelis, who advocates 'a dynamic evolutionary and historical approach' (Pitelis, 1993, pp. 2, 214–18) even though his own empirical research (Pitelis, 1987) seems to consist of econometric testing of theoretical hypotheses. Incidentally, game theory has been taken up in the effort to give a more mathematical grounding to biological evolutionary theory (Axelrod, 1990; Sigmund, 1993), and, in the process, theoretical biology has become detached from 'real' empirical biology (Rowe, 1993).

The best empirical historical work on organisational change within capitalist corporations has been carried out by business and economic historians, notably Alfred Chandler (1962; 1977) and William Lazonick (1992). Chandler came out of the institutionalist school of economic history associated with the journal *Explorations in Entrepreneurial History*, which was produced by a research centre at Harvard between 1948 and 1958 (Miller, 1979; McCloskey, 1990, p. 53). The major theoretical influences on this school came from economic sociology, primarily Schumpeter and Weber (Miller, 1979, p. 5; Chandler, 1988, ch. 11; 1962). Chandler's (1992b) evolutionary approach is distinctly Schumpeterian, and along with Lazonick (1991) he places great emphasis on the *process* of organisational innovation. Both Chandler (1984) and Lazonick are great advocates of the case study as the foundation for historical research. As Bernard Elbaum and William Lazonick put it in their outline of an institutional perspective:

> If we want to understand the operation of the capitalist economy as it exists in the real world, we have *to study* it . . . the case study approach is absolutely necessary to the development of a theoretical structure that can lay claim to capturing (as all good theory must) the essence of the economy it is purporting to describe (1982, p. 3)

Organisational and technological innovation, treated as an endogenous feature of the economy, tends to undermine static equilibrium models. In Nelson and Winter's (1982, p. 128) view, 'innovation' represents a change in routine; it cannot be predicted; and neither can its consequences.

The elaborate typologies of organisations developed by sociological organisation theory offer no more of an insight into the processes of organisational change than artificial economic models of natural selection leading to equilibrium. Organisational economics is caught between neoclassical economics, which predicts equilibrium in an imaginary world, and organisation theory, which merely categorises contingency in the real world. Whereas economists exclude data that does not fit into analytical models, sociologists force data into abstract typologies, exemplified by the 'ideal types' invented by Weber. If 'metaphors dominate physics and stories dominate biology' (McCloskey, 1990, p. 11), then economics may be afflicted by 'physics envy' (Ellerman, 1991, p. 558), but sociology is susceptible to the 'taxonomitis' that bedevilled early biology.

In order to transcend restrictive notions of equilibrium on the one hand, and overarching classification schemes on the other, evolutionism needs to emphasise the importance of explaining social change. Within economics, the close adherence of evolutionary theory, such as Nelson and Winter's, to biological analogy is, in Gustafsson's view 'a sign of its immature character'. Even so, Gustafsson concedes that, 'biological analogies are . . . closer to economic reality than the mechanical–physical analogy of neoclassical theory' (1991a, p. 26). Evolutionary theory is more likely to be able to accommodate social change and to distance itself from neoclassical notions of equilibrium if it emphasises the 'purposeful, voluntaristic nature of human activity' (Biddle, 1990, p. 19). However, a 'volitional' version of evolutionism, such as Commons' theory of 'purposeful, selection' (1951, p. 91), may not require any maintenance of the biological analogy, except for its differentiation from 'natural selection'.

Economy and society

There are problems with sociologists and organisation theorists invoking the arguments against economic imperialism in general to repulse organisational economics, which is largely concerned with organisations that are, after all, economic phenomena. The charge of economic imperialism may be no more than an attempt by sociologists to defend their boundary in a demarcation dispute with economists over who should have the franchise for studying organisations. This dispute can be bitter; when the economists have won, organisation theorists have been fired (Barney, 1990, p. 390). But it detracts from more substantive issues, two of which can be identified.

First, the distinction between economic and non-economic phenomena, and second, the universal applicability of the concept of the market. Swedberg *et al.* (1990) argue that, on the one hand, mainstream economics makes the mistaken assumption that the economic system in general, and markets in particular, can be analysed in complete isolation from the rest of society. On the other hand, they believe that if economic sociology is to be delineated from wider sociology, then it 'stands to benefit very much from a renewed interest in the concept of the economic system and its autonomy' (1990, p. 66). This leads on to the question posed by Swedberg of whether there is 'a non-social, purely "economic" area, that is surrounded by institutions', or whether '"the economy" consists exclusively of social institutions?' (Swedburg, 1991, p. 13).

In fact, it has proved very difficult for economic sociologists to distinguish the economy from the rest of society in terms of the economic functions that 'all economies . . . hold in common' (Holton, 1992, p. 17). It is a problem that is side-stepped by the neoclassical theory of the firm and mainstream organisa- tion theory, both of which abstract social organisation from social structure (Coleman, 1984, p. 87), a point picked up by their radical critics. Stephen Marglin, a radical economist, notes that in neoclassical 'models of the competitive economy' the firm 'is merely a convenient abstraction for the household in its role as producer and does nothing that households could not equally well do for themselves' (1976, p. 17). Radical organisation theorists criticise mainstream organisation theory because it obscures the historical specificity of the capitalist firm by 'providing concepts of "the organisation" . . . which are absolutely independent of any political economy' (Clegg and Dunkerley, 1980, p. 538). This means that neither the neoclassical theory of the firm nor the concept of an organisation in organisation theory are specific to an economic section of society or to any historical period.

Both Weberian-inspired theories of organisation and the neoclassical theory of the firm are abstractions that obscure the historical specificity of the capitalist firm, so that an organisation or a firm could correspond to just about every collectivity in any historical setting. In contrast, Schumpeterian- inspired economic sociology (Shionaya, 1991, pp. 213–15) and evolutionary economics (Nelson and Winter, 1982, pp. 39) present analyses that are more or less specific to capitalism. For example, Nelson and Winter explicitly recog- nise that: 'There are a great many different sorts of organisations, and it is implausible that a given collection of concepts and propositions would apply uniformly, or even usefully, to all of them.' They restrict their analysis to business firms concerned with survival and profits (Nelson and Winter, 1982, p. 96).

Martinelli and Smelser argue that the emergence of modern social science is predicated upon the historical 'differentiation of economic structures from social structures – for example the differentiation between economy and state . . . [and] the dissociation of kinship from economic production under the factory system' (1990, p. 2). This corresponds to Galbraith's position, which is that 'Economics . . . does not exist apart from the relevant economic life', primarily the prevalence of the market (Galbraith, 1987, p. 30). So the problem of the distinction, and the relationship between economy and society, only arises when dealing with societies in which economic and social institutions are differentiated, and it is not possible to read this differentiation back on to societies in which it did not exist.

The distinction between economy and society needs to be seen as the product of the differentiation of purposive economic organisation from more regularised and less reflexive social conduct (Giddens, 1986, pp. 199–203). The provision of, say, certain material goods, cannot be located within the economy or society except by historical research to find out whether it is governed by purposive economic organisations or by collectivities which are more or less unreflexive. The hallmark of the economic organisations of modern capitalism is probably their separation of production from consumption. If this separation is the product of specific historical types of economic organisation, notably the capitalist firm, then it does not make sense to reify such a separation by imposing it on other historical forms of organisation in which it is absent, such as, say, the medieval household.

Markets and organisations

Turning to the issue of the universal applicability of the market, the study of organisation is in itself a conceptual concession by economists. By using a reified metaphor of the market, economists have analysed a range of traditionally non-economic problems and apparently non-market activities as if they were market transactions (Sawyer, 1993, p. 25). In doing so economists have effectively extended their denial of the existence or importance of collective organisation from economic to non-economic arenas. According to Clifford Geertz, an economic anthropologist, the 'word market itself' has become 'as much an analytic idea as the name of an institution, and the study of it . . . as much a theoretical as a descriptive enterprise' (Geertz, 1992, p. 226).

Confronting the existence of organisation has compelled organisational economists to concede that markets themselves are 'institutions that exist to facilitate exchange' (Coase, 1990c, p. 7), or even that 'a market is as much an organization as is a bureaucracy' (Ouchi, 1980, p. 132n; Alchian and Demsetz, 1986, p. 111). Acknowledging the existence of organisations undermines the universal applicability of the market metaphor, because either organisations are different from markets, or else, even if the market metaphor is deemed to be universally applicable, markets as institutions have to be differentiated in order to include organisations. Williamson (1983, 1985) takes the first approach, distinguishing between markets and hierarchies, whereas Alchian and Demsetz (1986) take the second, by considering firms as a specific type of market. 'The view that the firm *is* a market, a particular pattern of voluntary exchange relations, and not a unitary actor at all' is, as Nelson and Winter say, distinctive 'for its intellectual boldness and for its faithfulness to the individualist tradition' (1982, pp. 54–5). Nelson and Winter see the 'firms as markets' and 'markets and hierarchies' perspectives as alternative ways out of the neoclassical blind alley in which the firm is portrayed as a black box.

Another important concession to the importance of organisation comes from the economist Albert Hirschman, in his essay on *Exit, Voice, and Loyalty* (1970). According to Hirschman, an organisation can learn about its failings from its members or its customers in two ways. First, a firm's customers or an organisation's members can exercise the *'exit option'*, by ceasing their purchases from the firm, or ending their membership of the organisation. This signals their dissatisfaction to the organisation, which will need to respond if it is to survive. On the other hand, a firm's customers or an organisation's members can exercise the *'voice option'* by expressing 'their dissatisfaction directly to management or to some other authority to which management is subordinate or through general protest addressed to anyone who cares to listen' (Hirschman, 1970, p. 4).

Hirschman believes that exit belongs to the realm of economics and voice to the domain of politics, with each discipline neglecting the other option. Exit is:

> the sort of mechanism economics thrives on. It is impersonal – one either exits or one does not; it is impersonal – any face-to-face confrontation between customer and firm with its imponderable and unpredictable elements is avoided and success and failure to the organization are communicated to it by a set of statistics; and it is indirect – any recovery on the part of the declining firm comes by courtesy of the Invisible Hand, as an unintended by-product of the customer's decision to exit.

Exit corresponds to what Williamson calls the 'discrete transaction paradigm', which has 'served both law and economics well' (1985, pp. 68–9). Williamson quotes Macneil to describe discrete transactions which are 'sharp in by clear agreement; sharp out by clear performance' (quoted in Williamson, 1985, p. 68).

Economists are biased 'in favor of exit and against voice' because they consider 'withdrawal or exit as the "direct" way of expressing one's unfavorable views of an organization'; but, as Hirschman observes, 'A person less well trained in economics might naively suggest that the direct way of expressing views is to express them!' (Hirschman, 1970, pp. 15–17). As for Friedman's view that exercising voice means resorting to 'cumbrous political channels' (quoted by Hirschman, 1970, pp. 16–17), this reflects how unintelligible normal human communication is to economists more than it reflects humanity's difficulties with communication.

Organisation theorists have criticised transaction cost economics for the empirical inadequacy of the dichotomy between markets and hierarchies. In doing so, Stinchcombe at least acknowledges that:

> It is a great advance to conceive that dichotomy as a variable to be explained, as Coase and his successors have done. But things in the world are hardly ever dichotomies, and they are especially unlikely to be dichotomies when the economy sets a large number of intelligent men and women looking for the intermediate ground. (1990, pp. 234–5)

Whether or not the economy sets intelligent men and women looking for the intermediate ground, the twofold classification scheme proposed by transaction cost economics has certainly set organisation theorists and sociologists searching for exceptions.

There are two parts to the alleged inadequacy of the markets and hierarchies dichotomy. The first is whether markets and hierarchies are specifically capitalist institutions. In Williamson's version of transaction costs, the ubiquity of markets is assumed, as revealed by his assumption that 'in the beginning there were markets' (1983, pp. 20–1). Debate has focused on whether markets can be logically, or were historically, prior to hierarchies (Fourie, 1993, p. 47). According to Williamson, organisations arise from market failures, and markets take over when there are organisational failures (1983, p. 20, n.1). Although he stresses that markets and hierarchies 'coexist' (Williamson and Ouchi, 1981, p. 387), the underlying assumption seems to be that hierarchies may change but markets remain the same.

The second part of the inadequacy of the markets and hierarchy dichotomy concerns the extent to which it captures the diversity of arrangements within a broadly capitalist framework. This issue has received more attention from organisation theorists. Stinchcombe affirms his 'assent to the core of the markets and hierarchies tradition' but seeks to extend it (Stinchcombe, 1990, p. 235). He finds 'social structures that work like hierarchies' constructed 'out of contracts between legally equal corporate bargaining agents in a market'. He therefore restates the Williamson hypothesis in a 'continuous form' (1990, pp. 195, 233). Williamson has gone some way towards accommodating the extension of the markets and hierarchies perspective with his acknowledgement that there is 'relational contracting' between parties within markets (1985), and 'hybrid' governance structures in addition to markets and hierarchies (1991).

Partly in reaction to the markets and hierarchies dichotomy, a literature has emerged within sociology promoting the 'idea of networks as a means of coordination. . . . In contrast to either hierarchy or market, networks coordinate through less formal, more egalitarian and cooperative means' (Thompson, 1991, p. 171). This is expounded by Thompson *et al.* in *Markets, Hierarchies and Networks* (1991). This is a very misleading book; it is intended as an introductory selection of readings for sociologists, but it does not include any excerpts from leading organisational economists such as Alchian, Coase, Demsetz or Williamson, who are given short shrift by various critics. According to the advocates of networks, 'the most important attribute of network operation [is] the formation and sustaining of *trust* within and between networks. . . . If it is price competition that is the central coordination mechanism of the market and administrative orders that of hierarchy, then it is trust and cooperation that centrally articulates networks' (Frances *et al.*, 1991, p. 15).

If it is being asserted that networks alone are predicated on trust, any instance of trust can be construed as a manifestation of networks, but then network becomes a residual catch-all category that absorbs all others.

However, it is a misrepresentation of transaction cost economics to suggest that trust and reciprocation are absent from either markets or hierarchies. Williamson himself points out that, 'trust is important and business men rely on it much more extensively than is commonly realized' (1983, p. 108). Williamson (1983, p. 107) cites with approval Stewart Macaulay's landmark paper, 'Non-Contractual Relations in Business', an empirical study which shows that a large proportion (over half) of most business is carried out without resort to formal agreements or contracts. This being at least in part because 'Such planning indicates a lack of trust and blunts the demands of friendship, turning a cooperative venture into an antagonistic horse trade' (Macaulay, 1992 [1963], p. 277). Williamson does not argue that trust is either absent or unnecessary within markets or hierarchies, but that forms of organisation that rely on trust alone are unsustainable: 'cooperative modes of economic organisation, by which I mean those where trust and good intentions are generously imputed to the membership, are very fragile. Such organizations are easily invaded and exploited by agents who do not possess those qualities' (1985, pp. 64–5).

That the importance of trust and its peculiar characteristics are recognised by organisational economists is clear from Arrow's treatment:

> trust has a very important pragmatic value, if nothing else. Trust is an important lubricant of the social system. It is extremely efficient; it saves a lot of trouble to have a fair degree of reliance on other people's word. (1974, p. 23)

Trust is easily undermined but difficult to establish and sustain, since it is, 'not a commodity which can be bought very easily. If you have to buy it, you already have some doubts about what you've bought. . . . The agreement to trust each other can not be bought . . . it is not even necessarily very easy for it to be achieved by a signed contract saying we will work with each other' (1974, pp. 23, 26). If networks are allegedly based on trust then it is reasonable to ask how that trust has come about.

The advocates of networks make the mistake of contrasting abstract models of markets and hierarchies with the diversity of actual arrangements. Their conclusion is that whereas once there may only have been markets and hierarchies, now there are networks as well, as if the model of markets and hierarchies corresponds to an earlier historical period instead of being an analytical dichotomy. Whereas transaction costs economists claim to be able to predict the circumstances under which markets or hierarchies will prevail, networks are advocated under virtually all circumstances. Thus a predictive model is sacrificed in favour of a taxonomy. The advocates of networks often seem to be saying little more than that markets and hierarchies are nasty but networks might be nice.

Jeffrey Bradach and Robert Eccles make the point that 'three-fold typologies which simply add a category to the market and hierarchy dichotomy' are misleading, because they 'rest on the premiss that market and hierarchy are mutually exclusive means to govern transactions' (1991, p. 276). Control mechanisms such as authority and trust as are found in both markets and hierarchies as well as relational contracting. The more general point is that markets, hierarchies, and any other arrangements which can be identified, are embedded in social contexts in which there are only certain amounts of trust at any given time.

Social contexts can be conceptualised as social networks, which is the approach of social network analysis. Confusion has inevitably arisen as a result of the unfortunate use of the same term, 'network', to describe the proposal for an alternative organisational form, as well as the social context within which organisations operate. This confusion has allowed the advocates of network forms of organisation to identify themselves with the well-established social network analysis, which is far from incompatible with transaction costs economics (Wellman and Berkowitz, 1988). Network analysis tends to be very statistical. It focuses on the linkages between a defined set of social entities, such as people or organisations (Knoke and Kuklinski, 1991, p. 175; Leinhardt, 1977, p. xiii). The interlocking directorates which connect corporations are a particularly good example (Burt, 1983). Leinhardt argues that by 'focusing attention on the ties between individuals' the network approach 'forces social scientists to think about constraints on individual behavior, constraints that are inherent in the way social relations are organized' (1977, p. xiv). Such constraints clearly pervade markets as well as all other organisational forms.

Stinchcombe is right to point out that the analytical dichotomy between markets and hierarchies does not translate readily into empirically identifiable ideal types, but there is a risk that a useful conceptual distinction will be undermined by sociologists obsessed with compiling an endless list of exceptional cases. A more important point is that since markets are embedded in social contexts, the 'pre-existence' (Pitelis, 1993, p. 18), ubiquity and homogeneity of markets cannot be assumed in the way that it is by Coase and Williamson.

Louis Putterman argues that 'the "ahistoricity" of markets is as much a projection of neoclassical methodological propensities as of the character of markets themselves' (1986a, p. 16). In Hirschman's terms it must be recognised that the categories of exit and voice are 'contrasting, though not mutually exclusive' (1970, p. 15), and voice is exercised in markets just as exit is exercised in organisations. The advocates of networks seem to accept that real markets correspond to the neoclassical model of the market, which means that another category, such as networks, is required to capture the diversity of actual arrangements. This only deflects attention away from research into the historical origins, contexts and diversity of markets (Anderson and Latham, 1986). As the Marxist historian E. P. Thompson points out, 'the "market" turns out to be a junction-point between social, economic, and intellectual histories, and a sensitive metaphor for many kinds of exchange' (1993, p. 259).

Mainstream and radical

Each of the dichotomies discussed so far can be interpreted in relation to their political orientation. Many sociologists see themselves as radicals, and they often identify economics with mainstream conservatism. There is a danger that this reduces the divergence between economics and sociology to the political differences between neoclassical free market liberals and sociologically informed advocates of reform and state intervention in the economy (Hirsch *et al.*, 1990, pp. 45–6; Block, 1990). Lex Donaldson, an organisation theorist, complains that sociology is often 'introduced to students as an inherently critical, anti-establishment, social movement, and the idea of science is treated as a sham' (1985, p. ix). Jay Barney reports an American Academy of Management meeting where comments could be heard like, 'all economists are greedy fascists', and the economists responded with, 'all behavioural scientists are mushy-headed liberals' (1990, p. 390). There is a danger that this name-calling can end up as 'vulgar political determinism' (McCloskey, 1990, p. 52), where any theoretical perspective is allegedly explained and therefore dismissed as simply an expression of its adherents' political beliefs. Besides, whereas Marxism has been largely excluded from mainstream economic debates, some organisational economists, notably Williamson (1980), have opened up a dialogue with Marxian and radical political economists, such as Samuel Bowles (1986) and Stephen Marglin (1976), who share an interest in the internal organisation of capitalist firms.

In Britain and the USA the dominant ideology in economics is definitely neoclassical, but neoclassical thinking is not necessarily linked to either right-wing or left-wing policies. It is probably fair to say that the typical thought pattern of academic economists up to the 1980s glorified 'laissez-faire micro-economics while at the same time favoring Keynesian interventionist macroeconomics' (Nelson and Sheffrin, 1991). This might mean that left-wing neoclassical economists could strongly oppose free market government economic policies but remain orthodox in relation to the theory of the firm and organisation. Fortunately, making a distinction between mainstream and radical theories of the firm and organisation is relatively straightforward compared to the rest of social theory. Putterman has expressed the division clearly: 'To be "mainstream" is almost by definition to believe in, or at least to be open to, the legitimacy of the capitalist firm and of the economic system in which it is embedded, while to be radical seems to require some display of hostility toward them' (Putterman, 1986a, p. 25).

There is a view that analytical economic modelling necessarily reflects a conservative ideological position because it 'inevitably understates the complexity of real phenomena' and imposes 'a normatively motivated closure' (Neimark and Tinker, 1987, pp. 662–4). But abstract modelling is not confined to neoclassical economics. Baran and Sweezy are among the most influential Marxian economists and they give one of the best arguments for modelling:

> Scientific understanding proceeds by way of constructing and analysing 'models' of the segments or aspects of reality under study. The purpose of these models is not to give a mirror image of reality, not to include all its elements in their exact sizes and proportions, but rather to single out and make available for intensive investigation those elements which are decisive. We abstract from non-essentials, we blot out the unimportant to get an unobstructed view of the important, we magnify in order to improve the range and accuracy of our observation. A model is, and must be, unrealistic in the sense in which the word is commonly used. Nevertheless, and in a sense paradoxically, if it is a good model it provides the key to understanding reality. (1968, p. 27)

Marxism has not been immune from obsessive modelling. Schumpeter derided those Marxists who tried to develop a 'pure theory of the capitalist machine' (1976, p. 74), and, as Hodgson points out, 'Examples of mechanistic modelling in the Marxian tradition are, unfortunately, not difficult to find' (1988, p. 301n).

Whether or not it is appropriate to make unrealistic assumptions for the purpose of building models is an issue that tends to be obscured because economists use their models as 'a set of idealized criteria for evaluating the correctness or incorrectness of existing economic arrangements and for guiding social policy' (Martinelli and Smelser, 1990, p. 3). Economists' policy advice 'comes to carry an implicit prescription that individuals always should act out of self interest' in order to realise the benefits of policies derived from an imaginary model of the world in which self interested behaviour is assumed (Davis, 1990, p. 752).

The assumption of rational maximising behaviour is not necessarily linked to *laissez-faire*, liberal social policies. Game theory has been used by rational choice Marxists, notably Jon Elster, to develop a theory of revolution (1990). Patrick Dunleavy, a radical political scientist, set out to show that the public choice models inspired by Olson (1971) were 'internally inconsistent and ideologically slanted'; but, ten years later, he ended up using public-choice theory to argue for a democratic socialist position (Dunleavy, 1991). So the methodological issues that arise from making assumptions in order to build models cannot be reduced to political differences.

The political implications of evolutionism and its association with social Darwinism have already been discussed. If there is a political dimension to the markets and hierarchies dichotomy, it is that those who are open to the legitimacy of the capitalist firm and the economic system in which it is embedded, or the possibility of its reform, tend to find markets, or at least more egalitarian sounding arrangements, within hierarchies, while radicals tend to see markets as hierarchical. The mainstream is epitomised by Alchian and Demsetz's view:

> It is common to see the firm characterized by the power to settle issues by fiat, by authority, or by disciplinary action superior to that available in the conventional market. This is delusion. The firm does not own all its inputs. It has no power of fiat, no authority, no disciplinary action any different in the slightest degree from ordinary market contracting between any two people. (1986, p. 111)

The radical view is indicated by the title of Pitelis's book, *Market and Non-market Hierarchies*; he regards 'the market itself as a hierarchy!' (1991, p. 8).

The dichotomy between markets and firms is important for Marxists and for Marxian influenced radicals in their treatment of work organisation (Hodgson, 1988, p. 199). From a Marxian viewpoint the existence of sustainable non-market, non-hierarchical modes of organisation within a framework of capitalist property rights would undermine the view that hierarchy can only be dispensed with by dismantling capitalist market institutions and property rights (Gustafsson, 1991a, p. 24).

The attempt to undermine the markets and hierarchies dichotomy is analogous to the search for a third way between capitalism and socialism. Like other third way literatures, the advocates of networks confuse description, prediction and prescription. Networks are clearly attractive to those who are not enamoured of either markets or hierarchies but who cannot countenance the possibility of changing radically the property rights within which these organisational forms are embedded. They end up portraying phenomena which can easily be explained by the various perspectives within organisational economics as inexplicable without the concept of networks. Thus they refer to:

> on the one hand an internal reorganization of the big corporation to allow a renewed flexibility and less bureaucratic style of operation, with semi-autonomous departments and divisions contracting amongst themselves in a network framework; on the other hand a re-emphasis on external flexibility with respect to supply contracting associated again with network-type structures. (Frances *et al.*, 1991, pp. 15–16)

For transaction cost economics this may amount to no more than a semantic dispute over whether increasing corporate flexibility can be adequately described using transaction costs terminology such as relational contracting (Williamson, 1992), or whether it really requires a new term such as 'networks'. But from radical and Marxian standpoints, describing even delayered, decentralised multinational capitalist corporations as egalitarian networks must be seen as dissimulation. The networks literature resembles the premature pronouncement of the 'coming demise of bureaucracy and hierarchy' by various management gurus such as Rosabeth Moss Kanter (1990, p. 351) and Tom Peters (1992). As the more perceptive management writers have pointed out, 'Peters does not actually mean the hierarchy will vanish in the sense that no one will be more senior than another', but that hierarchy will take a different form (Stewart, 1993).

Conclusion

The view taken here is that a clear-cut differentiation between organisational economics and organisation theory is difficult, not least because the differences between them cannot be reduced to a division across any single dimension reflecting the boundary between economics and sociology. Both disciplines have set up a series of dichotomies that turn out to be exaggerated or even false. There is clearly a preference for deductive, analytical model-building in economics, as opposed to empirical research and inductive theory in sociology. There is a tendency for model-building to displace historical research, but it is not possible to abstain from modelling completely without lapsing into empiricism. Organisational economics does at least depart from some of the more unrealistic assumptions that are made by neoclassical economics for the purposes of building models, and this offers the possibility of a convergence with organisation theory.

Economists have set up a false dichotomy between rational choice modelling and functionalist evolutionary theory. Both can be teleological, and evolutionary theory is no less susceptible to equilibrium analysis than rational choice, as is shown by the advance of game theory in biology (Poundstone, 1993). Historical research is best justified by stressing the importance of processes in historical change as opposed to equilibrium, not by insisting, as so many organisation theorists do, on elaborate typologies to replace useful conceptual dichotomies such as markets and hierarchies.

It may or may not be legitimate to use 'if . . . then' propositions derived from equilibrium models as the basis for forecasting quantitative changes in market prices. However, the evolutionary historical approach that is required for analysing organisations and institutions more or less rules out such detailed prediction. As an evolutionary economist, Boulding readily admits that evolutionary theory 'does not have very much predictive power' (1981, p. 44). McCloskey contends that '*Prediction is not possible in economics*' (1986, p. 15). A rather semantic counter argument is that 'denials of the power to predict' are themselves a form of prediction (Hutchison, 1981, p. 280). McCloskey also alleges that even though the theory of evolution is, 'one of the most successful of all scientific theories, [it] makes no predictions and is therefore unfalsifiable by prediction . . . its main facts, its dinosaur bones and multicolored birds, are things to be explained, not to be predicted' (1986, p. 15).

Evolutionary theory in biology does not abstain from prediction in the way that McCloskey implies. If it did so, 'survival of the fittest' would be a meaningless tautology, because fitness would be defined by survival. In fact, as Gould points out, 'Better survival is a prediction to be tested, not a definition of adaptation' (1991, p. 236). Darwin's proposition that natural selection is the mechanism of evolution was very much a prediction, and it has been confirmed by the discovery of genes. McCloskey is right in the sense that, although evolutionary theory has predicted the mechanisms of change, it cannot predict the outcome of change itself. By analogy, organisational economics cannot predict organisational innovations and institutional change, even if it can predict the mechanisms by which organisational change may take place.

The major criticism of mainstream neoclassical economics must be that it deliberately ignores issues of organisation (Stiglitz, 1991). The real existence of the firm is 'something of an embarrassment' for neoclassical theory (Putterman, 1986b, p. 24), and it is hard put to explain the existence of a vast body of management literature (Green, 1988, p. 308). Whereas neoclassical economics threatens to marginalise organisation theory by denying the importance, or even the existence of organisation, organisational economics threatens to compete with other disciplines in the study of organisations by taking organisation seriously (Williamson, 1985, p. 297). In the context of a general expansion of economics into sociology, and the reinvigoration of economic sociology, the development of organisational economics promises to undermine the boundary between the disciplines in the study of organisations. This could be an opportunity for opening up a dialogue between economics and sociology, rather than a threat to the continuation of sociological theory and research on organisations, which has always been one of sociology's strongest areas.

Organisational economics and organisation theory

Introduction

Organisation theorists and organisational economists tend to see each other as belonging to more unified camps than they really do. To be blunt, some organisation theorists try to lump all organisational economists together so that they can all be dismissed out of hand. On the other hand, organisational economists will often take one or two leading organisation theorists as representative, so that they can say they have taken organisation theory into account. Oliver Williamson (1990, p. 5) is a good example of a prominent organisational economist who tends to see organisation theory as more unified than it is. He seems to believe that organisation theory is derived from a few classic texts starting with Chester Barnard's *The Functions of the Executive* (1964 [1938]), followed by Herbert Simon's *Administrative Behavior* (1976 [1945]) and Philip Selznick's *Leadership in Administration* (1957). This clearly reflects an American bias. More importantly, it obscures the diversity within organisation theory.

The origins of organisation theory are usually traced to Max Weber's seminal writings on bureaucracy (Weber, 1991; Reed, 1992b, p. 237), but no mention of Weber can be found in Williamson's major works (1983, 1985). Much of organisation theory consists of modifications to and disagreements with Weber's work on authority and bureaucracy (Donaldson, 1985, p. 6; Clegg and Dunkerley, 1980; Perry, 1992). Organisation theorists have refined Weber's intuitive definition of power, but this literature is not referred to by organisational economists, most of whom prefer to explain the existence of organisations in terms of efficiency rather than power. The second part of this chapter explores the disagreement between organisational economists and organisation theorists over the meanings, and the relative importance, of efficiency and power. As a prelude to this, the first part of this chapter explores the meanings and significance of the concepts of organisations and institutions. These have been discussed less often, probably because there appears to be considerable agreement.

Organisations and institutions

Although organisational economics is associated with the revival of institutionalism within economics, the term 'institution' remains imprecise. For example, Pitelis (1993, p. 26), a radical economist, claims that in *The Economic Institutions of Capitalism*, 'Williamson (1985) fails to define either capitalism or institutions!' Furthermore, using the term *'institutionalism'* is likely to cause confusion, because it has 'disparate meanings in different disciplines' (DiMaggio and Powell, 1991, p. 1; Scott, 1994, p. 55). There are 'old' and 'new' versions of institutionalism within organisation theory and sociology, just as there are in economics.

The first issue to be addressed must be the possibility of making a distinction between organisations and institutions. The word 'organisation' suggests action and change, whereas 'institution' is associated with stability and continuity. This comes through in the use of the terms by both organisation theorists and organisational economists. In Henry Mintzberg's popular version of organisation theory: 'Organization . . . means collective action in the pursuit of a common purpose, a fancy way of saying that a bunch of people have come together under an identifiable label . . . to produce some product or service' (1989, p. 2). Richard Daft gives a more technical definition in a well-established textbook on organisation: *'organizations* are social entities that are goal-directed, deliberately structured activity systems with an identifiable boundary' (1992, p. 7).

These definitions of organisation from organisation theory are reassuringly similar to the definition of organisations given by Douglass North, the neoinstitutional economic historian: 'groups of individuals bound by some common purpose to achieve objectives'. On the other hand, North reckons that institutions 'are the rules of the game in a society or, more formally, are the humanly devised constraints that shape human interaction. . . . Institutions reduce uncertainty by providing a structure to everyday life'; institutions include both the formal and informal constraints 'that human beings devise to shape human interaction' (North, 1990a, pp. 3–5). Harvey Leibenstein (1987, p. 35), a more idiosyncratic organisational economist, sees most 'institutionalized and quasi-institutionalized arrangements . . . such as mealtimes, normal working hours, nature of meals, and sleeping times', as examples of 'invariant', or 'inertial behavior', which involves 'doing something more or less repetitive within a recognized pattern. . . . It is because of inertia that we are able, to a considerable degree, to make predictions about other people's behavior, and about the world in general'. Lynne Zucker is one of the leading lights in the new institutionalism in organisation theory. She has found a quote which seems to sum up discussion: 'The only idea common to all usages of the term "institution" is that of some sort of establishment of relative permanence of a distinctly social sort' (Hughes, 1936, p. 180, quoted in Zucker, 1991, p. 83).

Peter Berger and Thomas Luckmann's *The Social Construction of Reality* (1971) was a major impetus for the 'new' institutionalism in sociology and organisation theory (DiMaggio and Powell, 1991, p. 21). Berger and Luckmann devote a chapter to 'Institutionalization'. The process of institutionalisation is preceded by 'habitualization', whereby: 'Any action that is repeated frequently becomes cast into a pattern, which can then be reproduced with an economy of effort.' As well as economising on effort, 'Habitualization carries with it the important psychological gain that choices are narrowed' (Berger and Luckmann, 1971, pp. 70–1). This gives individuals 'psychological relief' from the burden of making continual decisions that would otherwise result from the human condition in which instinct is fundamentally undirected.

Institutionalisation itself occurs whenever two or more individuals recognise a typical pattern of habitualisation, which means that the habitual behaviour is beginning to transcend the individual and may be transmitted to other actors who were not part of the original process of habitualisation. Institutionalisation brings segments of human activity under social control by limiting choices and providing a framework in which choices can be made. According to Berger and Luckmann (1971, pp. 72–7), 'institutions generally manifest themselves in collectivities containing considerable numbers of people. . . . Institutionalization is incipient in every social situation continuing in time'. The most important gain from institutionalisation is that individuals are able to predict each other's actions. In terms of organisational economics, institutionalisation could be interpreted as economising on bounded rationality.

To illustrate the distinction between organisations and institutions, North (1990a) uses an analogy with competitive team sports, such as soccer. Institutions correspond to the formal and informal rules of the game, and organisations are the teams. The way the teams play is constrained, but by no means wholly determined, by the written and unwritten rules of the game; some teams consistently break the rules. Eventually both the written and unwritten rules may change in response to the changing ways in which the teams play the game. Thus the nature of the game changes over time. In the same way, organisations can change the formal and informal institutions by which they are constrained, but the outcomes of such changes may not necessarily be those the organisations intended. In the team game analogy, a team that enjoys an advantage by consistently cheating may lose out if the rules are changed as a result, or if every other team starts cheating in the same way. Furthermore, teams are also constrained by the ability of their players. Whilst existing players' skills may be developed, or new players substituted for old ones, the general implication of North's analogy is that organisations, no more than sports teams, cannot simultaneously and continuously change everything, from the players to the rules. There is a need for some consistency.

The types of social, political and economic organisations that come into existence, and the way they operate, is influenced by the institutional framework. In turn, organisations influence the institutional framework. North (1990a) emphasises the interaction between institutions and organisations and focuses on organisations as agents of institutional change. Extending North's distinction between organisations and institutions, and using the team game analogy, three sources of influence on the behaviour of an organisation can be set out (see Figure 4.1). These are: institutions (the formal and informal rules of the game); individual actors (the players); and the routinised activities of the organisation itself and other organisations (the past game-plans of the team and other teams).

The diverse approaches to organisations within economics and sociology give differing interpretations and attribute varying degrees of importance to these sources of influence on organisations. Of course, the distinction between actors, organisation and institutions is conceptual, and as such it is often difficult to sustain. Among both organisation theorists and organisational

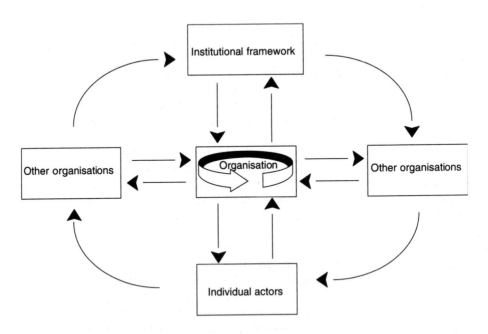

Source: Adapted from Williamson, 1992 and Scott, 1994.

FIGURE 4.1   Organisations and institutions

economists, the distinctions are often obscured. With Williamson, for example, the terms organisation and institution appear to be used interchangeably. But this seems to be almost inadvertent on Williamson's part, as in the following passage: 'complex organizations commonly serve a variety of economic and noneconomic purposes. That is plainly true of the economic institutions of capitalism' (1985, p. 2).

What is more significant is that Williamson and other organisational economists are more likely to deduce the form of organisations from strong behavioural assumptions and relatively fixed preferences of individual actors, even if they depart from the assumption that preferences are virtually fixed by biology, which is espoused by those such as Becker (1979) and Posner (1992). The behaviour and preferences that are influenced by participation in organisations – which Williamson (1992) refers to as 'endogenous preferences' – play a minor part in his explanatory framework. In other words, what Williamson does is effectively to collapse organisations between the combined pressures from the behaviour of individual actors and the institutional environment. To use the team game analogy again, in Williamson's framework, the outcome of any game can be predicted given knowledge about the nature of the players and the rules they are subject to.

There is also confusion as to the distinction between organisations and institutions within institutionalism in organisation theory. The central figure for the 'old' institutionalism in organisation theory is Selznick. According to Selznick, ' "to institutionalize" is to *infuse with value* beyond the technical requirements at hand', and 'the test of infusion with value is *expendability* . . . when value-infusion takes place . . . there is a resistance to change' (1957, pp. 17–18). Selznick, like Barnard, has been taken up by prescriptive management writers such as Peters and Waterman (1982, p. 85), because he suggests that the institutionalisation process is 'subject to conscious design and intervention' (Scott, 1987, p. 495). Even though it is prescriptive, Scott defends Selznick's 'treatment of institutionalization' as useful for the new institutionalism in organisation theory, on the grounds that it 'informs us *that* values are instilled; not *how* this occurs' (1987, p. 495). By emphasising the importance of values as institutions, as well as constraints such as the legal code, and the ways in which values can be changed, there is a danger that institutions are collapsed into organisations. It might appear that the rules of the game can be any rules that the players of a one-off game believe the rules to be.

Unfortunately, due to the influence of the organisational culture perspective (Morgan, 1986; Ott, 1989), a diluted version of the social construction of reality has found currency in organisation theory. There is a widespread misapprehension that research into the social construction of reality has to be qualitative and ethnographic. This can result in a misinterpretation of the process of institutionalisation that lends itself to the notion that institutions can be constructed and distorted almost at will. It has led many organisation theorists to misconstrue the conscious misrepresentation of socially constructed reality by organised actors as instances of the social construction of reality. Not unreasonably, organisation theorists who take the contingency view that, for the most part, an organisation's structure and behaviour can be explained by its context (Pugh, 1990), have been critical of this diluted version of the social construction of reality. Donaldson in particular maintains that the outcomes of human decision processes are largely determined by their environment, and that the 'human processes of perception, intention and so on' are 'epiphenomena' (Donaldson, 1991). From organisational economics, Williamson's view is that much that is studied as part of the social construction of reality is mere 'tosh (superfluous rituals)', that detracts from analysis of the 'core features of the institutional environment' (Williamson, 1995, p. 243). The fascination that ephemera seems to hold for many organisation theorists who proclaim themselves to be social constructionists has deflected discussion away from more important concerns, such as the extent to which the determining environment consists of universal phenomena, or historically specific socially constructed institutions.

Some of the new institutionalism in sociology tends to find 'institutions everywhere, from handshakes to marriages to strategic-planning departments'. The danger of this is that the preferences of individual actors are endogenised to such an extent that it is said that 'institutions constitute actors as well as constrain them' (DiMaggio and Powell, 1991, pp. 7–9). For some proponents of the new institutionalism in organisation theory, there is a tendency to reduce organisations themselves to institutions, given the extent of patterned behaviour that takes place within most large organisations. This is evident in the work of Zucker, who treats organisations *as* institutions, and describes organisations as 'the preeminent institutional form in modern society' (1983, p. 1). Fortunately, some of the best of the new institutionalism in organisation theory focuses on 'organizational structures and processes that are industry wide, national or international in scope' (DiMaggio and Powell, 1991, p. 9). A social constructionist perspective can be applied to longitudinal quantitative studies of large data sets (Fligstein, 1985). This allows a discussion of issues such as work organisation in general, rather than practices that are specific to a particular location or organisation which are the focus of the organisational culture perspective (Ott, 1989).

Paul DiMaggio and Walter Powell are American organisation theorists associated with the new institutionalism. In an influential article they have come up with the concept of the 'organizational field' in order to try to explain the 'startling homogeneity of organizational forms and practices' (DiMaggio and Powell, 1991, p. 64). An organisational field is defined as, 'Those organizations that, in the aggregate, constitute a recognized area of institutional life: key suppliers, resource and product consumers, regulatory agencies, and other organizations that produce similar services or products' (DiMaggio and Powell, 1991, p. 64). A virtue of this concept is that it rests in part on actors' recognition of the field. Within an organisational field there a tendency towards homogenisation of organisations. DiMaggio and Powell's term for this homogenisation is 'isomorphism', which is 'a constraining process that forces one unit in a population to resemble other units that face the same set of environmental conditions' (1991, p. 66).

DiMaggio and Powell (1991) emphasise that even when organisations are coerced into conformity, this coercion is exercised by other organisations within the organisational field. This dereifies the institutional rules. To use North's team game analogy yet again, it is as if the rules of the game are recognised as being dependent upon the governing body and the referee, who influence the game by making and enforcing the rules. Organisation theorists associated with the new institutionalism are less concerned with obvious coercion and more concerned with what DiMaggio and Powell describe as the mimetic and normative processes of isomorphism. Mimetic isomorphism occurs as a result of the tendency for organisations to imitate other organisations when faced with uncertainty. Normative pressures arise from the professionalisation of organisation members. Professional networks span organisations, and through these networks models of organisations are diffused. This recognises the importance of other teams and of the players in the team game analogy.

The confusion over the distinction between organisations and institutions within organisational economics arises in part from a failure to specify the institutional framework within which capitalist firms arise. To be more specific, the private property rights that are generally recognised to constitute capitalism are more or less taken as given. Taking the institutional framework as given tends to obscure the historical specificity of particular forms of organisation such as capitalist firms. Thus Coase's original question, 'Why is there any organization?' implicitly equates organisations with capitalist firms in the same way that functionalist organisation theory does. It also obscures the historical development of markets themselves as organisations (Ouchi, 1980, p. 132) or institutions, as Coase himself has recognised (1990c).

As an economic historian, North is concerned with broader issues than just the emergence of capitalist firms. He poses a more general question than Coase: 'What makes it necessary to constrain human interaction with institutions?' (North, 1991, p. 97), a question which is largely answered by Berger and Luckmann's exposition of the social construction of reality. Coase's question could be rephrased along the following lines: In the context of capitalist property rights, why have firms displaced markets to the extent that they have? As long as it is clear that capitalism is not assumed to be universal, then the institutions that constitute it can be taken as given to some extent in order to focus on the capitalist firm as a form of organisation, since all contemporary capitalist firms operate in a context of markets and nation states. If the discussion were to be extended to include an analysis of the context in which firms exist, then both markets and the state would require much more extensive treatment.

The important point that comes out of this discussion is that organisations can be said to be embedded in institutions, but the extent to which they are is necessarily disputed. Neoclassically inclined economists tend to press for economic theories of organisation to be formalised in such a way that they can be abstracted from the institutional environment and applied to collectivities in general (Alchian and Woodward, 1988, p. 77; Pollak, 1985). Against this, the few sociologists and organisation theorists who are prepared to countenance a contribution to the study of organisations from economics insist that economic organisations such as markets and hierarchies, 'are themselves embedded in broader systems of social relations' (Granovetter, 1992a, p. 65; Stinchcombe, 1990, p. 344). The concept of embeddedness elaborated by Mark Granovetter allows for a distinction to be made between economic organisation and social institutions without collapsing the economic into an undifferentiated social system, which is what all too many functional sociological perspectives end up doing.

Economic organisations are embedded in other institutions and social structures in two senses. First, there is the embeddedness in institutions that are more structural – most importantly the explicit enforcement of property rights through the state and the legal system. Although these can be thought of as social structures it is important to recognise that they are enacted by other purposive organisations. Second, there is the embeddedness, or 'imbeddedness' as North calls it, in informal or cultural constraints. According to North, it is this type of embeddedness that explains why change tends to be incremental rather than discontinuous (1990a, p. 6). Even drastic changes in the social structure, such as revolution and the redefinition of property rights, are unlikely to change economic organisations in the ways envisaged because of the embeddedness of cultural constraints. It also explains why it is difficult for nation states to emulate each other, in the way that Western industrial economies such as Britain have sought to emulate Japan's perceived success, since it is difficult to identify and change the important informal constraints that make up national cultures (Hamilton and Biggart, 1988; Whitley, 1992).

Even though it is widely accepted that contemporary capitalist institutions encourage experimentation, only a few organisational or technological inventions are ever turned into widely diffused innovations (Stinchcombe, 1990). Some of the sociological reasons for this are explained by Neil Fligstein:

As it turns out, there have not been many organizational innovations in the past hundred years. This reflects the fact that managers in organizations are generally highly constrained and that to change the course of the large firm requires taking huge risks. Equally important, managers and entrepreneurs have a stake in what exists. They have an organizational story about what the organization does and how it does it. Those who are in control generally base that control on existing organizational strategy and structure. This illustrates one of the central insights of organization theory: organizations tend not to change what they are doing because of deep-seated interests to continue business as usual. Only when those interests can be changed do organizations strike out on new courses of action. (1990, p. 9)

The boundary between institutions and organisations is clearly not fixed, since it is through purposive collective activity, that is, organisation, that actors are able to change the routines and rules, that is, the institutions, within which they organise. However, actors cannot change every routine and rule all at once. If they could do so they would have no need for either organisations or institutions. Roughly speaking, approaches to the study of organisations that are party to, or could be party to, the disputes between organisation theory and organisational economics, are divided over the emphasis that should be accorded to the constraints on capitalist firms from the external institutional framework, including the regularities in individual actors' behaviour, or the capacity of capitalist firms to influence external institutions such as property rights and individual behaviour.

Efficiency and power

A few sociologists (Stinchcombe, 1990; Zald, 1987) and organisation theorists (Barney and Ouchi, 1986; Barney, 1990; Hesterly *et al.*, 1990) have welcomed organisational economics, but most have been more or less sceptical about it (Oberschall and Leifer, 1986; Francis *et al.*, 1983). A major objection to organisational economics is that it emphasises efficiency and neglects power in its explanations of economic organisation. This is seen by radical organisation theorists in particular as 'a totally unsociological perspective' (Morgan, 1990, p. 180). The dispute over whether efficiency or power best explains the existence and form of organisations comes close to being a manifestation of disciplinary, methodological and political disagreements between certain factions in organisational economics and organisation theory. The major theme of a conference assembled to discuss the implications of Williamson's markets and hierarchies perspective was, 'The debate over the relative attractiveness of efficiency and power as the fundamental concepts in economic organization' (Francis *et al.*, 1983, p. 7) 'Economists (and some organisation theorists) tended to contend that organizations are all about efficiency; sociologists (and other organization theorists) retorted that organizations are all about power' (Turk, 1983, p. 189). The sociologists and organisation theorists interpreted the division as 'an expression of the divergence in "world view" between the majority of economists and the majority of sociologists' (Francis *et al.*, 1983, p. 7). Disagreement over the relative importance of efficiency and power also features in the dispute between mainstream organisational economics and radical political economy that has followed in the wake of Marglin's (1976) seminal paper on work organisation.

The division between organisational economics and organisation theorists is epitomised by the exchange between Williamson and Ouchi (1981) and Charles Perrow (1981). Williamson and Ouchi defend their markets and hierarchies perspective against Perrow, a radical organisation theorist, who criticises them for ignoring power. Williamson and Ouchi maintain that:

> Inasmuch as power is very vague and has resisted successive efforts to make it operational, whereas efficiency is much more clearly specified and the plausibility of an efficiency analysis is buttressed by ecological survival tests, we urge that efficiency analysis be made the center piece of the study of organizational design. This does not imply that power has no role to play, but we think it invites confusion to explain organizational results that are predicted by the efficiency hypothesis in terms of power. (1981, p. 364)

According to Williamson's version of transaction cost economics, along with most agency theorists, as well as those organisation theorists, such as Donaldson (1991), who take a contingency approach to the study of organisations, efficiency is an overriding constraint on organisations, and power is more or less ephemeral. Williamson's major proposition is that 'the economic institutions of capitalism have the main purpose and effect of economizing on transaction costs' (1985, p. 17). He sees this as an expression of efficiency and the thrust of his 'efficiency hypothesis' is 'that more efficient modes [of organization] will eventually supplant less efficient modes – though entrenched power interests can sometimes delay the displacement' (1985, pp. 236, 125). Williamson and Ouchi submit that: 'power considerations will usually give way to efficiency – at least in profit-making enterprises, if observations are taken at sufficiently long intervals, say a decade' (1981, p. 363).

Although Perrow concedes that there is 'something to be said for [the] efficiency argument', he construes it as a normative defence of hierarchically-organised big business. Although not uncritical of the market, Perrow prefers market transactions to hierarchy because 'hierarchy necessarily gives power to the few' (1981, pp. 372, 386). According to Perrow:

> The historical evidence on the growth of large firms is striking and attests to various forms of market power and government support that have little to do with organizational efficiency. The major industries of the United States – oil and chemicals, iron and steel, automobiles, electrical goods, food processing, railroads, and now electronics and television – are as concentrated as they are not because the leading firms saved on transaction costs or were more efficient in other ways, but because they could control the market, labor, and government and were backed by powerful financial interests. (1986, p. 247)

Williamson complains that the concept of power is 'so poorly defined that power can be and is invoked to explain virtually anything', although he concedes that 'efficiency stands in need of refinement as well' (1985, p. 237). However, clarity in the use of the terms 'efficiency' and 'power' is sadly lacking in the dispute between mainstream organisational economics and radical organisation theory. Drawing on the broader debates in economics and sociology, the various meanings of, first, efficiency and then power in organisational economics and organisation theory are set out and compared. The two concepts of power that are highlighted, the 'processual' and 'institutional' perspectives (Fincham, 1992), are then related back to the discussion of organisations and institutions.

Efficiency

Buchanan, a neoclassically-inclined economist, assesses the moral and efficiency arguments for and against the market. According to Buchanan, the most widely accepted concept of efficiency in economics is that developed by Vilfredo Pareto: 'a state of a given system is Pareto Optimal if and only if there is no feasible alternative of that system in which at least one person is better off and no one else is worse off' (Buchanan, 1985, p. 4). This is a subjectivist view of efficiency, since, as Arrow puts it, whatever else is meant by 'better' or 'efficient', it certainly means that: 'one situation, one system, or one allocation is better than another if every individual feels it is better according to his own individual values'; but, at the outset, Arrow points out that efficiency can only be achieved through the price system 'under certain very special assumptions' (1974, pp. 19–20).

In Louis Putterman's view, 'The Pareto criteria of efficiency' is 'so deeply embedded in the language and analytical structure of modern economics, that it is virtually impossible to use economic analysis without referring to it' (1990, p. 38). Perhaps surprisingly, radical political economists such as Bowles and Gintis (1993) have made even less effort than many mainstream organisational economists to distance themselves from Pareto optimality, even though there are serious problems with invoking it once the neoclassical model is abandoned. For a start, if a 'Pareto Optimal equilibrium state' is to prevail, then the conditions of an ideal market need to be met, and these include zero transaction costs *or* perfect competition with no externalities. It is quite clear that, 'the case for the market on grounds of efficiency depends on the extent to which actual markets do approximate, or can be modified to approximate, the ideal market' (Buchanan, 1985, pp. 14–15).

Some neoinstitutional economists, such as Eggertsson, have noted that: 'In the basic neoclassical model, which assumes zero transaction costs, there is no logical rationale for contractual arrangements such as various types of firms or even money. The logic of such arrangements becomes apparent when transaction costs are added to the model' (Eggertsson, 1990, p. 22). This means that it is difficult to see how economic outcomes derived from the basic neoclassical model of an ideal market can be 'used as a yardstick of efficiency in real-world situations' (Eggertsson, 1990, p. 22). Similarly, Papandreou recognises that it is difficult to use a model of the ideal market without 'avoiding the "nirvana" criticism of comparing the real world to utopian ones' (1994, p. 263). Demsetz criticises the 'nirvana' approach to public policy in economics on the grounds that it, 'implicitly presents the relevant choice as between an ideal norm and an existing "imperfect" institutional arrangement' (1991, p. 3). Coase has called it 'blackboard economics' (1990a, p. 28), because it is concerned with the operation of a system that only exists 'in the minds of economists' (1993b, p. 229). This means that it is problematic, to say the least, to characterise organisations or institutions as efficient in anything like a Pareto optimal sense if the very existence of such organisations and institutions is both evidence of the absence, and a violation of, the conditions required for Pareto optimality.

In a generally sympathetic review of Williamson's work, James Malcomson has set out the incompatibility of Pareto efficiency criteria and transaction cost economics:

> Economic efficiency is a characteristic of equilibria in what one might call 'well-functioning' perfectly competitive markets. The catalogue of exceptions to efficient markets is long and, for the most part, well known. . . . What should however be emphasized is that the twin pillars on which so much of Williamson's argument rests are precisely conditions under which markets either are not perfectly competitive . . . or, if perfectly competitive, do not function well. . . . It seems therefore that an essential feature of the world Williamson is interested in (and, I am only too happy to admit, the one I am interested in since it has a lot of features of the world we live in!) is not one in which one can simply *assume* that economic efficiency will win out in the end. (1984, p. 126)

Radical economists, such as Paul Marginson, are critical of Williamson and other organisational economists on the grounds that, 'The efficiency of particular outcomes has to be demonstrated and not presumed' (Marginson, 1993, pp. 142, 150). Unfortunately, they have not yet specified a clear alternative to the Pareto criteria for efficiency. Like the organisational economists they criticise, these radical economists seem to believe that the meaning of efficiency is more or less self-evident, when clearly it is not.

It is important to note that the perfectly competitive model plays an ideological role. Putterman suggests that it is not unreasonable to ask 'whether economists did not design their definition of efficiency precisely so as to fit the theoretical properties they see in a competitive economy' (1990, p. 67). The model purports to show that under certain conditions prices and output will merely reflect the preferences of consumers constrained by the prevailing technological possibilities with no interference from firms or any other organised interests. The allegedly efficient outcomes of such a situation are sacrificed it there are any interventions by organised collectivities, especially the state. According to the neoclassical vision, 'the firm has no independent power to determine what is produced, how it is produced, or how income is distributed' (Lazonick, 1991, p. 63). Perfect competition is not unlike the imaginary situation of 'perfect spontaneity' described by the sociologist Emile Durkheim. If 'labor is divided spontaneously' then 'social inequalities exactly express natural inequalities' (Durkheim, 1947, pp. 377–8). Not only is such spontaneity compromised by any instance of coercion, but also by the 'hereditary transmission of wealth' (Durkheim, 1947, p. 378), an essential feature of most capitalist economies (Putterman, 1990, p. 79).

Pareto efficiency is compromised when there is any departure from perfect competition, but since all real-life situations depart significantly from the perfectly competitive model, economists have to use their discretion in deciding whether existing situations are more or less efficient, usually resorting to political expediency. In other words, although economists know that their theoretically constructed firms bear little or no resemblance to the firms that exist as empirical entities (Machlup, 1967, pp. 9–10), many of them are prepared to keep quiet about it if it serves what Galbraith (1987) would call the 'convenient social virtue' of defending actual firms from any interference. On the other hand, critics of large corporations call on the neoclassical theory of monopoly to argue that the market power of corporations should be constrained because it stifles efficiency, even though they well know that an efficient perfectly competitive situation is unattainable in the real world.

Transaction, or organisational, costs might be thought of as the costs that would be incurred in moving towards an efficient Pareto optimal equilibrium state. It could then be said that a Pareto optimal state would prevail were it not for the costs of achieving such a situation, 'in which at least one person is better off and no one else is worse off', being greater than the potential benefits to that person. However, to follow this line of argument would reduce efficiency to a tautology because any and every existing situation could be construed as efficient, no matter how little resemblance it bore to the conditions for Pareto optimality, on the grounds that it is efficient given the costs that prevent the optimal state coming about. Papandreou believes that a 'particularly discouraging feature' of such an approach is that it seems to 'lead to the unpalatable conclusion that any institution that exists must be optimal otherwise wealth-maximizing agents would have exploited any "attainable" improvements' (1994, p. 253).

Organisation theorists can be forgiven for failing to notice the scepticism towards any notion of efficiency among a few economists associated with the new institutionalism since the problems associated with any subjectivist concept of efficiency, once transaction costs and other conditions are admitted, are glibly glossed over by most organisational economists. For example, in their textbook of organisational economics, Paul Milgrom and John Roberts (1992) give a brief outline of what they mean by 'efficiency', which is deceptively prosaic in the light of the discussion by Eggertsson (1990) and Papandreou (1994). Milgrom and Roberts give a definition of the 'efficiency principle':

If people are able to bargain together effectively and can effectively implement and enforce their decisions, then the outcomes of economic activity will tend to be efficient (at least for the parties to the bargain).

They then make the assertion that:

Much of our analysis of organizations is based on the efficiency principle. We try to understand existing arrangements as efficient choices, and we interpret changes in these arrangements as efficiency-enhancing responses to changes in the environment within which the arrangements exist. (1992, p. 25)

In other words the 'existing arrangements' are simply assumed to be efficient, even though the absence of the circumstances in which such an assumption can be made is the whole basis of organisational economics.

The objection to Milgrom and Roberts is that any existing arrangements can only be assumed to be efficient in terms of reflecting the choices or preferences of individuals if the conditions of perfect competition are fulfilled. If all markets were efficient in the first place, that is, if transaction costs were zero, then any choices made 'would always be efficient' (North, 1990a, p. 8). However, once the conditions of perfect markets are violated, as they are by the existence of organisations, then outcomes can no longer be presumed to be efficient in terms of maximising individual actors' subjectively defined utility. Actors can only be assumed to have devised arrangements in which they can bargain effectively if they start from a situation in which they *can* bargain effectively. It simply cannot be assumed that they have made such arrange-ments if they start from a situation in which effective bargaining is impeded, and it is the universality of impediments such as bounded rationality that is the starting point for organisational economics.

By a sleight of hand, neoclassical economists, and organisational economists such as Milgrom and Roberts, supplant Pareto efficiency as a criterion of evaluation with a tautological assumption. Unless the conditions that allow for 'efficient choices' to be made are clearly specified, it is merely a tautology to assert that 'existing arrangements' are the outcome of efficient choices, since if the conditions for efficient outcomes are not adequately specified, any and all situations can be construed as efficient. If the conditions, such as perfect competition, in which there will be efficient outcomes, are relaxed, or are vague enough in the first place, then efficiency can be invoked to describe any situation that is to the liking of economists. If they like the existing set up, then they have sufficient discretion to be able to characterise it as being efficient.

The neoclassical methodology consists of working out a set of assumptions such that something resembling the existing situation is the logical and, by implication, the efficient outcome. Those organisational economists who use this methodology to claim that existing arrangements represent efficient outcomes have not broken from the circular reasoning that is prevalent in neoclassical theory, which 'confuses the question of efficiency with existence' (Hodgson, 1988, p. 214). This is what is known as Panglossian economics 'After Voltaire's Dr Pangloss, who pronounced: "Things cannot be other than they are. . . . Everything is made for the best purpose. Our noses were made to carry spectacles, so we have spectacles. Legs were clearly intended for breeches, and we wear them" ' (quoted by Gould, 1992, p. 114), the 'belief that whatever there is, is there for a reason' (McCloskey, 1986, p. 15). Taking the fact of existence itself to indicate that an arrangement is optimal in some sense is inevitably tautological, but economists are rarely prepared to admit or defend their use of tautologies, given the 'strong pejorative overtones' that the word has in economics (Jensen, 1983, p. 330). In order to avoid tautological assertions, Eggertsson specifically eschews the word 'efficiency', and he relegates his reasons for doing so to a brief footnote:

> Efficiency is an unmeasurable characteristic of models. If we assume that agents are rational maximizers, all models yield efficient outcomes – regardless of whether transaction costs are zero or positive. Efficiency is a logical consequence of the assumptions in models assuming maximizing behavior. (1990, p. 102n)

While neoinstitutional economists such as Papandreou (1994) and Eggertsson (1990) have expressed scepticism towards any concept of efficiency, or even abandoned it, they have given less attention to the reasons for the retention of a subjectivist notion of efficiency by most other economists. Neoclassical economists are well aware that defining actors' wants or needs in terms other than actors' own subjective definitions of their wants or needs runs into the problem of relativism. They are keen to retain a subjectivist version of efficiency, such as Pareto optimality, as a bench-mark for assessing efficiency, since they believe that by positing subjective 'utility' maximisation as a generic goal of the economy they can avoid admitting to any problems of relativism in defining what is efficient (Mirowski, 1988, p. 210). Although this position is untenable since even Pareto optimality is 'morally controversial' (Buchanan, 1985, p. 10; Putterman, 1990, p. 40). An 'unimprovable' optimal situation is no 'big deal' for those who start out with nothing, 'all they are sure of is not getting any worse off' (Sen, 1982, p. 86).

The more fundamental point is that the attempt to define efficiency in terms of subjective utility maximisation reflects the desire of economists to retain a distinction between positive and normative judgements. However, this distinction itself, and with it the notion of some positive, non-relative definition of efficiency, is under threat once bounded rationality is admitted, and the assumption of bounded rationality underpins organisational economics (Simon, 1976, p. xxviii). This is because, 'One little-recognized consequence of our bounded rationality is that we lack the capability to sharply separate our values from our knowledge' (Nelson and Winter, 1982, p. 382). This would suggest that the definition of important concepts such as efficiency or power necessarily reflects differences in human values, unless organisational economists are claiming unbounded rationality for themselves while attributing bounded rationality to everyone else.

Among radical organisation theorists there are those who barely mention efficiency, let alone define it, and if they do so it is only in order to criticise the efficiency position of other social theorists. This is because they believe that efficiency is virtually meaningless. No one can be against efficiency, they say (Power and Laughlin, 1992, p. 130), but that only goes to show that the word is 'loaded with political content' and that 'language serves interests' (Nord and Jermier, 1992, p. 206). Paradoxically, although they appear to be diametrically opposed to each other, the radical organisation theorists who oppose the concept of efficiency and the economists who adhere to efficiency both turn out to share an extreme subjectivist position in which the human subject is conceived of as 'a disembodied self' (Callinicos, 1989, p. 25). Whereas economists seek to avoid relativism in their subjectivist definition of efficiency, radical organisation theorists seek to avoid defining efficiency as a capitulation to relativism.

Not all social theorists have been as reluctant as neoclassical economists or radical organisation theorists to specify efficiency in terms of essential human needs which reflect universal features of human nature. These essentialist definitions of efficiency are clearly unable to avoid the problem of relativism, not least because human needs are not merely physical, such as the need for adequate nourishment; human beings also require 'love, respect and friendship' and 'a freedom and breadth of intellectual and physical self-expression' (Geras, 1983, p. 96). Beyond simple reproduction of the species, human need is notoriously difficult to define, since it inevitably involves an assessment of the quality of human life (Nussbaum and Sen, 1993), and any such assessment would have to take into account subjective preferences.

It is extremely difficult, if not impossible, to develop any criteria of efficiency based on objectively defined human needs. Most radical organisation theorists are extremely sceptical of any attempt to incorporate humanistic notions of efficiency into an explanation of organisational change. Furthermore, they allege that the humanists who appeal for essential human needs to be met, 'proceed to commit atrocities in the name of those they claim to know and serve' (Knights and Willmott, 1989, p. 539). Similarly, the 'concept of basic needs' as a criterion of evaluation 'meets criticism from neoclassical economists', who 'argue that any attempt to distinguish between "basic needs" and "mere wants" must lead to distinctions which are arbitrary, inherently paternalistic, and potentially dictatorial' (Putterman, 1990, p. 43).

The humanists' objection to the neoclassical view that actors merely maximise their subjectively defined utility is that it seems to deny that human beings are *'embodied'*, and as such share some needs which are more than merely subjective. Marxist humanists pose the question: 'is it really plausible to say that if human beings photosynthesized . . . this would make no difference to their history?' (Callinicos, 1989, p. 25). However, the assertion that human beings do not photosynthesise is hardly sufficient to explain the whole of human history: 'The fact that human beings must survive in the material environment in which they live tells us nothing about whether what they do in order to survive plays a dominant role in social transformation' (Giddens, 1986, p. 243; Berger and Luckmann, 1971, pp. 65–70; Rueschemeyer, 1986, pp. 41–2).

Radical humanism has been very much a minority position among organisation theorists. There are few who would endorse the 'general Marxist postulate' as stated by Stinchcombe: 'that there is a long-run tendency for the relations of production to assume a form in which the activities of production are efficiently and effectively done'; Stinchcombe believes that if an environment is exploited efficiently then it will support more humans, and according to the 'principle of social evolution . . . more efficient modes of exploitation tend to succeed less efficient ones' (1983, pp. 8, 31). At least one of the problems with this is that of reconciling an increase of physical output with the subjective preferences of actors. In other words, the effectiveness of an activity 'can only be evaluated in relation to the ends of the activity'; even so, Stinchcombe contends that, 'If the principle of evolution works perfectly, then there is usually a unique exploitative system determined by a given technology and a given environment' (1983, p. 31). This position would be condemned by most organisation theorists and sociologists as technological determinism (Clegg and Dunkerley, 1980, pp. 237–56). However, it is worth noting that those theorists who are often accused of technological determinism, notably Joan Woodward, are well aware of the danger of degenerating into a 'circular . . . argument that an arrangement works because it exists', and the need to specify efficiency criteria (Woodward, 1969, p. 200).

In common with Stinchcombe, Williamson invokes evolution in support of his efficiency hypothesis. Williamson maintains that his argument, 'relies in a general, background way on the efficacy of competition to perform a sort between more and less efficient modes and to shift resources in favour of the former', although he admits that this is an 'intuition' which would 'benefit from a more fully developed theory of the selection process' (1985, p. 23). Unless it can be demonstrated that the selection environment selects according to efficiency criteria such as facilitating choice or meeting identifiable human needs, this argument also reduces to a tautology, that the fittest survive, with fitness being defined purely by survival. Hodgson (1988, p. 216) sets out the argument against the view that the mere prevalence a particular form of organisation, such as the capitalist firm, is evidence of its superior efficiency:

The most that can be concluded is that there is some evidence of the relative efficiency of the capitalist firm in the context of a given type of social, economic and political environment. The current make-up of financial institutions, government policies, case law, etc., clearly favour the traditional firm. If this environment were to change (and it could) then we may be able to find 'evidence' of the 'superiority' of a quite different form of organization.

It is only in a footnote that Williamson claims to subscribe to 'weak rather than strong-form selection, the distinction being that "in a relative sense, the *fitter* survive, but there is no reason to suppose that they are *fittest* in any absolute sense"' (Williamson, 1985, p. 23n, quoting Simon, 1983). Therefore Williamson concedes the point that only 'comparative efficiency' (1993b, p. 107) can be claimed for the capitalist firm, but he fails to acknowledge the implications of this concession for his efficiency propositions. Williamson misunderstands the nature of the evolutionary process. In the first place, the inference of efficiency from the proliferation of an organisational form is gratuitous: 'the fact that the cockroach has proliferated and survived, as Friedrich Hayek reminds us, does not give the cockroach moral value' (Bowles and Gintis, 1993, p. 97).

Second, as Neil Kay (1993, p. 254) has consistently maintained, 'natural selection arguments have not been applied properly by Williamson'. This criticism is particularly important in assessing Williamson's accounts of the development of work organisation and the capitalist corporation (Chapters 6 and 8 below). According to Kay, it is not sufficient to conduct an analytical comparison of 'alternative feasible' forms of organisation, as Williamson (1993b, p. 105) does, in order to demonstrate the relative efficiency and explain the prevalence of existing organisational forms. To do so is fundamentally ahistorical. Competition simply does not 'perform a sort between' all feasible forms of organisation. Instead, as new forms of organisation appear, the nature of the competitive environment itself changes, and the relative efficiency of organisational forms within that environment changes. As Kay explains:

> Natural selection selects from what actually exists. It does not generate new forms but selects out inferior forms as a consequence of competition from superior forms *after* the appearance of the latter, not before such appearance. (1993, p. 253)

By the way, Demsetz prefers a *'comparative institution* approach in which the relevant choice is between alternative real institutional arrangements' (1991, p. 3).

What Williamson does is to reify the selection environment by failing to recognise that organisations themselves are a significant part of that institutional environment. The boundary between organisations and their selection environment, conceptualised here as the boundary between organisations and institutions, is by no means fixed. In order to make Williamson's 'microanalytic and comparative institutional research' (1985, p. 238) more historical and evolutionary he would have to add two elements. First, an account of the superior efficiency of particular forms of organisation relative to the other forms of organisation with which they have co-existed, and second, a theory of innovation in order to explain the appearance of particular forms of organisation in a specific institutional environment. It should be said that Williamson's writings provide invaluable preparation for such historical research.

An historical account of the relative efficiency of particular organisational forms needs to take account of path dependency, which, put simply, means that 'where you end up depends on where you've been' (Bowles and Gintis, 1993, p. 97). Latterly, Williamson (1993b, p. 104) has claimed that he agrees with 'the proposition that evolutionary processes are path dependent', but this agreement is qualified. First, he reckons that path dependency 'does not preclude comparative efficiency assessments of alternative feasible forms, but some forms may be privileged by their evolutionary origins'. Second, 'we are still awaiting a demonstration that path dependency has large and wide-spread effects'. The basis for Williamson's second, supplementary, qualification seems to be the debate over the relative superiority of the QWERTY typewriter keyboard. This is a distraction. Williamson's disregard for path dependency when it comes to organisational forms is epitomised by his assertion that it was, 'Not by history but by logic' that the owners of capital became the owners of enterprise (Williamson, 1985, p. 324), and the way his argument for the existence of conglomerates 'relies on a combination of *a priori* theorizing and related natural selection considerations' (Williamson, 1983, p. 171).

Neoinstitutional economists, such as North, have made efforts to incorporate path dependency into their analysis. For a long time North has recognised the need to endogenise social and institutional variables into economic history. These are the major sources of change in an economy that are held constant by most economists, such as: 'technology, population, property rights and government control over resources' (1971, quoted by Gustafsson, 1991a, p. 27). In his later work North has explicitly 'abandoned the efficiency view of institutions' (1990a, p. 7). In contrast to Williamson's subordination of history to logic, North explicitly allows for choice in history by introducing path dependence into his analysis, in order to try to prevent his stories sounding 'inevitable' or 'foreordained'. North's account of history is not intended to be 'a story of inevitability in which the past neatly predicts the future. . . . Path dependence means that history matters. We cannot understand today's choices . . . without tracing the incremental evolution of institutions'; however, 'Once a development path is set on a particular course, the network externalities, the learning process of organizations, and the historically derived subjective modelling of the issues reinforce the course' (North, 1990a, pp. 98–9, 100).

Path dependence shifts the focus from a static comparison of efficiency towards an emphasis on the capacity for organisational change. North distinguishes between allocative efficiency and adaptive efficiency. Allocative efficiency corresponds to the most efficient allocation of existing resources, as described by Pareto optimality. Adaptive efficiency, on the other hand, means the provision of incentives to encourage 'the efforts required to explore alternative ways of solving problems' (North, 1990a, pp. 80–1). Similarly, Demsetz sees the basic problem as: 'the design of institutional arrangements that provide incentives to encourage experimentation (including the development of new products, new knowledge, new reputations, and new ways of organizing activities) without overly insulating these experiments from the ultimate test of survival' (Demsetz, 1991, p. 19). North recognises that 'allocative and adaptive efficiency may not always be consistent' (1990a, p. 81).

Stinchcombe offers a Marxist version of path dependency in his book, *Economic Sociology*: 'Institutional structures are transformed because they give rise to incentives and pressures to change them . . . the theory of how movements of the economy as a whole gives rise to such incentives for changing the form of class relations is a theory of the enterprise in a capitalist market . . . the social and technical organization of production is therefore created by enterprises that are shaped by the institutional order' (1983, pp. 3–4). The Marxist view is that in the institutional context of capitalist property rights the relative efficiency that capitalist firms enjoy is predicated upon the exploitation of labour.

In his later book, *Information and Organizations* (1990), Stinchcombe draws extensively on Chandler's business history (1962), Williamson's (1985) organisational economics, and the forerunners of organisational economics such as March and Simon (1961), in order to analyse the subparts of capitalist firms that constitute his unit of analysis. Of special interest is Stinchcombe's account of how inventions, both technical and organisational, are turned into innovations. This process is not routinised or institutionalised, and for it to be successful the actors involved need a theory, or a mental picture, not only of how their innovation will work, but of how and why it will be introduced.

The distinction between allocative and adaptive efficiency is echoed by Stinchcombe when he contends that the most salient characteristic of modern society is not the most efficient use of existing technology but the rate of innovation (Stinchcombe, 1983, p. 111). A similar point is made by other organisation theorists, such Peter Clark and Neil Staunton (1993, pp. 1, 5, 12), who identify the fundamental dilemma of 'balancing and blending' efficiency and innovation. They propose that organisation theory should focus on 'innovation rather than efficiency'. They add a note of caution and warn that an overemphasis on innovation can lead to a neglect of 'exnovation', by which they mean 'the problems of the removal of existing practices so that they can be replaced'.

A strength of North's and Stinchcombe's analysis is that they give an insight into the process whereby the appearance of new forms of organisation is, at least partially, consciously willed. Organisational change is the outcome, be it intended or unintended, of actors' competing pictures, their 'subjective models' (North, 1990a, p. 9) of existing and future situations. A problem with both Stinchcombe and North is that although they take account of path dependency, they retain an implicit view that organisations and institutions can be assessed as efficient according to criteria other than their relative efficiency in a specific institutional context. Stinchcombe's criteria are essentially humanistic, whereas North emphasises economic growth, which is in practice the most favoured measure of efficiency among contemporary economists (Putterman, 1990, p. 43). This goes back to the problem of relativism; the difficulty of assessing individuals' and societies' success in achieving their objectives in circumstances where their choices cannot be assumed to be efficiently made or expressed. The problem is that what constitutes efficiency itself is path dependent.

It must be self-evident that any and all existing human arrangements are efficient in some minimal essentialist and subjectivist senses in terms of both meeting sufficient human needs for some human beings to be able to reproduce themselves and reflecting at least a degree of choice on the part of those living human actors. Any organisational economists or organisation theorists who claim that organisations are efficient would have to show that organisations are efficient in more than this minimal sense if efficiency is to mean anything more than existence. By the way, perfectly fulfilling actors' choices in a perfectly competitive model is not sufficient to ensure the continuation of an economic system; it is feasible that all the members of a society could starve to death while it meets all the requirements of perfect competition and is Pareto optimal (Putterman, 1990, p. 79).

A more generally accepted view in organisation theory is that while there may be universal human needs, as the humanists claim there are, and although actors do make choices, as the neoclassical economists assert, these needs and choices are always socially mediated by the existing institutions. Thus, as the radical organisation theorist, Stewart Clegg, puts it, 'The efficiency imperative can rarely be untangled from the institutional framework within which calculations both of what efficiency is and how it is to be achieved are made' (1990, p. 98). This sociological view is appropriately described by Neil Fligstein as 'The Social Construction of Efficiency', which 'does not assume the rationality of action or some absolute standard of efficiency' (1990, ch. 9).

Power

Turning now to a discussion of power, the first point to make is that sociologists and organisation theorists acknowledge that there are competing definitions of power. They have gone to considerable lengths to set out the major conceptions of power, but organisational economists have not consulted the literature in which this is done. Williamson, for example, refers to 'the power hypothesis' (1993b, p. 107), as if there is only one. Following Lukes' influential essay, *Power: A Radical View*, most sociologists and organisation theorists would accept that power is an '"essentially contested concept" – one of those concepts which "inevitably involve endless disputes about their proper uses on the part of their users"' (Lukes, 1974, p. 26 quoting Gallie, 1955–6). This is because 'power is one of those concepts which is ineradicably value-dependent', which means that: 'both its very definition and any given use of it, once defined, are inextricably tied to a given set of (probably unacknowledged) value-assumptions which predetermine that range of its empirical application' (Lukes, 1974, p. 26). This recognises the problem of relativism in relation to power and attempts to overcome it, at least partially, by encouraging reflexiveness about underlying values. Some social theorists would maintain that just about every concept worth using in social theory is necessarily contested. This would include 'efficiency, productivity, individual and social welfare', just as much as power, justice, democracy, exploitation and alienation (Rueschemeyer, 1986, p. 52).

Robin Fincham (1992), an organisation theorist, has distilled two versions of power from organisation theory: 'processual' and 'institutional' perspectives. The processual perspective equates power with Machiavellianism and locates it in the achievement of intended strategies by individuals and groups. This corresponds to the intuitive view of power set out by Weber: 'In general, we understand by "power" the chance of a man or of a number of men to realize their own will in a communal action even against the resistance of others who are participating in the action' (1991, p. 180).

In contrast to the processual view of power, the institutional perspective sees power as being embedded in the constraints imposed on organisations (Giddens, 1986, p. 15). It is acknowledged that this type of power is 'hard to identify if one looks for a contest of wills' (Rueschemeyer, 1986, p. 12), but Lukes argues that power should not only be associated with 'actual, observable conflict', since 'the most effective and insidious use of power is to prevent such conflict from arising in the first place' (1974, pp. 22–3). It is generally agreed that: 'Ultimately, the resolution of this issue involves assumptions about the different parties' *objective* interests' (Rueschemeyer, 1986, p. 12). However, in the absence of a subjective expression of interests, it is difficult to avoid resorting to an essentialist assertion that interests are constituted by objective needs.

Clearly, there is disagreement as to what sort of evidence is required in order to demonstrate that the exercise of power is connected to 'the achievement of sectional interests' (Giddens, 1986, p. 15). If a processual view of power is taken, then evidence of overt conflict is required. If an institutional perspective is taken, then the relative absence of conflict may well constitute evidence of the exercise of power. What seems reasonably clear is that the most effective forms of power need to be explicitly exercised only rarely. From a simplistic humanistic viewpoint, power results from the unequal distribution of the resources required to meet human needs: 'If people's basic needs are not met, they cannot survive. Those who have a large command over economic resources have power over others who have a lesser command over economic resources and typically a critically limited ability to meet their needs' (Lutz and Lux, 1988, p. 122). This means that power can be said to have suppressed efficiency if it frustrates the fulfilment of human needs which otherwise could be met. Radical anti-humanist organisation theorists, such as Knights (1990), have attempted to develop a subjectivist perspective in which institutional power can be said to have been exercised without invoking essential human needs. That this work is often tortuous attests to the difficulty of the task. The danger is that if subjectivity itself is said to be constituted by power, then the exercise of choice is merely a reflection of power and is virtually meaningless.

Both mainstream organisational economists and radical political economists seem to be under the misapprehension that there is, or ought to be, a ready-made definition of power, and the definition that they use generally corresponds to the intuitive, processual power perspective. According to Williamson and Ouchi: 'power explains results when the organization sacrifices efficiency to serve special interests. We concede that this occurs. But we do not believe that major organizational changes in the commercial sector are explained in these terms. The evidence is all to the contrary' (1981, p. 364). Radical economists such as Marglin (1976) and Marginson (1993) dispute Williamson's evidence, but they seem to be agreed on his implicit definition of power. It is revealing that Marglin (1976, 1991) and Marginson (1993) use the terms power and control interchangeably. According to Marginson: 'Power or "control" models of the firm have emphasized the coercive nature of employer authority. The essence of the authority relation is seen to lie in the ability of the employer to force workers to do things which they would not otherwise do' (1993, p. 155). This corresponds to the processual view of power in that it implies that the exercise of power occurs when identifiable special interest groups within organisations are able to achieve their expressed objectives in the face of opposition that is articulated by other special interest groups.

Although the dispute over efficiency and power has centred on work organisation, Williamson's interpretation of power comes through more clearly in his discussion of vertical integration (1985, pp. 124–5). Williamson's contention is that power, or domination theory, is refuted by historical examples where wealthy and powerful groups have been undermined by organisational innovations which render their positions redundant. Williamson poses two questions: first, why would wealthy and powerful special interest groups 'ever permit economic activity to be organized in ways that removed power from their control'?, and, second, why does 'power leak out selectively' (Williamson, 1985, p. 124), with the positions of power being appropriated by certain groups and not others? In answer to the first question, the disappearance of particular positions does not mean that the sectional group which fills those positions necessarily loses wealth and power. As Williamson himself puts it, 'The aphorism "if you can't beat them, join them" is often the way by which such interests secure relief' (1985, p. 237). This suggests that entrenched interest groups are able to find favourable positions to fill in new forms of organisation. The second question would appear to confirm rather than refute a power perspective, in that it suggests that when a sectional interest group loses out, the benefits from efficiency enhancing organisational innovations are diffused unevenly.

From an institutional perspective, power is constituted by the ability to construct and ensure the continuation of institutional constraints on organisations. Williamson actually concedes that 'power may have a lot more to say about the institutional environment that it does about the institutions of governance. Rules of the game that privilege one group in relation to another for reasons that are lacking in merit are insidious' (1993b, pp. 112–13). However, this is very much an afterthought on Williamson's part. These constraints would include the institutional measures of relative efficiency, most notably profitability, which is predicated upon the maintenance of capitalist property rights. Mainstream organisational economists, in common with most economists, simply presume that increases in profitability correspond to increases in 'the efficiency with which society's resources are used' (Caves, 1980, p. 79). This conflates the relative efficiency of the capitalist firm in a context of capitalist property rights with some notion of absolute efficiency. Such an assumption is evident in Williamson's assertion that efficiency gains from new forms of work organisation are 'diffused throughout society' (1985, p. 235). Such an assumption begs enormous questions about the relationship between work organisation and the distribution of wealth and power, which Williamson does not even begin to address.

North's neoinstitutional economic approach comes close to the institutional perspective on power. North (1990a, pp. 7, 58–9) recognises that rulers devise property rights 'in their own interests' and transaction costs result in typically inefficient property rights prevailing. As a result, it is possible to account for property rights that do not produce economic growth being widespread throughout history and in the present. Here North does not go far enough, since the preference for economic growth itself is historically specific and almost certainly benefits some groups in society at the expense of others. Ultimately, power has to be admitted into North's analysis because in modern interdependent economies, agreements have to enforced by coercion, and those who exercise coercion will use that force in their own interests.

In effect, the significant choices facing organisations in North's path-dependent analysis are the choices that affect the institutional constraints within which organisations operate. This is similar to the notion of 'strategic choice' set out by John Child in one of the most influential papers in organisation theory. Child maintains that:

'strategic choice' extends to the context within which the organization is operating, to the standards of performance against which the pressure of economic constraints has to be evaluated, and to the design of the organization's structure itself. (1972, p. 2)

Acknowledging strategic choice involves recognition that the power exercised by the dominant coalitions in organisations such as corporations play a significant part in constructing the institutions which constitute the efficiency criteria by which their organisations are assessed. This is captured by Giddens when he describes the 'capitalist enterprise' as 'both typical of modern organizations and one of the main sources of innovation generating the circumstances in which they have arisen'; Giddens goes so far as to suggest that a distinctive characteristic of modern capitalism is that corporations become increasingly disembedded from the institutional framework of nation states (1986, pp. 183, 205).

Conclusion

More heat than light has been produced in the dispute between mainstream organisational economists and radical organisation theorists which has been dominated by diametrically-opposed factions on both sides. These factions have presented the concepts of efficiency and power as being absolute and mutually exclusive alternatives. This has obscured the scope for dialogue between organisational economics and organisation theory concerning the meanings of efficiency and power and their relative importance in understanding organisations.

It turns out that mainstream organisational economists in general (and Williamson in particular) have gone to great lengths to try to refute what they see as the power hypothesis in favour of their own efficiency hypotheses. However, Williamson has targeted a processual version of power and overlooked the institutional perspective, which may be more compatible with organisational economics. This is understandable for several reasons. First, the predominant view of power in the organisational behaviour literature is a processual view (Thompson and McHugh, 1990, p. 141). Second, the radical political economists who have been in dispute with Williamson have been equally unclear about which version of power or efficiency they prefer. Finally, the radical organisation theorists who are most vehement in their opposition to organisational economics take a subjectivist position and tend to reject any concept of efficiency.

Two points should be borne in mind when radical organisation theorists proclaim that 'Organisations are all about power' (Littler, 1990, p. 72; Turk,

1983, p. 189) in an attempt to dismiss organisational economics. First, several economists associated with neoinstitutionalism, (Demsetz, 1991; Eggertsson, 1990; North, 1990a; Papandreou, 1994), are not convinced that only efficient organisations and institutions prevail. Second, the radical organisation theorists' sloganeering is not only directed against organisational economics, they are equally scathing about humanistic Marxists for assuming that efficiency belongs to 'the essence of capitalism' (Clegg, 1990, p. 226).

Within Marxism there is a general perception of the need to transcend the false dichotomy between Marxist theory that is 'based on a necessitarian, deterministic logic which emphasises iron laws, a strict succession of stages, the inevitability of the proletarian revolution' on one side, and, on the other, 'attempts to soften Marxism's core by stressing indeterminacy, complexity, the importance of [action], the relative autonomy of the political etc.' (Mouzelis, 1988, p. 107). Marxists seem to believe that the way forward for them is to extend Marx's analysis of capitalism to the contemporary institutional context, so as 'to incorporate the concrete institutions and processes (e.g. multinational corporations and banks, trade networks, and accompanying changes in state forms) which have developed over the last century' (Burkett, 1991, p. 65). Marxists (Armstrong, 1989; Green, 1988; Pitelis, 1993; Stinchcombe, 1990) have increasingly been prepared to borrow from the new and neoinstitutional economics in order to analyse the institutions of capitalism.

The dispute over efficiency and power reflects the division between mainstream and radical perspectives in relation to organisations. To characterise the capitalist firm as an efficient form of organisation, as many organisational economists do, implies that the existence of the capitalist firm is inevitable if human actors are able to make rational choices in the absence of coercion. This implication needs to be demonstrated rather than assumed once it is admitted that the conditions for Pareto optimality are an impossibility, since in the real world boundedly rational human actors make choices subject to coercion from institutions which enforce agreements. The view that power is equally, or more, important in explaining the prevalence of the capitalist firm is radical to the extent that it throws into question the inevitability and desirability of such organisations and the institutions which sustain them by suggesting that they reflect sectional rather than societal interests. However, the disagreement over the legitimacy of the capitalist firm will never be resolved by appeals to efficiency criteria. The concept of bounded rationality ought to bring organisational economics closer to organisation theory, by compelling the economists to concede that values are inevitably incorporated in any efficiency criteria.

Perhaps surprisingly, it is Demsetz, a mainstream property rights theorist, who believes that 'The "great debate" is not properly about efficiency but about which set of preferences, or perhaps which political weighting of citizen preferences, is most desirable. "Most desirable," of course, constitutes an appeal to standards of a higher order' (Demsetz, 1991, p. 46). Efficiency could only be used as a neutral criterion for assessing forms of organisation if there was 'virtually complete consensus about needs, wants and values' (Rueschemeyer, 1986, p. 45). The implication of Pareto optimality is that something approaching such a consensus might be possible if certain conditions prevailed. It is only in the absence of consensus about what is efficient that it is worth debating what it means.

PART 3

CHAPTER 5

Divisions of labour and hierarchy

Introduction: revival of debates

There has been a revival of interest in the organisation of work across the social sciences. This has come about more or less independently within organisational economics, radical and Marxian political economy, industrial sociology, and economic history, so the potential for interdisciplinary debate has yet to be realised. If it is remembered that work organisation was central to the classical political economy of Adam Smith, and Karl Marx and Friedrich Engels, then a contemporary discussion of divisions of labour and hierarchy in work organisations needs to start with an explanation for the demise of earlier interest.

Heterodox economists blame the hegemony of neoclassical orthodoxy for the neglect of work organisation. The point is made forcefully by Stephen Marglin, the radical economist. His attack on capitalist hierarchy in the seminal article 'What Do Bosses Do?' (1976 [1974]) has been central to the renewal of interest in work organisation. Marglin argues that the assumptions made by mainstream neoclassical economists exclude consideration of work and organisation:

> perfect competition has virtually nothing to say about the organization of production! Indeed, even the firm itself, a central economic institution under capitalism, plays no essential role in models of the competitive economy; it is merely a convenient abstraction of the household in its role as producer and does nothing that households could not do equally well do for themselves. (1976, p. 17)

This is a reiteration of the argument (detailed in Chapter 1), that in the neoclassical theory of the firm the firm is treated as a 'black box'. Since this argument is a mainstay of mainstream organisational economics, it is by no means an exclusively radical argument. According to neoclassical theory, organisation within the firm is assumed to be the same for given combinations of labour and capital inputs. Price changes for capital or labour affect the quantities of either that are purchased by the firm, and affect output accordingly. It is assumed that there is an appropriate, exogenously determined technology for each combination of capital and labour inputs. Any reflection on the problematic distinction between technology and organisation is avoided, since organisation is exogenised and subsumed under the categories of capital or labour, so that qualitative differences between technologies are not discussed. This effectively denies the importance of work organisation.

Marglin notes that neoclassical economics can have little to say about management within the firm because, 'In the competitive model, there is no scope for supervision and discipline except for that imposed by the market mechanism.' (1976, p. 29) Hierarchy within capitalist firms is not so much defended by the neoclassical model: rather it is ignored or denied. Williamson mounts a defence of hierarchically organised production derived from transaction cost economics. As a prelude to this he concedes that 'New Left' critics, such as Marglin, have a 'legitimate complaint that neoclassical economics makes little useful contact with organization of work issues' (1980, p. 6; Putterman, 1986, p. 317).

The 'Marglin debate' (Magnusson, 1991, p. 203) can be seen as a reaction against the limitations of neoclassical economics by neoclassically trained economists, like Marglin himself (1991, p. 228). As a professor of economics at Harvard University, Marglin presumably found himself compelled to deal with neoclassical economists. The same cannot be said of the 'labour process debate' (Littler, 1990) that developed in response to Harry Braverman's book *Labor and Monopoly Capital* (1974). (The meanings of some Marxist terminology, such as the 'labour process', will be explained later. For an excellent guide to any Marxian terms which are unclear, readers should refer to *A Dictionary of Marxist Thought* (Bottomore, 1991). Braverman was an ex-craft worker and an active socialist. His book is in part a reaction against what he calls 'questionnaire-sociology'. The impression given by Braverman is that up to the 1970s academic sociologists, no less than neoclassical economists, accepted the idea that the organisation of work is technologically determined: 'from this point of view, the only important matter, the only thing worth studying, is not work itself but the reaction of the worker to it, and in that respect sociology makes sense' (1974, p. 29). For a time, industrial sociology, especially in Britain, succumbed to 'Bravermania' (Littler and Salaman, 1982), even though Braverman was scathing about academic sociologists. Industrial relations, and to a lesser extent organisation theory, have also been influenced by the labour process debate (Burrell, 1990, pp. 275–6). Unfortunately, Braverman died soon after the publication of his book, so he did not have the chance to give more than a brief response (Braverman, 1976) to the debate he had started.

Braverman alleges that the preoccupation of sociologists and psychologists with the orientation of workers' towards work rather than the organisation of work itself reflects their concern to assist management in the 'habituation' of workers to 'degenerated forms of work' (1974, pp. 140–1, 151; Baritz, 1960). Dietrich Rueschemeyer, a sociologist, provides an overview of social theory in *Power and the Division of Labour*. He accepts that, 'Increased monotony of work or heightened job insecurity . . . have been of little concern to entrepreneurs unless workers' morale or the politics of labour relations seemed affected'; however, he identifies a wider tendency for social theorists to focus 'their attention more on the consequences of division of labour than on its causes' (1986, pp. 48, 15). This tendency started almost as soon as Adam Smith's ideas became common knowledge and can be found in the work of Alexis de Toqueville, Jean-Baptiste Say and Emile Durkheim, who outlines the earlier authors (Durkheim, 1947, pp. 46–7).

The general neglect of the causes as opposed to the consequences of the division of labour and hierarchy in the organisation of production is not confined to either neoclassical economics or academic sociology. A similar criticism could be levelled at many ethnographic accounts of work by sociologists and historians, and indeed workers themselves, who unquestionably take the side of the workers against their employers. An obvious and outstanding example is the collection of interviews by Studs Terkel; *Working: People Talk About What They Do All Day and How They Feel About What They Do* (1985 [1972]).

Turning to the record of Marxism, although an analysis of the capitalist labour process takes up much of the first volume of *Capital*, Marx's three volume critique of political economy, it has not always occupied a central place in Marxist economics. Up to the 1970s, socialist economists criticised neoclassical economics for upholding the grossly unequal distribution of income under capitalism as being efficient. Socialists did not tend to criticise neoclassical economics for its neglect of production. A typical socialist polemic against neoclassical economics argued that 'income distribution, the division of society's annual product among the members of society, is *the* central question' for socialist economists, and income is distributed '*according to relative power*' (Nell, 1972, pp. 80, 95).

Monopoly Capital by Baran and Sweezy (1968) is arguably one of the most important contributions to Marxist economic theory since V. I. Lenin (Friedman, 1977, p. 28; Lazonick, 1991, p. 279). Baran and Sweezy contend that the only way for contemporary monopoly capitalism to sustain economic demand and avoid unemployment and economic crises is by ever-increasing expenditure on advertising and arms, and the production of more and more useless goods. This involves enormous waste and means that genuine human needs are not met.

Whatever its strengths are, Baran and Sweezy admit that a shortcoming of their critique of the capitalist economy is that it:

resulted in almost total neglect of a subject which occupies a central place in Marx's study of capitalism: the labour process. We stress the crucial role of technological change in the development of monopoly capitalism but make no attempt to inquire systematically into the consequences which particular kinds of technological change characteristic of the monopoly capitalist period have had for the nature of work, the composition (and differentiation) of the working class, the psychology of workers, the forms of working class organization and struggle, and so on. These are all obviously important subjects which would have to be dealt with in any comprehensive study of monopoly capitalism. (1968, p. 22)

Braverman saw his work very much as a supplement to Baran and Sweezy, but it is not without difficulty that he tries to integrate his study of work organisation into their analysis of monopoly capitalism (Rowlinson and Hassard, 1994). As Braverman himself puts it, 'Baran and Sweezy deal less with the movements of production than with the movements of its outcome, the product' (1974, p. 253).

Marxist fundamentalists, whose inspiration comes from an exegesis of Marx's writings (Fine and Harris, 1979), adhere to a theory of crisis derived from the third volume of Marx's *Capital* (1981, pp. 319–66). According to this theory, an economic 'collapse of capitalism' is inevitable because of an inherent tendency for the rate of profit to decline, which results in capitalists ceasing to invest in the means of production (Mandel, 1981, p. 86). Braverman's view is that for most of the twentieth century the fundamentalist theory of crisis was in the ascendancy:

The working philosophy of Marxism . . . focused increasingly not upon the profound inner nature of capitalism and the worker's position within it, but upon its various conjunctural crises. In particular, the critique of the mode of production gave way to the critique of capitalism as a mode of distribution. (1974, p. 11)

During the 1970s Marxists increasingly came to acknowledge the shortcomings in the Marxian theory of crisis (Van Parijis, 1980). However, in Stinchcombe's opinion although most Marxists have rightly accepted that Marx's theory of crisis is mistaken, they have gone about the job of reconstructing Marxism 'in the wrong way. They have usually taken the tack that Marx's theory was "too economic", and so have tried to add a theory of politics, rather than to repair the core of Marxist theory, the theory of the enterprise' (1983, p. 5).

Braverman's and Marglin's original and contemporaneous contributions to the revival of interest in work organisation are often lumped together (Bowles, 1986; Friedman, 1990b, p. 182; Thompson, 1989), especially since both are identified with the New Left radicalism of the 1960s. However, the different trajectories of the labour process debate and the Marglin debate reflect many of the divergencies within the discussions of work organisation that cut across the obvious political divisions. Whereas the starting point for the Marglin debate is a critique of neoclassical economics, for the labour process debate it is a critique of the technological determinism which once prevailed in industrial sociology and organisation theory.

The methodological differences between the Marglin debate and the labour process debate reflect the cleavage between economics and sociology. Marglin believes that since the 'social sciences are not experimental', egalitarian work organisation cannot be tested empirically and compared with hierarchical work organisation (1976, p. 14). He therefore combines historical research and economic modelling to explain how the hierarchical organisation of work came about. In doing so, Marglin follows the approach to work organisation found in classical political economy (Berg, 1994, ch. 3). Frank Stephen contends that Adam Smith's famous discussion of the pin factory 'was sustained at the conceptual level. He was not analysing the organization of a particular pin factory' (1984a, p. 3). For Marx too it was important that his account of the origins of capitalist production should be 'true both historically and conceptually' (1976, p. 439; Berg, 1994, p. 61).

Both mainstream and radical economists have followed Marglin's conceptual approach by attempting to model various forms of work organisation. In his article 'The Organisation of Work', Williamson offers a defence of hierarchy and what amounts to a mainstream reply to Marglin. Williamson endorses Marglin's contention as to 'the non-experimental nature of the social sciences', but instead of pursuing historical research Williamson submits 'that a great deal can be discovered about the efficiency of alternative work modes by an abstract assessment of their transactional properties' (1980a, p. 12). Samuel Bowles, a Marxist economist, sets out to develop the 'microeconomic logic of the Marxian model' in order to contrast it with the models of the production process in neoclassical and transaction cost economics (1986, p. 329).

Turning to the labour process debate in industrial sociology, initially a series of empirical case studies of the labour process were carried out which were deemed to confirm or refute the deskilling thesis (Wood, 1982; Zimbalist, 1979). These studies were often ethnographic, in the tradition of the shopfloor studies in industrial sociology that include Tom Lupton's *On the Shopfloor* (1963) and Donald Roy's 'Banana Time' (1973 [1960]; Burawoy, 1979). Feminist labour process writers, such as Anna Pollert (1981), have extended the coverage of shopfloor studies beyond the infamous '3 Ms': the male, manual, manufacturing workers so often idolised by left-wing industrial sociologists (Thompson, 1989, p. 5). It is difficult to know what can be said about such writings in relation to conceptual economic models. Economists might concede that they can be emotionally moved by such literature but deny that they could be intellectually persuaded by it.

Subsequently, the labour process debate became much more theoretical, but it is not theoretical in the sense of constructing conceptual models as in theoretical economics. Labour process theorists are more concerned with the philosophical issues that would lead them to question the underlying assumptions in economists' models. Although labour process theory often consists of tortuous ontological and epistemological reflection, the vital theme that comes out of it is the problem of the so-called 'subjective factor', which refers to the difficulty of integrating an understanding of the 'psychology of individual identity' and the formation of collectivities and social movements by workers into theoretical accounts of the labour process (Thompson, 1990, p. 114; Knights, 1990; Willmott, 1990). This has become a relatively self-contained debate with little or no point of contact with the discussions of work organisation elsewhere in economic history or radical political economy, let alone organisational economics.

All of this means that even though there has been a revival of interest in work organisation, the sources of it are so disparate that it would be misleading to speak of a unified debate. Nevertheless, some linkages can be made. In order to facilitate and structure a dialogue between the diverse views on work organisation from different disciplines, four stylised positions are set out in this chapter (see Figure 5.1). In relation to existing forms of work organisation, the four perspectives consist of: first, a defence of divisions of labour and hierarchy on efficiency grounds; this is the stance of most mainstream organisational economists, of whom Williamson (1980a) is probably the most forthright. Second, a critique of excessive divisions of labour and hierarchy; this is the position of most mainstream organisation theorists, of whom Child (1984) is a good example. Third, the predominantly Marxist critique of the distinctive capitalistic characteristics of divisions of labour and hierarchy. Finally, a rejection of the necessity for any specific divisions of labour or forms of hierarchy, which is claimed by radicals, of whom Marglin (1976) is the exemplar.

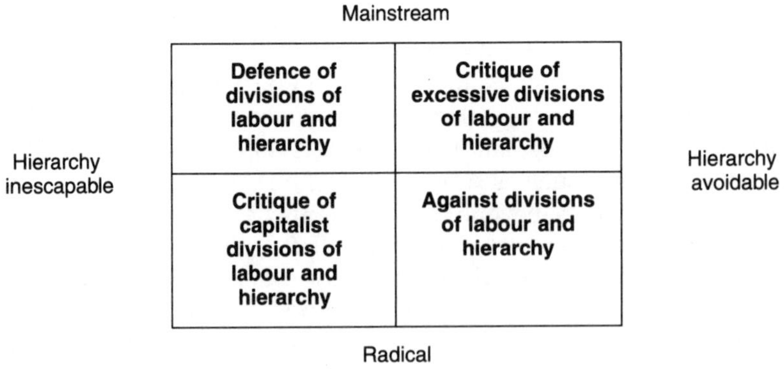

Mainstream

Defence of divisions of labour and hierarchy	Critique of excessive divisions of labour and hierarchy
Critique of capitalist divisions of labour and hierarchy	Against divisions of labour and hierarchy

Hierarchy inescapable (left)   Hierarchy avoidable (right)

Radical

FIGURE 5.1 Perspectives on work organisation

Defence of divisions of labour and hierarchy

The mainstream defence of capitalist work organisation can be said to start with Adam Smith's famous account of the division of labour in a pin factory. Smith contrasts one person carrying out every operation in the production of pins with a division of labour where, say, ten people each carry out two or three separate, simplified operations, which, according to Smith leads to a phenomenal 'increase of the productive powers of labour' (1976, p. 9). He gives three reasons for the increase in output from the division of labour. First, each worker becomes more dexterous at a single operation. Second, time is saved which would otherwise be taken up by each worker moving from one operation to the next. Third, the invention of new machinery is facilitated by the division of labour, either by the workers actually carrying out an operation, or by the specialised makers of the machines, who are also working under a division of labour.

Smith is concerned with the division of labour between operations. This does not, in itself, suggest the need for the exercise of any authority over the individual operatives. Co-ordination between operations that have been divided does not enter into the discussion, instead the only limit to the division of labour is, as Smith put it, 'the extent of the market' (1976). This implies that the division of labour arises spontaneously and that co-ordination between the divided operations is carried out by the market. Smith is therefore concerned with the horizontal division of labour between operations, rather than the vertical division of labour between superiors and subordinates which is characteristic of a hierarchy.

Two problems with Smith's argument can be highlighted at this stage. First, Rueschemeyer (1986, p. 201n) points out that although it is rarely noticed, there is 'a fundamental contradiction between the productivity claims made on behalf of competition and those made on behalf of division of labour'. The division of labour results in 'a pattern of ever-widening interdependence among specialized, non-competing units', whereas competition, 'requires many similar units that produce in parallel fashion the same or very similar goods and services'. Competition implies duplication while the division of labour suggests specialisation and, ultimately, monopoly. They are therefore contradictory tendencies.

Second, as Ugo Pagano notes in his survey of the economic literature on work organisation, 'Smith was largely unable to understand that the division of labour was coordinated, in the case of his own celebrated example [the pin factory], by means other than the market' (1985, p. 2; Demsetz, 1988). As a result, he only considers what North (1990a) would call the transformation costs of production. There are also the transaction costs to be considered, the costs of making agreements between the operatives at each stage of production. Intuitively, it would seem likely that transaction costs will rise as the division of labour increases because of the greater number of transactions that have to be made between increasingly heterogeneous operatives.

In contrast to Smith's view that one of the advantages of the division of labour is that it develops skill, Charles Babbage believed that it lessened the need for skilled workers. As the Lucasian Professor of Mathematics at Cambridge University, Babbage is perhaps best known for his contribution to the development of the computer. He outlined what is known as the 'Babbage principle' in his book *On the Economy of Machinery and Manufactures*:

> That the master manufacturer, by dividing the work to be performed into different processes each requiring different degrees of skill and force, can purchase exactly that precise quantity necessary for each process; whereas, if the entire work is executed by one workman, that person must possess sufficient strength to carry out the most laborious of the operations into which the art is divided. (Babbage, 1832, pp. 137–8, quoted by Pagano, 1985, p. 12)

Pagano maintains that, 'The division of labour within the firm', following the Babbage principle, appears to be 'independent of the kind of society in which it is performed. It seems to be a rather simple rule by which we can economize on the human skills and strength necessary for the production of wealth' (1985, p. 17).

Incidentally, Babbage's views on the cause and effect of the division of labour are the opposite to Smith's. Smith acknowledged that the limited capabilities of workers are a deleterious consequence rather than a cause of the division of labour:

> In the progress of the division of labour, the employment of the far greater part of those who live by labour, that is, of the great body of the people, comes to be confined to a few very simple operations, frequently to one or two. But the understandings of the greater part of men are necessarily formed by their ordinary employments. The man whose whole life is spent in performing a few simple operations, of which the effects too are, perhaps, always the same, or very nearly the same, has no occasion to exert his understanding, or to exercise his invention in finding out expedients for removing difficulties which never occur. He naturally loses, therefore, the habit of such exertion, and generally becomes as stupid and ignorant as it is possible for a human creature to become. (Smith, 1976, pp. 302–3; quoted by Pagano, 1985, p. 17)

In order to rectify this, Smith advocated at least minimal universal education at public expense.

The mainstream defence of capitalist hierarchy in contemporary organisational economics tends to take the horizontal division of labour as given. Of more concern is the issue of whether the co-ordination between divided operations should take place across markets or within firms, under the direction of an employer. The latter gives rise to the employment relationship, a subject on which there is generally acknowledged to be substantial common ground between many mainstream areas of organisational economics and Marxian or radical political economy.

It has been said that 'The attack on – or defence of – contemporary economics must begin with Paul Samuelson', as the author of the most widely used textbook in economics and the leading exponent of 'bourgeois economics' (Silk, 1978, p. 3). It is appropriate that Williamson, from transaction cost economics (1980a, p. 7), as well as Marglin, from radical political economy (1976, p. 47, nt 5; 1984, p. 163, nt 3), and Bowles, as a Marxist (1986, p. 331), all quote an aphorism from Samuelson, famous in economics (also cited by Berg, 1991, p. 174; Lazonick, 1991, p. 184; Marginson, 1993, p. 138), to show the indifference of neoclassical economics towards work organisation: 'in a perfectly competitive market it doesn't really matter who hires whom: so have labor hire capital'. (Samuelson, 1957, p. 894) This statement effectively sidesteps the whole issue of the employment relationship.

It is widely accepted by organisational economists that the employment relationship is of special interest with regard to issues of organisation. Simon (1986) defines an employment contract as a situation in which a worker 'agrees to accept the authority of' an entrepreneur, 'and the latter agrees to pay the former a stated wage . . . This contract differs fundamentally from a sales contract – the kind of contract that is assumed in ordinary formulations of price theory'. With a sales contract, 'the seller is not interested in the way in which his commodity is used once it is sold, while the worker *is* interested by what the entrepreneur will want him to do'. If workers became completely passive after entering into an employment contract, then virtually all the problems of managing production, which are major concerns for organisational behaviour and production engineering, would disappear (Simon, 1986, pp. 103–4; 1976, pp. 115–17). Yet this is exactly what is suggested by standard textbook economic theory, which assumes 'complete' labour contracts in which all activity to be carried out by workers is specified in advance.

In transaction cost economics it is recognised that within an employment relationship workers are not contracted to carry out a specific task; instead, they submit to the direction given by the buyer of their labour services. This is clear from the major forerunners of transaction cost economics, Ronald Coase and John Commons. According to Coase, the existence of a firm is virtually synonymous with an employment relationship (Masten, 1993), since a firm is, 'likely to emerge in those cases where a very short term contract would be unsatisfactory. It is obviously of more importance in the case of services – labour – than it is in the case of the buying of commodities' (Coase, 1990b).

In Coasian terms, a firm can almost be defined by the existence of an authority relationship in which, within certain limits, labour is directed. Coase is careful to note that 'it is not possible to draw a hard and fast line which determines whether there is a firm or not. There may be more or less direction' (1990b). Penrose also notes that although a firm can be defined as an area of 'authoritative communication', the actual boundary is difficult to draw, given the existence of 'various kinds of "cross currents" of "authoritative communication", particularly those arising from outside the firm' (Penrose, 1959, p. 20). This would appear to anticipate the notion that firms are embedded in networks. Although Coase has not contributed directly to the debate over work organisation, it is evident that he sees the subordination of the worker to the authority of an entrepreneur as the essence of the supersession of the market, and the distinguishing mark of a firm. Coase cites the direction of labour in production as evidence that there are situations other than direction by the state in which planning supplants co-ordination by the price mechanism: 'If a workman moves from department Y to department X, he does not go because of a change in relative prices, but because he is ordered to do so' (Coase, 1990b).

This point is similarly well made by Commons:

> As a bargainer, the modern wage-earner is deemed to be the legal *equal* of his employer, induced to enter the transaction by persuasion or coercion; but once he is permitted to enter the *place of employment* he becomes legally *inferior*, induced by commands which he is required to obey. The distinction is clear if the two sets of terms are distinguished as the bargaining terms of employer and employee, or rather of owner and wage-earner, and the managerial terms of foreman or superintendent, and workman. (1961, pp. 60–1)

As will be seen later in this chapter, Commons' interpretation of the employment relationship is in fact closer to the Marxian view than to contemporary transaction cost economics.

Not all organisational economists are agreed on the significance of the employment relationship. Alchian and Demsetz focus on property rights issues within the firm. According to them there is nothing special about the employment contract, since 'almost every contract is open-ended in that many contingencies are uncovered' (Alchian and Demsetz, 1986, p. 113n). In other words there is no such thing as a complete contract in any context. They maintain that it is not the employment relationship but team production that is the defining characteristic of the firm. They deny that employers have any 'authoritarian directive or disciplinary power' over workers:

> To speak of managing, directing, or assigning workers to various tasks is a deceptive way of noting that the employer continually is involved in renegotiation of contracts on terms acceptable to both parties. Telling an employee to type this letter rather then to file that document is like my telling a grocer to sell me this brand of tuna rather than that brand of bread. (Alchian and Demsetz, 1986, p. 112)

Alchian and Demsetz believe that a firm is characterised by team production, in which all the members of the team make contracts with one *centralized contractual agent* instead of trying to make separate contracts with each other.

They define a firm as 'a specialized market institution' in which contracts for team production can be made; in their view, a firm is not an organisation in which employers can tell workers what to do (Alchian and Demsetz, 1986, pp. 112, 132).

According to Alchian and Demsetz, once technology makes team production more productive than individual production, capitalist firms may emerge. It is fair to say that they are obsessed with 'shirking' among team members. In terms of game theory, this is the problem of free riders. They believe that the best way to overcome shirking is to have a centralised contracting agent who can meter the inputs of each team member and adjust their contracts accordingly. If the output from team production exceeds the output of individual production sufficiently to cover the additional costs of 'organising and disciplining team members', then team production will displace individual production (Alchian and Demsetz, 1986).

The centralised contracting agent becomes an employer because, according to Alchian and Demsetz, the best incentive for him or her to monitor the rest of the team effectively is to be assigned a claim to the residual rewards that are left over after the rest of the team have been paid for their inputs. An employer in a classical capitalist firm is defined by Alchian and Demsetz as the possessor of a 'bundle of rights: (1) to be a residual claimant; (2) to observe input behavior; (3) to be the central party common to all contracts with inputs; (4) to alter the membership of the team; and (5) to sell these rights' (1986, pp. 118–19). Notice that these rights do not include any authority over the workforce, in contrast to the models which stress the distinctiveness of the employment relationship. This line of argument is extended by Yoram Barzel, a neoinstitutional transaction cost economist, who suggests that, as a residual claimant, the entrepreneur will be ready to commit his or her own capital, 'In order to persuade others to work for him' (1987, p. 103). Furthermore, having agreed a contract and fixed their pay with the employer, other members of the team are relieved of the difficult task of monitoring their employer's performance.

Among organisational economists, Alchian and Demsetz are closest to being an extension of the neoclassical mainstream in that they do not present a defence of hierarchy within capitalist firms at all: they simply deny that the employment relationship is hierarchical. Nevertheless, Alchian and Demsetz should not be dispatched along with the neoclassical mainstream, since even though they characterise firms as markets, they do differentiate between various forms of market institution. They compare what they call 'the classical proprietorship' with other types of firm, such as profit-sharing and socialist firms, which are in effect workers' co-operatives. The essence of their case is that 'in the context of free association and choice of economic organization' it is the classical proprietorship or the corporation which prevails, whereas other types of firm only exist if the state enforces political preferences (Alchian and Demsetz, 1986, p. 124).

Williamson thinks that Alchian and Demsetz, in common with most conventional accounts of the organisation of production, resort too readily to an argument based on the technological indivisibility of production. Williamson concedes that there are instances of non-separability, but he maintains that they are not as common as is usually supposed, and they are nowhere near frequent enough to explain the prevalence of capitalist firms. Besides, 'indivisibilities . . . are neither necessary nor sufficient for market contracting to be supplanted by internal organization' (Williamson, 1983, p. 60). This highlights the variety of contracting arrangements that are possible even for a large indivisible industrial plant enjoying technological economies of scale (Williamson *et al.*, 1986, p. 137).

Mainstream defences of capitalist work organisation can be divided into two types: those which rely on technology to explain the existence of firms, and those which avoid doing so. The former is largely an extension of the neoclassical position and can be characterised as technological determinism. Williamson's case against technological determinism is that only the existence of very small groups can be explained in terms of technological 'non-separabilities'; most capitalist corporations are far larger than the work teams that are suggested by Alchian and Demsetz's analysis. Since Williamson believes that 'non-separabilities are much less widespread than is commonly believed', he goes on to discuss organisational rather than technological reasons for the existence of hierarchically organised firms (1983, p. 49).

Williamson's analysis of work organisation comes in two parts (1983, p. 41): an exposition of the employment relationship (1983, ch. 4; Williamson *et al.*, 1986); and a justification of the hierarchical and capitalistic form of most organisations in which workers are employed (1980a; 1983, ch. 3; 1985, ch. 9). The employment relationship arises in the first place simply because it means that the exact operations to be carried out do not have to be specified in the employment contract. It is reinforced where workers acquire task-specific or firm-specific skills in an on-the-job context, when a premium wage or a long-term contract will discourage labour turnover (1983, p. 59). Furthermore, firms employing workers provide internal labour markets, as described by Doeringer and Piore. Within 'the *internal labor market* . . . the pricing and allocation of labor is governed by a set of administrative rules and procedures', which can be 'distinguished from the *external labor market* of conventional economic theory where pricing, allocating, and training decisions are controlled directly by economic variables' (1971, pp. 1–2).

Hierarchy is justified on the grounds that each employee need only reach an agreement with one or a few individual decision-makers, rather than every other member of an organisation. A major problem for mainstream organisational economists such as Coase, Williamson, and Hess (1983), who, unlike Alchian and Demsetz, accept that the employment relationship is hierarchical, is to explain why workers would submit to authority in the absence of coercion. To acknowledge the ubiquity of hierarchy within capitalist firms means accepting that the conditions of voluntary market exchange that are axiomatic for neoclassical economics are almost universally violated. This compromises the classical liberal defence of capitalism which maintains that aside from the state the pattern of all economic activity is determined by voluntary exchanges between individuals.

Coase intuitively accepts that it is unlikely that firms arise because some individuals prefer to work under the direction of someone else and are prepared to accept less pay in order to do so (Coase, 1990b). Essentially, organisational economists recognise that what they have to show is that 'the authority vested in the employer is mutually beneficial' for both the employer and the worker. Hess tries to do this by building a model that explains how employers desire authority because of the uncertainties they face, and workers are willing to submit to authority because their income is supplemented by such submissive behaviour (Hess, 1983, pp. 97, 110).

Another problem for Williamson and Hess and their ilk is that even if their justification of hierarchy is fairly convincing, it does not explain why hierarchy should necessarily take the form of capitalist firms, in which all the means of production are owned by one party. According to Williamson, peer groups are only slightly less efficient than capitalist firms. Peer groups can be taken to mean workers' co-operatives, where the means of production are held in common ownership and leadership positions rotate among organisation members or are subject to periodic election. Williamson reckons that capitalist firms have the edge, since they are able to economise on the unequal distribution of decision-making skills by having permanent bosses who possess the required capabilities (Williamson, 1983, p. 52; 1985, pp. 217–18). This pessimistic assessment of the distribution of abilities echoes Babbage.

Williamson explains the absence of workers' co-operatives and the prevalence of capitalist firms in terms of the reluctance of workers to accept slightly lower wages from co-operatives in order to escape the oppressive authority of capitalist factories. He is also dismissive of the view that workers' co-operatives are frustrated by a shortage of capital. On the one hand, if workers were prepared to take a lesser wage, co-operatives could survive and expand with retained earnings (1980a, p. 33), and on the other, it is unlikely that they would be discriminated against by lenders of capital, since 'venture capitalists are unprincipled in their search for profit. Capital displays an inexorable tendency to equalize returns at the margin' (1985, p. 266).

Ultimately, Williamson falls back on his own jaundiced view of 'human nature as we know it' as the reason for the absence of workers' co-operatives (1980a, p. 33). Remember that, as well as being inherently unequal in their capacities to make decisions, Williamson believes that human beings are predisposed to 'lie, cheat, steal, mislead, disguise, obfuscate, feign, distort and confuse' (1985, p. 51n). By asserting a constancy of human nature and a fixed distribution of human capabilities, Williamson avoids the problem that work organisations might be susceptible to change in response to changes in factors such as workers' attitudes and readiness to take decisions: what labour process theorists would call the 'subjective factor', and what Williamson himself referred to, in his earlier work, as 'atmosphere' (1983, pp. 37–9).

In his discussion of atmosphere, Williamson emphasises that *'technological separability does not imply attitudinal separability'*. What he means by this typically opaque phrase is that even though internal organisation can easily be replaced by markets for exchanges between technologically separate activities, to do so can undermine the more satisfying and less calculative atmosphere that internal organisation often provides. Internal organisation is more likely than markets to foster 'quasi-moral' involvement and 'reciprocity' among organisation members (Williamson, 1983, pp. 37–8, 258).

It is worth quoting Williamson at length on the consequences of taking atmosphere into account:

> Recognition that alternative modes of economic organization give rise to differing exchange relations, and that these relations themselves are valued, requires that organizational effectiveness be viewed more broadly than the usual efficiency calculus would dictate. Thus, modes of organization or practices which would have superior productivity consequences if implemented within, and thus would be adopted by, a group of expected pecuniary gain maximizers, may be modified or rejected by groups with different values. For one thing, favorable productivity consequences may no longer obtain – which is to say that efficiency and a sense of well-being (that includes, but transcends, equity) are intrinsically (nonseparably) joined. In addition, preferences for atmosphere may induce individuals to forego [sic] material gains for nonpecuniary satisfactions if the modes or practices are regarded as oppressive or otherwise repugnant. (1983, pp. 38–9)

While Williamson is more concerned with how atmosphere considerations may explain a preference for internal organisation as opposed to markets, and how markets can undermine reciprocity, there seems to be no reason why the argument could not be extended to a comparison between workers' co-operatives and capitalist firms. Williamson concedes that it is conceivable that a co-operative 'structure will be so satisfying to its members that it will result in greater productivity per unit than the same group would realize if organized as a hierarchy', but, predictably, he thinks this is 'doubtful' (1983, p. 55n). A case could well be made that the prevalence of hierarchy has undermined the reciprocity and involvement that would make workers' co-operatives not only preferable but also more efficient.

The concept of atmosphere therefore threatens to undermine the whole of Williamson's justification for capitalist hierarchy. A few sociologists have seized on atmosphere as the loose thread they can pull to unravel Williamson's model of work organisation. Atmosphere is a residual category, intended by Williamson (1983) to explain phenomena that are otherwise inexplicable in quantifiable transaction costs terms. As such it is, 'high in justificatory value, but low in explanatory value' (Bauer and Cohen, 1983, p. 83):

> Constructs of this nature always seem to turn up as a lame afterthought to elaborate theoretical schemes whose authors have come to doubt the closure of their systems. After all, if atmosphere and social norms carry the weight attributed to them, it would not be necessary to create the complex and ingenious institutional checks and balances which these writers spend most of their time deducing. (Braendgaard, 1983, p. 170)

The implication of this is that by an inculcation of norms and the concomitant improvement in atmosphere, work could be intensified and shirking virtually abolished, such that any form of work organisation could become more efficient. It is not surprising that Williamson has lost interest in the concept of atmosphere. In a footnote to their article, 'Understanding the Employment Relation', Williamson *et al.* give a lame excuse for omitting atmosphere from their discussion: 'Failure to include atmosphere does not imply that we think it unimportant. But the concept is somewhat difficult to explicate in what is already a rather long paper' (Williamson *et al.*, 1986, p. 141 [1975]).

In Williamson's subsequent writing on the organisation of work (Williamson, 1980, 1984) he makes no mention of atmosphere, and it does not even appear in the index to *The Economic Institutions of Capitalism* (1987), his most comprehensive statement of the markets and hierarchies perspective. He does make a brief allusion to 'the evidence relating job satisfaction to productivity' which, 'Curiously,' he says, 'discloses little or no association between the two' (Williamson, 1980a, p. 35; 1987, p. 270). If job satisfaction is taken as an indication of atmosphere, then two issues need to be explored. First, the reasons for the subordination of job satisfaction to productivity, and second, the possible effects on the efficiency ratings of different forms of work organisation if atmosphere, or job satisfaction, were to be included as a component of efficiency criteria as well as productivity. Williamson has not taken up either of these issues.

Three matters arising from the efficiency defence of capitalist hierarchy can be taken up in discussing each of the other perspectives. First in defending (or denying) the existence of capitalist hierarchy, mainstream organisational economists are in danger of obscuring the diversity of hierarchically organised capitalist firms. This is highlighted by the critique of excessive divisions of labour and hierarchy which focuses on the various forms and degrees of hierarchy.

Second, the defence of hierarchy is separated from the defence of the capitalist firm in the critique of capitalist divisions of labour and hierarchy. Although they have modelled the problem in different ways, organisational economists seem to agree that 'collaboration among people is often subject to shirking' (Barzel, 1987, p. 103), and this gives rise to hierarchy, with bosses trying to minimise shirking. But the variety of explanations for the relationship between hierarchy and the capitalist firm given by organisational economists themselves suggests that the relationship is problematical. Williamson concedes that 'ownership is only weakly related to hierarchy' (1985, p. 239). It is important not to confuse two separate questions: 'Why are there bosses?' (Hess, 1983, ch. 7) and 'Why are capitalists the bosses?' (Eswaran and Kotwal, 1989). The answers to each question are not necessarily the same.

Finally, neither the technological nor organisational mainstream explanations for the capitalist firm give much attention to what causes the division of labour in the first place; they tend to take it as given. That, is they assume, either that operations are inseparable, as do Alchian and Demsetz, or that operations are separable, as does Williamson, rather than considering the processes whereby operations are separated or combined over time. Neimark and Tinker make this point in their radical critique of Williamson. They argue that he 'does not question the origins of the technologically separate interfaces that define transactions; rather he takes them as given' (Neimark and Tinker, 1987, p. 668). The relationship between hierarchy and divisions of labour is elaborated by Marglin, who disputes the necessity for divisions of labour and hierarchy.

Critique of excessive divisions of labour and hierarchy

Mainstream organisation theorists are more concerned with the choices to be made within the context of the capitalist firm than with any alternatives to it. These are, after all, the only choices that are open to the managers of capitalist firms, and it is they who are often seen as the beneficiaries of organisation theory as taught in business schools. Organisation theorists often portray management as a ubiquitous function. This overlooks the extent to which management, as a specialised activity, is predicated upon the existence of a division of labour and hierarchy. Nevertheless, by ignoring the choice between markets and hierarchies, organisation theorists have highlighted the choices that exist within capitalist hierarchies. As a leading proponent of a strategic choice perspective in organisation theory, Child offers a useful overview of organisational choices in his textbook, *Organization* (1984). Two issues examined by Child will be taken up here, to show how the markets and hierarchies dichotomy can obscure the choices to be made within firms. First, the division of labour, which generally comes under the heading of 'job design' in mainstream organisation theory and organisational behaviour, and second, the extent of hierarchy: what Child refers to as 'tall' or 'flat' organisation.

Child explicitly acknowledges that 'there is a conflict of interests inherent in the employment contract which, if it remains at the forefront of employees' minds, will tend to sustain an active and probably collectively organized resistance to managerial control' (1984, p. 138). This goes much further than most mainstream organisation theorists towards accepting that the need for management control itself is predicated on the existence of the employment relationship, and it reflects Child's long-standing engagement with radical and Marxian ideas. But Child's theme is that 'the variation found in job and work design even under similar contextual conditions suggests that there is often a degree of choice between alternatives' (1984, p. 25). The implication is that managerial strategies have to be examined in order to explain differences in job design (Child, 1985), otherwise the diversity of job design that prevails even within broadly capitalist institutions will be obscured.

The implication of mainstream organisation theory is that excessive divisions of labour and the consequent degradation of work within capitalist firms is an unintended consequence of several managerial strategies. The advocates of 'job redesign' maintain that if the trends towards increased specialisation and reduced discretion for workers could be reversed, then the performance of organisations would almost certainly improve. Simon has pointed out that this view rests on an assumption that 'the happy employee is the productive employee' (1976, p. 289), even though there is little evidence to support this, as Williamson has noticed. It could be said that mainstream organisation theory, and organisational behaviour even more so, takes the employment relationship as given and is concerned with how 'atmosphere' can be fostered in organisations that have hired workers. The general impression is that atmosphere will improve if the division of labour is at least moderated. This means that issues to do with the employment relationship itself are put to one side. On the other hand, it could be said that organisational economics takes atmosphere as given in order to analyse the employment relationship and hierarchy.

Turning to the issue of hierarchy, Williamson implies that there is a more or less fixed relationship between the number of transactions that are internalised by a firm and the number of levels of hierarchy. This is because bounded rationality limits managers' span of control. The span of control refers to the number of subordinates formally reporting to a manager. Williamson suggests that, 'If any one manager can deal directly with only a limited number of subordinates, then increasing firm size necessarily entails adding hierarchical levels.' He qualifies this by noting that firms can increase in size without necessarily adding hierarchical levels so long as the top levels in the hierarchy only intervene selectively in the lower levels. This means that not all information has to be transmitted from the bottom to the top of the hierarchy, nor all decisions communicated from the top to the bottom, thus reducing the problems of attenuation through the hierarchy (Williamson, 1985, pp. 134–5).

Child (1984, ch. 3) supports the view that the length of hierarchies increases in a predictable way as the total number of employees in an organisation rises. This is not surprising, remembering that Child's enunciation of the strategic choice perspective was in part a qualification to his earlier work as a contingency theorist, where he examined the size of organisations as a variable. Child maintains that there are significant choices between having a 'taller' hierarchy, with more hierarchical levels than average for the number of employees in an organisation, and a 'flatter' hierarchy, with fewer levels than average: 'Basically,' Child writes, 'there is choice between increasing levels of management or increasing spans of control as the size of an organization rises.' Reviewing 'the arguments for and against tall and flat structures', Child suggests that 'the weight of argument comes down against tall structures'. This is largely because tall structures can lead to the attenuation of information flowing up and decisions coming down through the levels in the hierarchy. As well as this, while the top levels of the hierarchy will be overloaded with information, the lower levels will have limited opportunities to exercise their decision-making capabilities, possibly leading to reduced performance on their part.

An interesting point about Child's analysis is that he suggests sociological reasons for the proliferation of taller hierarchies, even though flatter hierarchies seem to be preferable. Taller hierarchies can result from the unintended consequence of other management objectives. For example, a taller structure can arise from the provision of a career structure for managers, a form of internal labour market within an organisation which offers advancement through hierarchical levels. There is also the problem that as an organisation contracts in size, the number of levels in the organisation tends to remain the same. The managers assigned to reduce numbers interpret this as a call to dispense with some of their subordinates. Williamson actually gives a good description of this problem:

> Managers are notably reluctant . . . to abolish their own jobs, even in the face of employment guarantees. The problems with such guarantees are that while continued employment may be secure, assurances that status will be maintained when a position is eliminated, and that promotion prospects will not be upset upon removal from a promotion ladder are unenforceable. (1985, p. 152)

A problem for the defence of capitalist firms by mainstream organisational economists is that it can be construed as a defence of excessive hierarchy, as if the only alternative to existing hierarchical structures is a co-operative or a reversion to the market rather than a reduction in the levels of hierarchy. The general defence of hierarchy may obscure Child's argument that many organisations 'would benefit from a reduction in the number of levels they already have' (1984, p. 65). On the other hand, the critique of tall organisations, and the call for flatter managerial hierarchies, should not be confused with radical attacks upon the very existence of hierarchy. It is often difficult to differentiate calls for the amelioration of hierarchy from more radical demands for the abolition of hierarchy.

A similar point has to be made in relation to Leibenstein's (1986) and Aoki's (1984) game-theoretic arguments for co-operation between managers and workers within firms. Put very simply, they model the firm as a prisoner's dilemma, with managers and workers representing the two prisoners. They argue that if management and workers can be induced to co-operate rather than to defect, then they can both enjoy superior payoffs. Aoki posits 'two major modes of work organisation and inter-workshop co-ordination practised within modern firms': these are the traditional hierarchical mode and an emerging co-operative, participatory mode (Aoki, 1990, pp. 27–9). The latter, co-operative mode, is generally looked upon more favourably. However, it is clear that participation does not constitute worker control, a point that has long been recognised by radical writers on industrial relations (Ramsay, 1985). For a start, participation does not extend to strategic decisions within a firm; these are still firmly under the control of management (Cowling and Sugden, 1993, p. 73).

Authors such as Leibenstein and Aoki draw attention to the limitations of treating the hierarchical firm 'as a homogeneous entity' (Cowling and Sugden, 1993, p. 73). What they do not do is to explain or challenge the existence of hierarchical capitalist firms in general. They tend to reify the categories of management and workers, as if the two are readily identifiable parties (Rueschemeyer, 1986, p. 78) locked into a prisoner's dilemma with each other. Game theory needs to explain the existence of the hierarchical capitalist firm in the first place before setting up the options between the more or less co-operative forms it can take. Otherwise, game theorists, like organisation theorists, are in danger of assuming the universality of capitalist firms, as if the only alternative is between one form of capitalist firm and another.

The choices to be made within capitalist firms are captured in terms of trust in Alan Fox's book on industrial relations *Beyond Contract* (1974). According to Fox, if organisations fail to sustain a high-trust dynamic then they are likely to succumb to a low-trust dynamic. Where there is a low-trust dynamic, workers are given little discretion by management, there is close supervision, rigorous enforcement of the rules and punishment for failure. Workers perceive that the managers behave as if the workers cannot be trusted, and the workers' response is to behave as if they cannot be trusted. The dynamics of the situation generate 'a spiral of institutionalised distrust' (Fox, 1974, p. 102). In contrast, where workers are assumed by managers to share a 'moral involvement' in the organisation's goals and values and are granted significant discretion, a high-trust dynamic can be set in train. Robert Holton (1992) has distilled the choices that can be made which might foster low trust or high trust in terms of six dimensions along which organisations can encourage or discourage self-interested behaviour (these are set out in Table 5.1). In summary, it can be said that tall organisations undermine trust, while trust sustains flat organisations. However, high trust is difficult to create and sustain, and there is a tendency for management 'to assume that changes in

TABLE 5.1   Encouragement or discouragement of self-interest

Variable	Encourages self-interest	Discourages self-interest
Patterns of interaction	Minimal interactions with others, e.g. fluid labour markets based on single migrant workers, temporary or high turnover of labour; occupations with a heavy emphasis on individual promotion.	Close interactions with others, e.g. occupational communities where workplace and residence are stable and coincide for most of the workforce; occupations with group job rotation
Basis of rewards	Rewards accrue to individuals, e.g. steep salary structure reinforced by individually assessed tax structure.	Rewards accrue to group, e.g. co-operative, teamwork-based labour.
Measurement of effort	Effort of individuals can be measured, e.g. piece rates, personal evaluations.	Effort of individuals cannot be measured, e.g. large indivisible projects based on teamwork and job transferability.
Work design	Minimise interdependence, e.g. Taylorist breakdown of worktasks; surveillance of individual worker.	Maximise interdependence, e.g. co-operative effort; activity defying precise contractual specification.
Leadership and authority	Preference for stable leadership, e.g. individual leaders taken to be omni-competent and positions held continuously.	Rotating leadership, e.g. all regarded as potential leaders, and hence skills develop in group context.
Hierarchy	Tall hierarchy, e.g. rewards unequally distributed such that access to better rewards requires pursuit of self-interest.	Flat hierarchy, e.g. greater participation and less inequality puts less premium on self-interest to advance.

Source: Holton, 1992, p. 86.

the high-discretion direction would invariably generate consensus on ends and means' (Fox, 1974, p. 116).

Issues of trust have been addressed increasingly in terms of corporate or organisational culture. According to Reve, in terms of organisational economics 'the essence of organizational culture' is that through an infusion of shared values 'trust replaces monitoring and control, thus creating transaction cost-efficient governance structures compared to traditional hierarchical contracts'

(1990, p. 152). North puts it more succinctly: 'morale building is a substitute at the margin for investing in more monitoring' (1990a, p. 66). Variability in culture, morale, or norms (Sen, 1982, p. 7) is now routinely invoked to explain variations in economic performance between firms and nations. Any trade-offs that have to be made in creating culture are rarely discussed. Corporate culture is like atmosphere – it is a residual category that is invoked unthinkingly but which threatens to undermine most economic models of the firm. Without denying the existence of something that might be understood as culture, it would probably be a good idea to assume that, within firms and nations at least, it is fairly constant and difficult to change.

With the critique of excessive hierarchy there is a tendency to confuse description, prescription and prediction (as was noted in Chapter 3, in relation to the advocates of network forms of organisation). More co-operative forms of capitalist firm, with flatter hierarchies incorporating job redesign and a less extreme division of labour, are seen as being more desirable, but their advocates are hard put to explain the relative absence of such forms of organisation, given their alleged superiority. As a substitute for finding forms of organisation they would like, these theorists often end up renaming the forms of organisation that actually exist, to make them sound more acceptable. Engels' comment from his short piece 'On Authority' seems apposite: 'These gentlemen think that when they have changed the names of things they have changed the things themselves' (1969, p. 378).

Critique of capitalist divisions of labour and hierarchy

As a starting point for looking at Marxist interpretations of work organisation it would be useful to reiterate the extent of agreement between Marxian and transaction cost economists concerning the employment relationship. Marx makes a distinction between labour power, the human capacity for work, and actual labour. It is worth quoting him at length to sample his exasperation and ironic tone as he makes his point:

> The consumption of labour-power is completed, as in the case of every other commodity, outside the market or the sphere of circulation. Let us therefore, in company with the owner of money and the owner of labour-power, leave this noisy sphere, where everything takes place on the surface and in full view of everyone, and follow them into the hidden abode of production, on whose threshold there hangs the notice 'No admittance except on business'. Here we shall see, not only how capital produces, but how capital is itself reproduced. The secret of profit-making must at last be laid bare. (Marx, 1976, pp. 279–80)

There is clearly a similarity between the markets and hierarchies dichotomy in transaction cost economics and the Marxian distinction between labour

power and labour, which is, according to Bowles, 'perhaps the most fundamental distinction in Marxian economics'. In Bowles' view, what is 'Central to
the Marxian approach' is 'the distinction between those social relationships
that take the form of market exchanges between firms and other ownership
units, on the one hand, and relationships of command that take place within
firms' (1986, pp. 333, 333n, 352). Putterman remarks that 'in at least one sense,
namely his sharp delineation of firm and market, Marx belongs firmly in the
camp of Coase, Simon, and Williamson' (1986a, p. 26).

Some Marxist economists, such as Francis Green (1988, 1992), accept that by
'making a slight change in the hard core of the neoclassical paradigm', namely
questioning 'the assumption of complete labour contracts', organisational
economics has injected 'social relations' into the analysis of production. This
means that the standard Marxist critique of neoclassical economics, that it
ignores production and relegates it to the realm of engineering, is misplaced
when it comes to organisational economics, which recognises the special
nature of the employment relationship. The similarity between Simon's
critique of the neoclassical treatment of the employment relationship and
the Marxist critique (Hodgson, 1982b, p. 65n) has only rarely been noticed by
mainstream organisational economists (Goldberg, 1980, pp. 249–50) or neoclassically inclined economists (Bartlett, 1989, p. 122).

Whether or not Marxian and transaction costs analyses of production can be
said to have converged (Green, 1988, 1992; Young, 1992), it is certainly true
that their agreement about the special nature of the employment relationship
has at least opened up an arena for dialogue which was previously ruled out
by neoclassical assumptions. However, the limited agreement between Marxist and transaction cost economists does not extend to all organisational
economists. Alchian and Demsetz are so anxious to legitimise the capitalist
firm that, 'For them not only is there no exploitation or alienation, there is no
power or authority in employment at all' (Bartlett, 1989, p. 122). They have
brought the wrath of radicals such as Hodgson upon themselves for trying to
present 'the firm as a market', and the employer as merely 'an orchestrator of
a "market" within the firm'. For Marxists and radical institutionalists, 'One
reason why the work of Oliver Williamson and his followers is superior to that
of Alchian and Demsetz is that a distinction between market and non-market
institutions is firmly upheld' (Hodgson, 1988, pp. 196–9).

Having noted the immediate similarities between the Marxist and transaction costs critiques of the neoclassical neglect of production, it is necessary to
explain that the Marxist approach has very different origins. Marx follows
most nineteenth-century political economy by reasoning in terms of value.
According to Marx, the value of a commodity is determined by the average
socially necessary labour time that is needed for its production. This goes for
labour power as much as any other commodity. So the value of labour power
is determined by the labour time necessary to produce and reproduce a
worker. In Marx's model of the capitalist economy he assumes that the wages

paid by employers in exchange for labour power are equal to the value of the labour power. This means that Marx assumes that the exchange of wages for labour power is, in a sense, a fair exchange, since the owner of labour power (the worker) receives in wages the full value of his or her commodity. Although Marx recognises that at times employers are in a position to force down wages below the value of labour power, it is important to realise that in his model of capitalism in its 'pure form' it is assumed that employers pay the 'full price' for labour power so that the workforce is reproduced both daily and across generations (1976, p. 279).

Marx developed his concepts of labour and labour power partly in response to Pierre-Joseph Proudhon, the influential self-educated anarchist philosopher. Marx 'readily accepted Ricardo's belief that products under capitalist conditions already exchange at prices proportionate to their values' (Thomas, 1985, p. 228). As a result, Marx locates the exploitation of workers by their employers in the labour process, and unlike Proudhon, he does not believe that the exploitation of workers can be ended by establishing a fair exchange between workers and employers in the market. Putterman summarises the point succinctly:

> Marx himself went to great lengths to insist that the employer and employee contract voluntarily and as equals. The crux of his theory may be seen to be an argument that exploitation occurs *inside the factory gates* and not in market exchange – an argument that might appear arcane from the standpoint of *value theory*, yet one that retains some conceptual significance. (1986a, p. 6n)

The special feature of labour power as a commodity is that in its use, as labour, it can create more value than is required for its own production. In value terms, the importance of the distinction between labour power and labour is that it shows how employers are able to extract surplus value from labour power in the labour process. This locates exploitation in production rather than exchange. What is not clear is whether Marx's distinction between labour power and labour, and his focus on the labour process, is inextricably linked to the labour theory of value. If it is, then this creates serious problems for making connections between Marxist political economy and organisational economics. Ernest Mandel is a leading Trotskyist who has written the introductions for recent editions of *Capital*. In his introduction to Volume I he wrote, 'No part of Marx's theory has been more assaulted in the academic world during the last seventy-five years than his theory of value' (1976, p. 38). The main criticism of the labour theory of value is that, 'Contrary to what he [Marx] thought possible, prices cannot be reduced to quantities of labour' (de Vroey, 1982, pp. 34, 37).

The labour theory of value has increasingly 'come under widespread attack' within Marxism (Callinicos, 1989, p. 71). One of the many lines of argument against it is derived from Piero Sraffa's notoriously difficult book, *The*

Production of Commodities by Commodities (1960). The technicalities and mathematical foundations of the Sraffian argument are beyond the scope of this work, but since it has had some influence on the labour process debate, it is worth discussing. In *Marx After Sraffa*, Steedman (1977) gives an assessment of the Sraffa-based critique of Marxist political economy which at first sight seems reassuring for the study of the labour process. Steedman maintains that 'the concepts of labour, labour power and of surplus labour', as well as the 'emphases on the labour process, on coercion therein, and on the everchanging nature of the labour process resulting from both workplace conflicts and the competitive struggle', are unaffected by the Sraffian critique, because they are independent of Marx's 'reasoning in value magnitudes' (Steedman, 1977, p. 206). In a later paper, Steedman admits that once it is accepted that the concept of labour power is redundant in value terms, 'The only real force of Marx's insistence that it is labour-power (or the disposal over it) that is sold by the worker is that labour contracts are never absolutely precise – perhaps necessarily so' (Steedman, 1982, pp. 151–3). But this is very much an afterthought on Steedman's part; it does not lead him to analyse the labour process.

Sraffian Marxists, like neoclassical economists, take production as given (Bradby, 1982, p. 117; de Vroey, 1982). Steedman's discussion of 'an "abstract" capitalist economy' illustrates the point. When analysing the relationship between wages, profits and prices of production, he assumes that 'production relations' are ' "frozen" and taken as determined exogenously . . . the shopfloor balance of forces are (hypothetically) held constant'. Although Steedman claims that this does not deny the importance of the labour process (1977, pp. 16–17), it does separate the analysis of the labour process from the rest of Marxian political economy, in the same way that mainstream neoclassical economics is separate from organisation theory and studies of management. What is more, in terms of what Sraffians actually do, it is quite simply wrong to suggest, as Wright, a leading Marxist, has done, that both Sraffa and the labour theory of value 'direct class analysis towards the investigation of the labour process' (1981, p. 161; Bradby, 1982, p. 115).

Fortunately, those Marxist, and Marxian influenced, economists who are engaged in debate with organisational economics over the labour process have for the most part distanced themselves from the labour theory of value without diluting the distinction between labour power and labour. According to Bowles, the distinctiveness of Marxian microeconomics 'has little to do with the labor theory of value' (1986, p. 330). Hodgson (1988) is now a self-styled radical institutionalist, but he started out as a Marxist and along the way was identified with the Sraffian critique of the labour theory of value (Hodgson, 1982a). Since the 1970s he has made a habit of demolishing Marxist shibboleths by pointing out how little they actually meant to Marx (Hodgson, 1974, 1975). In the case of the labour theory of value, Marx never made clear what was meant by it: 'In fact,' says Hodgson, 'as far as I am aware, he never used the term' (1982b, p. 60). If it is accepted that the labour theory of value is not vital to Marxism, then the difference between Marxian political economy and organisational economics turns on the extent to which the distinction between labour power and labour and the need for hierarchy are universal or specific to the capitalist employment relationship.

This is picked up by Victor Goldberg in his article, 'Bridges Over Contested Terrain' (1980), which attempts to reconcile Marxist and radical political economy with organisational economics. He argues that the distinction between labour power and labour is central to mainstream organisational economics as well as Marxist analysis, but he maintains that 'The employment relationship is not, as the radicals suggest, unique', because,

> Most exchange relationships will entail, in varying degrees, the type of gap between promise and execution implicit in the labor–labor power distinction. The appearance of uniqueness arises from the fact that the assumptions of conventional microeconomic analysis preclude the existence of such a gap. (1980, p. 253)

In a well-known paper Leibenstein makes a similar point: 'it is one thing to purchase or hire inputs in a given combination; it is something else to get a predetermined output of them' (1986, p. 169). However, Goldberg is careful to note that 'exchange relations are not ahistorical; they take place within a specific social context', which means that 'the gap between promise and execution' will take various historical forms (1980, p. 253).

Hodgson suggests that labour and labour power are, like the labour process, universal categories which bear 'no specific and exclusive relation to a particular mode of production', even though in Marxist literature they have 'tended to take on a different meaning, referring to the specific relations of capitalist production' (1982b, p. 62). This appears to go some way towards conceding Goldberg's point that the employment relationship is merely a particular historical manifestation of what could be thought of as a universal problem of agency.

There is some confusion, because Marxists have tried to make two separate but related points. First, the reason that most Marxists, following Marx, refer to production as the labour process is because this emphasises that production is, in fact, a process which occupies actual time and space. It should be borne in mind that in neoclassical 'microeconomics textbooks, all production seems to take place on the head of a mythical pin' (Bartlett, 1989, p. 129). Furthermore, the term 'labour process' underlines the inseparability of labour from production. As Cohen puts it in his defence of Marx, 'Labouring activity is not used in production: it *is* production' (1978, p. 43). In Marx's own words, 'The use of labour-power is labour itself' (Marx, 1976).

This means that an agency problem only arises if labour is involved. Labour is not simply one among many factors of production, since without it production cannot take place. What is more, as Marxists and radicals have repeatedly emphasised, unlike other factors of production such as a machines or raw materials, 'labor is embodied in people' (Bowles, 1986, p. 333), it 'cannot be disassociated physically from its possessing agent' (Hodgson, 1982a, p. 208). This is in sharp contrast to neoclassical economics, where, 'The fact that labor is not only owned by individuals but lies inextricably bound within their minds and bodies is simply irrelevant' (Bartlett, 1989, p. 121).

While Marxists are adamant that labour is the essential and universal component in production, which means that it is more accurate to speak of production as a labour process, their second point is that the appearance of labour power as a commodity available for sale is by no means a universal phenomenon. Marx is quite clear on this point:

> [N]ature does not produce on the one hand owners of money or commodities, and on the other hand men possessing nothing but their own labour-power. This relation has no basis in natural history, nor does it have a social basis common to all periods of human history. It is clearly the result of a past historical development. (1976, p. 273)

The availability of labour power as a commodity depends upon the existence of 'free' workers. By this, Marx means that workers must be doubly free: in the positive sense that as 'a free individual' the worker 'can dispose of his labour-power as his own commodity'; and free in the ironic sense that 'he has no other commodity for sale, i.e. he is rid of them, he is free of all the objects needed for the realization of his labour-power' (Marx, 1976, pp. 272–3).

The availability of labour power as a commodity rests on the existence of a specific set of property rights (as was noted in Chapter 2), namely the exclusion of workers from the means of production by the enforcement of private property on the one hand, and on the other the prohibition of slavery. The latter point is alluded to by both Marx (1976, p. 271) and Coase (1990b). A few organisation theorists have recognised that ultimately this means that managerial authority consists of 'the right to exclude' workers from production (Marsden, 1993, p. 104), which is underpinned by the readiness of the state to enforce property rights. The existence of this specific set of property rights is taken for granted in transaction cost economics, while Alchian and Demsetz (1986) see the emergence of these property rights as the outcome of a neutral efficiency imperative. They rule out any interference of political preferences in the allocation of such property rights. They allege that this only happens when property rights are devised to facilitate the emergence of alternative types of firm, such as workers' co-operatives.

According to Bowles, therefore, although 'the Coasian view of the capitalist economy as a multiplicity of mini-command economies operating in a sea of market exchanges' presents 'a well-developed model of the firm as a social organization', it is only 'superficially indistinguishable from the Marxian view' (1986, pp. 352, 342). The Coasian view obscures the coercive separation of workers from the means of production, which the availability of labour power as a commodity is predicated upon, and is evidenced by the involuntary unemployment that plays a central part in the Marxian theory of the capitalist economy. As Neimark and Tinker put it in their polemic against Williamson, 'the technological separability of labor services from the means of production, which establishes the employer–employee relationship, is taken as given rather than being recognised as the historical outcome of social processes' (1987, p. 669). If it could be shown that the labour contract, which workers apparently enter into freely, is, in fact, underpinned by 'the coercion machinery of the state' (Rueschemeyer, 1986, p. 46), this would undermine the mainstream assumption that workers voluntarily submit to the employment relationship and capitalist authority because it is efficient for them to do so.

Having highlighted the differences between Marxism and organisational economics, it might seem surprising that Marx does not seem to be too far from mainstream organisational economics in his belief that hierarchy is necessary for co-operation in production to take place. This is made quite clear in the following passage from *Capital*:

> All directly social or communal labour on a large scale requires, to a greater or lesser degree, a directing authority, in order to secure the harmonious co-operation of the activities of individuals, and to perform the general functions that have their origin in the motion of the total productive organism, as distinguished from the motion of its separate organs. A single violin player is his own conductor: an orchestra requires a separate one. (Marx, 1976, pp. 448–9)

Engels extends the argument from the orchestra to the cotton spinning mill, the railway, large-scale industry in general, and large-scale agriculture (Engels, 1969b, pp. 377–8). Williamson concedes that the symphony orchestra is one of the few examples of true technological non-separability (1985, p. 88, n. 4). By the way, it is reported that, 'The Russians apparently tried a leaderless orchestra shortly after their revolution but soon gave it up as unworkable' (Mintzberg, 1989, pp. 265–6).

The disagreement between Marxism and the mainstream concerns the pathological reasons for hierarchy within capitalist production. According to Marx (1976, ch. 13), while a directing authority is necessary for all social labour, in the context of the capitalist firm, where social labour is exploited by the capitalist, 'the necessity increases for some effective control' over the workers. This is because the workers do not own the equipment or the raw materials used in production, and they are only paid for their labour power, not according to the product of their labour.

The capitalist's direction of production is therefore 'twofold in content', according to Marx. On the one hand, direction by some authority is a necessity in any 'social labour process for the creation of a product', and this role is fulfilled by the capitalist in capitalist production. On the other hand, in the capitalist labour process, direction takes on a 'despotic' form, since it is also required to ensure the exploitation of labour. A defining feature of 'capitalist production, properly speaking', is that the capitalist is 'relieved of actual labour' and,

> hands over the work of direct and constant supervision of the individual workers and groups of workers to a special kind of wage-labourer. An industrial army of workers under the command of a capitalist requires, like a real army, officers (managers) and N.C.O.s (foremen, overseers), who command during the labour process in the name of capital. (Marx, 1976, p. 450)

Marx alleges that apologists for capitalism try to identify the universal requirement for direction that arises out of co-operation with the specific form of direction 'which is made necessary by the capitalist and therefore antagonistic character of that process'. Against this, Marx insists that, 'It is not because he is a leader of men that a man is a capitalist; on the contrary, he is a leader of industry because he is a capitalist' (1976, p. 450). Herein lies an explanation for the discrepancy between the managers and informal leaders in production that is often observed by industrial sociologists (Strauss, 1992; Dalton, 1992), yet almost never mentioned by mainstream economists. If the authority relationship in capitalist production were to arise consensually in anything like the way mainstream organisational economics suggests that it does, then presumably there would be no such divergence between the official managers and the unofficial leaders among the workforce, who in practice frequently direct team production. It requires considerable credulity to believe, as Williamson appears to, that capitalist bosses comprise the 'few individuals who have superior information processing capacities and exceptional oratorical and decision-making skills' (1983, p. 52).

In fact, workers have shown considerable ingenuity in collectively regulating their output in order to be able resist management's attempts to speed them up. This suggests that team production needs to be analysed at the shopfloor level, with rate busters being seen as free riders just as much as the shirkers are (Clawson, 1980, p. 263), since both gain by undermining the collective solidarity of the workforce. It is this capacity for solidarity and self-organisation that socialists hold up as a foretaste of workers' self-coordination.

The twofold character of the capitalist direction of production is captured by Richard Edwards' distinction between 'co-ordination', which is a requirement of 'all social production', and 'control', which is a specific requirement of capitalist production. Co-ordination can be achieved by various means: tradition; co-operation among workers; or, as production increases, by establishing a separate group of managers. As long as the managers, no matter how numerous, remain accountable to the whole workforce, then they are merely carrying out co-ordination (1979, pp. 16–17). It might be supposed that co-ordination requires a flatter hierarchy, and control a taller hierarchy, as if the pathological capitalist requirement for control were superimposed upon, and could be distinguished from, the hierarchy required for co-ordination. But, as Dan Clawson points out, the distinction between co-ordination and control is 'analytic' rather than empirical, and 'most acts of supervision contain elements of both' (1980, p. 22).

Given that capitalists have no interest in the proliferation of managers and supervisors, who are, after all, only wage labourers themselves, there is no inconsistency in the Marxian analysis of capitalist production between the exercise of control and the pursuit of flatter hierarchies by capitalists. In contrast to game theorists, Marxists see co-operation in production as a prerequisite for control, not an alternative to it. This means that turning up cases of flatter, more co-operative, firms, be they real or imagined, does not of itself undermine the Marxist view that hierarchical control of some sort is necessary for capitalist firms.

The Marxist case is that the phenomena that are variously referred to as control (Edwards, 1979), surveillance (Bowles, 1986), metering (Alchian and Demsetz, 1986), or monitoring (Williamson, 1985), are of greater necessity within a capitalist labour process because the capitalist owners of the means of production need to ensure that sufficient labour is extracted from the labour power purchased from propertyless workers. The capitalist labour process is seen as a process of redistribution that puts workers' time at the disposal of capitalists (Marx, 1976, p. 667). In both Marxism and organisational economics, the analysis of the labour process is an attempt to identify the underlying logic of work organisation. For Marxists, the prevailing forms of control in the labour process are explained by the institutional constraints of capitalist property rights, which ensure that labour power is available as a commodity that can be purchased and exploited in the labour process; this then produces and reinforces inequalities between workers and capitalists. For organisational economics, the prevalence of the capitalist firm and associated property rights is explained by superior efficiency.

Marxist contributions to the labour process debate have elaborated the various control strategies pursued by management in the capitalist labour process. According to Braverman's (1974) deskilling thesis, work is inevitably degraded in the capitalist labour process as a result of an inexorable tendency for conception to be separated from execution. Braverman's argument is based on the Babbage principle (Pagano, 1985, p. 18n), which he believes to be 'fundamental to the evolution of the division of labor in capitalist society' since it exemplifies the 'most common mode of cheapening labor power . . . break it up into its simplest elements' (Braverman, 1974, pp. 81–2). The end result of this process is the 'creation of a hierarchy of skills with no job-specific skills at the bottom' (Pagano, 1985, p. 15), where workers are interchangeable and the conception and planning of all activities is the prerogative of an ever-smaller group of managers. In other words, within capitalism there is an inexorable tendency towards a polarisation between an ever smaller minority of thinkers and an ever-larger majority of deskilled doers.

Other Marxist labour process theorists have objected to Braverman's account of the capitalist labour process and qualified it by pointing out that in order to overcome the resistance of workers, managers have often pursued strategies other than deskilling. Andy Friedman (1977) has offered a fairly self-explanatory dichotomy between management strategies such as deskilling which attempt to achieve 'direct control' over workers, and strategies which attempt to involve workers in production through granting them 'responsible autonomy'. Either strategy can be pursued according to the state of the labour market and the extent of worker resistance. This is reminiscent of the dichotomy between the high-trust and low-trust dynamics described by Fox (1974).

The main objection to Braverman within labour process theory is his neglect of the subjective factor (Thompson, 1990). To some extent, there is a parallel between this neglect and the abandonment of atmosphere in Williamson's version of transaction cost economics. Within labour process theory there has been an increasing emphasis on subjectivity, and the importance of workers' and managers' perceptions and expectations in shaping the labour process as opposed to economic imperatives. Critics of Braverman, such as Craig Littler and Graeme Salaman, reject the view that there can be a 'universal framework' for analysing capitalism and assert that 'there can be no theory of *the* capitalist labour process'; instead, they have settled for devising ever 'more complex typologies' of 'labour control strategies' and an elaborate 'sociological classification of industries and periodizations of change'. The justification for their taxonomitis is that 'capitalist reality is more complex' than Braverman imagined it to be (Littler and Salaman, 1982; Reed, 1992, pp. 161–2).

Against this emphasis on subjectivity it can be argued that although the labour process is 'a *social* process', in which 'workers and capitalists have an active relationship, involving the clash of different purposes and intentions' (Hodgson, 1982a, p. 203), nevertheless the forms of organisation through which that clash takes place are shaped by the institutions of capitalist property rights. Thus within capitalist firms, managers confront workers who, if they are organised at all, are likely to be organised into trade unions. Stinchcombe (1983, pp. 182–4) complains that by concentrating on the subjectivity of workers and managers and the 'games' they play with each other in production, labour process theorists such as Burawoy divert attention away from the decisive political question of the incentive structures (that is, the property rights) within which the games are played out. According to the revolutionary interpretation of Marx, the economic power of property ownership is 'so strongly cemented that only the political organization of the working class in its most extreme form – violence – would be able to break it' (Gustafsson, 1991a, p. 24). This means that any resistance by workers that falls short of the revolutionary abolition of capitalist property rights can only deflect management control strategies; it cannot do away with the need for control itself within the capitalist labour process. In other words, there is a big difference between workers winning an occasional game against the capitalists, and workers changing the rules so that the distinction between capitalists and workers no longer exists.

Against divisions of labour and hierarchy

Much of the contemporary debate about the division of labour and hierarchy has been in response to Marglin's (1976) radical polemic against capitalist hierarchy. Marglin is an idiosyncratic economist. He is one of the few economists who appears to be able to work comfortably within both radical and mainstream perspectives (Bellinger and Bergsten, 1990, p. 708). Having trained as a neoclassical economist, he came under the influence of Marx, but his relationship with Marx is ambivalent. Marglin advises all economists to read Marx: even if they end up being 'deeply critical' of Marx, as Marglin has, he reckons that they will at least realise the importance of 'values and beliefs' in shaping our views of the economy (Marglin, 1991, p. 225). This seems about as likely to inspire any mainstream economist to tackle *Capital* as the postmodernists' claim that it is an 'incisive deconstruction of political economy' (Neimark, 1990, p. 104). Berg's assessment is that Marglin draws on Marx but without the 'Marxist hagiography' (Berg, 1991, p. 173). In fact, Marglin does not even cite Marx in his major articles on work organisation (Marglin, 1976, 1984, 1991), even though (as will be seen in the next chapter), he parodies Marx and quotes directly from the same sources.

Marglin takes up Adam Smith's discussion of the pin factory and attempts to refute Smith's three arguments for the advantages of the division of labour. First, an increase in the dexterity of workers from the division of labour and specialisation implies the acquisition of skill, but Marglin finds little evidence of any skilled work in the records of an early-nineteenth-century pin factory. The different jobs in the factory were paid at more or less the same rate, which suggests that workers were easily replaced and 'that the mysteries of pin-making were relatively quickly learned' (1976, p. 20). Second, to save time transferring between activities it is only necessary for operations to be separated and for workers to continue at a single activity long enough for the set-up time to become an insignificant proportion of the time spent on that activity. Thus, Smith's 'dichotomy between specialization and the separate crafting of each individual pin seems to be a false one' (Marglin, 1976, p. 20). As for the propensity to invention, Marglin finds this 'not terribly persuasive' because invention would be more likely if each worker had some understanding of the total process of production.

Marglin's explanation for the detailed division of labour and the prevalence of 'specialization as well as separation of tasks' (1976, p. 20) is that it creates a role for the capitalist as the intermediary between the workers carrying out separate activities; 'without specialization, the capitalist had no essential role to play in the production process'. However, what is 'conspicuously absent' from Marglin's model is 'an explanation of how an inessential role can be maintained in the face of competition or why the capitalists could not expropriate all the surplus through money-lending' (Eswaran and Kotwal, 1989, p. 162).

In the end Marglin falls back on external factors to explain the persistence of hierarchy, namely 'socialization' (1984, p. 151), in the family (1991, p. 246), the school and the factory itself (1976, p. 14). In other words, Marglin invokes assumptions that are very similar to neoclassical economics in order to construct his conceptual model. Although, he rails against neoclassical economists for their assumptions about human nature (1991): when it comes to it, Marglin's account of hierarchy rests on a residual argument, socialisation, just as much as Williamson's relies on a pessimistic view of human nature. The difference between Marglin and Williamson is that socialisation is presumably susceptible to change, whereas 'human nature as we know it' must be more or less immutable.

Some interesting experimental evidence from social psychology (Humphrey, 1985) suggests that subordinates within hierarchical organisations can come to overvalue their managers' competence and undervalue their own and their fellow workers' abilities even without prior socialisation. This is because subordinates have limited information about their own decision-making abilities, since they are rarely asked to make decisions, whereas managers are not only required to make decisions, but they can also control their contact with subordinates so that managers' work is less open to inspection. As Mintzberg puts it, 'managers have formal and easy access to each of their subordinates' (1989, p. 18). Thus the hierarchical structure of organisations itself can generate a belief among both managers and workers that the managers have greater ability to make decisions.

The major difference between the radical rejection of divisions of labour and hierarchy and the Marxist approach is that the radicals explain hierarchy in terms of a pervasive desire for domination, whereas 'one of Marx's central claims is . . . that exploitation *explains* domination' (Callinicos, 1989, pp. 71, 163). Radical organisation theorists often misunderstand Marx's distinction between labour and labour power. For example, in their major text, Clegg and Dunkerley state that 'what the worker sells to the capitalist in return for his wages is his labour power. Marx maintains that this cannot be a fair exchange' (1980, pp. 457, 467). As has already been made clear, Marx (1970, p. 16) went to considerable lengths to establish that under normal conditions this is a fair exchange. Perrow is as confused as Clegg and Dunkerley, if not more so. He seems to think that Marx's concept of surplus value only applies to exceptional situations where excessive profits are made at the expense of low wages (Perrow, 1986, p. 225), whereas Marx's model of capitalism assumes that a surplus is extracted under normal conditions with an average rate of profit and fair wages for workers.

Marglin disputes the Marxian view that the existence of capitalist firms is predicated upon the separation of workers from the means of production. He argues that although, individually, workers do not have access to sufficient capital to set up on their own, collectively they do have access, and their trade union funds could be invested in workers' co-operatives:

> It is a story in itself why worker-owned enterprises have failed to develop in the womb of capitalism – except, *in extremis*, to forestall plant closures. Suffice it to say that the failure cannot be explained in terms of capital costs.

> It is hardly coincidental that Karl Marx formulated his analysis of capitalism precisely during the rather limited time period in which the capital barrier effectively limited entry to a single class. But if it is understandable why Marx was led to identify capital costs as the most important barrier to entry, it is less easy to explain why latter-day Marxists have not, in the light of the historical specificity of the conditions of Marx's day, re-examined the basis of capitalism (Marglin, 1984, p. 163, n. 2).

Marglin contends that, 'For some time preservation of the boss–worker hierarchy has required tacit acceptance by unions; present day unions lack the will for change, not the strength' (1976, p. 25). What Marglin means by 'strength' is not what Marxists usually take it to mean, namely the capacity to overthrow capitalist property rights by revolution. Instead, Marglin believes that unions have strength in terms of sufficient funds to invest in labour-managed enterprises operating within capitalist property rights. He supports his argument with reference to the alternative forms of work organisation that have appeared from time to time.

Marglin also cites Trist and Bamforth's well known paper, 'Some Social and Psychological Consequences of the Longwall Method of Coal-Getting' (1984 [1951]), which is a mainstay of mainstream organisation theory. Trist and Bamforth explain how the mechanised 'longwall' method of coal-getting introduced into British coalmining after the Second World War failed to produce the anticipated improved output. They put this down to the break-up of the small groups which operated under the previous hand-got system, where 'Leadership and "supervision" were internal to the group, which had a quality of *responsible autonomy*' (Trist and Bamforth, 1984, p. 393). Output improved under the new longwall system when innovations in the social organisation of the miners were introduced, which once again granted a degree of responsible autonomy to work groups.

According to Marglin, managers in general will not remove levels of hierarchy and allow autonomous work groups, since this introduces the possibility that workers will set up on their own without bosses. Management was prepared to do so in the special circumstances of mining where workers could be denied access to the means of production because of 'the physical scarcity of coal seams' (Marglin, 1976, p. 25). This clearly shows that, unlike Marx, Marglin equates bosses with managers and supervisors. In Marglin's view bosses create divisions of labour in order to perpetuate a superfluous role for themselves as managers and supervisors co-ordinating production. Therefore, from Marglin's perspective, the movement from direct control to responsible autonomy is seen as a direct threat to the bosses' existence, since 'without specialization, the capitalist had no essential role to play in the production process' (1976, p. 20). In contrast, from a Marxist point of view, a reduction in the number of levels in management hierarchies is merely a way of ensuring exploitation with fewer managers.

Marglin reveals his naïvety in his celebration of 'the reintroduction into the mines of self-integrating, non-specialized non-hierarchical work groups' (1976, p. 25). This illustrates how the amelioration of excessive divisions of labour associated with the human relations movement in industry comes as a revelation to neoclassically trained economists. Richard Butler, a mainstream organisation theorist, warns against romanticising the responsible autonomy in the longwall method of coal-getting:

> it was still hard work, dangerous, and damaging to health, but the social organiza-tion provided support for the miners who had to work in these conditions. The social structure was also a support against an exploitative management which not only applied to coal mining but also to many other occupations. (Butler, 1991, p. 111)

Trist and Bamforth suggest that responsible autonomy was reintroduced in part because the improvement in the economic situation in Britain following the Second World War resulted in 'a greater intolerance of unsatisfying or difficult working conditions, or systems of organization, among miners' (1984, p. 414). Marglin fails to see any potential for the resistance to management from work groups to generate a revolutionary challenge to capitalist property rights; instead, he seizes on the possibility of them setting up on their own as independent workers' co-operatives, presumably within existing property rights. The Marxist argument is that with the availability of labour power for sale as a commodity, exploitation arises almost inevitably, and with it the need for hierarchical control of one form or another. The Marxist view is that this undermines the possibility of associations of independent producers emerging, which is Marglin's implied preference.

Conclusion

The four perspectives outlined in this chapter can be set out in terms of their own preferred forms of work organisation (see Figure 5.2): first, the

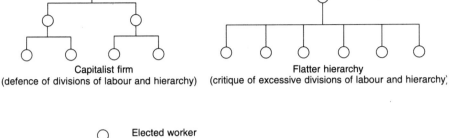

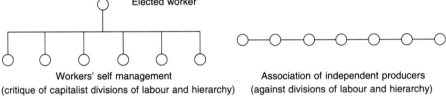

FIGURE 5.2 Preferred forms of work organisation

capitalist firm; second, 'flatter' management structures; third, workers' self-co-ordination; and finally, a non-hierarchical association of independent producers.

The argument from radical perspectives, such as Marglin's, is that it is possible to conceive of non-hierarchical work organisations operating within a market framework with safeguards against exploitation. The difference between this and the mainstream critique of excessive divisions of labour and hierarchy is often blurred, because part of the argument for less specialisation and a flatter hierarchy is that it improves efficiency by reducing resistance from disgruntled workers. Against both of these positions, if the prevalence of hierarchy can be explained in terms of the efficiency of the hierarchical capitalist firm, then differentiations based on the degree of hierarchy within capitalists firms should not detract from the general defence of hierarchy itself. The Marxist view is that the radical attacks on hierarchy itself, such as Marglin's, are easily discredited and give an opening for the defence of hierarchy on efficiency grounds to be confused with a defence of the specific form of hierarchy in the capitalist firm. From the Marxist perspective, all capitalist firms are necessarily exploitative, whatever their degree of hierarchy, and furthermore, exploitative capitalist firms will prevail unless the capitalist property rights which allow workers to be excluded from the means of production are abolished. According to the Marxist view, only the removal of the historically specific market interface that separates workers from the means of production could abolish the need for control and allow for workers' democratic self-co-ordination. In other words, if workers could not be excluded from access to the means of production, then co-ordination of production, albeit by hierarchy, would have to be based on consent.

Historical transformations in work organisation

Introduction

According to Maxine Berg, author of *The Age of Manufactures* (1994), a major reconsideration of the Industrial Revolution in Britain, it is largely due to the influence of Marglin and Braverman that, 'economists and economic and social historians can no longer write of industry and labour without consideration of the labour process' (1984, p. 165). However, their influence has been felt in the debates concerning two fairly separate historical transformations in work organisation. Marglin's account of the origins of capitalist hierarchy refers to the emergence of the 'factory system' during the period in British history from 1760 to 1830 commonly known as the 'Industrial Revolution' (Ashton, 1968). This is the period analysed by Marx (1976), following Engels' classic study, *The Condition of the Working Class in England* (1969a).

Albeit that Braverman himself is historically rather ill informed (Nelson, 1980, p. xin), in so far as it is historical at all, the labour process debate shifts attention away from the rise of the factory system in Britain to the emergence and diffusion of Frederick Taylor's (1967 [1911]) ideas about scientific management in the USA. Daniel Nelson (1975) sees scientific management as one component of what he calls the 'new factory system' which developed between 1880 and 1920, while Dan Clawson (1980), who is much more supportive of Braverman, identifies scientific management with the bureaucratic transformation of US industry between 1860 and 1920.

These two historical transformations in work organisation are explained differently by the various perspectives. To start with, Williamson adopts what he calls a 'microanalytic and comparative institutional research strategy' (1980a, p. 12), by which he means a comparison of different abstract models of production. He outlines six alternative modes of work organisation, ranked according to their alledged efficiency, starting with the least efficient:

1. *Communal.* Work stations are owned collectively by a group of workers, but it is 'every man for himself' when it comes to production. Each worker follows his or her own work in progress and sells the final product in the market. There is communal ownership and an absence of hierarchy. This scores well for work intensity but scores badly for just about everything else. It is difficult to make contracts with outside specialists, equipment is badly utilised, and the system is unresponsive to product or process innovations.

2. *Putting-out.* A merchant–co-ordinator supplies raw materials and owns all the work in progress, but individual 'entrepreneurs' own their equipment and perform the basic operations in their own homes in batches, so that work is moved from home to home under the direction of the merchant–coordinator. Work intensity and equipment utilisation are good, but there are chronic problems with quality and theft from the merchant–co-ordinator.

3. *Federated.* Work stations are located side by side in a common facility, but each work station is owned by a specialist worker. Work is transferred by contract between operations. Each worker proceeds at his or her own pace, provided that a buffer inventory is kept at the prescribed level. This system is hypothetical, since it is doubtful whether it has ever been widely used, but it would be the least hierarchical, with no supervision. Again, work intensity and equipment utilisation are good, but there are difficulties with the level of inventory needed, responsiveness to innovations, and contracts with specialists.

4. *Inside contracting.* All the equipment, raw materials, final product and work in progress are owned by a single capitalist, but between the supply of all raw materials and the sale of the final product, production is delegated to an inside contractor who supervises the work, hires the workers, and receives a negotiated piece rate from the capitalist. This arrangement is useful for capitalists who have no technical knowledge of production. It scores well for contracting with specialists and work intensity but scores badly for equipment utilisation and system responsiveness.

5. *Peer group (workers' co-operative).* Work stations and all materials are owned collectively and workers are paid on the basis of a share in the group output rather than individual output. Workers can rotate activities, or specialise. In order to ensure co-ordination, 'leaders' can be elected to make operating decisions, but not strategic decisions. To ensure that a rigid hierarchy does not emerge, it is necessary to rotate the leadership roles. This system scores well in terms of responsiveness and keeping inventories low, but there are problems with work intensity because of the lack of individual incentives and the opportunity for shirking.

6. *Authority relation (capitalist firm).* A capitalist owns all the equipment and inventories and workers enter into an employment relationship with the capitalist, which entails incomplete contracting and necessitates the workers being subjected to detailed supervision. Although this system scores badly for

work intensity and local innovation, since workers have little incentive to work harder or to innovate, it scores well on every other criterion because the capitalist is in a position to contract with specialists, take up innovations, ensure that inventories are kept low, that equipment is fully utilised, and that workers do not steal too much.

It has to be said that Williamson's efficiency ranking seems arbitrary. In the first place, he makes nine explicit assumptions, of which one of the most controversial must be that, 'Replacement investment occurs routinely and investment for expansion purposes is ignored' (1980a, p. 13). This rules out differentiation between forms of work organisation that are more or less effective at securing investment. He then scores the six modes of work organisation positively or negatively against eleven 'efficiency indicators', to give each mode an 'efficiency rating'. If nothing else, it must be obvious that his method is almost unmanageable and very difficult to summarise. No set of efficiency criteria or rankings could possibly constitute the sort of incontrovertible self-evident truths that Williamson implies they must be, given his view that efficiency can be operationalised effectively. It is fair to ask whether, perhaps even unconsciously, Williamson has worked backwards, constructing efficiency criteria to deliver the ranking order he already had in mind. For one thing, the equal weighting assigned to each efficiency criterion seems perverse. Thus, while capitalists may be relieved to find that the 'authority relation' is the most efficient mode, underlining their legitimacy, they might be more than a little surprised to find that the two allegedly most efficient modes, the peer group and the authority relation, suffer from poor work intensity. Williamson's response might be that it is this very weakness of the authority relation, which explains why the managers of capitalist firms study organisational behaviour in the vain hope that theories of motivation will reveal the elusive secret of how work can be intensified without organisational change (Thompson and McHugh, 1990, pp. 274–80).

Williamson believes that his ranking of forms of work organisation corresponds to the chronological order in which each mode has appeared historically (1985, p. 231). However, the communal and federated modes do not correspond to any historically significant forms of work organisation; they are only included because they are 'logically possible' (Neimark and Tinker, 1987, p. 668n), and workers' co-operatives can hardly be said to have been prevalent immediately prior to capitalist firms. So although Williamson alludes to a historical progression from the least to the most efficient modes, he offers no explanation as to why history has taken the course that it has, and there would appear to be no good reason why the authority relation should not have appeared at the outset. Even if the authority relation is the most efficient mode of work organisation, Williamson does not even address the question of why it has appeared so late in human history. As Marginson, a radical critic, observes, 'Showing that one form of work organization has desirable efficiency properties as compared to another says nothing about the causal process by which it arose' (1993, p. 149).

In evolutionary terms, Williamson says nothing about the mechanisms by which new forms of work organisation appear (Kay, 1993, p. 253). In Williamson's version of evolution, new species can appear fully formed without any intermediate stages, but this violates the principles of Darwinian natural selection (Gould, 1992). A more convincing evolutionary model would have to suggest reasons for the particular course of history. This would have two elements lacking in Williamson's account. First, the context in which new forms of work organisation arose and why they were superior in that context. Second, the incentive structures within each historical mode of work organisation which inhibited or facilitated the emergence of new forms of organisation. Williamson's allusion to history is fallacious, since his logic takes little or no account of the actual path that history has taken.

Turning to Marglin, he emphasises 'the importance of *history* in the radical analysis and its absence from the mainstream analysis' (1991, p. 229). Amongst radical historians (Berg, 1991, p. 173) and labour process theorists it is generally accepted that Marglin's article, 'What Do Bosses Do?' is a major historical study (Storey, 1983, p. 48; Thompson, 1989, p. 73). But Marglin has referred to his work as both 'history' (1991, p. 245) and 'theorizing' (1984, pp. 146, 149). In fact it would be more accurate to say that Marglin's argument consists of a conceptual model with selective historical illustrations, and as far as some historians are concerned, 'his history is not what it should be' (Landes, 1986, p. 621). This is suggested by the subtitle to his original article: 'The Origins and Functions of Hierarchy in Capitalist Production'. What Marglin does is to weave historical research on the 'origins' of capitalist hierarchy into an economic model of its 'functions'. The result is a narrative in which it is often difficult to disentangle the historical data from Marglin's implicit modelling.

The Industrial Revolution in Great Britain

In 'What Do Bosses Do?' Marglin sets out three questions:

[W]hy, in the course of capitalist development, the actual producer lost control of production. What circumstances gave rise to the boss–worker pyramid that characterizes capitalist production? And what social function does the capitalist hierarchy serve? (1976, p. 14)

Marglin approaches these issues through an examination of the rise of the factory during the Industrial Revolution in Britain. He argues that there were two decisive steps which deprived workers of control over both the product and the process of production. First, the development of the minute division of labour, characterised by the putting-out system. Second, the development of a centralised organisation, characterised by the factory system (1976, p. 14).

Marglin maintains that under the putting-out system, capitalists subdivided work in order to ensure a co-ordinating role for themselves. Although Marglin offers no explanation as to how the capitalist arose in the first place, he anticipates the argument that if the capitalist was superfluous then he would have been eliminated by competition from integrated producers. Berg puts the question succinctly: 'Why didn't the individual workman just set up shop for himself, producing for the market rather than the capitalist?' (1991, p. 174). Marglin poses the question and attempts to answer it:

> Why didn't some enterprising and talented fellow organize producers to eliminate the capitalist putter-outer? The answer is that there was no profit in such a line of endeavour. If the organizer became a producer himself, he would have had to settle for a producer's wage. His co-workers might have subscribed a dinner or gold watch in his honour, but it is doubtful that their gratitude would have led them to do much more. To glean rewards from organizing, one had to become a capitalist putter-outer! The point is that no collusion was necessary between the men of talent, enterprise, and means that formed the capitalist class of the putting-out days. It was in the interest of each as well as the interest of all to maintain the system of allocating separate tasks to separate workmen. Not much wit was required to see that their prosperity, as well as their survival as mediators, depended on this system. (1976, p. 21)

The passage just quoted reveals many of the weaknesses in Marglin's argument. The existence of the 'organiser' is simply taken as given, as is the profit maximising behaviour of the 'men of talent, enterprise, and means'. The absence of collusion between them fulfils the requirement of a neoclassically trained mind that collective action is excluded from the explanation. His excuse for not finding any 'Hard evidence that "divide and conquer" rather than efficiency was at the root of the capitalist division of labour', is that, 'One cannot really expect the capitalist, or anybody else with an interest in preserving hierarchy and authority, to proclaim that production was organized to exploit the worker' (1976, p. 21). In other words, the lack of evidence is the evidence!

Marglin argues that 'The entrepreneurial personality derives its social virtue from an every-man-for-himself individualism, from a specific social context. It is not an immutable human nature, a universal social virtue of these traits, that makes individualism into the basis of our social organisation' (1984, p. 151). However, he fails to explain how, at the outset, the 'men of talent, enterprise, and means' who subdivided work in the putting-out system could be possessed of an 'entrepreneurial personality' before their own actions had created an appropriate social context for their behaviour. Berg points out that, in effect, Marglin invokes an individualistic 'dominant ideology' in order to support his assumption that 'in an individualistic society the upwardly mobile will not seek alternative modes of organisation or self-sufficiency; they will seek to join the capitalists. But the actual history of this ethic of individualism is much more complex' (Berg, 1984, p. 168).

Conceptually, Marglin fails to explain how the capitalists were able to subdivide operations under the putting out system so as to ensure a role for themselves without first subjecting those operations to observation. Marx makes the point in his critique of Proudhon:

> The development of the division of labour supposes the assemblage of workers in a workshop. . . . For M. Proudhon, who sees things upside down, if he sees them at all, the division of labour, in Adam Smith's sense, precedes the workshop, which is a condition of its existence. (1978, p. 133)

According to Berg, the dependence of the outworkers was 'caused by differences in access to credit, since the master manufacturer could control the outworkers' product markets by monopolizing credit markets – an aspect of the putting-out system which has received minimal analysis' (1991, p. 178),

As for the transfer from the putting-out system to the factory, Marglin explains this very simply. Putting-out undermined the workers' control over the product, then the move to the factory wiped out the workers' control over the process of production. It was in the capitalists' interests that workers be required to choose between whether to work, or not to work at all, instead of how hard or how long to work. The factory gave the capitalists control over the pace of work, so that workers no longer had any control over how hard they would work. Marglin emphasises that 'the discipline and supervision afforded by the factory had nothing to do with efficiency, at least as this term is used by economists. Disciplining the work force meant a larger output in return for a greater input of labour, not more output for the same input' (1976, p. 36).

The factory also gave the capitalist control over materials, whereas under the putting-out system embezzlement, dishonesty and laziness on the part of the workers had been a problem for the capitalists. Marglin stresses that 'an end to embezzlement and like deceits changed the division of the pie in favour of capitalists' (1976, p. 36), and he has consistently defended 'embezzlement and fraud' by outworkers as the exercise of resistance which secured a 'fringe benefit' for workers (1991, p. 237). Williamson produces four objections to the view of embezzlement as 'income redistribution': first, investment decisions will be distorted; second, embezzled goods are traded on inefficient black markets; third, the cost of efforts to police against the losses; and fourth, compensation will favour the shirkers and embezzlers, those in the population 'who are most prepared to lie, cheat, and steal' (1985, pp. 212, 233–4). Williamson asserts that it is 'simply wrong' to maintain that embezzlement and the like are merely redistributive measures with no consequences for efficiency (1984, p. 107).

In economic history, much of the 'dispute over the origins of factory production' has centred 'on the extent to which technological factors can be disentangled from organizational ones' (Berg, 1994, p. 190). The economic historian, David Landes, author of the influential book *The Unbound Prometheus: Technological Change and Industrial Development in Western Europe from 1750 to the Present* (1969), returned to the fray with a belated riposte to Marglin titled 'What Do Bosses Really Do?' (1986). Berg accuses Landes of reasserting historical determinism: 'history led by technology', in which technology marches forward, 'fulfilling its preordained logic in overcoming all previous production barriers' (Berg, 1991, pp. 174, 183). In fact, Landes endorses Marglin's argument that 'the motivation for the move from putting-out to factory was the employer's desire to gain control over the work process', since it is this model of explanation that he originally put forward in *The Unbound Prometheus*.

Landes disagrees with Marglin's view that control 'was enough to give the factory an edge and make it a dominant mode of production'. According to Landes, 'A factory . . . is not simply a large production unit or workshop', which had appeared centuries before the Industrial Revolution for a variety of reasons, such as the 'noxious or noisome nature' of production. A factory is defined by the use of 'power-driven machines', and in industries where these were not developed 'there was nothing one could do in a large shop that one could not do as well and cheaper in the home of the worker' (Landes, 1986, pp. 602–4) . . . 'what made the factory successful in Britain was not the wish but the muscle: the machines and the engines. We do not have the factories until these were available, because nothing less would have overcome the cost advantage of dispersed manufacture' (1986, p. 607).

It should be noted that putting-out did not disappear with the rise of the factory: it continued throughout the nineteenth century, as Marx was well aware, partly because the rise of the factory system and technological innovations therein constantly created and recreated a reserve army of labour which could be recruited into the low-paid 'sweated' industries. In a major study, *Outwork in 19th-Century Britain*, Duncan Bythell maintains that outwork 'remained an integral part' of large-scale manufacturing, 'under the auspices of private capitalists' (1978, p. 13); in fact, homeworking persists to this day (Phizacklea and Wolkowitz, 1995). The feature of putting-out which Marx does not discuss is the predominance of women engaged in this work; indeed, Marxist analysis has been accused of being '*sex-blind*' (Hartmann, 1979). Putting-out was one way in which relatively cheap female labour could be tapped, which in the case of many women and children, would otherwise not be used (Berg, 1994, p. 145; Bythell, 1978, pp. 250–1).

The widespread use of female and child labour both in putting-out and in factories demonstrates the importance of the relationship between new forms of work organisation and the social structures which already existed – something that is overlooked by economists such as Marglin and Williamson. On the one hand, existing social structures were imported into the early factories. Before more formal management hierarchies were developed, capitalists hired men to supervise women and children, relying on the subordination of women and children to men which existed in the pre-industrial family unit. Thus the management of factories and in turn the forms of resistance developed by male-dominated trade unions reinforced the patriarchal relations from the pre-capitalist family (Lazonick, 1978, pp. 8–10). This means that to some extent the division of labour within the workplace was, 'an effect of the social hierarchy and not its cause' (Berg, 1994, p. 156). On the other hand Berg describes how women workers were often employed in the early factories and workshops in order to by-pass existing social structures, such as traditional artisan customs, when new methods of production were being introduced (1994, p. 149).

Summing up the development of work organisation during the Industrial Revolution, Berg writes:

> Recent research on the enormous diversity of manufacturing organization even within a single industry – with putting-out, workshops and sweating existing alongside and complementary with a diverse factory sector – has muddied the waters of a once clear stream of unilinear development in the rise of the factory system. (1994, pp. 195–6)

She argues that, 'The close interdependencies between small-scale and large-scale producers, and the capacities within both organizational forms for innovation, undermine assumptions of a sharp divide between the factory system and artisan or domestic industry' (1994, p. 198).

Berg's argument echoes Pollard's earlier polemic against the history of work organisation being written as a neat series of logical stages. According to Pollard, putting-out, or

> [S]ubcontract . . . does not itself form a 'stage', but may be compatible with different stages of development of industrial capitalism, according to technical and commercial needs and managerial competence. It survives, in many forms, into the factory age; and in some industries it survives until today, and is not necessarily inefficient or anachronistic. It is, in fact, only the dogmatism of classical political economy as developed in the nineteenth century, which looked upon the capitalist-owner-entrepreneur, facing an individual propertyless worker, as the 'normal', highest, finite form of organization, which has led us to ignore or minimize the importance of surviving systems of subcontract, group-contract or cooperation . . . . (1968, p. 53)

As well as their neglect of diversity in work organisation throughout history, a major objection to the work of both Williamson and Marglin is that, typically for economists, they fail to contextualise the emergence of the putting-out system. Despite Marglin's disclaimers (1984, p. 158), his view that the capitalists inserted themselves between producers and the market romanticises the position of the pre-industrial independent producer. However, factories had to be inserted into the society of the eighteenth century that has been described as a 'moral economy', which can be defined as an economy where 'claimants to a commodity can invoke non-monetary rights to that commodity, and third parties will act to support *these* claims – when, for example, community membership supersedes price as a basis of entitlement' (Tilly, quoted in Thompson, 1993, p. 338). Being particularly sensitive to the inequalities between men and women, and between children and adults, Berg is wary of any nostalgic sentimentality for the pre-industrial community, since it was 'neither egalitarian, nor was it free of power and subordination' (1994, p. 165).

The essential point is that, in contrast to Williamson and Marglin, a long series of leading sociologists (Durkheim, 1947; Weber, 1930) and historians (Ashton, 1968; Pollard, 1968) have recognised that a prerequisite for the Industrial Revolution and the rise of the factory was the need for a fundamental challenge to the 'traditionalism of labor', meaning 'The workers' widespread reluctance to change a customary way of life' (Bendix, 1963, pp. 34–46), and a transformation in worker's orientation to work. Among other things, a new psychological sense of time was required, and, as the clock became ubiquitous (Ashton, 1968), workers had to learn the lesson that 'time is money' (Thompson, 1993).

Pollard (1968, p. 243) is adamant that: 'the modern industrial proletariat was introduced to its role not so much by attraction or monetary reward, but by compulsion, force and fear. It was not allowed to grow as in a sunny garden; it was forged, over a fire, by the powerful blows of a hammer'. He believes that the 'typical framework' for the emergence of 'modern industrialism' is 'that of dominance and fear, fear of hunger, of eviction, of prison for those who disobey the new industrial rules. Hitherto, the experience of other countries at a similar stage of development has not, in essentials, been very different'. If it can be demonstrated that, at the outset at least, the rise of the capitalist and the factory depended upon the coercion of workers, rather than their voluntary submission to an employment relationship, then this goes some way towards undermining the view that the evolution of successive forms of work organisation can be explained by a logic of efficiency.

In Pollard's (1968, pp. 193–6) opinion, the coercive aspect of the rise of the factory is not only evidenced by the enclosures in England, which created a class of workers without the means for subsistence, but also by the widespread 'association of the idea of the factory with unfree labour' during the Industrial Revolution. One of Pollard's themes is that the big landowners in the pre-industrial economy, followed by the big capitalists in the early industrial economy, enjoyed sufficient political power to be able to invoke coercive, state-sanctioned, 'extra market means . . . when the market threatened not to produce the right results for them' (1968, p. 39).

The problem with Pollard's analysis is that, in common with much of Marxist analysis, it tends to obscure important differences in the patterns of 'proletarianization and state intervention' between countries and over time (Burawoy, 1985, p. 99). This comes out in the major sociological. study of industrialisation by Reinhard Bendix (1963). Like Pollard, Bendix notes that there was 'widespread resistance to factory employment' during the Industrial Revolution in England, and that the distinction between work and state-sponsored punishment for poverty 'became blurred' (1968, pp. 35, 42). However, when comparing England and Russia, Bendix makes the point that one of the most important preconditions of industrialisation in the West was 'the relative independence of economic activities from government regulations'. The major difference in the condition of workers in England and Russia during industrialisation was that the English workers were freer than their Russian counterparts from any claim on or attachment to the land. This meant that there was less need to use extra market coercion to compel the English workers to work in the factories compared to the Russian serfs, who neither could nor would leave the land to work in the factories unless they were forced to do so (1968, pp. 118, 177).

Although the concept of a moral economy has been challenged (Holton, 1992, p. 41), the point remains that what is at issue between historians and sociologists is whether or not, and by what means, the first factory workers were forced to work in factories. When Williamson assumes, albeit for the sake of 'expositional convenience', that 'in the beginning there were markets' (1975, p. 20), he obscures the fact that the market for labour power was predicated upon the 'creation of a landless industrial work force' (Bendix, 1968, p. 176), and this was usually achieved by extra-market means of one sort or another.

This debate is largely missed by Marglin as well. This is because his paper, 'What Do Bosses Do?' is as much a polemic against Marx and Engels as it is against mainstream economics. Marglin (1976, p. 13) starts off with a quote from Engels' brief article 'On Authority', where he says that: 'Wanting to abolish authority in large-scale industry is tantamount to wanting to abolish industry itself, to destroy the power loom in order to return to the spinning wheel' (1969b, p. 377). Marglin concludes his paper by paraphrasing Marx. In *The Poverty of Theory*, an early work of Marx's and a polemic against the anarchist Proudhon, Marx writes: 'The hand-mill gives you society with the feudal lord; the steam-mill, society with the industrial capitalist' (1978 [1847]). Marglin turns this round when he makes the following statement: 'The steam mill didn't give us the capitalist; the capitalist gave us the steam mill' (1976, p. 41; 1991, p. 236).

Marglin's (1976, 1991) argument is that Marx and Engels are technological determinists. He maintains that because they accept that particular technologies require hierarchy, they end up by merely proposing to swap one form of hierarchy, capitalist hierarchy, for another, socialist hierarchy, instead of advocating non-hierarchical production with different technologies. It is not worth resorting to an exegesis of Marx's work here. However, it should be pointed out that Rosenberg (1982, pp. 34–7), an influential writer on technology and economics, maintains that apart from the polemical outbursts, which are often quoted, Marx was clearly not a technological determinist. Instead, Marx was one of the first analysts of work organisation to see the importance of studying the history of technology as an expression of 'the social relations' in human life (Marx, 1976, p. 493n).

The new factory system in the United States

The second significant historical transformation for the debates over work organisation is the emergence of the 'new factory system' in the USA between 1880 and 1920. This saw the emergence of large plants incorporating technological innovations, managerial hierarchies and sophisticated techniques for the management of labour (Nelson, 1975, p. ix). An important part of the new factory system was the scientific management movement identified with Taylor (1967). Braverman sees Taylorism as the ultimate expression of the tendency towards the separation of conception from execution. The centre-piece of Taylor's scientific management is the idea that scientific studies of each 'task' can be used by managers as the basis for instructions to workers specifying the most efficient method of carrying out a task and the time allowed for doing so. Taylor advocated that workers should be paid an individualised piece rate on the satisfactory completion of their tasks in the time allowed. According to Braverman, behind the commonplaces associated with scientific management, the 'stopwatch, speed-up, etc. . . . there lies a theory which is nothing less than the explicit verbalization of the capitalist mode of production' (1974, p. 86).

There appears to be a measure of agreement between Marxist writers such as Braverman (1974) and Clawson (1980) on one side and transaction cost economics represented by Williamson (1985) on the other, over the reasons for the inside contracting system being superseded by the capitalist authority relation. The difference, of course, is that the Marxists see the improved profitability of the capitalist authority relation as a redistribution from the workers to the capitalists, whereas Williamson sees it as an expression of enhanced efficiency.

Inside contracting is 'simply a system which carries the marketplace right inside the factory' (Clawson, 1980, p. 124). By replacing the market relationship between the capitalist and the contractor with a bureaucratic relationship the capitalists were able to subject the labour process to direct observation. What Taylor did was to argue the case, and devise various techniques for doing just this: 'he learned what workers already knew. This was no easy task, and it is something other managers did not do' (Clawson, 1980, p. 234; Francis, 1983, pp. 109–10). By studying the labour process, Taylor was able to divide work into discrete 'tasks'. This shows that the technological separability of activities, which Williamson takes as given, is actually the outcome of an organisational innovation, namely scientific management. The interfaces between each potentially separable activity across which transactions can take place are therefore inserted by organisation; they are not simply given at the outset within markets.

A general criticism of both Marx and Braverman is that their empirical historical research is inadequate because they take the pronouncements of capitalist ideologues such as Andrew Ure, Charles Babbage and Frederick Taylor at face value. Lazonick (1979, 1983) and others (Piore and Sabel, 1984, p. 45) are sceptical of Marx's and Braverman's description of workers being subject to an inevitable process of 'deskilling and homogenisation' (Elbaum *et al.*, 1979). They argue that this overlooks three vital relationships that affect the development of the labour process. First, the capacity of workers to resist deskilling, second, the effects of inter-capitalist competition which weakens capitalists in relation to labour; and finally, the importance of divisions between workers. On the last point, the effect of gender divisions needs to be taken into account since deskilling is often associated with feminisation, whereby previously skilled occupations that are filled by men become pre-dominantly female occupations as the work is deskilled (Berg, 1994, p. 187).

Clawson has tried to counter the argument that 'Taylorism was primarily an ideology with little practical significance', by listing the extent to which Taylorism was implemented, but as he himself says, in order to make a convincing argument, 'It matters not only what happened, but why it happened' (1980, pp. 27, 224). Even so, empirical research continues to turn up cases where Taylorism has been adopted where previously it was thought to have been rejected (Rowlinson, 1988).

Conclusion

The Industrial Revolution and the rise of the new factory system are especially important for contemporary debates since they have become identified with the marginalisation and demise of preferable alternatives to the forms of work organisation associated with the factory and mass production. This has set off a dialogue between radical economists and sociologists on one side and historians on the other. Marglin seems to believe that the technology of the factory itself shapes the hierarchical organisation of work decisively, but that it is the exercise of power in the first place which determines the choice of technology. In effect, Marglin ends up arguing for alternative technologies to be found which do not require hierarchy. Since capitalists cannot be expected to invest in technologies that would make their own role superfluous, Marglin looks to the trade unions to invest in small workshop enterprises (1984, p. 163).

Marglin's position is similar to Piore and Sabel's in their book, *The Second Industrial Divide* (1984), which has been well received, especially by business school academics, but much criticised by Marxist economists (Williams *et al.*, 1987). Piore and Sabel have advocated a return to craft production based on the development and use of emerging information technologies. These technologies have presented an opportunity to choose the course of future of development in work organisation, just as there was a choice between craft production and mass production at critical points during the nineteenth century, when the mass production model won out. The contemporary choice facing corporations, nations, and most importantly, industrial regions, is between continuing with mass production, which is becoming increasingly untenable as the mass markets which once supported it continue to fragment, and the alternative of flexible specialisation.

Piore and Sabel claim to have found an example of flexible specialisation in:

> the networks of technologically sophisticated, highly flexible manufacturing firms in central and northwestern Italy. Flexible specialization is a strategy of permanent innovation: accommodation to ceaseless change, rather than an effort to control it. This strategy is based on flexible – multi-use – equipment; skilled workers; and the creation, through politics, of an industrial community that restricts the forms of competition to those favoring innovation. For these reasons, the spread of flexible specialization amounts to a revival of craft forms of production that were emarginated at the first industrial divide. (1984, p. 17).

Piore and Sabel's argument appears to be that with the rise of mass production it was not only craft production itself that was marginalised. The Industrial Revolution was accompanied by an ideological revolution in which even the socialist opponents of capitalism, most notably Marx, could not see that craft production represented a viable 'alternative to craft production as a model of technological advance' (1984, p. 28). As a result, 'Proudhon's vision of socialism as self-managed co-operatives linked through market ties' was increasingly derided (Stark, 1992, p. 50).

In contrast to Proudhon (and latterly Marglin, and Piore and Sabel), Marx appears to have believed that, as a result of protest by factory workers organised through trade unions, new forms of work organisation would arise within the factory. Instead of seeking a return to craft production through the development of alternative technologies, Marx saw the possibility and need for formulating *'a theory of the alternative (social) ways to run a given type of technical system'* (Stinchcombe, 1983, p. 9). In a more formal way, this is what Williamson sets out in his comparative institutional assessment of alternative forms of work organisation.

Most historians, sociologists and economists are more or less sceptical about the possibilities or desirability of a return to small-scale craft production. On the basis of her study of the Industrial Revolution, Berg (1991, p. 191) is doubtful as to whether Marglin's, or Piore and Sabel's, notion of a 'non-hierarchical flexible road' is, or ever was, conceivable within a market framework with essentially capitalist property rights. Berg seems to see craft production as being synonymous with the putting out system, or outwork, and on this basis she is sceptical of any suggestion that a return to craft production would signal any improvement in conditions for workers. Similarly Bythell (1978, pp. 252–3) uses his study of outwork in Britain during the nineteenth century to criticise the utopian notion of a return to small scale production expounded by Schumacher in his popular book, *Small Is Beautiful* (1973). In Berg's view, outworkers, whether or not they are skilled craft workers, can be controlled by capitalists through credit and leasing arrangements just as effectively as through supervision in the factory. If anything, putting out lessens the chances of effective protest by workers since: 'Dispersal mythifies and complicates the capital–labour relationship; it weakens organized labour and exploits a cheap labour force, especially women' (Berg, 1991, p. 191). Landes (1986, p. 606), the mainstream historian, and Berg, the radical, both make the same point: 'small bosses are still bosses' (1994, p. 206). If anything, within small workshops the bosses are more likely to be autocratic men exercising arbitrary control over women and children (Bendix, 1963, p. 26).

It must be quite clear by now that the studies of the Industrial Revolution and the new factory system do not furnish neat confirmation for any of the radical or mainstream perspectives on work organisation. Mainstream historians (Landes, 1986; Nelson, 1980) are probably right to complain that Marglin and Braverman have raided secondary historical sources selectively to find support for their radical views. However, radical historians have probably not complained so much about mainstream economists raiding history, since economists such as Williamson, and Alchian and Demsetz, have hardly consulted history at all to support their arguments in favour of capitalist forms of work organisation.

CHAPTER 7

Ownership and control

Introduction

There are longstanding debates in both sociology and economics about the significance of the modern corporation. Many social scientists contend that since the economy has become increasingly dominated by large corporations there has been a fundamental transformation of society. These commentators believe that contemporary society bears very little resemblance to the models of capitalism developed by classical, neoclassical and Marxist economics. This is because those models emerged during the nineteenth and early twentieth centuries, before the ascendancy of the modern corporation had become apparent. According to this view, established economic theories need to be modified or rejected, not so much because they are internally inconsistent, but because they have been rendered redundant by changing circumstances.

Those who proclaim the transformation of society by the modern corporation often characterise contemporary capitalism as 'managerial' (Chandler, 1977), 'corporate' (McDermott, 1991; Marris and Mueller, 1980), 'monopoly' (Baran and Sweezy, 1968) 'organized' and or more recently 'disorganized' (Offe, 1985; Lash and Urry, 1987), thus differentiating it from previous eras of capitalism (Bottomore, 1985, p. 2; Rowlinson and Hassard, 1994; Wheelock, 1986). Some go further, to suggest that it is no longer appropriate to describe contemporary society as capitalist at all, meaning that the general technological or organisational dynamics that characterise all large bureaucracies, whether capitalist or otherwise, have transcended the specifically capitalist features of the economy. They are more comfortable with descriptions of society as 'industrial' (Galbraith, 1967), or, latterly, 'post-industrial' (Bell, 1974; Scott, 1985, pp. 16–17); a 'society of organizations' (Mintzberg, 1989, p. 1; Perrow, 1991) rather than a capitalist society.

Debates about the significance of the modern corporation have taken place within and between different disciplines and political perspectives. According to Neil Fligstein, a leading organisational sociologist, 'The question of who controls the large modern corporation is one of the most enduring of modern social science' (Fligstein and Brantley, 1992, p. 280). Mike Reed, another sociologist, endorses this view. Introducing what he calls 'the separation thesis', Reed declares that, 'the debate about the separation of ownership from control in modern industry focuses upon the most significant economic, political, organisational and technological changes that have occurred' during the twentieth century (1989, p. 129).

Broadly speaking, the view that managers, rather than the owners of capital, have come to dominate modern corporations can be described as 'managerialism'. (This is not to be confused with managerialism in the sense of accepting and reinforcing the legitimacy of management, which is also prevalent in organisation theory (Thompson and McHugh, 1990, pp. 18–19).) Although there are many versions of managerialism, the basic managerialist thesis is that the separation of ownership from control in modern corporations is either the cause or the effect of the managers of corporations having the ability to pursue their own objectives, which diverge significantly from the objectives that would otherwise be pursued by the owners of corporations. The managerialist thesis is captured well by one of the propositions put forward by the business historian, Alfred Chandler, in *The Visible Hand*, his seminal historical study of the emergence of the bureaucratic industrial enterprise in the USA: 'an enterprise controlled by its managers can properly be identified as managerial, and a system dominated by such firms is called managerial capitalism' (Chandler, 1977, p. 10). Chandler has extended the characterisation of the USA as managerial capitalism to the rest of the Western world and Japan (Chandler and Daems, 1974, 1980).

The opponents of managerialism argue that the separation of ownership from control is not as pervasive as the managerialists believe it is. Or else, even if there has been a separation of ownership from control, the managers of large corporations are subject to similar pressures and pursue more or less the same objectives as the capitalists who previously both owned and controlled firms.

Concern about the effects of the separation of ownership from control goes back at least as far as Adam Smith. He was critical of joint stock companies on the grounds that their directors,

> being the managers rather of other people's money than their own, it cannot well be expected, that they should watch over it with the same anxious vigilance with which the partners in a private copartnery frequently watch over their own. . . . Negligence and profusion, therefore, must always prevail, more or less, in the management of the affairs of such a company.

With this in mind, Smith believed that unless they were granted monopolistic privileges, joint stock companies would not be able to compete against private individuals (Smith, 1976, vol. 2, p. 265). Smith's was very much the predominant view, reiterated by John Stuart Mill (1899, p. 390; quoted by Winter, 1993,

p. 182), during the nineteenth century. It was 'based on bitter experience as well as on fashionable economic reasoning' (Pollard, 1968, p. 23). For contemporary managerialists, such as J. K. Galbraith (1987), the supersession of owner-operated firms by management-controlled corporations throws into doubt the relevance of Smith's analysis for understanding and legitimating modern capitalist economies.

The roots of actual managerialism, the realisation that a separation of ownership from control might become pervasive and have profound implications for the workings of a capitalist economy, are to be found in Marxist writings, starting with Marx himself, followed by evolutionary socialists, such as Eduard Bernstein (Bottomore, 1985; Zeitlin, 1989), and then evolutionary and institutional economists, primarily Veblen and Commons. However, two books in particular crystallised the managerialist thesis. These are, *The Modern Corporation and Private Property* (1967 [1932]) by Adolfe Berle, a lawyer, and Gardiner Means, an economist, and *The Managerial Revolution* (1962 [1941]) by James Burnham, a political philosopher.

Berle and Means' book has been described as 'one of the most influential books of the twentieth century' (Moore, 1983, p. 235), even though the ideas they presented by were not particularly original (Hessen, 1983, p. 279): Berle and Means saw their research as an extension of Veblen's work. However, their book was the most coherent exposition of the managerialist critique of corporations that had yet appeared, and, unlike many of their managerialist predecessors, they presented detailed empirical research to back up their arguments. The book engendered a research tradition which brings together law and economics, and in recognition of its influence a conference was held to commemorate the fiftieth anniversary of its publication. The papers presented appeared in a special issue of the *Journal of Law and Economics* (Landes *et al.*, 1983).

Berle and Means collaborated on a research project designed to assess the extent and significance of management control of large American corporations. The centrepiece of their work is a survey of the 200 largest American corporations at the beginning of 1930. They identified five types of control of corporations. The first three types of control have a legal basis, which consists of the right to vote for a majority of the stock of a corporation. First is control through almost complete ownership of the corporation's stock, such as in privately-owned family firms. Second is straightforward majority control of stock. Third is control through a legal device without majority ownership, especially 'pyramiding', which was of concern in the USA at the time. This 'involves the owning of a majority of the stock of one corporation which in turn holds a majority of the stock of another – a process which can be repeated a number of times' (Berle and Means, 1967 [1932], p. 72)

For most corporations, however, Berle and Means argue that control does not have a legal status, but rests on a strategic position. This is achieved in one of two ways, which constitute the fourth and fifth types of control: either through control of a minority of shares, often as little as 10–15 per cent, but where no other group is able to organise a majority of the voting stock; or else where share ownership is so widely diffused that no individual or group is able to mobilise even a minority shareholding to control the corporation, then management is able to exercise control and becomes a virtually self-perpetuating body. Their evidence is summarised in Table 7.1.

Berle and Means developed the thesis that the ownership of large publicly quoted corporations has become separated from effective control. They believed that with the increasing separation of ownership and control, a 'corporate system' had emerged (Berle and Means, 1967 [1932], p. 1). Along with institutional economists such as Veblen and Commons, Berle and Means believed that the corporate system they described contradicted the basic assumptions of classical and neoclassical economics. These assumptions had led economists since Adam Smith to warn against allowing managers to exercise responsibility on behalf of the owners of companies, as this would undermine efficiency. This throws into question the adequacy of public policies based on classical assumptions, since the question of who does control corporations obviously has implications for the issue of who *should* control corporations. Commenting on the book fifty years on, Means still maintained that the evidence presented in *The Modern Corporation* begs the question:

> How can public policies that can work reasonably well when most enterprises are small, closely held, and highly competitive, be expected to work when an important part of production is carried on by giant enterprises with dispersed ownership and fewer competitors? (1983, p. 300)

In a review of the reception given to *The Modern Corporation*, Stigler and Friedland set out the legacy of Means' contribution to economics:

TABLE 7.1   Control of the 200 largest American companies at the beginning of 1930

	By number (%)	By wealth (%)
Management control	44	58
Legal device	21	22
Minority control	23	14
Majority ownership	5	2
Private ownership	6	4
In hands of receiver	1	negligible
Totals	100	100

Source: Berle and Means, 1967 [1932], p. 94.

the belief that the economy was no longer effectively competitive; the belief that ownership and control were fully separated in most large corporations; the strategic role of giant corporations in the economy; the beginning of measurement of concentration of production, using census data; and the belief that prices of large companies were unresponsive to the conditions of demand and supply (administered prices). (1983, pp. 258–9)

This legacy clearly constitutes the major part of managerialism.

Stigler and Friedland maintain that most economists 'continued to apply traditional profit-maximizing theory', as if *The Modern Corporation* had never been written (1983, p. 259; Galbraith, 1987, pp. 198–9). One of the leading Marxist critics of managerialism, Maurice Zeitlin, reckons that Berle and Means are 'widely cited but seldom read' (1989, p. 77). Even so, the emergence of behavioural and managerial theories of the firm within economics can be seen as a response to the managerialist challenge to orthodox economic theory. Furthermore, the relationship between the owners and managers of corporations has become synonymous with 'the agency problem', and in Douglass North's view, Berle and Means deserve credit for addressing the agency issue 'long before anyone else' (1983, p. 270).

Burnham's contribution to the managerialist thesis is more journalistic than academic, and he can easily be criticised for his wild predictions (Child, 1969, p. 41). For example, he believed that a European superstate would emerge in the wake of German expansion during the Second World War. However, it was Burnham who coined the phrase, 'the managerial revolution', and the importance of this should not be underestimated (Scott, 1985, p. 228; Chandler, 1977, p. 515, n. 5). Burnham's theory of the managerial revolution is more concerned with the nature of management control within corporations and large bureaucracies in general, rather than the specific relationship between types of ownership and the control of corporations from outside.

According to Burnham, whatever the nature of ownership, the managers of large bureaucracies are able to exercise effective control because of their special knowledge and access to information inside their organisations. Burnham argued that a managerial revolution was taking place in all industrial societies, be they capitalist, socialist or Fascist, although the revolution was nearer to completion in Soviet Russia and Nazi Germany. This is because the transition from capitalist society to managerial society is only finished when the 'limited state' of capitalism is replaced by an 'unlimited' managerial state which completely abrogates the remaining capitalist property rights that still restrain, if only minimally, managers in capitalist corporations (1962, p. 113).

An insight into Burnham's political background is helpful in understanding how, as a philosopher, he came to write a book about economic and sociological issues (Nichols, 1969). He had previously been a Trotskyist, but he disagreed with Leon Trotsky about the nature of the Soviet Union (Trotsky,

1971). From the time of his exile from Russia until his murder by one of Stalin's agents, Trotsky was one of the fiercest socialist critics of Stalin's betrayal of the Bolshevik revolution, long before most Western socialists. However, Trotsky continued to believe that there were aspects of the Soviet Union that should be defended by socialists, and that it could still be characterised as a 'workers' state'.

Burnham disagreed with Trotsky. Burnham believed that there had actually been a bureaucratic counter-revolution and that the Soviet Union, along with Nazi Germany, could be characterised as a bureaucratic centralist state. He broke from Marxism in 1939 when he parted with Trotsky's political organisation. Although *The Managerial Revolution* 'can be read as an anti-communist polemic' (Nichols, 1969, p. 34), and Burnham is adamant that socialism is impossible (1962, p. 69), his language is resonant of his Marxist background. This comes through vividly in his use of metaphors, such as, 'the struggle for power' by managers, and managers replacing capitalists as 'the dominant or ruling class' (1962, pp. 72, 76).

Burnham takes Berle and Means' research as 'a powerful confirmation of the theory of the managerial revolution'. However, he maintains that there is a 'basic deficiency' in their analysis. This is because:

> whatever its legal merits, the concept of 'the separation of ownership and control' has no sociological or historical meaning. Ownership *means* control; if there is no control, then there is no ownership. . . . If ownership and control are in reality separated, then ownership has changed hands to the 'control' and the separated ownership is a meaningless fiction.

Burnham reinterprets the phrase 'separation of ownership and control' to mean 'separation of control over access to the instruments of production from control over preferential treatment in distribution'. He believes that such a separation is untenable and that sooner or later the owners who merely receive a share of declared profits without any control over access to production itself will lose out to the managers who do control production. Burnham asserts that, 'Control over access is decisive, and, when consolidated, will carry control over preferential treatment in distribution with it.' Control over access includes 'the all-important prerogative of hiring and firing . . . as well as organization of the technical process of production', both of which will be exercised in such a way as to ensure that management control is enhanced and becomes increasingly opaque to outsiders (1962, pp. 87–102).

Although Burnham presents hardly any evidence to back up his argument, his work suggests a different line of enquiry to Berle and Means. Burnham's argument is that *actual*, as opposed to merely *legal*, ownership of corporations must be derived from effective control of production, whereas Berle and Means adhere to the view that various types of control of corporations are derived from different patterns of legal ownership. Burnham's theory of the managerial revolution suggests sociological research into the process of change inside organisations, as exemplified by Chandler's historical research into the internal organisational structures of industrial enterprises (Chandler, 1962, 1977, 1990). On the other hand, Berle and Means initiated a more 'statistical approach' to the relationship between ownership and control (Nichols, 1969, p. 21). Even though Berle and Means' work was 'nakedly empirical', and they 'had no systematic theory of the causes or consequences of the separation of ownership and control' (Stigler and Friedland, 1983, p. 258; North, 1983, p. 270), their work is more akin to economists' preference for testing hypotheses derived from models against quantifiable published data. Each type of research can be found in the literatures both for and against managerialism, so that the debate over managerialism is not merely a manifestation of methodological differences between economics and sociology.

In a review of managerialism, Theo Nichols (1969), a sociologist, divides managerialism into two camps: sectional and non-sectional. This has proved to be a useful distinction which has structured discussions in sociology (Child, 1969; Reed, 1989, p. 147, n. 33; Scott, 1985, pp. 18–20). Sectional managerialists are those who argue that management control of corporations has had adverse consequences, with managers using their power to pursue their own, sectional, interests. In contrast, non-sectional managerialists argue that once managers are freed from the constraints of ownership they will, or can be influenced to, exercise power in a way that is socially responsible.

Against both the sectional and non-sectional managerialist schools, Nichols counterpoises the 'Marxist school', which disputes the extent and significance of the separation of ownership from control. However, whilst managerialism is opposed by many Marxists, it is more often criticised, though for very different reasons, by mainstream economists, especially organisational economists who have taken the managerialist challenge seriously. Marxist anti-managerialists argue that the control of corporations is subordinated to the sectional interests of a class of capitalist owners. In contrast mainstream economists maintain that even if there has been a separation of ownership from control, the managers who control corporations are constrained to do so efficiently by the combined pressures from product, labour, and capital markets.

Discussion on this issue between organisational economists and organisation theorists has been confused. This is partly because the economists seem to see nearly all sociologists and organisation theorists as managerialists. Furthermore, economists equate managerialism with the sectional managerialist perspective. Dialogue could easily be frustrated if the only possible debate is seen as one between diametrically opposed camps. These would consist of mainstream organisational economists opposing managerialism on one side, facing radical sociologists and organisation theorists supporting sectional managerialism on the other. However, as already noted, Marxists are opposed to managerialism just as much, if not more, than organisational economists, and most mainstream organisation theory can be characterised as non-sectional managerialism. To allow for a more constructive dialogue four perspectives can be set out to structure discussion. These are: non-sectional anti-managerialism; non-sectional managerialism; sectional anti-managerialism; and sectional managerialism (see Figure 7.1). It should be noted that unlike other attempts to structure discussions about the control of corporations (Hirsch *et al.*, 1990, p. 51), the four perspectives set out in this chapter are intended as a typology of theories, not a typology of corporations. To confuse the two runs the risks of implying that different theories are only appropriate for alternative forms of organisation. The view taken here is that one aspect of each theory is the extent to which it accepts or tries to explain the diversity of corporate forms.

FIGURE 7.1   **Perspectives on managerialism**

Non-sectional anti-managerialism

The managerialist thesis is fiercely contested by leading organisational economists. They accept that the managerialist critique highlighted inadequacies in the neoclassical theory of the firm. Whereas neoclassical economists see firms as mere cyphers for product markets and markets for factors of production, organisational economists emphasise the specific nature of the constraints on the managers of firms from capital and labour markets, constraints which can be both internal and external to a corporation. Organisational economists tend to reject the managerialist view that the owners of large corporations have lost almost all control over the way corporations are operated. However, they argue that to the extent that there has been a separation of ownership from control it has arisen for efficiency reasons, rather than because managers have been able to usurp the power of owners.

Criticisms of the neoclassical theory of the firm may have been prompted by the managerialist critique, but it should be emphasised that the responses to the critique, such as the managerial and behavioural theories of the firm, and finally organisational economics, are not synonymous with an acceptance of the managerialist thesis. The managerial theory of the firm within economics responded to the challenge of managerialism by analysing the motivation of managers in terms of neoclassical assumptions. However, these modifications to the theory of the firm apply just as much to classical capitalist firms as to management-controlled firms.

Demsetz (1988, p. 189) points to the danger that managerialism confuses the firm of economic theory with the firm of a previous era, as if the neoclassical model corresponds to a type of firm that did once exist in reality but which has now been superseded by the large corporation. This obscures the point that the neoclassical model was never anything more than a theoretical construct. As its advocates have reiterated, the neoclassical model was not intended to be a realistic representation of the firm. It can be argued that Berle and Means in particular commit the 'fallacy of misplaced concreteness' (Machlup, 1967, p. 9). That is, they compare the model of the firm in neoclassical price theory with the empirical reality of existing corporations in order to demonstrate that the latter have superseded the former, as if the former was ever more than a theoretical construct. Demsetz reiterates the point that, 'It is a mistake to confuse the firm of economic theory with its real-world namesake' (1988, p. 189).

As for the behavioural theory of the firm, it is not only management-controlled firms that are compelled to satisfice. All firms facing uncertainty, which means in effect all firms in the real world, are compelled to satisfice rather than to maximise. Managerialists themselves, such as Marris and Mueller (1980, p. 41), seem unclear as to whether the question of satisficing or maximising should be settled theoretically or empirically. If it is deemed to be an empirical question, then the implication is that only management-controlled firms satisfice and therefore require managerial or behavioural models to explain their behaviour.

While the managerial theory of the firm was in part a reaction to the managerialist critique of neoclassical theory, the body of theory that has become known as 'managerial economics' is by no means synonymous with managerialism. It has to be admitted that confusion is bound to arise when such similar terms are used to label two related and partly overlapping schools of thought. To concede that managerial discretion is important enough to be incorporated into a model of the firm does not amount to admitting that capitalism has been superseded by a corporate economy in which corporate management wields decisive influence. A case in point is Oliver Williamson's version of transaction cost economics.

Williamson incorporated managerial objectives into a model of the firm in his earlier work (1964, 1986a [1963]), which, as he says, 'emphasized the distortions that result from managerial discretion' (1993a, p. 105). However, it would be a mistake to continue to characterise Williamson's later contributions to the development of organisational economics as managerialist on the basis of his previous contribution to managerial economics (see Nichols, 1969, p. 94). In his later work on transaction costs, Williamson goes beyond the managerial theory of the firm in order to focus on the internal organisation of firms (Marris and Mueller, 1980, p. 37). His preferred 'research strategy is to start from managerial discretion premises and then inquire into what means can be or have been devised to bring discretionary excesses *under control*' (1993a, p. 105). Williamson does not deny that there is a potential conflict of interests between owners and managers, given 'managerial preferences (for salary and perquisites) and stockholder preferences (for profits)' (1983b, p. 363). Rather he maintains that 'to observe that ownership and management are separated does not establish that ownership is thereafter wholly lacking in control' (1985, p. 145). Like most anti-managerialists, Williamson is sceptical about the extent to which ownership control has been superseded by management control of corporations. He believes that it is a 'rare firm that is not subject to the discipline of the capital market to some degree, however attenuated its influence may be' (1980, p. 194).

Williamson's (1985, p. 299) view is that Berle and Means mistook the increasing size of corporations and the separation of ownership from control as a manifestation of the assumption of control by the managers of corporations. Williamson maintains that this is understandable, since Berle and Means did not realise that what was in fact happening was that firms were able to internalise transactions that previously took place in the external capital market as a result of organisational innovations taking place within corporations. These organisational innovations, primarily the multidivisional structure (discussed in the next chapter), which did not become apparent until later, meant that corporations were better placed to make decisions about investments internally than were investors in the external capital market. Williamson does not deny that this exacerbates the issue of 'managerial discretion' that is highlighted by the managerialist literature: 'Strategically situated as it is, the management is able to present (screen, distort, manipulate) information in ways which favor its own agenda. Albeit subject to limitations . . . managerial discretion is not for nought' (1985, p. 318).

Williamson also accepts that there are costs associated with bureaucracy in organisations (1985, pp. 148–9). These costs arise because it is difficult for organisations to replicate the high-powered incentives that exist in markets, so they are more likely to forgive failures on the part of managers. This is exacerbated by the tendency of managers to underestimate the complexity of a situation, and to overestimate their own capacity to manage complexity. Williamson calls this 'the propensity to manage', and while it is often well-intentioned, he acknowledges that there is a reprehensible aspect to it when managers take advantage of organisations to pursue their own subgoals.

There is an implicit assumption in Williamson's argument that if managers enjoyed even greater discretion and were immune from paying any penalty for the costs of bureaucracy, then organisations would displace markets to an even greater extent than they have done. If managers enjoyed unlimited discretion then there would be no limits to the growth of corporate bureaucracies, but limits clearly do exist. What is more, there are discernable patterns in the relationships between factors such as industry, ownership, and the growth of firms, which are the subject of the literature on industrial organisation. These relationships presumably would not exist if managerial discretion were unconstrained.

Williamson is more concerned with elaborating the incentives and the internal structures for governing corporations, awkwardly known as governance structures, that have been developed within the corporation and which constitute it as an internal capital market. He is less interested in the control mechanisms developed by the external capital market, which check the discretion of corporate managers. It is only in passing that he alludes to the 'refinement of takeover techniques' which expose incumbent managers to the risk of dismissal after their firm has been taken over (1985, p. 314; 1993a, p. 104). According to Williamson, putting too much emphasis on the relationship between corporate managers and the external capital market obscures the importance of organisational forms and organisational innovations within corporations which have facilitated the internalisation of transactions from the external capital market (1983b, p. 356).

Agency theorists have concentrated on explaining how the separation of ownership from control has arisen for efficiency reasons, and how corporate managers, the agents, remain constrained to act in the interests of owners, the principals. Agency theorists point to two sources of constraint on corporate managers (Jensen and Meckling, 1986, p. 228). First, there is the market for the firm itself, the capital market, where there is supposedly the ever-present threat of takeover for under-performing firms. Second, there is the competition from other potential managers, 'the managerial labor markets, both within and outside of the firm' (Fama, 1986, p. 200).

In defending divisions of labour and hierarchy within capitalist firms, organisational economists advance efficiency reasons to explain how the capitalists are almost invariably the bosses. According to Alchian and Demsetz's (1986) property rights analysis, the capitalist, who is the owner-manager in the classical capitalist firm, enjoys the rights to the residual rewards from the firm after the other members of the firm have been paid according to agreed performance criteria. There is nothing to stop the owner-manager enjoying the residual rewards in the form of on-the-job consumption. As Demsetz says, nowhere is it written that the owner-manager 'prefers to consume only at home' (1983, p. 381). On-the job consumption might include a range of non-pecuniary benefits, such as those listed by Jensen and Meckling:

the physical appointments of the office, the attractiveness of the secretarial staff, the level of employee discipline, the kind and amount of charitable contributions, personal relations ('love', 'respect', etc.) with employees, a larger than optimal computer to play with, purchase of production inputs from friends, etc. (1986, pp. 216–17)

Less benign benefits might include the indulgence of the owner-manager's racial and sexual prejudices and proclivities in the selection, promotion and treatment of other members of the firm.

This is an important prelude to the agency argument, since it establishes that managerial discretion is not unique to corporations where ownership is separated from control; rather, it is a phenomenon which arises in any situation that departs from the neoclassical ideal. In the capitalist corporation the owner-managers have the right to sell their claim to the residual rewards. The alienability of such rights has several advantages, which are outlined by Fama and Jensen (1983). First of all, the claims to the residual rewards of the firm carry risks, starting with the risk that there will be zero or negative residual rewards. Alienability allows the risks associated with the residual claims to be spread between multiple owners, each of whom is able to spread his or her risks by owning shares in a number of firms. This makes it more likely that these risks will be undertaken (Jensen and Meckling, 1986), and may lessen the extent of the residual claims that are required to attract investment in the corporation. In Demsetz's view, the existence of a capital market gives shareholders who do not agree with the management group an 'escape hatch', and this minimises the costs of complex negotiations which would otherwise have to take place to enable the shareholders to make their views known to the management group (1988, pp. 113–14).

Alienability of the residual claims also allows for the specialisation of management. Fama and Jensen make a distinction between decision-making and risk-bearing. They argue that this separation is by no means peculiar to large corporations, since it is common to other complex organisations such as large professional partnerships and non-profit organisations. One reason for this is that managerial, or decision-making skills, 'are not necessarily tied to wealth or willingness to bear risk' (1983, p. 330). Robert Hessen (1983) similarly redefines the separation of ownership from control as one manifestation of the more general phenomenon of the separation of investment from management. Without such a separation, 'careers as managers would only be open to the heirs of private fortunes or those who had married money. But there is little reason to think that heirs or fortune hunters are superior managers – even if there are enough of them (which there are not) to supply the necessary capital' (Hessen, 1983, p. 285).

In the terminology that is more familiar to organisation theory and organisational behaviour, the separation of risk-bearing from decision-making improves the process of management selection and succession. Without such a separation, not only would a change of management have to wait for a transfer of ownership, but a transfer of ownership would necessitate a change of management. These are problems that confront private companies which are owned and managed by a single family and where it could be said that the residual rewards are consumed in part in the form of ensuring continuing family control of the firm.

The issue of management succession is addressed succinctly by Stinchcombe in his book, *Economic Sociology*. He notes that 'part of the advantage of a corporate form of organization of capitalism is that the *operative* part of the property system – namely, corporate ownership of the means of production – does not have to be reorganized on the death of a property owner' (1983, p. 230). This means, for example, that widows can be dominant among the inheritors of wealth, even though elderly women are often not generally 'socially eligible for the roles of running national corporations' (Stinchcombe, 1983, p. 230; Burnham, 1962, p. 98). The separation of ownership from control is therefore one way in which organisations are able to outlive their founders. It may also mean that since the owners are removed from the organisation they are less likely than owners who are also managers to indulge managers' preferences for enjoying on-the-job non-pecuniary rewards.

Although the separation of ownership from control can be presented as an efficient prerequisite for ensuring smooth transitions when either the owners or the managers of corporation are changed, anti-managerialists back up their argument by pointing to the rare occasions when conflicts do arise. These events, which can be referred to as critical episodes, usually occur when managers patently fail to act in accord with the wishes of shareholders. The outcome of these episodes is particularly important as a rejoinder to the charge that the dilution of ownership among a multitude of shareholders effectively robs the shareholders of the power to discipline management. Demsetz summarises the counter argument:

> [W]hen the need arises, dispersed ownership will become sufficiently concentrated to give proper guidance to, perhaps to 'boot' out, an ineffective management. This congealing of ownership may take the form of a takeover, a rebellion by a group of cooperating shareholders, or the acquisition of large shareholdings by one or a few shareholders. These events, because they are possible, and, indeed, actually do take place, put a constraint on management even when they are not currently operative. (1983, p. 387)

Martin Ricketts reiterates the argument. He notes that there is nothing to say that a particular company's shares must be widely dispersed continuously, so that:

> The degree of concentration or dispersion is capable of changing over time. It may appear *at any given moment* that shareholdings are dispersed and management has

great discretionary power. But financial capital can congeal suddenly and unexpect-
edly. A dominant interest can emerge which changes the top management and
consigns the existing top managers to the labour market. (1987, p. 253)

The boundary between firms and the external capital market is susceptible to
change as organisational innovations take place. On the one hand, firms may
increase in size if, as a result of innovations, they are better able to undertake
investment decisions internally than are investors in the external capital
market. On the other hand, organisational innovations in the external capital
market may counter the growth of firms and curb the increase in managers'
autonomy by improving external investors' capacity to ensure the pursuit of
profit and to discipline under-performing corporate managers. It can be
argued that recent improvements in external capital markets have created a
more competitive 'market for corporate control' (Chandler, 1990, p. 621).

Two complementary developments can be seen as devices which have
disciplined corporate managers and compelled them to divest their corporations of operations which have been under-performing. First, the improvement in takeover techniques, through devices such as leveraged buyouts.
Second, the increased awareness of managers, both inside and outside a
corporation, that with the help of the external capital market they are able
to separate operations from corporations if they believe those operations are
under-performing and could be managed better. Thus there have been waves
of leveraged management buy-outs and buy-ins in Britain and the USA. Steve
Thompson and Mike Wright have followed these developments closely in
Britain. They see the boundary between the firm and the market changing in a
dynamic way, with internal organisation displacing external markets in the
first instance, but transactions reverting to the external market as innovations
occur there. They have referred to management buy-outs as 'the remarriage of
ownership and control'. They believe that buy-outs facilitate the introduction
of more appropriate accounting control systems, especially at the strategic
level in firms (1993, pp. 233–5).

Increasing shareholder activism, the reassertion of shareholders' rights and
the questioning of executive remuneration packages that occurred in Britain
and the USA during the 1980s can be understood as a response to the growth
and diversification of firms and an attempt to ensure that corporate managers
act in the best interests of shareholders. Organisational economists have been
well placed to contribute to the ensuing debate over corporate governance,
which has mainly been concerned with the membership and structure of
company boards of directors, rather than the climate in which, or the
processes whereby, corporate decisions are made. More orthodox neoclassical
economists and enthusiasts of *laissez-faire* capitalism are hard put to discuss
the adequacy of measures to curb managerial discretion when, as Williamson
points out, they commonly deny the existence or significance of managerial
discretion in the first place (1985, p. 319). Having said that, it should be noted

that organisational economists generally endorse the prevailing arrangements for corporate governance rather than recommend radical change. Virtually all organisational economists give priority to the protection of shareholders, which is seen as being synonymous with the agency problem. If the interests of other stakeholders are considered at all, then predictably reasons are found to rationalise their lack of representation in the running of corporations (for example, Williamson, 1985, pp. 302–11).

Most mainstream organisational economists adhere to an efficiency argument against managerialism. Although they concede that some separation of ownership from control has taken place, they maintain that such a separation can be explained in terms of efficiency. While corporate management may enjoy significant discretion, this by no means constitutes complete autonomy from external capital markets, so that managers are still constrained, if not to maximise profits, then at least to secure an acceptable level of profitability. Like nearly all mainstream economists, most organisational economists vaguely presume that the interests of shareholders are synonymous with the interests of society as a whole, and that by being constrained to act in accord with those interests managers are being compelled to behave efficiently.

Organisational economists adhere to the mainstream neoclassical view that in the absence of state interference, firms are ultimately constrained by consumer preferences. This is expressed clearly by Fama and Jensen: 'Absent fiat, the form of organization that survives in an activity is the one that delivers the product demanded by customers at the lowest price while covering costs' (1983, p. 301). Their intention is to explain how the survival of firms in which ownership and control are separated is compatible with the assumption that only efficient forms of organisation can survive. Making such an assumption amounts to a denial that different forms of organisation and distributions of ownership have any significant effect on what is produced and how the product is distributed. In other words, organisational economists are more or less indifferent to any implications of the separation of ownership from control for the changing class structure of society since, for them, as for neoclassical economists in general, social class is not a consideration (Pitelis, 1987, p. 34). Even to discuss social class might imply that firms are susceptible to influence from collectivities other than the state.

The identity of shareholders is not explored in mainstream organisational economics. Shareholding is assumed to be widespread, or at least shareholders' interests are taken to be heterogeneous and non-sectional. Therefore there is no discussion of the significance of the separation of ownership from control for changing patterns of social class. Class is a term which finds as little resonance in mainstream organisational economics as it does in orthodox neoclassical economics. The general conclusion of the non-sectional anti-managerialist view of corporations is that if corporate managers are better able to make risky investment decisions than are individual shareholders, then corporations should only be interfered with in order to allow shareholders to ensure that corporate management keeps within certain measurable and enforceable parameters of profitability.

Organisational economists have tended to characterise managerialism in general as a radical critique of the capitalist corporation. Thus Demsetz (1991) is scathing of the view that corporations have come to exercise a malevolent influence in society, a view which he associates with Galbraith's major statement of managerialism in *The New Industrial State* (1967). This means that organisational economics can be interpreted as a neo-liberal defence of the capitalist corporation against outside interference, especially from the state (Holton, 1992, pp. 90–6).

The existence of corporations and managerial discretion is something of an embarrassment for the liberal defence of capitalism derived from orthodox neoclassical economics, since corporations compromise the neoclassical model of an efficient economy. This means that, if pressed, neoclassical *laissez-faire* economists should be compelled to condemn the large corporation as mono-polistic, and possibly even a threat to capitalism itself. Unlike their more orthodox neoclassical colleagues, organisational economists are able to con-cede that the managers of corporations do enjoy considerable discretion, and that this is problematic. However, the autonomy enjoyed by managers is said to be a by-product of the institutional arrangements by which more efficient investment decisions can be made. This means that mainstream organisational economics may provide a more robust legitimation of the capitalist corpora-tion than *laissez-faire* neoclassical economics. This is because organisational economics defends a more realistic version of the capitalist corporation, whereas the orthodox neoclassical *laissez-faire* defence of capitalism is derived from a model of an efficient economy in which the large corporation plays no part.

Non-sectional managerialism

Non-sectional managerialism can be said to rest on two arguments, which appear at first sight to be contradictory: these could be called the divergence and convergence theses. On the one hand, the diversity of managerial strategies that can be pursued within broadly similar institutional arrange-ments suggests that the constraints of property rights are not major determi-nants of the structure and behaviour of organisations. On the other hand, it can be argued that organisational and technological imperatives, as determi-nants of the structure and behaviour of organisations, transcend property rights institutions. This is confirmed by the apparent convergence of bureau-cratic organisations operating within very different institutional settings. The divergence thesis takes the institutional setting of capitalism as given in order to highlight the degree of variation that is possible within and between capitalist firms. The convergence thesis highlights the extent of similarities between capitalist firms and other types of bureaucratic organisation. These are not necessarily mutually exclusive arguments, since the underlying theme of both theses is that an argument derived from property rights alone is hard put to explain the similarities or differences between bureaucratic organisations. Both arguments pervade mainstream organisation theory, which tends to abstract organisations from their institutional setting.

It is fair to say that 'Much organization theory is implicitly based on a premise of "managerialism"', at least in the minimal sense that, 'the ownership of large corporations is dispersed among thousands of stockholders who are not actively involved in the day-to-day operations of the organization, and this separation of ownership and control allows entrenched managers broad discretion' (Davis, 1991, p. 583). It could hardly be otherwise, since if corporate managers did not enjoy significant discretion then there would be little if any justification for studying decision-making within large organisations. There would be even less point to the exhortation to managers to adopt a humane approach to the management of employees that constitutes courses on organisational behaviour in business schools.

The discussion of bureaucracy in organisation theory really starts with Weber. Weber identified six defining characteristics that go to make up the 'ideal type' of modern bureaucracy (1991, pp. 196–8):

1. A principle of fixed rules and regulations;
2. Hierarchy, with the lower offices supervised by the higher ones;
3. Written records, 'the files';
4. Management as a specialised activity that requires expert training;
5. Management as a full-time activity; and
6. Management reduced to following a set of general rules which managers have to learn and which constitute their special knowledge.

An ideal type is a template distilled from historical studies which allows for a typology of authority. Weber identified three ideal types of authority: *legal–rational*, which characterises bureaucracies; *traditional*, typified by hereditary monarchies; and *charismatic*, exemplified by religious social movements, such as Christ and his disciples.

According to Weber, 'The decisive reason for the advance of bureaucratic organization has always been its purely technical superiority over any other form of organization' (1991, p. 214). In the popular American literature on management and organisations, Weber is often misrepresented as having 'doted on bureaucracy' (Peters and Waterman, 1982, pp. 5, 92). Nothing could be further from the truth. Far from extolling the virtues of bureaucracy, Weber was profoundly disturbed by the all-pervasive tendency towards rationalisation that he saw in all spheres of life. He believed that in modern societies even the charismatic leaders of social movements inevitably succumb to routine, and that bureaucracy will endure no matter which political philosophy prevails: 'Not summer's bloom lies ahead of us, but rather a polar night of icy darkness and hardness, no matter which group may triumph externally now' (1991, p. 128). The only escape from the 'iron cage' of rationality is an individual 'mystic flight from reality for those who are gifted for it' (Ibid.). Weber's pessimism was compounded because he did not see himself as gifted in any spiritual sense.

In the opening to his essay on bureaucracy, Weber argues that, 'It does not matter for the character of bureaucracy whether its authority is called "private" or "public"' (1991, p. 197). This would appear to indicate that Weber believed that bureaucracy transcends property rights. However, in his essay on class, he maintains that 'the existence of capitalistic enterprise presupposes' protection of 'the possession of goods, *per se*, and especially the power of individuals to dispose, in principle freely, over the means of production. The existence of a capitalistic enterprise is preconditioned by a specific kind of "legal order"' (1991, p. 185). This passage is in part a concession to the Marxist view that property rights, established through revolutionary upheavals, are more important than ideology in determining the dominant form of organisation in society. Weber's classic text, *The Protestant Ethic and the Spirit of Capitalism* (1930) is generally seen as an antidote to Marx's economic reductionism. Weber identifies the asceticism of Protestant religious sects, such as the Quakers, with the rational pursuit of profit and the emergence of the capitalist enterprise. He emphasises the importance of ideology in changing property rights. Thus the relationship between bureaucracy and property rights in Weber's work is open to different interpretations (Parkin, 1982, p. 92).

One theme that emerges from Weber's (1991) essays on sociology is that modern bureaucracy is predicated upon a series of separations, starting with the separation of workers from the means of production and culminating in the separation of ownership from control, which Weber saw as an element of 'high capitalism' (Gerth and Mills, 1991, p. 68). These separations mean that bureaucracy is free from external constraints in the sense that the members of a bureaucracy do not have divided loyalties. Bureaucratic officials become increasingly dependent on the bureaucracy itself rather than any outside interest for their position and therefore owe their allegiance to the bureaucracy.

Whether it is as state administrators, organisers in political parties, or the managers of capitalist enterprises, bureaucrats increasingly hold sway over charismatic leaders because only the bureaucratic officials are able to provide rationally debatable reasons for their actions. In Weber's view, 'charisma rejects all rational economic conduct' (1991, p. 247), it is thus inimical to capitalism, since:

> it is primarily the capitalist market economy which demands that the official business of the administration be discharged precisely, unambiguously, continuously, and with as much speed as possible. Normally, the very large, modern

capitalist enterprises are themselves unequalled models of strict bureaucratic organization. Business management throughout rests on increasing precision, steadiness, and, above all, the speed of operations. (1991, p. 214)

This means that a truly charismatic capitalist entrepreneur is a rarity, if not a contradiction in terms. Even if the occasional charismatic entrepreneur is thrown up, he or she will soon be replaced by career-orientated bureaucrats. More likely, the so-called 'charisma' of capitalist entrepreneurs is the highly rational product of corporate image-makers.

Weber notes that although 'bureaucracy promotes a "rationalist" way of life . . . the concept of rationalism allows for widely differing contents' (1991, p. 240). This allows for both a mainstream and a radical interpretation of Weber. The mainstream view is that bureaucracy is merely a technical instrument, which in itself is neutral in its effect on society. Once the restrictions imposed by capitalist owners are removed, then the managers of bureaucratic corporations can be induced to follow various socially responsible courses of action. Rationality ensures that whatever objectives are selected, they can be pursued efficiently, albeit with a tendency to emphasise objectives where achievements are more easily measurable (Mintzberg, 1989, p. 332). Mainstream organisation theorists are open to the criticism that, as far as most of them are concerned, 'Bureaucracy means efficiency' (Perrow, 1991, p. 743), it is an unpleasant necessity.

The radical view latches on to Weber's pessimism, and the distinction he makes between formal and substantive rationality. Within capitalist bureaucracies, purely formal rationality prevails, emphasising rational calculability without regard for the desirability of an objective in terms of substantive rationality, 'meaning rationality from the point of view of some particular substantive end, value or belief' (Brubaker, 1983, p. 4). Thus bureaucracies are equally at home producing fast food (Ritzer, 1993), promoting equal opportunities (Pringle, 1988), manufacturing condoms, or planning genocide (Bauman, 1989).

Neoclassical economics is highly susceptible to the radical Weberian critique, given the claims of economists that economic policy-making techniques can be refined independently from moral considerations of economic objectives. The point is illustrated by Friedman's belief that a clear distinction can be made between positive economics, which 'is, or can be, an "objective" science', and normative economics, which is concerned with ethical judgements (1953, p. 3). When government officials or corporate executives defer, as they often do (Galbraith, 1987, pp. 264–5), to economists who disclaim any moral agenda, substantive rationality can be said to have been subordinated to formal rationality.

Non-sectional managerialists acknowledge that in a society dominated by large organisations there is a general problem of controlling bureaucracies, which could be interpreted as the agency problem. According to Coleman

(1990), a rational choice sociologist, the profit-making corporation is merely the most salient among many corporate actors that have come to dominate society. In Mintzberg's view, the difficulties in ensuring that bureaucracies are socially responsible 'arise more from the size of an organization and its degree of bureaucratization than from its form of ownership' (1989, p. 307). Organisation theorists and sociologists who adhere to this view are open to the criticism that they fail to 'appreciate the distinction between corporate size and corporate power' (Frank, 1992, p. 164). The implication of this criticism is that the increased size of corporate bureaucracies can be explained by reasons other than the power of corporate managers. If this were not the case, there would be virtually no limits to the growth of corporate bureaucracies, or at least no explanation for the different growth rates of corporate bureaucracies in different industries.

Chandler (1962, p. 400, n. 5; 1988, pp. 304–5), the business historian, is one of the most forthright in putting forward a non-sectional managerialist defence of bureaucracy that is partly derived from Weber. It is Chandler's contention that:

> The rise and continuing growth of this [the industrial] enterprise and its contribution to American economic expansion cannot be explained by orthodox economics. For economists of the conventional school a statement that economic growth was paced by a few hierarchical enterprises competing in an oligopolistic manner is a contradiction in terms. For them and for most scholars, bureaucracy means inefficiency and oligopoly means misallocation of resources by a few firms that collect monopoly rents based on their market power (1990, p. 227).

Chandler's views are clearly at odds with nearly all economists, given that the term bureaucracy is rarely used affirmatively by economists, including organisational economists (Meyer, 1990b, p. 156). Chandler has consistently defended bureaucracy in industrial enterprises on efficiency grounds (1962, p. 37). Although Chandler accepts that private business enterprise and public civil or military organisation are 'all bureaucracies in Max Weber's sense of the word – hierarchies manned by professional officers – and so have features common to that social form', he argues that there are fundamental differences between them (1962, pp. 322). This represents a difference between Chandler and Weberian organisation theory.

One of Chandler's major propositions is 'that once a managerial hierarchy had been formed and had successfully carried out its function of administrative coordination, the hierarchy itself became a source of permanence, power, and continued growth' (1977, p. 8), and he does not deny that market power 'could, of course, be misused in predatory or antisocial ways'. But he maintains that such power requires 'a sound economic base', and this derives mainly from the 'organizational capabilities – the facilities and skills' developed by the managerial hierarchies within large, bureaucratic industrial enterprises (Chandler, 1990, p. 227, 1992). Chandler's endorsement of Weber overlooks Weber's disenchantment with the rationalism that is the inevitable concomitant of increasing bureaucracy. Instead bureaucracy, or organisational capabilities, are seen more or less as neutral technical instruments that can be picked up and used for almost any purpose, be it good or ill. It is this view, that bureaucracy can, at least potentially, be tamed and put to good use, that typifies non-sectional managerialism.

The general line of argument in organisation theory follows Burnham rather than Berle and Means, in that the autonomy of corporate managers is held to be predicated upon their special expertise as much as, if not more than, the dispersion of share ownership. Again, it is Chandler who summarises this position, when he stresses that 'management control cannot be measured in terms of the amount of stock held'. He alleges that managers gained control of industrial enterprises 'because they, not the outside directors, had the knowledge, experience, and information required to make and implement the strategies essential to keep such enterprises profitable' (1990, p. 192). This is partly endorsed by dissenting economists, such as Galbraith, who have advanced a managerialist thesis. Whereas anti-managerialists have developed new theoretical perspectives to counter managerialism, Galbraith defers to organisation theory as taught in business schools for an understanding of the firm as a 'bureaucratic structure and organization' (1987, p. 288; 1967, pp. 130–1). Burnham took Veblen to task for characterising engineers, rather than managers, as the emerging new class which would usurp the owners of capital. However, by reifying bureaucracy itself as the source of managerial autonomy, and emphasising managers' organisational rather than technical expertise, the managerialist thesis is in danger of missing the real variations in influence enjoyed by professional groups possessing different types of specialist expertise.

Rueschemeyer argues that the extent of the separation of ownership from control is greatest where professional groups have been able to monopolise a specific body of knowledge. He points to the autonomy enjoyed by professionals in medicine, a highly capital-intensive industry:

> Perhaps the greatest tribute to the professional power of physicians is the fact that by and large hospitals and their equipment are put at the disposal of doctors by public and charitable funds. In hospitals doctors control, but with few exceptions do not own, the means of their work. The degree of their control varies across and within countries and over time, but it is the strongest control exercised by any occupational group that does not own the means of its production – the most powerful university faculties constituting perhaps an exception. (Rueschemeyer, 1986, p. 128)

Rueschemeyer concedes that expert occupations have been able to dilute the concentration of power based on property through their collective organisation and control of knowledge. However, he maintains that this is a far cry from saying that the power of sectional interests based on property ownership has 'become irrelevant or even muted'. This is at least in part because capitalist interests have been able to co-opt corporate executives and managers by paying them with capital shares (Rueschemeyer, 1986, pp. 135, 140). In other words, while there is a need to understand how the actions of corporations are modified by the outlook of their managers and executives, these can be and are constrained by the agency structures devised by the owners of corporations. The diversity of corporate strategies should not be mistaken as evidence for complete managerial autonomy.

Unlike non-sectional anti-managerialists, and organisational economists in particular, non-sectional managerialists have discussed extensively the implications of the separation of ownership from control for the class structure of societies. However, class is generally discussed in more 'anodyne' (Scott, 1985, p. 266) terms than it is in either of the sectional literatures, whether anti-managerialist or managerialist. Managerialists tend to speak of 'elites' rather than 'classes', thus playing down any Marxist connotations. One of the themes of managerialism is the dissipation of the old capitalist ruling class whose power rested on the ownership of property, consisting primarily of controlling interests in family firms. This class is said to have been replaced by a class of salaried managers: a new 'business class' (Chandler, 1977, p. 1). Galbraith coined a new term to describe the newly-dominant class as he saw it: 'the Technostructure'; the technostructure extends beyond the 'management' of an enterprise, which Galbraith sees as an 'imperfectly defined entity' – instead, the technostructure 'embraces all who bring specialized knowledge, talent or experience to group decision-making' (1967, p. 71).

While non-sectional managerialists may concede that the old capitalist ruling class could be narrowly defined by property ownership, the new managerial class is not so cohesive or clearly bounded. With the displacement of capitalist entrepreneurs and their heirs by salaried bureaucrats with suitable educational qualifications, the class structure is supposedly less rigid, with greater social mobility and easier access to the positions in which the important decisions for society are made (Scott, 1985, p. 247). Chandler's conclusion is that class distinctions have become 'blurred' as a consequence of the rise of the managerial enterprise and the emergence of a 'class of managers' (1977, p. 500).

In so far as non-sectional anti-managerialists discuss the issue of class at all, they are likely to dispute the existence or cohesiveness of either the old capitalist class or the new managerial class. They would point to the problems of organisation, such as free-riding, which would make it unlikely that individuals sharing similar economic positions could come together to express and pursue a common interest. Organisational economics is therefore well placed to furnish theoretical arguments to reinforce Weber's objection to Marxism, that 'a class does not in itself constitute a community' (1991, p. 184). Thus Demsetz criticises Galbraith's view of a unified technostructure dominating a 'monolithic business world'. According to Demsetz, the business world is 'extremely heterogeneous in objective': it is characterised by 'diversity of interest' combined with 'rivalry in the market-place' (1991, pp. 172–3).

Managerialists maintain that although corporations may well be disciplined through their product, labour and capital markets, this discipline is likely to be exercised by other large, bureaucratic, management-controlled organisations, rather than by disparate, unorganised, individual consumers, employees, or shareholders. Thus management-controlled bureaucracies may constrain each other through various means, but bureaucratic organisations of one form or another prevail. This argument comes through in the dispute between managerialists and anti-managerialists over the importance of the critical episodes, in particular takeovers, when corporate managers might appear to be disciplined effectively. As Williamson puts it, managerialists see takeovers and mergers 'as manifestations of managerial discretion *by the firm proposing the takeover*'; by contrast, anti-managerialists, such as himself, focus on the limitation of managerial discretion in firms targeted for takeover (1993a, p. 104).

Galbraith maintains that such critical episodes are infrequent, because most of the time the technostructure enjoys autonomy from outside interference on the basis of retained earnings within the corporation. If, say, investment is needed and the firm is showing losses, then the rights of outsiders, such as bankers or others, 'to inquire and intervene will have to be conceded. They cannot be told to mind their own business. Thus does a shortage of capital, though limited in time and place, promptly revive the power of the capitalist. And it is in times of such failure of earnings, and then only, that the stockholder of the large corporation can be aroused' (Galbraith, 1967, p. 81).

As economists and non-sectional managerialists, Marris and Mueller (1980) address specifically the agency literature in which the threat of takeover is held up as a major constraint on managers. They emphasise that, in practice, takeovers are carried out by other managerial organisations, or else by 'wheeler-dealers' who are likely to leave the top management intact. Writing in 1980, they concluded that 'All the empirical work to date supports . . . [the] . . . contention of considerable slack in the takeover mechanism' (p.42). In the mid-1990s, they might have cited the emergence of leveraged management buy-outs and buy-ins as further evidence that divestment is likely to be driven by inside or outside coalitions of managers backed by the bureaucratic, management-controlled shareholding organisations such as pension funds (Thompson and Wright, 1993; Pitelis, 1993, p. 39).

As an organisation theorist, Mintzberg also argues that although it is true that stock ownership can become concentrated very quickly, with one or a few corporations or financial institutions amassing considerable shareholdings in a company, this merely bumps the agency problem up one level, 'to the question of who can control the controller. . . . Thus, while there may occasionally be shareholder *autocracy* – control of the corporation by a single important shareholder – there is never likely to be shareholder *democracy* – true control of the management by many small shareholders' (Mintzberg, 1989, p. 323). Mintzberg looks further than the threat of takeover from other management controlled corporations. He concedes that 'external influencers', be they shareholders, government or any other interested party, may actually win in their occasional confrontations with internal management

> social legitimacy is, after all, on the side of the external constituency the organization is supposed to serve. But the external influencers are likely to lose out eventually, at least if the organization grows rather large, simply because they cannot control the great many internal decisions made on a daily basis. In effect, though they may win the wars, they are likely to lose the peace. (1989, p. 291)

Sectional anti-managerialism

Radical opposition to managerialism has come almost exclusively from Marxists of a more or less fundamentalist hue. In their commentary on the reception given to Berle and Means within economics, Stigler and Friedland note that 'the most vigorous attack on Mean's statistical findings has come, not from defenders of the private enterprise system, but from Marxists: a villain is apparently even more important to a theory than a hero' (1983, pp. 246–7). However, Marxists find themselves in a paradoxical position, because in f *Capital*, vol. 3, ch. 27, Marx himself makes some observations that could be construed as anticipating the emergence of the managerial enterprise.

Marx believed that the formation of joint-stock companies would make it possible for 'enterprises that merely yield an interest' to develop. His assessment of the implications of this is almost prescient:

> Transformation of the actual functioning capitalist into a mere manager, in charge of other people's capital, and of the capital owner into a mere owner, a mere money capitalist. (1981, p. 567)

> This is the abolition of the capitalist mode of production within the capitalist mode of production itself, and hence a self-abolishing contradiction, which presents itself *prima facie* as a mere point of transition to a new form of production. It presents itself as such a contradiction even in appearance. It gives rise to monopoly in certain spheres and hence provokes state intervention. It reproduces a new financial aristocracy, a new kind of parasite in the guise of company promoters, speculators and merely nominal directors; an entire system of swindling and cheating with respect to the promotion of companies, issues of shares and share dealings. It is private production unchecked by private ownership. (Ibid., p. 569)

Probably the most consistent and vehement Marxist critic of managerialism is the American sociologist Maurice Zeitlin (Scott, 1985, p. 230). He has attacked managerialism in a series of articles collected in his book, *The Large*

Corporation and Contemporary Classes (Zeitlin, 1989). Zeitlin, and other Marxist anti-managerialists such as Michel deVroey (1980), have tried to interpret Marx in such a way as to show that whatever Marx meant in the passage quoted above, it is not compatible with managerialism. Zeitlin maintains that not only has Marx's meaning been lost in translation from the German, but also that Marx only makes sense in relation to Hegel. In Zeitlin's opinion, when Marx writes of 'the abolition of the capitalist mode of production within the capitalist mode of production itself', this 'can only be jibberish in English . . . unless it is understood in its Hegelian sense of preserving while negating, recreating while abolishing. . . . Thus, the large corporation, as a new form of "social capital," re-creates "private capital" while abolishing it. Certainly, this is Marx's intended meaning' (1989, p. 46). This tortuous and semantic argument is more or less impenetrable to anyone who does not share the Marxist Fundamentalists' penchant for the exegesis of *Capital*.

It is hard to say whether or not Marx himself believed that the separation of ownership from control would change the nature of capitalism. His observations are little more than speculation. Far too much is often read into fragments of Marx's writings by his latterday adherents. However, it is clear that, for contemporary Marxists, more is at stake than merely 'what Marx really meant' (Nichols, 1969, p. 44). They see managerialism as a threat to their political perspective, which is why they are so keen to distance Marx, their mentor, from managerialism.

As Nichols realises, if Marxists were to accept that 'ownership and control were in fact separated this could weaken their theoretical justification for radical as opposed to reformist policies' (1969, p. 67). The reason for this is that revolutionary Marxists justify their call for the revolutionary overthrow of capitalist property rights on the grounds that capitalism cannot be reformed. By this they mean that individual capitalists cannot be persuaded to treat labour differently by moral arguments because capitalists are the personification of a dynamic arising from capitalist property rights. This dynamic ensures the preservation of a capitalist class, if not the survival of individual capitalists. Piecemeal reforms in one enterprise or another can only ever be a temporary accommodation of resistance from workers, and they are inevitably undermined.

Managerialism opens the way for what Nichols describes as the reformist 'belief that managers are more manageable than capitalists' (1969, p. 66). If managers are no longer constrained by capitalist property rights and the need to preserve the privileges of capitalist owners, then managers may be more susceptible to pressures to become socially responsible, such as in what they decide to produce, and in how they manage labour. What is more, if managerial enterprises are not constrained by the dynamics of the capitalist economy, then managers in general should be able to manage the economy in such a way as to avoid the economic crises that many Marxists believe are inherent in a capitalist economy driven by competition between capitalists.

The Marxist case against managerialism rests on the assertion that a capitalist social class continues to exist. Whether or not they accept that there has been a separation of ownership from control, Marxists maintain that 'the fundamental dynamics of the capitalist mode of production' remain unaltered (deVroey, 1980, pp. 225, 226). This is because the continued existence of a capitalist class is predicated upon its ability to impose sufficient control over corporations for it to secure a share of the surplus that is at least enough to ensure its perpetuation.

Zeitlin rejects just about every aspect of the managerialist thesis. He contends that 'separation of ownership and control' is an example of the 'pseudofacts' which come to 'bedevil' all sciences from time to time (1989, p. 37). Zeitlin is partially supported by John Scott, in his book *Corporations, Classes and Capitalism* (1985), which is a survey of the various literatures relating to managerialism. Instead of a separation of ownership from control, Scott maintains that the 'depersonalization' of property associated with the modern corporation has led to what C. Wright Mills called a 'managerial reorganization of the propertied class' (1956, p. 147, quoted by Scott, 1985, p. 238). If there has been a separation of ownership from management, then, in deVroey's (1980) view, it amounts to no more than a 'functional differentiation' within the capitalist class. According to this thesis, the vast family fortunes of the capitalist class are no longer tied to the vagaries of individual enterprises. The fortunes of the capitalist class are in fact all the more secure for being diversified.

Within the corporation the interests of the capitalists are safeguarded by the directors and executives. Though they may not be the largest single share-holders in their own corporation, the directors and executives are likely to be drawn from a 'pool' of wealthy share-owners (Scott, 1985, p. 245). Marxists go beyond the non-sectional anti-managerialist argument of organisational economics by asserting that corporations are not only constrained by the external capital market, but also that ownership interests are co-ordinated, so that corporations are in fact constrained by the sectional interests of the capitalist class. The capitalist class is held together and ensures that its members within corporations look out for each others' interests through an intricate network of general social interaction and actual kinship relations (Zeitlin, 1989, p. 37).

While the managers of large corporations may enjoy considerable leeway so long as the interests of the capitalist owners are safeguarded, during critical episodes the 'allegedly controlling management' can be decimated by intervention from outside, often by the banks representing ownership interests. Zeitlin's 'general proposition' is that 'those who really have control can decide when, where, and with respect to what issues and corporate policies they will intervene and exercise their power' (1989, p. 24). This is remarkably reminiscent of the analysis of critical episodes, already outlined above, by organisational economists such as Demsetz (1983) and Ricketts (1987) from a non-sectional anti-managerialist perspective. The major difference is that, unlike the non-sectional anti-managerialists, Zeitlin maintains that behind the sudden co-ordination of ownership interests during critical episodes there lies the manipulation of interlocking directorates and other networks by an 'inner group' of well-placed directors who represent the interests of a cohesive capitalist class (1989, p. 68).

Marxist anti-managerialists, such as Zeitlin, line up with mainstream economists when they argue that, 'The conduct of the large corporation . . . whether under management control or ownership control, is mainly determined by the market structure – the nature of competition, products produced, and the constraints of the capital (and labor) markets' (1989, p. 25). Stinchcombe is much less hostile to the managerialist thesis than Zeitlin; even so, he contends that 'the control system of the market' makes the 'formidable hierarchical' corporation 'somewhat less fearsome'. Although Stinchcombe accepts that it may seem 'unbelievable', he still maintains that the 'great corporations controlling the American economy are actually subject to market forces that they cannot control, but which control them' (1983, p. 167).

Against managerialism again, Andrew Friedman, a Marxist labour process theorist, reiterates the view that there is an underlying trend towards des-killing of workers in capitalist firms, even though managers pursue alternative strategies when they are compelled to do so by labour market pressures and resistance from workers. To explain this, Friedman invokes the law of value, 'a law which is enforced by competition' (1990a, p. 4). Support for this view can be drawn from the pricing procedures of large corporations, which confirm the Marxian theory that the process of production is the centre of gravity for market prices (Semmler, 1982, p. 111). John Kelly, another Marxist labour process theorist, argues that managerial strategies aimed at conceding greater industrial democracy are likely to be undermined because: 'If large corporations are to continue in competitive markets then they will have to ensure that their labour productivity, unit costs, product quality and other salient dimensions of competitiveness are kept broadly in line with their rivals' (1988, p. 217).

Friedman explains diversity in labour management strategies in terms of 'management error' (1990b, p. 180; 1977). This implies that, for each situation, there is only one labour management strategy that is compatible with the interests of capitalist owners, whether or not managers realise this. Peter Armstrong (1989) offers a more robust refutation of the managerialists divergence thesis. Perhaps surprisingly, given that Armstrong is a fairly fundamentalist Marxist, he draws on agency theory developed by Jensen and Meckling (1986) to discuss 'the *effect* of capitalism on the labour process'. Armstrong takes from agency theory the view that the 'management problem' is that 'of ensuring that managers, so far as is possible, make decisions which are in the interests of ownership' (Armstrong, 1989, pp. 309, 311). A diversity of management strategies is more or less inevitable, not only because different incentive structures for management are constructed, but also because the costs of information and computation make it impossible for owners to assess all management strategies (Jensen and Meckling, 1986).

Zeitlin maintains that it is 'necessary to explore in detail not only the institutional but the *class* relations in which large corporations are situated' (1989, p. 37). However, while organisational economists have analysed the institutional settings of large corporations in order to refute the managerialist thesis, Marxists have concentrated on class relationships. Although there are differences within Marxism concerning theories of competition and monopoly, there is agreement that the 'institutional framework' within which accumulation takes place needs to be elaborated (Wheelock, 1983, p. 19; Burkett, 1991, p. 65; Semmler, 1982, p. 109). Within Marxist theory there is a need to dereify both the market and the corporation so that they can be analysed as historically specific institutions, as they are beginning to be analysed in organisational economics.

If, as Marxist economists maintain, there is an increasingly institutionalised rate of profit in modern capitalism (Eatwell, 1982, p. 218), then the institutions, primarily capital markets, through which this institutionalisation takes place need to be analysed. On the whole, Marxists have failed to do this. However, as Armstrong has demonstrated, organisational economics, such as agency theory, can be used to illuminate the institutions through which class relations are mediated. In relation to the management of labour, it is clear that changes in ownership or changes in the incentive structures for managers can have significant effects on the labour process within corporations. For example, the increased influence of financial institutions during critical episodes may force corporations to minimise risks and maximise profits by lowering labour costs (Stearns, 1990, p. 196).

Non-sectional arguments against managerialism from organisational economics are to some extent compatible with Marxian sectional anti-managerialism. The major disagreement between them is whether the external constraints on corporations, especially from the capital market, merely ensure efficiency or, in addition, safeguard the sectional interests of the capitalist class. Stinchcombe argues that an analysis of the incentive structures for the various participants in a corporation, be they workers, managers or shareholders, inevitably 'brings up the question of who gets to set up the incentive system'. For Marx, this was 'ultimately a political question' (Stinchcombe, 1983, p. 182). The Marxist position is that the incentive structures not only have to be efficient in eliciting effort from workers and managers within the corporation, as organisational economics suggests, but they also have to ensure that a small class of capitalists, who may or may not be represented within the management of a corporation, are guaranteed a disproportionate share of the national income. According to the sectional anti managerialist perspective, any corporation in which the interests of the capitalist class are seriously threatened can expect intervention from outside.

Sectional managerialism

Whereas non-sectional managerialists see the results of a managerial revolution as being beneficial, or at least potentially, benign, sectional managerialists perceive the ascendancy of the management-controlled corporation as a major manifestation, or even the prime cause of the malignant bureaucratisation of society. The sectional managerialist position is shared by radical organisation theory and radical political economy. Given the Marxist background and sympathies of many radical organisation theorists and political economists, it is not surprising that the sectional managerialist and sectional anti-managerialist camps shade into each other.

Zeitlin alleges that, in managerialist imagery, the management of large corporations is characterised as a self-perpetuating oligarchy (1989, p. 64). Stinchcombe qualifies this with his definition of the corporation as 'a self-perpetuating oligarchy sensitive to market pressures' (1983, p. 178). Neither organisational economics nor Marxian political economy denies that corporate management has some capacity to safeguard its own position, so the distinction between managerialism and anti-managerialism rests on the degree of emphasis that is given to management's autonomy.

Baran and Sweezy's position can be characterised as a form of 'Marxist managerialism' (Scott, 1985, p. 26), insofar as they claim to adhere to Marxism and yet they appear to 'accept that a managerial revolution has taken place, so that control of the giant corporation rests in the hands of management' (Sawyer, 1979, p. 135; Zeitlin, 1989, p. 9). A fundamental difference between mainstream managerialism and Baran and Sweezy's position, is that the latter 'do not see the emergence of a managerial class as changing the basic objective of the firm, which remains the reaping of profits' (Sawyer, 1979, p. 136; Pitelis, 1987, p. 15). They believe that 'the giant corporation' has transformed capitalism, but they reject the view that 'the managements of big corporations form some sort of separate, independent, or "neutral" social class' (1968, p. 46).

The major difference between Baran and Sweezy and Marxist anti-managerialism is that Baran and Sweezy locate power 'inside rather than outside the typical giant corporation'. This means that even if the major goal of modern corporations remains long-term profit maximisation, as Baran and Sweezy maintain it does (1968, pp. 30, 37), this results from the psychological orientation of managers within large corporations rather than from the external constraints exerted by capitalist owners. Baran and Sweezy conflate external institutional constraints upon corporate management and managers' subjective aspirations:

> Business is an ordered system which selects and rewards according to well-understood criteria. The guiding principle is to get as near as possible to the top inside a corporation which is as near as possible to the top among corporations. Hence the

need for maximum profits. Hence the need to devote profits once acquired to enhancing financial strength and speeding up growth. These things become the subjective aims and values of the business world because they are the objective requirements of the system. The character of the system determines the psychology of its members, not vice versa. (Baran and Sweezy, 1968, pp. 53–5)

Zeitlin disputes the view that outside control of corporations is no longer important. He argues that 'Baran and Sweezy's formulation tends to reify if not hypostatize "giant corporations", and to lead to a managerialist impression of a sort of "capitalism without capitalists".' He cites another Marxist managerialist, the British historian Eric Hobsbawm, who goes 'so far as to assert that "the real members of the ruling class today are not so much real persons as organisations"' (Zeitlin, 1989, p. 44) Zeitlin identifies Marxist managerialism with what he calls the 'interorganizational paradigm' which prevails in sociology and organisation theory (1989, pp. 44, 112).

According to Zeitlin, the 'interorganizational paradigm' portrays the large corporation as merely one form of organisation attempting to preserve its autonomous existence in an uncertain interorganisational environment composed of large corporations and other forms of organisation. Organisation theorists assume that all forms of large organisation inevitably succumb to the inexorable historical process of bureaucratisation, which effectively robs the capitalist class of its control over corporations. They believe that corporations, like other large bureaucratic organisations, are self-perpetuating and virtually invulnerable to outside interests. All forms of bureaucratic organisation are administered by propertyless managers (Zeitlin, 1989).

The radical, sectional, version of managerialism in organisation theory reflects Weber's disenchantment with bureaucracy. Thus Perrow (1991) sees society as increasingly subordinated to the need for bureaucratic organisations to perpetuate themselves. In a 'society of organisations' . . . 'the organization redefines the needs of citizens in organizationally convenient forms, including the convenience of easy control'. Perrow refers to the dominant organisations as 'large employing organizations', rather than capitalist corporations, thus playing down any specifically capitalist features. He alleges that these large employing organisations are creating 'a rationalized, controlled, surrogate society'. The organisation is becoming the major supplier of all the most important social functions, from sex therapy to funeral services, and the 'arbiter of their availability' (Perrow, 1991, pp. 753–4).

George Ritzer is more explicitly Weberian than is Perrow. Ritzer (1993) has written a popular reiteration of Weber's bureaucratisation thesis. Like most managerialists, Ritzer highlights the ability of private sector corporate bureaucracies to subordinate the market to their own requirements. He does this by describing the contemporary process of rationalisation as 'McDonaldization'. According to the 'McDonaldization' thesis, society is increasingly succumbing to the obsession with 'efficiency, calculability, predictability, and greater control through the replacement of human by nonhuman technology': this is symbolised by McDonalds' fast food. Echoing Weber's pessimism, Ritzer sees little chance of escape from what he calls 'the irrationality of rationality' in 'The Iron Cage of McDonaldization'.

Marxist managerialists, namely Baran and Sweezy, also see corporations as having the ability to control their product markets. Writing in the late 1960s, they castigated their Marxist contemporaries for failing to come to terms with the 'affluent society'. While they accept that the Great Depression of the 1930s 'accorded admirably' with the Marxian theory of capitalist crisis, the USA enjoyed two decades after the Second World War 'without the recurrence of severe depression' (1968, p. 17). Subsequently, of course, fundamentalist Marxists have taken Baran and Sweezy to task for failing to anticipate the onset of yet another capitalist crisis (Harman, 1984; Mandel, 1981, p. 34).

In Baran and Sweezy's view, once the economy is dominated by giant corporations, economic crises become avoidable, because those who manage the corporations 'look ahead and calculate with great care. It is their initiative that sets the economy in motion, their power that keeps it moving, their policies that get it into difficulties and crises'. By implication, because the relationship between corporations is one of 'reciprocity, which enjoins corespective behaviour as surely as competition does', it is unlikely that the big business community will allow crises to occur (1968, pp. 60, 62, 82). In Baran and Sweezy's opinion, if crises do occur, they are the outcome of mismanagement of the economy and a breakdown of corporate relations. They do not accept the view of Marxist fundamentalists (Harman, 1984, pp. 148–54), that crises are the inevitable consequence of capitalist accumulation.

According to Baran and Sweezy's model of the capitalist economy, there is a tendency for a surplus from production to increase. This surplus allows society room to manoeuvre to avoid economic crises (Desai, 1979, p. 114). However, the rising surplus needs to be absorbed. This is achieved by a massive expansion of 'the sales effort' and the creation of artificial consumer needs, as well as the growth of civilian and military government spending to ensure effective demand (Baran and Sweezy, 1968). Each of these measures obviously reflects a view that large bureaucratic organisations, be they public- or private-sector, are able to act in harmony with each other in order to subordinate society to their requirements. The problem with Baran and Sweezy's work is not merely that they admit to neglecting the labour process (1968, p. 22; Friedman, 1977, p. 29), but that their analysis of monopoly capitalism is essentially similar to a liberal critique of the market power of large corporations. This directs attention away from corporations' control over process of production (Semmler, 1982).

In relation to the labour process, the diversity of strategies pursued by management is generally interpreted as confirmation of the managerialist view, in line with the divergence thesis. For example, labour process theorists Littler and Salaman conclude 'that the linkage between the logic of capital accumulation and transformations of the labour process is an indirect and varying one' (1982, p. 257, 265). They imply that the internal dynamics of corporations override any external constraints from capitalist ownership interests and that the requirement to compete in product markets leaves room for alternative strategies to be pursued in the management of labour. Michael Burawoy, another leading labour process theorist, suggests that, as a result of the separation of ownership from control, variations between the labour process 'might appear not only between different fractions of capital but also within the firm itself' (1985, p. 46).

In line with Baran and Sweezy, the sectional managerialist view seems to be that management control over the labour process is not essential for profit-ability so long as corporate control over product markets can be achieved (Littler and Salaman, 1982, p. 257; Thompson, 1989, p. 231). Littler claims that it is not possible to locate a 'managerial logic' linking the market to the labour process, because 'the separation of ownership and control' makes any linkage between 'corporate and labour-management strategies' problematical (1990, p. 82). The implication of much labour process theory is that to the extent that corporations are relieved of the immediate pressures of external competition, corporate management is relieved of external constraints, such as those implied by the law of value. Therefore, management enjoys some leeway in its choice of strategies . If corporate managers choose strategies for managing labour which deskill and subordinate labour, they do so in order to reinforce their own position, and not because they are compelled to do so by the combined pressures to compete in product markets and to secure an adequate rate of profit for capitalist owners.

Burnham outlined the consequences of the managerial revolution for the labour process. These have been echoed by latterday labour process theorists, from Braverman (1974) onwards, as well as radical organisation theorists. Having secured power by their ability to exclude the capitalists from control over production, Burnham believed that corporate managers are unlikely to allow skill and understanding of production to be diffused throughout the workforce of their corporations:

> In comparison with the organization of industry in the period prior to modern mass-production, the individual tasks, with the notable exception of a comparatively small percentage, require relatively less skill and training on the part of the individual worker . . . it takes a couple of weeks to make a worker ready to take his full place on a production or assembly line. Even so-called skilled work today usually needs no more than a few months' training. But, conversely, at the same time today a small percentage of tasks requires very great training and skill . . . within the process of production, the gap, estimated both in amount of skill and training and in difference of type of function, between the average worker and those who are in charge, on

the technical side, of the process of production is far greater today than in the past. (1962, p. 79)

The sectional managerialists' position is exemplified by the following statement from Marglin:

> Acquisitive societies – precapitalist, capitalist or socialist – develop institutions whereby collectivities determine the rate of accumulation. In modern capitalist society the pre-eminent collectivity for accumulation is the corporation. It is an essential social function of the corporation that its hierarchy mediate between the individual producer (and shareholder) and the market proceeds of the corporation's product, assigning a portion of these proceeds to enlarging the means of production. (1976, p. 15).

Marglin's position seems to be that the existence of the modern corporation is best explained in terms of the corporate hierarchy's need to perpetuate itself.

The amorality of bureaucratisation is summarised by Robert Jackall, one of several pessimistic contemporary Weberians: 'Bureaucracy breaks apart the ownership of property from its control, social independence from occupation, substance from appearances, actions from responsibility, obligation from guilt, language from meaning, and notions of truth from reality' (Jackall, 1988). A few radical Weberians claim to reject 'Weber's fatalism about the relations between bureaucracy and industrial society' (Thompson and McHugh, 1990, p. 44), but on the whole the Weberian position can be characterised as pessimistic resignation to the inevitability of bureaucratisation. The classic statement of Weberian-type pessimism remains Robert Michels' *Political Parties*. Michels formulated the 'Iron Law of Oligarchy', according to which: 'It is organization which gives birth to the dominion of the elected over the electors, of the mandatories over the mandators, of the delegates over the delegators', and by extension, managers over owners. Michels declared: 'Who says organization says oligarchy' (1962, p. 365).

From this pessimistic viewpoint, any radical social movements which challenge capitalist corporations are themselves likely to succumb sooner or later to rationalisation. As these social movements become better organised in order to deal with corporations they are compelled to develop bureaucracies of their own. The bureaucracies are inevitably run by career-orientated bureaucrats, who come to see the organisation's purpose as being synonymous with preserving a role for themselves. This amounts to organisational fetishism, whereby all bureaucratic organisations exist primarily to perpetuate themselves and provide careers for bureaucrats rather than to meet any genuine human need. The only way to challenge, or at least to live with, bureaucratic organisations is to develop ways of producing and consuming, such as co-operatives and small businesses, that are less likely to become bureaucratised.

Conclusion

There are significant similarities and differences between the various positions on managerialism set out in this chapter. In the first place, managerialism is seen as a threat by both mainstream organisational economists, representing non-sectional anti-managerialism, and sectional anti-managerialists, represented by Marxist economists. For the Marxists, managerialism threatens to undermine the justification for the revolutionary overthrow of capitalism, since it suggests that strategies pursued by workers and other groups in society that fall far short of the abolition of capitalist property rights are sufficient to deflect corporate managers from profit-maximising strategies. Similarly, by diluting the imperative for profit maximisation and granting significant discretion to corporate management, managerialist theories weaken the neoclassical argument that, because profit maximisation can be equated with efficiency, private business should not be interfered with, except for instances where inefficient monopoly persists. Thus, although Marxists and mainstream organisational economists are sharply divided as to the legitimacy of the capitalist firm, there is scope for cross-fertilisation in so far as they are both concerned to establish that what they are opposing or defending is the capitalist corporation, not diffuse management-controlled bureaucratic organisations.

Although Weber's concept of bureaucracy as an ideal type has come under criticism for its reification of bureaucracy (Clegg and Dunkerley, 1980, ch. 4), Weber's theory of bureaucracy remains the usual starting point for organisation theory. Following Weber, mainstream organisation theorists have played down the importance of the constraints on bureaucratic organisations from property rights institutions personified by external ownership interests. Instead, they have examined the facilities that diverse forms of organisation have for responding to the pressures from multifarious external and internal constituencies. It follows that the best way to alter the behaviour of organisations, or to make organisations more efficient or responsive, is not by abolishing or amending the institutional arrangements within which firms operate, as is advocated, respectively, by Marxist political economy and mainstream organisational economics. Instead, the strategies pursued by managers within bureaucratic organisations can be changed by influencing their perceptions and priorities.

Some of the issues that separate the various positions on managerialism can be thought of in terms of the concept of corporate culture. Both the non-sectional and sectional anti-managerialist camps have largely neglected 'the existence and nature of organizational culture', meaning the 'normative framework within which the . . . processes of decision-making take place' (Nichols, 1969, pp. 95–6). In contrast, the concept of corporate culture has proved to be immensely popular in business schools, where it is used by mainstream organisation theory to celebrate the extent of cultural diversity within and between corporations. Radical organisation theorists would allege that this celebration of diversity is dissimulatory to the extent that it obscures the relative cultural conformity that has been highlighted throughout the twentieth century by authors such as William Whyte, in *The Organization Man* (1960). If anything, there is an overarching culture of bureaucracy in almost all large organisations which worships efficiency and productivity, science and technology (Alvesson, 1987, 1993). In essence the culture of bureaucracy elevates rational means above human ends.

Finally, there is a similarity between non-sectional anti-managerialist, non-sectional managerialist, and sectional managerialist perspectives in that all three perspectives 'deny the potential importance of capitalist control of corporations through share-ownership' (Pitelis, 1987, pp. 34, 113 n. 3). Non-sectional anti-managerialists, such as most organisational economists, deny the existence or significance of organised collectivities pursuing sectional class interests in relation to the capitalist firm. For example, it is very briefly and only in passing that Williamson acknowledges that the insularity of bureaucracies might give rise to internal oligarchies (1983a, p. 127; 1985, p. 264), and this is as much as anything in order to demonstrate that the issue is almost completely ignored in the agency literature (1993a, p. 108). While both non-sectional and sectional managerialists acknowledge the importance of intra- and inter-organisational coalitions between the officials in bureaucracies, such as the dominant coalitions of managers in corporations, the non-sectional managerialists are more likely to believe that the influence of such coalitions is offset by what Galbraith (1952) called the 'countervailing power' of other bureaucracies. By and large it is only sectional anti-managerialists, mainly Marxists, who assert that corporations are subject to decisive pressure from extra-organisational sectional interests, namely the capitalist ruling class.

CHAPTER 8

Development of the modern corporation

Introduction

The debates about the significance of the corporation in contemporary societies have often taken place without sufficient reference to historical and comparative studies of the emergence and development of the corporation. In part, this is a result of the view that the modern corporation is merely a contemporary manifestation of bureaucratic tendencies. Weber (1991, p. 204) saw the 'large modern capitalist enterprise' as simply a purer form of the bureaucratic ideal type found at various times and places in history since ancient Egypt. Galbraith (1987, p. 42) has portrayed organisations such as the British East India Company, which lasted from 1600 to 1874, as antecedents of the modern multinational corporation. Business historians, notably Chandler and Daems, have dismissed much of the literature on the modern corporation, typified by Galbraith's *The New Industrial State*, as 'factless theorizing' (1980). Chandler (1962, 1977, 1990), along with other business historians such as his colleague, Lazonick (1992), have produced detailed histories dealing with the rise of the modern corporation. Their studies draw upon both survey and case study research based on internal company documents.

Three historical developments have generated the most interest. First, the transformation of the American economy that occurred with the rise of the corporation. This is the subject of Alfred Chandler's monumental study, *The Visible Hand*, which identifies the relevant period as the 1840s to the 1920s (1977, p. 5). Second, the development and diffusion of what is known as multidivisional structure within corporations, starting in the USA. Again, the most important study is by Chandler, in his earlier book *Strategy and Structure* (1962). Finally, the increasing significance in the world economy of the multinational corporations based in industrialised countries has generated a literature in its own right.

196

Origins of the modern corporation

It is well worth giving a summary of some of the major points in *The Visible Hand* (1977) as a starting point for looking at the rise of the corporation. Chandler reckons that the 'fundamental changes in the organization of American business enterprise and of the economy came before World War I', and 'the managerial revolution in American business' was complete by the middle of the twentieth century, which is when his story ends. His story begins in the 1840s, at a time when the American economy bore a reasonable resemblance to the market economy described by Adam Smith, with most economic activity being co-ordinated by the invisible hand of the market. In this context, Chandler allows that 'owners managed, and managers owned their enterprises'.

While conceding that the first large factories developed in cotton textiles, Chandler (1977) maintains that the textile industry was not particularly significant in 'the development of modern industrial management'. This is because, although the textile factories had to deal with the novel problems of managing waged labour, they did not centralise the basic management functions of marketing, production, finance and purchasing in one enterprise. Hence, Chandler's account is at odds with almost all 'discussion of the industrial revolution' in Great Britain, where, as Pollard (1968, p. 110) points out, the cotton industry is accorded a central part. Compared to Pollard's account of modern management in Britain, Chandler plays down the significance of the management of labour in relation to the development of modern management in the USA Chandler has been criticised for ignoring 'the importance of factory organization as means of disciplining workers', treating it as 'an external "given" for managers' (Du Boff and Herman, 1980).

It is in the American railways of the 1850s and 1860s where Chandler finds 'the first modern business enterprises' (1977, p. 81). The technology of the railways called for co-ordination in order to ensure, first safety, and then efficiency. Such 'unprecedented organizational efforts . . . led to the creation of a managerial hierarchy, whose duties were carefully defined in organizational manuals and charts'. In order to deal with the constant flow of information, top and middle managers learned how to exercise 'control through statistics'. Thus it was on the railways that organisational innovations such as the line-and-staff concept, whereby managers with line authority are responsible for managing their operations according to standards set centrally by staff executives, originated. Accounting, legal and financial innovations followed, and these enabled the railway enterprises to manage the vast funds which were needed for investment.

The managers employed in the railway companies came to regard their work as a career, and much more so than, say, the agents who managed the textile mills on behalf of their owners. In Chandler's (1977) view, the railway managers constituted the first 'administrative bureaucracy', and as such they 'began to take control of their own destinies'. In time, these managers had to learn to share the 'most critical decisions' with investment bankers in order to get access to sufficient capital to finance the growth of the railway enterprises. As a consequence of periodic bouts of intense competition it became apparent that the managers' 'organizations remained intact', even after bankruptcy, when only one or two senior managers would be removed. Although Chandler himself is a managerialist, his historical account could well support the anti-managerialist argument that, far from usurping the shareholders, it was the original owner-managers who accepted the possibility of a dilution of their control in order to have access to additional capital. They expected to continue to control their companies so long as they managed well, with only limited interference from shareholders, in extreme circumstances (Hessen, 1983, p. 288).

Chandler (1977) charts a haphazard process of diffusion by which the organisational innovations from the railways spread throughout other transportation and communication enterprises. The infrastructure resulting from this process opened up markets and facilitated the development of mass distribution, followed by mass production. This, in turn, fuelled the growth of managerial enterprises in other industries. In Chandler's (1988, p. 298) view, his account of the rise of the corporation somewhat undermines the econometricians' debate about the importance of the railways for economic growth in the USA during the nineteenth century. The debate was sparked off by Robert Fogel's book, *Railroads in American Growth* (1964), a milestone in the use of econometrics in the new economic history. Fogel's argument is neatly summarised by his fellow econometrician, McCloskey (1990, p. 91; 1986, p. 117).

What Fogel does is to imagine what would have happened if there had not been railways; it is a classic counterfactual analysis. He supposes that roads and canals would simply have been better, and production would have been located nearer to consumption. On this basis, Fogel attributes to the railways a mere 5 per cent of US national income in 1890, equivalent to only two years of economic growth. If it is accepted that the 'greatest invention of the nineteenth century accounted for only a small part of economic growth, at most' (McCloskey, 1990, p. 92), this tends to undermine technological determinism, which views individual technological innovations as all-important for explaining economic development. Instead, Fogel's analysis focuses attention towards the institutional prerequisites for economic growth. McCloskey concedes that Fogel's counterfactual argument is susceptible because: 'If Fogel had developed a theory of invention to draw a less vague picture of road transport he would have faced the problem that the very theory would have predicted the invention of the railroad' (1990, p. 94). It would have to: since railways were invented, their invention would have to be explained by a theory of invention. Chandler (1988, p. 298) takes a different and opposing tack from Fogel's. Instead of positing a theory of invention, Chandler maintains that the importance of the railways was in fostering organisational developments as much, if not more than, in facilitating economic growth through transportation.

Although Chandler has been criticised (Du Boff and Herman, 1980; Piore and Sabel, 1984, p. 26) for obscuring the historical choices that were made in relation to technology and organisation, *The Visible Hand* remains the classic starting point for studying the modern corporation. Chandler's critics (Du Boff and Herman, 1980, p. 109) acknowledge that the significance of Chandler's contribution to business history is that he focuses on the *'process* of structural transformation in business enterprise'. In relation to the emergence of the corporation Chandler (1977) emphasises how the sophisticated systems and autonomous subsystems by which the vast railway enterprises were administered did not come about through a blind 'evolutionary process'. In each case, the organisational innovations were conscious responses to new managerial challenges, and, as often as not, Chandler claims, a named individual can be credited with an innovation such as a new form of organisational structure.

The multidivisional structure

In Williamson's (1985, p. 279) opinion, the 'most significant organizational innovation of the twentieth century' was the development of the multidivisional structure by American companies in the 1920s. However, the importance of the multidivisional structure, otherwise known as a decentralised structure, the M-form (Williamson, 1986b, p. 69), or the multidivisional form (MDF) (Fligstein, 1985), was not widely recognised until the 1960s when Alfred Chandler analysed its development. Before then, according to Chandler, most management texts were more concerned with 'the management of the individual field unit rather than the larger enterprise' (1962, p. 284). In so far as it was noticed at all, the M-form was identified with decentralisation at General Motors (Sloan, 1986 [1963]). Chandler's *Strategy and Structure* (1962), was a 'pathbreaking study' which came out of business history and 'simply by-passed' the existing literature on management and organisations (Williamson, 1985, p. 279).

According to Chandler's (1962, pp. 13–14) strategy-structure thesis, different structures arise as a result of the different strategies of growth pursued by companies. In the first place, he distinguishes between strategy, which is the 'planning and carrying out' of growth and structure, that 'the organization devised to administer these enlarged activities and resources'. Chandler identifies four steps through which the multidivisional structure emerged: first, expansion by volume gives rise to an administrative office for one function in one local area; second, following geographical dispersion a departmental structure and headquarters are created to administer the local field units; third, vertical integration of different types of function requires a central office and multidepartmental structure (for the functional structure, see Figure 8.1); and finally, diversification, where the development of new products and growth on a national and international scale leads to the 'formation of the multidivisional structure with a general office to administer the different divisions.' (1962, p. 14)

Chandler gives an outline of the multidivisional or 'decentralized' structure (see Figure 8.2):

> At the top is a *general office*. There, general executives and staff specialists coordinate, appraise, and plan goals and policies for a number of quasi-autonomous, fairly self-contained divisions. Each division handles a major product line or carries on the firm's activities in one large geographical area. Each division's *central office*, in turn, administers a number of departments. Each of these departments is responsible for the administration of a major function – manufacturing, selling, purchasing or producing raw materials, engineering, research, finance, and the like. The *departmental headquarters* in its turn coordinates, appraises, and plans for a number of field units. At the lowest level, each *field unit* runs a plant or works, a branch or district sales office, a purchasing office, an engineering or research laboratory, an accounting or other financial office, and the like. (1962, p. 9)

From a preliminary survey of fifty of the largest American industrial enterprises Chandler (1962, pp. 3, 284) demonstrated how widespread the multidvisional structure had become, and identified which companies were its innovators. He selected four companies for further in-depth research: E. I. du Pont de Nemours & Co.; General Motors Corporation (both of these companies began to reorganise soon after the First World War); Standard Oil Company (New Jersey) (which started its reorganisation in 1925); and

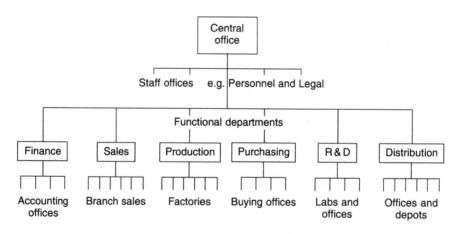

Source: Adapted from Chandler, 1990.

FIGURE 8.1   The functional structure

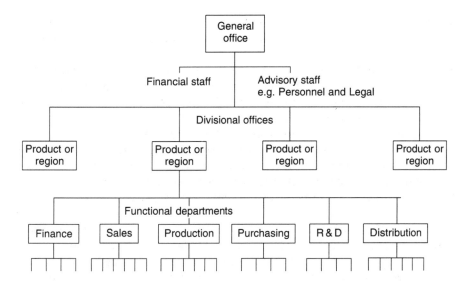

Source: Adapted from Chandler, 1990.

FIGURE 8.2   The multidivisional structure

Sears, Roebuck and Company (which reorganised in 1929). For each of these four companies Chandler was confident that the adoption of the multidivisional structure represented a 'creative innovation' in the sense intended by Schumpeter's use of the term. That is, they 'were making a creative response to new needs and new conditions' that 'went beyond existing practices and procedures'. The executives of the four firms 'began to develop their new structure independently of each other and of any other firm. There was no imitation. Each thought its problems were unique and its solutions genuine innovations. . . . In time the innovations became models for similar changes in many American corporations'. The subsequent diffusion of the multidivisional structure represented 'an adaptive response', which involved major changes for the firms making the response, but which 'stayed within the range of current custom' (Chandler, 1962, p. 284).

Chandler charts two routes to diversification and divisionalisation: through the internal generation of new products within one firm; or through two or more firms joining together by merger, acquisition or federation. The first route would tend to result in a centralised, multifunction firm trying to manage several product lines, while the second route would result in a decentralised but uncoordinated holding company. Chandler's case studies of Du Pont and General Motors are exemplify the two routes. Du Pont was a diversified but centralised company which needed to decentralise by creating autonomous divisions, whereas General Motors was composed of autonomous divisions which required the creation of a centralised general office to provided co-ordination.

Du Pont's growth up to the First World War was based on the manufacture of explosives. Even before the war the company's executives, who were all members of the du Pont family, were concerned about relying too heavily on one product. After the war, when government orders for explosives declined, the company began to diversify to ensure throughput for its plants and to use its expertise in the chemicals industry. Problems began to develop and the first response, in 1919, was to put in place a 'carefully worked-out centralized, functionally departmentalized structure', but this only exacerbated the company's difficulties. Du Pont was losing money on products where other firms were making money.

There was disagreement within du Pont over the cause of its difficulties. Some members of the company were convinced that the problem was in organisation, but others believed that there was a fault in a particular function, namely selling, or that the centralised structure would work if there were more accurate statistics. By the first half of 1921 the company had made a net loss of $2.5 million, suffering losses in all parts of the company except explosives: diversification seemed to be bringing only difficulties and deficits. Finally, in September 1921, a new structure was put into effect. This was the first multidivisional structure in an industrial enterprise. It consisted of five separate, autonomous, multidepartmental product divisions and, 'a general office with staff specialists and general executives. Each division had its own functional departments and its own central office to administer the several departments' (Chandler, 1962, p. 111).

The multidivisional structure served the company well: 'Losses were soon converted into profits and never again – not even in the middle of the depression of the 1930's – did the company face a crisis as severe as that of 1921' (Chandler, 1962, p. 112). Chandler's explanation for its success is that once the senior executives in the general office were no longer bothered by 'operating duties', they then 'had the time, information, and more of a psychological commitment to carry on the entrepreneurial activities and make the strategic decisions necessary to keep the over-all enterprise alive and growing and to coordinate, appraise, and plan for the work of the divisions' (1962, p. 111–12).

In contrast to du Pont, the founder of General Motors, William C. Durant, expanded the company by acquiring control of other automobile manufacturers and parts suppliers after his initial success at Buick. By 1920, however, General Motors was facing bankruptcy. In the loosely-federated structure the divisions had absorbed vast funds for investment, and when the automobile market collapsed later in the year it was difficult to find enough cash to just cover the payroll. The plan for reorganisation that was to save the company was introduced by Alfred P. Sloan, Jr, the head of one of the parts suppliers that Durant had bought out in 1916. A general office was created with an executive committee. The 'strong and independent managers' from the divisions were removed from the overall direction of the company. This allowed General Motors to be transformed from a federation of firms into a 'single integrated enterprise'. With uniform accounting and statistical methods, and inter-divisional billing, it was possible for the general office to assess the performance of the divisions in terms of return on investment. Chandler distils the alternative routes which led the two companies to the same divisional structure:

> At du Pont, it was the attempt to handle the company's various new product lines within the older centralized functionally departmentalized structure which caused the difficulties. At General Motors, the problem had been the integration and coordination of many almost completely independent operating divisions. (1962, p. 115)

The multidivisional structure adds an additional layer of bureaucracy to industrial enterprises. Divisionalisation is part of the process that resulted in hierarchies with six or more levels of management becoming widespread during the twentieth century (Chandler and Daems, 1980, p. 1; Child, 1984, p. 59). This point is sometimes obscured by organisation theorists, such as Clegg (1990, p. 80), who vainly see divisionalisation as an amelioration of bureaucracy. While divisionalisation represents decentralisation of operational decisions, defined by Chandler as *'tactical'*, dealing with the day-to-day activities necessary for efficient and smooth operations, there is clearly centralisation of what Chandler calls the *'strategic* decisions', which are 'concerned with the long-term health of the enterprise' (Chandler, 1962, p. 11).

Although the existence of an extra layer of bureaucracy appears at first sight to be wasteful, Chandler (1962, p. 16) believes that continued growth without such structural adjustment in companies leads to 'inefficiency'. The implied counterfactual is that if companies do not reorganise after growth (that is, if structure does not change in response to strategy) then market competition will either force companies out of business or compel them contract in size and reverse diversification. As Chandler is well aware, such decomposition of corporations does occur, and each division in a multidivisional company could undoubtedly operate independently as a separate company if the general office did not offer some advantage over independent competitors. Chandler's explanation for the success of the multidivisional structure is that:

> it clearly removed the executives responsible for the destiny of the entire enterprise from the more routine operational activities and so gave them the time, information, and even psychological commitment for long-term planning and appraisal. Conversely, it placed the responsibility and necessary authority for the operational administration in the hands of the general managers of the multifunction divisions. (1962, p. 309)

Chandler maintains that although the functional and multidivisional structures have 'developed many variations', and they have occasionally been mixed to form a matrix structure, they remain the 'only two basic organizational structures . . . for the management of large industrial enterprises. The 'centralized, functional departmentalized' structure 'has been used primarily by companies producing a single line of goods for one major product or regional market'. The 'multidivisional, decentralized structure' is found predominantly in companies 'manufacturing several lines for a number of product and regional markets' (1977, p. 463).

Williamson has elaborated a useful sixfold classification scheme for corporate structures (see Table 8.1) (1983a, pp. 151–4, 1985, pp. 279–94, 1986b, pp. 69–77). This typology is intended in part to guard against an 'overassignment' of companies to the M-form category. Companies which appear at first sight, or claim to be, multidivisional may not, in fact, be so if they either lack a strong co-ordinating general office, which means that they remain essentially holding companies, or they are only nominally divisionalised, 'with the general office maintaining extensive involvement in operating affairs', which means that they are still largely centralised (Williamson, 1983a, p. 151).

Williamson's explanation for the success of the M-form is that it operates as a 'miniature capital market' in which: 'Investment proposals from the divisions are solicited and evaluated by the general management. The usual criterion is the rate of return on invested capital' (1983, p. 147). The M-form gives the executives in the general office better access to information for making investment decisions than investors in the external capital market. They also have more expertise with which to assess that information. There is a crucial difference between the H-form and the M-form in their treatment of financial surpluses, or profits, earned by divisions:

> In the H-form, these tend to be retained for reinvestment at the discretion of divisional management. Capital investment under this system, therefore, tends to go with past success. In the M-form, however, divisional surpluses are pooled and reallocated among divisions by the general office on the basis of expected, future yield, after evaluation of competing divisional bids. (Cable, 1988, p. 16)

This means that the general office needs to be sufficiently distanced from the operating divisions so that the executives do not succumb to the subgoals of particular divisions at the expense of the enterprise as a whole.

It should be obvious that much of the contemporary writing on corporate strategy (Moore, 1992), especially in terms of portfolio planning, is predicated upon the existence of the M-form. Chandler notes (1962, n. 1) that he 'did not have the opportunity to read Edith T. Penrose, *The Theory of the Growth of the Firm*' until after he had finished the manuscript for *Strategy and Structure*. This is unfortunate, since Penrose (1959, p. 175) realises that the M-form not only functions as an internal capital market, it also facilitates the market for

TABLE 8.1 Williamson's typology of corporate structures

1. **Unitary or Functional (U-form)**
   Traditionally organised, centralised, functionally departmentalised enterprise, appropriate in most small- to lower-middle-sized firms. (Du Pont before reorganisation.)

2. **Holding company (H-form)**
   Enterprise without internal control apparatus, divisions often affiliated with parent company through subsidiary relationship. (General Motors before reorganisation.)

3. **Multidivisional (M-form)**
   Divisionalised enterprise, separation of operating from strategic decision-making, internal control apparatus assembled and systematically employed.
   Two subcategories:
   D1 highly integrated M-form, essentially common final products.
   D2 diversified final products and services.

4. **Transitional multidivisional (M'-form)**
   M-form in process of adjustment, organisational learning involved, or newly acquired parts not yet brought into regular divisionalised relationship to parent enterprise

5. **Corrupted multidivisional (M̄-form)**
   Requisite control apparatus provided but general management has become extensively involved in operating affairs, appropriate distance relation missing, therefore M-form performance over long run cannot reliably be expected.

6. **Mixed (X-form)**
   Divisionalised but some divisions essentially holding company subsidiaries, others under close supervision of general management. Unlikely to continue indefinitely because rational structures should thrive in the long run, but aberrant cases will persist at any one time.

Source: Adapted from Williamson, 1986b.

corporate control in the external capital market. This is because self-contained divisions can be bought and sold with minimal disruption to the organisation as a whole.

According to Hoskisson *et al.*'s 1993 review of the literature on the M-form, among economists, there has been, at least until recently, general support for Williamson's 'M-form hypothesis', which postulates 'that firms with an M-form structure would outperform firms that operated with other organizational forms' (Hoskisson *et al.*, 1993, p. 270). Richard Rumelt's classic study of divisionalisation, *Strategy, Structure, and Economic Performance* (1974), consists of a statistical study of the 500 largest industrial firms in the USA listed annually by *Fortune* magazine over the period from 1949 to 1969. Rumelt concludes that 'Firms with product-division structures had rates of growth that, on average, were significantly higher than those of firms with other types of organizational structures' (1974, p. 152). Williamson's view is that, in the long term, 'rational structures should thrive, but aberrant cases will appear and occasionally persist' (1983a, p. 154). The prevalence of the M-form is therefore evidence of its superior efficiency. It has been successful because it 'permits the firm simultaneously to realize strategic responsiveness and operating efficiency and in the process internalize certain failures in the capital market with net beneficial consequences' (Williamson, 1986b, p. 54).

Williamson's evolutionary schema for corporate structures has come in for criticism on the grounds that, like his classification of forms of work organisation (discussed in Chapter 6), it violates the natural selection model of evolution. Neil Kay gives an account of the problem in the following passage:

> Williamson's description of the evolutionary process has the effects the wrong way round if he wishes to invoke natural selection. In natural selection it is the appearance of the superior form which causes problems for the inferior form, not problems in the inferior form stimulating the adoption of a superior form. Natural selection selects from *available* forms, not the set of all existing and potential forms. In natural selection, the form does not 'defeat itself', as Williamson suggests . . . it is competition form other forms that defeats it. In natural selection the relatively efficient win; if the U form has over-extended itself and run into problems of diseconomies of scale, a natural selection interpretation would identify limits to the size of firms, with smaller, more specialized firms competing successfully against larger ones, not organizational innovation. (1991, p. 146)

Kay seems to go too far in the passage just quoted, since he seems to imply that the set of available forms is fixed, which rules out organisational innovation. In evolutionary terms, there are two related problems with Williamson's account of the M-form. First, while he acknowledges that organisational innovation is important, he offers no analysis of the process by which it occurs. Second, he takes the environment as given, which overlooks the issue raised by Kay, that the environment changes with the appearance of new organisational forms. Chandler certainly gives an account of the process of organisational innovation. However, it is not clear whether he takes the environment as given to the extent that the emergence of the M-form in one company or another was more or less a foregone conclusion, or whether he believes that the adoption of the M-form itself by some companies created new environmental conditions for all companies. Chandler's strategy–structure thesis can be interpreted either way.

Chandler has certainly been misrepresented as being overly mechanistic, notably in the popular book by Peters and Waterman. For them Chandler captures the idea that 'a strategy of broad diversification *dictates* a structure marked by decentralization. Form follows function. . . . Get the strategic plan down on paper and the right organization structure will pop out with ease, grace and beauty' (Peters and Waterman, 1982, p. 4). While this might have been near to the truth for companies which embarked upon a strategy of diversification as late as the 1960s and 1970s, when they could call in management consultants to introduce a multidivisional structure almost immediately, nothing could be further from the truth for the innovators of the multidivisional structure back in the 1920s. The adoption of the new structure was no more automatic than the adoption of the strategy of diversification. Chandler makes it clear that there was delay, and structure 'was often slow to follow strategy, particularly in periods of rapid expansion' (1962, p. 16). However, at times, Chandler seems to suggest that the economic environment faced by companies was both given and ultimately deterministic:

> Although each company had a distinct and unique history, nearly all followed along this general pattern. Because all of them operated within the same external environment, these chapters in the collective history of the enterprise as an economic institution followed roughly the underlying changes in the over-all American economy. (1962, p. 385)

If this is Chandler's view, then much of the detailed description in *Strategy and Structure* would appear to be redundant, it would merely constitute anecdotal illustration of the M-form hypothesis.

In his defence, it should be said that Chandler focuses on the often painful 'process of innovation', as much as on 'the conditions calling for change'(1962, p. 299). Stinchcombe reckons that the 300-odd pages of history that Chandler devotes to tracing 'how and why the multidivisional structure was invented and adopted' makes his *Strategy and Structure* look 'like a case of a functional argument with individual-level explanations, which is not the same as a simple rational actor model at the individual level'. In other words, Stinchcombe believes that Chandler not only explains how the environment created opportunities and problems for individual actors, namely the executives in diversified companies, he also gives a convincing account of how those executives responded to their environment. According to Stinchcombe, Chandler's recognition of the need for this type of evidence is indicated by his inclusion of 'a large number of named individuals' (1990, p. 109). Chandler stresses that the construction of a new structure 'called for time, thought, and energy', so that 'executive experience and personality helped determine the course and rate of structural adaptation and innovation', which suggests a degree of path dependency. If path dependency were entirely absent there would be no place for Chandler's assertion that the study of a company's internal business documents and letters is necessary in order to 'reveal the details of structural reorganization' (1962, pp. 283, 380).

According to Chandler, the underlying reason why strategies changed, calling for changes in structure, was as a 'response to the opportunities and needs created by changing population and changing national income and by technological innovation.' Growth strategies were not determined mechanistically by changes in the economy; instead:

> the awareness of the needs and opportunities created by the changing environment seems to have depended on the training and personality of individual executives and on their ability to keep their eyes on the more important entrepreneurial problems even in the midst of pressing operational needs. (1962, p. 15)

Radical critics, such as Du Boff and Herman (1980), are not satisfied with what they see as Chandler's rather anodyne account of the success enjoyed by the companies which were the first to adopt the M-form. In a review of Chandler's work, they criticise his neglect of power. They argue that in Chandler's framework 'power seems to be an incidental consequence of the growth of large firms: it is thrust upon managers by technological advance, widening markets, and the drive for efficiency'. They allege that Chandler depicts managers as 'virtual pawns of technology', and this obscures the importance of managers' preference for technologies which enhance their own position. Taking General Motors, they argue that the adoption of the multidivisional structure is not sufficient to explain the company's success, 'General Motors' affluence has also been a consequence of its ability (and that of the industry as a whole) to externalize the social costs of automobilization'. The costs of pollution, increased speed without regard for safety, the 'neglect and decay of mass transport and central cities, and promotion of land-intensive suburbanization have all been absorbed by society at large, with only belated attention to the balance of costs and benefits. Externalization of this magnitude reflects sheer economic power' (Du Boff and Herman, 1980, p. 107). However, since Du Boff and Herman do not demonstrate the relationship between the exercise of this economic power and the adoption of the multidivisional structure, it is difficult to avoid the conclusion that in common with many other radicals and Marxists, they are largely indifferent to the internal structure of large capitalist corporations.

The M-form, and corporate structure in general, has received more detailed attention from the new institutionalists in organization theory, notably Neil Fligstein. In the first (1985) of a series of articles which culminated in his book, *The Transformation of Corporate Control* (1990), Fligstein traces the diffusion of the M-form among the hundred largest American firms by asset size between 1919 and 1979. He notes the extent of the take up of the M-form: 'In 1929 only 1.5 per cent of the firms had adopted the MDF, while by 1979 this had risen to 84.2 per cent'. However, rather than simply invoking natural selection and proclaiming the efficiency of the M-form, as most economists do, Fligstein analyses the processes whereby it was disseminated. From his data, Fligstein concludes 'that those in control of large firms acted to change their organizational structures under three conditions: when they were pursuing a multiproduct strategy; when their competitors shifted structures; and when they had a background in the organization such that their interests reflected those of the sales or finance departments' (1985, p. 388). The gist of Fligstein's argument is that the diffusion of the M-form was by no means determined by its superior efficiency, but rather that once it had emerged it became accepted as the appropriate response to crises within corporations, in part because it enhanced the influence of dominant sections within management, namely sales and finance (1990, pp. 275–7).

Whether or not the emergence and diffusion of the M-form confirms or refutes the managerialist thesis is an issue over which Chandler and Williamson, most notably, are at odds. Chandler seems to see the separation of ownership from control and the rise of the managerial enterprise, as charted in *The Visible Hand* (1977), as a precondition for the emergence of the M-form. This is because the founders of firms, the empire builders, were rarely responsible for the reorganization of their companies: they were too extrovert and were not interested in issues of organization and structure. The organization builders were more likely to be the professional managers who came after the founders. The professional managers were more reserved, studious types, with a narrower range of interests. They focused on business problems and were 'less involved in extracurricular activities' (Chandler, 1962, p. 316). They were more like contemporary professional administrators of corporations, in that they neither owned nor controlled large blocks of shares in the companies they managed, nor did they have family ties with large shareholders.

In contrast to Chandler, the economists, especially Williamson (1985) and Rumelt (1974), see the diffusion of the M-form as a refutation of the managerialist theses proposed by Berle and Means (1967) and Galbraith (1967). Williamson believes that the M-form effectively recreated the discipline of the external capital market within corporations so that they were able to grow, giving the appearance of increased managerial autonomy. Rumelt argues that huge corporations have not arisen as result of their ability to control product markets, but rather as a consequence of the M-form, from their ability to decide relatively quickly, compared to external investors, which product market, or even which industry, to invest in. While the M-form may ensure that the general office curbs managerial discretion at the divisional level, it is not clear that the general office is necessarily constrained to act in the best interests of shareholders (Stephen and Thompson, 1988, p. 180). Nor is it clear that the M-form has not simply allowed corporations to shift investments to product markets which are more easily controlled from those which are less easily controlled.

If Williamson and Rumelt's counters to the managerialist thesis are correct, and on the face of it they would appear to be, then this also provides a counter to the managerialist view that management pressure on the labour process is lessened because firms no longer compete through cheapening labour in order to compete in product markets (Knights and Willmott, 1990, pp. 13–15; Littler and Salaman, 1982, p. 257). Such a view assumes that corporations are unified entities, and that workers in monopolistic corporations automatically share in monopoly profits. Against this, seeing the corporation as an internal capital market allows for what could be called the decomposition of capital. This would mean that the M-form would ensure that, as must be obvious to all but the most optimistic managerialists, workers in, say, final assembly or design, do not necessarily benefit from advantages that their corporation enjoys in, say, accounting or distribution.

As yet, the implications of the M-form for the management of labour have not been widely explored. By his own admission, Chandler has consistently ignored the management of labour (1962, p. 284, 1990, p. 13; McCraw, 1988, p. 20). Several British authors (Gospel, 1992; Marginson *et al.*, 1988; Purcell and Ahlstrand, 1994) have started to consider the relationship between the adoption of the M-form and the management of labour. Paul Marginson (1988) in particular has argued that British companies adopted the M-form in the 1960s in order to regain control over labour. While the evidence is inconclusive as yet, what is surprising is that the connection between corporate strategies and structures, and the management of labour, have not been discussed at length before. Williamson in particular has analysed both the multidivisional structure and the employment relationship in terms of transaction costs (1980a, 1983d, 1985). However, he has not sought to make any connection between the two, even though it would seem obvious that additional layers of bureaucracy in corporate hierarchies might affect the 'atmosphere' of work organization.

Chandler's work on the origins of the corporation, managerial hierarchies, and the multidivisional structure, has spawned a comparative literature which assesses the importance of the development of the corporation and managerial hierarchies in various capitalist countries (Chandler and Daems, 1980; Daems and Van der Vee, 1974). For fairly obvious reasons, the countries that have generated most interest for comparisons with the USA are Britain, Germany, and Japan. Each has been associated with distinctive types of capitalism, and each, in turn, have been identified as the leading industrial economy in the world. Chandler's general thesis is set out at great length in *Scale and Scope* (1990), his comparative study of the hundred largest manufacturing companies in the USA, Britain and Germany from the end of the First World War to the beginning of the post-World War Two era. He distinguishes between the three countries in terms of the rate at which managerial hierarchies developed, their relations with owners, and relations between firms. He then characterises the USA as competitive managerial capitalism, the Great Britain as personal capitalism, and Germany as co-operative managerial capitalism. Chandler's view is that economic development in Great Britain was retarded in comparison with the USA because the families that owned firms in Britain failed to cede control to salaried managers as quickly as in the USA. This meant that firms were unable to acquire the organisational capabilities that ensue from the development of managerial hierarchies and the adoption of innovations such as the M-form.

The multinational corporation

There are vast, but largely separate, literatures dealing with the rise and significance of multinational corporations (MNC). It is a subject that has received considerable attention from organisational economists (Pitelis and Sugden, 1991), but much less from organisation theorists (Ghoshal and Westney, 1993, p. 1). Depending on the definition that is used, examples of multinational enterprises in Europe can be found as early as the 1780s, but they 'developed dramatically in the 1960s and 1970s' (Levy-Leboyer, 1989, p. 1). It was investment by US corporations in Europe from the 1950s onwards which precipitated debates about the nature of multinational corporations (Fieldhouse, 1989).

The labels used to describe multinational corporations reflect the various connotations attached to them from various perspectives (Pitelis and Sugden, 1991, p. 14). Sociologists tend to use the term 'transnational corporation' (TNC). This has negative connotations, in that for many commentators institutions that transcend the nation state are viewed with suspicion because they are seen as existing in order to suppress the democratic decisions of nation states. However, this is to pre-empt analysis, and in any case the term 'transnational' has recently acquired a more specific meaning, to refer to multidivisional companies that have divisional headquarters in separate countries and where those divisions have a global mandate. Economists (Buckley and Casson, 1992) often prefer the term 'multinational enterprise' (MNE), possibly because the word 'enterprise' has a more positive ring to it.

Sociologists in general have paid more attention to the MNC than have organisation theorists. However, dialogue between economics and sociology has been limited. In their review of the literature on MNCs, Bornschier and Stamm, economic sociologists, define MNCs, as 'decision-making centres owning income-generating assets in at least two countries' (1990, p. 203). They identify two main orientations to MNCs, 'neoconventional' and 'critical'; these can be taken to correspond to 'mainstream' and 'radical'. The neoconventional, or mainstream, approach encompasses most of the theories of MNCs that have developed from organisational economics and generally stress the economically positive side of MNCs. Bornschier and Stamm see the mainstream approach as emanating from business schools and MNCs themselves, in response to the extensive criticism of MNCs during the 1960s and 1970s. However, the emergence of economic theories of the MNC was just as a much a response to the perceived inadequacies of existing economic theories of international trade in relations to MNCs, which parallels the general critique of the economic theory of the firm and the emergence of organisational economics (discussed in Part 1).

A crucial difference between radical and mainstream theories of MNCs is that whereas mainstream economic theories have been developed specifically to explain the existence of MNCs, radical theories are generally part of a much wider analysis of the relative economic development and underdevelopment of interdependent nation states. A common feature of these radical theoretical perspectives is the notion, prevalent in sociology, that there is a 'core' and 'periphery' within labour markets, and that these are, in part, manifested in a core and periphery among nation states. There are unequal capitalist exchange relations between the developed national economies in the core, and the underdeveloped national economies in the periphery. Rejecting the view that less-developed national economies merely need to pass through various stages of development, radical theories emphasise that underdevelopment in the periphery is a necessary corollary of development in the core. This situation is constantly reproduced through a permanent dependency relationship between the periphery and the core. In pursuing strategies of development, the nations in the periphery are compelled to become dependent on the core economies, which then perpetuate underdevelopment in the periphery. MNCs are seen as one of the mediators of capitalist dependency relations which have replaced direct colonial domination.

Three broad hypotheses can be identified in the radical literature (Bornschier and Stamm, 1990). First, that the economic advantages of MNCs' direct investments in underdeveloped economies are unequally distributed between the MNCs and the host countries, so that the MNCs absorb the economic gains that might otherwise be reinvested in the host countries. Second, MNCs distort the host economies by displacing domestic production, utilising inappropriate technology and distorting consumer tastes. They are also held responsible for worsening income distribution. Finally, MNCs can pervert or undermine the political system in the host country. More recently, MNCs have been the focus of attention in relation to the so-called 'new international division of labour', whereby cheap migratory labour is no longer drawn into the core countries from the peripheral countries; instead capital migrates from the core to the periphery to find the cheapest and most pliant labour, and this is facilitated by the governments in host peripheral countries which undertake to subordinate labour on behalf of the MNCs and provide favourable conditions for investment for MNCs (Froebel *et al.*, 1981).

Because they are designed to explain underdevelopment rather than the existence of MNCs, radical theories do not address adequately the issue of foreign direct investment (FDI) by MNCs between countries in the core, even though this constitutes by far the largest part of FDI. The explanation radical theories would be most likely to proffer would be to differentiate the core countries internally into a core and periphery. This would fit with the current concern with so-called 'social dumping', where MNCs relocate between core countries to take advantage of cheaper labour and less restrictive labour regulations, such as the ability to hire and fire at will.

In the same way that neoclassical theories of international trade explain the existence and efficiency gains of trade between nations but do not specify the form that trade will take, so radical theories do not really specify why unequal capitalist exchange relations should take the form of FDI by MNCs. Essentially, the radical hostility to MNCs is based on their alleged distortion of market structure; that is, their exercise of monopolistic or oligopolistic market power through such devices as transfer pricing. This is similar to the liberal critique of large corporations. Marxian hostility to 'big capitals' and the 'rhetoric of opposition to giant corporations, multinational enterprises' has only rarely been criticised within the Marxian tradition, on the grounds that it directs attention away from exploitation in production and towards a view of big capital exploiting small capital, which obscures the possible 'progressive (for socialism) effects of concentration and centralization of capital' (Bryan, 1985). More recently, it has been argued not only that an integration of radical sociological and mainstream economic approaches to the MNC is long overdue (Bornschier and Stamm, 1990), but that since Marxism lacks a theory of MNCs, Marxists should look specifically to the 'neoliberal' critique of mainstream neoclassical economics developed by organisational economists following Coase in relation to the MNC (Pitelis, 1991).

As a response to the inadequacies of the theory of the firm in relation to the MNC, an economic theory of the MNC developed the 'application of the Coasian concept of internalization' to the MNC independently of Williamson's 'markets and hierarchies' perspective, according to Mark Casson, one of the leading proponents of the transaction costs, or internalisation approach to MNCs (Casson, 1987, p. 6). The 'internalization approach' to MNCs is derived from 'institutional economics and the theory of property rights' and poses the question: ' "Why are plants in different countries brought under common ownership and control?" The answer is "Because the transaction costs incurred in intermediate products markets can be reduced by internalizing these markets within the firm" '. The claim of the theory of transaction costs is to be able to 'explain why, in certain industries and at certain times, an MNE prevails and, in other industries and at other times, a cartel' (Casson, 1987, pp. 6–7).

Williamson's contribution stresses the significance of the M-form in explaining why portfolio investment has been superseded by FDI in certain industries (1985). Williamson argues that restraint of trade, through oligopoly, could be achieved by portfolio investment, which is supported by the evidence that MNCs are not equally prevalent in all oligopolistic industries. MNCs are of importance where there is a continual transfer of technology because of the problems of transferring technology across a market interface. There are problems, first of recognising an appropriate technology, second of disclosure of information concerning the technology, and finally of team organisation. Often, a 'consulting team' has to be organised by the seller of the technology in order to overcome start-up difficulties. Technology transfer is especially difficult across national boundaries. While FDI would be an extreme response for a one-off technology transfer, it is probably necessary where there is a continuous technology transfer. According to Williamson, this is the best explanation of why MNCs are concentrated in certain industries, including chemicals, drugs, automobiles, food processing, electronics, electrical and non-electrical machinery, non-ferrous metals and rubber, whereas there is little FDI in other industries such as tobacco, textiles and apparel, furniture, glass, steel and aircraft. The M-form enables firms to manage foreign subsidiaries as semi-autonomous operating units. Since US firms adopted the M-form ahead of firms in other countries, this explains why US firms were among the first MNCs.

While advocating that Marxists look to Coasian internalisation theory for a theory of the MNC, Pitelis (1991) argues that neither radical nor mainstream approaches to the MNC have much to say about the relationship between MNCs and the nation state. There is a general view that the importance and influence of the nation state is in decline in relation the MNC, and that MNCs 'are the most powerful agents involved in contemporary economic restructuring' (Whitaker, 1992, p. 198). Pitelis makes three points which would suggest that even if there is such a tendency there are limits to the extent to which the nation state will be eclipsed by the MNC. First, MNCs have been able to increase their power over labour and the nation state because of the relative flexibility of their operations. This suggests that MNCs *need* a system of nation states and national labour in order to be able to exploit this advantage. Thus, although there is an integrated world economy, the decentralised social and political structure of the world economy gives rise to MNCs (Bornschier and Stamm, 1990), or rather, there are alternative forms of decentralisation. Paradoxically, this suggests that strengthening the nation state at the expense of international economic institutions gives rise to the possibility of MNCs. Pitelis's (1991) second point is that public choice theory derived from institutional economics can be used to explain why state officials, politicians and bureaucrats are unlikely to surrender their special interests voluntarily to international bodies.

Pitelis's third point concerns the role of labour. The achievements of political parties supported by labour movements in areas such as welfare benefits tend to be country-specific. Labour movements are therefore likely to support the nation state, and for electoral reasons governments will be affected by this. Pitelis suggests that the way forward for labour movements is to try to restrict the mobility of MNCs and to increase their commitment to labour in host countries. He argues that MNCs have an interest in nation states, and that nation states have an interest in ' "*their*" transnational capital'. MNCs promote growth and investment, and the rivalry between nation states takes the form of rivalry between 'their' MNCs. The success of a nation's MNCs affects its ability to share in the benefits of 'transnationalization' through taxation of repatriated profits. In fact, Pitelis does not go far enough in explaining the radicals' rhetoric of hostility towards MNCs. For many radical critics of MNCs, the underlying suspicion is probably that transnationalisation by MNCs is primarily a means to frustrate their preferred strategy of nationalisation. For labour movements, the alternatives would appear to be between lining up with the nation state, which would involve strengthening the position of state officials and politicians, reversing transnationalisation in favour of nationalisation in some sense and sacrificing any progressive gains made by MNCs, or developing strategies of internationalisation in labour movements to counter the specifically capitalist logic of MNCs.

Conclusion

It is clear from an examination of the major developments of the corporation that in large sectors of most modern capitalist economies, corporations that are managed by extensive hierarchies, organised along the lines of the M-form and often operating in two or more countries, enjoys relative efficiency in comparison with smaller units co-ordinated through the market. Most organisational economists and organisation theorists would probably agree with John Cable's assessment that 'it can safely be said that, though not all M-form adoptions have been entirely successful, the M-form has often been a triumph in business efficiency terms'. However, the mainstream organisational economists would probably prefer to skip over his proviso that the effects of the M-form in terms of broader economic efficiency 'have yet to be established beyond reasonable doubt' (1988, pp. 35–6).

In relation to labour, radical organisation theorists, sociologists and economists have emphasised the way in which corporations suppress institutions which favour labour. However, they have not examined how this might have been done in relation to specific corporate organisational structures. On the other hand, mainstream organisational economists and business historians have examined corporate organisational structures extensively, but they have largely ignored the role of labour. There is clearly a need to integrate studies of the management of labour and the analysis of corporate structures.

It would seem likely that both the M-form and the MNC have allowed corporations to become increasingly disembedded from their institutional environment so that they are able to select institutional settings which favour their own relative efficiency. The challenge posed by the multinational, divisional corporation is that increasingly detailed empirical research and sophisticated theoretical analysis is called for in order to refute the managerialist thesis that the corporation has taken on a life of its own largely unconstrained by the interests of shareholders, not to mention labour and consumers, or even nation states.

CHAPTER 9

Conclusion

Perspectives

There is tension between organisational economics and organisation theory. While economists may think it is a 'healthy' tension (Williamson, 1995, p. 207), sociologists and organisation theorists are wary. The organisational economists might believe they have entered into a joint venture with organisation theory, but organisation theorists fear that the study of organisations is being hijacked by economists. The first part of this conclusion draws together the themes from the discussions of work organisation, and ownership and control. A framework is set out so as to facilitate dialogue by locating organisation theorists and organisational economists in relation to each other. The second and third parts identify further obstacles to debate, and suggest ways to overcome them.

Four fairly coherent perspectives in relation to the capitalist firm emerge from the discussion in Part 3 of the book (see Figure 9.1). These are divided along two dimensions. On the mainstream side there are efficiency and strategic choice perspectives, as opposed to the radical side, where exploitation and power perspectives are located. The other dimension is more difficult to define, but corresponds to the degree of emphasis on organisations or institutions. Efficiency and exploitation perspectives focus on the institutional constraints on organisations, while the autonomy of organisations is stressed by strategic choice and power perspectives. Now each perspective can be dealt with in turn.

First, there is an efficiency perspective, which includes most mainstream organisational economists. Within this perspective there are those theorists, such as Williamson (1985), who would characterise the capitalist firm as the culmination of efforts to economise on transaction costs that arise from universal features of the institutional environment, notably the bounded rationality and opportunism of human actors. This constitutes a relatively naïve and optimistic form of functionalism. On the other hand, there are

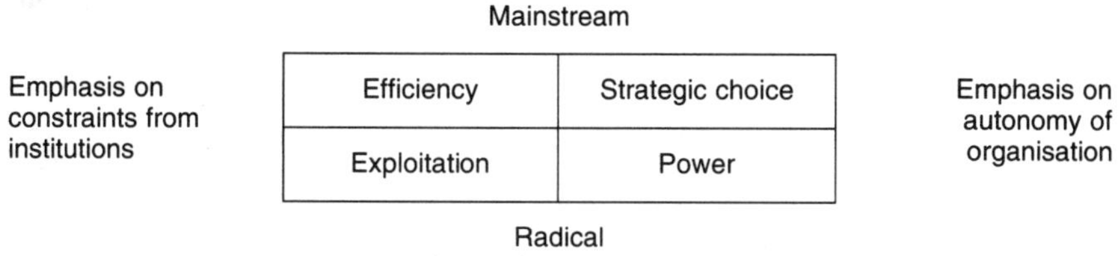

Mainstream

Emphasis on constraints from institutions	Efficiency	Strategic choice	Emphasis on autonomy of organisation
	Exploitation	Power	

Radical

FIGURE 9.1   Perspectives on the capitalist firm

theorists such as North (1990a) who do not argue that existing forms of organisation are by definition functional. North endorses the relative efficiency of capitalist firms because he is favourably disposed towards the institutional framework of liberal democratic capitalism which gives rise to capitalist firms. He believes that the institutions of capitalism encourage experimentation and economic growth through competition in both political and economic markets and effective enforcement of agreements.

Divisions of labour and hierarchy are defended from an efficiency perspective on the grounds that they are universal and essential features of work organisation, hierarchy being the only feasible alternative to co-ordination by the market. While it is predicted that hierarchy would arise even in workers' co-operatives, the employment relationship in capitalist firms is seen as the best means of securing output. The extent of the separation of ownership from control of corporations is disputed, but to the extent that there has been such a separation its existence is explained in terms of a benign functional split between investment and management, which is found in one form or another in most large organisations. This position is characterised as non-sectional anti-managerialism.

The second perspective is strategic choice, which is preferred by many mainstream organisation theorists. According to this perspective, the extent of divisions of labour and hierarchy could be ameliorated in most organisations, and there is a risk that the defence mounted by the efficiency perspective will obscure the scope for improvement. The separation of ownership from control is more or less taken as given. The managers of corporations, in common with those who have positions in the hierarchy of all bureaucratic organisations, are seen as being sufficiently free from interference by shareholders and other outside interests to be able to pursue benign, socially responsible objectives. This constitutes a non-sectional managerialist position.

A third perspective is that the existence of capitalist corporations is largely explained by the exploitation of workers. From this perspective, which corresponds mainly to a Marxist view, it is accepted that divisions of labour and hierarchy are efficient, and also that they could be ameliorated, but that they take a particular, and pathological, form which is constrained to reproduce inequalities and to preserve the privileged position of a capitalist class. As with the efficiency perspective, the extent of the separation of ownership from control is disputed. It is maintained that corporations are not only constrained by competition in markets, but also remain subject to control by an externally coordinated sectional interest, namely the capitalist class. This view can be characterised as sectional anti-managerialism.

Finally, there is the power perspective, which is advocated by radical political economists and organisation theorists. From this viewpoint, acceptance that divisions of labour and hierarchy are efficient almost inevitably results in a defence of a particular form of hierarchy. Instead, it is argued that divisions of labour and hierarchy mainly arise and are retained in order to provide privileged positions for bosses to fill. It is accepted that there has been a separation of ownership from control, and that the managers of large corporations, in common with the bureaucrats in all large organisations, are free to pursue their own sectional interests. Thus they constitute a self-perpetuating oligarchy. This positions corresponds to sectional managerialism.

The relationship between the four perspectives can be illustrated by using the team game analogy (Chapter 5) to discuss divisions of labour and hierarchy (Chapter 6). The efficiency view is that teams which have clearly defined roles and a hierarchy, analogous to capitalist firms, are more effective. They will almost always win, no matter what the rules of the game are. The power perspective takes a completely different view: that certain players, analogous to capitalist bosses, have rigged the rules of the game so that tightly organised teams with rigid hierarchies will win in order to ensure a superior position for themselves. If the rules were different, then teams that were organised along more egalitarian lines would stand more chance of success. The strategic choice view would be that the dispute between efficiency and power perspectives obscures the extent to which teams with more loosely defined roles and a less rigid hierarchy might succeed, even with the existing rules of the game. The exploitation perspective takes the view that some definition of roles and a degree of hierarchy will always be necessary, but that the existing rules ensure the perpetuation of an enormous and unnecessary difference in the rewards received by players in different positions in the teams.

These four perspectives are by no means intended as watertight categories, and they do not correspond to discrete schools of thought. So, for example, although strategic choice is strongly associated with John Child (1972), it is a strength rather than a weakness that his strategic choice thesis is seen as 'an eclectic combination' (Donaldson, 1985, p. 136). The limitations of this fourfold categorisation are readily admitted. It is not meant to be applicable to the whole of social theory, but is offered as a starting point for organisation theorists and organisational economists to explore their similarities and differences.

Paradigms

The idea of a fourfold categorisation of theories will be familiar to organisation theorists who, unlike most economists, often locate their own positions by providing a 'road map of social theory and organization studies' (Morgan, cited in Marsden, 1993, p. 99). Depending on their perspective, each theorist draws different boundaries within and around organisation theory. It is generally accepted that there is enormous diversity in organisation theory. Since the 1960s it 'has become much more pluralistic – some might even say anarchistic' (Reed, 1992a p. 1). Whether organisation theorists like it or not, they generally recognise that it is 'no longer fashionable' to present the development of organisation theory as an evolutionary progression 'towards a more theoretically advanced and empirically inclusive explanatory framework' (Reed, 1992b, p. 37).

One of the most influential 'road maps' in organisation theory is Gibson Burrell and Gareth Morgan's (1979) fourfold classification of sociological paradigms. Burrell and Morgan allocate one paradigm to each of four quadrants divided by two axes (see Figure 9.2). The four paradigms are: functionalist; interpretive; radical structuralist; and radical humanist. The radical humanist and radical structuralist paradigms are part of the sociology of radical change in that they stress conflict and its potential to transform society, rather than the order and stability which is taken as given by the interpretive and functionalist paradigms that are part of the sociology of regulation. On the other hand, the radical humanist and interpretive paradigms emphasise actors' subjective realm in explaining social action, whereas the radical structuralist and functionalist paradigms stress the role of societal constraints. From an examination of the assumptions underpinning theoretical statements Burrell and Morgan assign various theoretical positions to one of their four paradigms.

According to Burrell and Morgan: 'most organisation theorists, industrial sociologists, psychologists and industrial relations theorists approach their subject from within the bounds of the functionalist paradigm' (1979, p. 28).

fig ᴸ

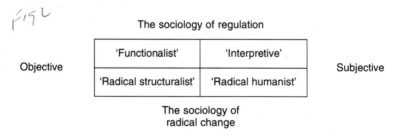

The sociology of regulation

'Functionalist'	'Interpretive'
'Radical structuralist'	'Radical humanist'

Objective   Subjective

The sociology of
radical change

Source: Adapted from Burrell and Morgan, 1979, p. 22.

FIGURE 9.2   Sociological paradigms

Opponents of functionalist organisation theory have offered two explanations for this. First, the study of organisation theory and organisational behaviour is a mainstay of business school programmes. As aspiring managers in large corporations, the students on such programmes are unlikely to be receptive to the questions raised by paradigms other than functionalism. Second, and of more significance here, the concept of organisation is problematic in all but the functionalist paradigm where it originated. As Burrell and Morgan point out, the radical humanists' approach would be more of an 'anti-organisation theory'.

From the radical structuralist paradigm there have been attempts to construct a Marxian alternative to mainstream organisation theory. This is problematic, since the term 'organisation' is an unfamiliar one within Marxism. Donaldson argues that, since Marxism is a theory of society, 'it can be called a theory of organization only by stretching the use of that phrase beyond the point where it retains any utility' (1985, p. 128). Marxists and radical organisation theorists take issue with the sharp distinction between organisation and society that is prevalent in functionalism. They argue that organisations cannot be studied outside their societal context. Their objection to functionalist definitions of organisations 'in terms of families arranging picnics' is that it deflects 'attention from the fact that organization theory is active in business and the predominant form in which business is organized is the corporation' (Marsden, 1993, p. 103). In other words, the suggestion that there can be a generic concept of organisation obscures the specificity of the capitalist corporation (Thompson and McHugh, 1990, p. 3).

While the fourfold categorization of theories outlined in this volume clearly owes a lot to Burrell and Morgan's paradigms, there are two reasons for not wanting to identify them too closely. First, forcing diverse theories of organisation from sociology and psychology into Burrell and Morgan's four paradigms makes for some strange bedfellows (Hassard, 1993, p. 68). The paradigms would certainly be stretched to accommodate organisational economics, which Burrell and Morgan largely ignored. They would probably put most economic theories of organisation into the functionalist paradigm, especially given the economists' liking for mechanical and biological analogies, which is a favourite way of understanding the social world for functionalists (1979, p. 26). However, in Burrell and Morgan's schema, functionalism is characterised as being objective rather than subjective. Although neoclassical economics, from which organisational economics is largely derived, is just as teleological as either functionalism or radical structuralism, it emphasises the centrality of the revealed subjective preferences of individual actors as opposed to the constraints of social structures (Elster, 1990).

Second, there is a danger that if the four perspectives are identified as paradigms they might be used to close down debate. The paradigm idea is popular in sociology and organisation theory, even though there is little agreement about what the concept means. It originates from Thomas Kuhn's book, *The Structure of Scientific Revolutions* (1970 [1962]), which is a historical study of the physical sciences. Kuhn's view is that one theory usually dominates each scientific domain, this theory being the dominant paradigm. Problems arising within any scientific field are conceptualised in terms of the dominant paradigm and its particular way of seeing the world. Scientific revolutions occur when the dominant paradigm is displaced, generally by theorists working outside, or on the margins of, the scientific community in question.

The idea that there is a parallel between the paradigms identified by Kuhn in physical science and divisions within social science is attractive to Marxist (Allen, 1975) and radical (Burrell and Morgan, 1979, p. 384) critics of mainstream organisation theory. The paradigm concept allows authors such as Burrell and Morgan to portray themselves, somewhat heroically, as challenging the dominant functionalist paradigm from the margins of sociology. According to Burrell and Morgan, 'To be located in a particular paradigm is to view the world in a particular way', and to move from one paradigm to another is to experience something like a 'conversion experience' (1979, p. 25). This means that a paradigm represents something more than just 'a perspective, theory, discipline, school, or method' (Hassard, 1993, p. 76).

Since a paradigm is a world view, communication between paradigms is difficult, if not impossible, and following Burrell and Morgan there has been much debate, neatly summarised by John Hassard (1993), as to whether paradigms are, in fact, incommensurable. Again, paradigm incommensurability is attractive to Marxians and radicals because it allows them to dissociate themselves from the dominant paradigm (Ackroyd, 1992). Vic Allen (1975) was one of the first to try to outline a Marxist version of organisation theory. He strongly endorses paradigm incommensurability and regards 'the notion of a synthesis between qualitatively different conceptual approaches as an intellectual travesty'. He goes on to make the assertion that all social theories 'serve one political purpose or another in that they are assisting to preserve a structure or to change it' (1975). This smacks of vulgar political reductionism. In response, it is tempting to dismiss paradigms, as Steve Ackroyd, another organisation theorist, has done. He sees the paradigm idea as a 'pernicious' attempt to 'limit the number and type of approaches to organizations accepted as having any validity' (1992, p. 104).

Given the obvious absence in organisation theory of any readily identifiable dominant paradigm akin to the dominant paradigms found in natural science, or orthodox economics, it would appear that talk of paradigms is most permissable where it is least applicable. A comment made by McCloskey, the economic historian, seems apposite: 'Kuhn's notion of revolutions of thinking in physics as shifts in paradigms has been of course grossly overworked, applied mindlessly to shifts far from revolutionary in fields far from physics' (1986, p. 136). The notion of paradigms has been used to exaggerate the differences in organisation theory. In their debates about paradigms,

222 Organisations and Institutions

organisation theorists have tortured themselves with philosophical problems of epistemology and ontology (Hassard, 1993, pp. 67–8). However, it is as well to remember that the use of four boxes as a heuristic device is all too familiar in sociology. It is most closely identified with Talcott Parsons, an arch-functionalist if ever there was one, so much so that in a review of his work Mike Lessnof refers to Parsons' 'tetramania' (cited in Sklair, .1981). For didactic purposes, four quadrants have proved useful for sociology and organisation theory. There is no need to dispense with them as a heuristic device so long as it is not suggested that one formulation can accommodate all social theory.

A positive outcome from the notion of paradigms is that it has encouraged sociologists and organisation theorists to become more reflexive about their own position in relation to others. This has fostered diversity and discouraged organisation theorists from attempting to construct an overarching theoretical synthesis which incorporates all other theoretical perspectives. However, this process may have gone too far in organisation theory. The concept of paradigms is associated with postmodernism, as epistemology, and the idea that theories can only ever be properly judged within the paradigms from which they developed (Hoksbergen, 1994). Postmodernists accept that there are many incompatible pictures of the world, while modernists seek to find agreement about one picture of how the world actually is. The pull of postmodernism has led to a position of extreme relativism, scepticism and subjectivism in sociology, and many organisation theorists have bemoaned its influence (Thompson, 1993). It has exacerbated fissiparous tendencies in organisation theory (Ackroyd, 1992), and has led to self-indulgent, introspective reflection being seen as more prestigious than empirical research or genuine theory construction.

In contrast with organisation theory and sociology, postmodernism has had relatively little influence in economics, but it has begun to 'reshape' the discipline in a positive way, encouraging economists to 'write and talk about what they do' (Ruccio, 1991, p. 502). In a series of books, starting with *The Rhetoric of Economics* (1986), McCloskey has argued that economists can enhance their self-understanding through reflection on the way they converse among themselves. In McCloskey's view, an increase in self-awareness among economists should improve their relationships with other disciplines. However, he believes that it need not stop economists doing what they do best, and it has certainly not stopped McCloskey himself pursuing his own line of econometric research.

Economists enjoy constructing mathematical models, but they would be in a better position to engage with other disciplines if they were to reflect on the way in which they incorporate their own values into their models. Dialogue with other disciplines would be facilitated if more economists were prepared to admit, along with McCloskey, that:

the problem of choosing a model is that of choosing a human point of view. It is something done by us, not by God, and is therefore not absolute and not inhuman. One is going to be driven insane if one tries to find a nonhuman point of view within a hopelessly human problem. (1991, p. 35; Galbraith, 1987, p. 261)

However, neoclassically-orientated economists may be reluctant to relinquish universalistic claims for their models since it is the predictive pretensions of their models that has secured their dominance in the market for economic ideas (Bellinger and Bergsten, 1990). As one commentator wryly observes, 'if improved prediction is denied as a scientific objective for economists, it would certainly seem difficult to . . . discern what precisely economists in business and government are being paid to do' (Hutchison, 1981, p. 280). Economists' models lend themselves to making predictions in the form of 'if . . . then' propositions (Akerlof, 1984, pp. 2–3). All too often, economists are prepared to forget that the 'if' component of their propositions is composed of assumptions that are generally unrealistic and are necessarily informed by ethical and political value judgements (Hutchison, 1981). This allows economists to peddle their predictions as neutral forecasts that can relieve corporate and government bureaucracies of the burden of decision-making (Galbraith, 1987, pp. 264–5).

Mainstream organisational economists might be reluctant to concede that their models, which appear to demonstrate that the capitalist corporation is efficient, are a reflection of their values and their belief in the legitimacy of the capitalist corporation. However, reflection on the values that underpin economic models of organisation might induce some useful discussion about what it is that theorists prefer about one form of organisation or another. Unfortunately, any notion of reflexivity is sadly lacking in organisational economics, and yet it is something that organisational economists could best acquire through dialogue with organisation theory. If organisation theory has had too much of postmodernism, organisational economics has not had enough.

Periodisation

Another obstacle to dialogue between organisational economics and organisation theory is the increasingly prevalent view in organisation theory that society is entering a new period of increasingly rapid technological and organisational change. The resulting instability means that it is difficult, if not impossible, to develop models or theories that will capture anything more than a momentary aspect of societal or organisational change. Mike Reed (1992b, p. xiii), a radical Weberian organisation theorist, complains that: 'the belief that we are living through a period of profound instability and disorganization has crystallized into something of a "new orthodoxy"'. This new orthodoxy means that organisation theorists are increasingly keen to generate new theories, if only to be able to appear relevant to the popular business press, which is filled with allegedly innovative ideas intended to improve the competitiveness of organisations. Thus the editors of *Organization Science*, Richard Daft and Arie Lewin, wrote an editorial essay titled: 'Where Are the Theories for the "New" Organizational Forms?'. They appealed for articles that 'develop new knowledge, theories and research about new organizational forms and ask new questions about evolving organizational paradigms' (1993, p. vi).

Post-modernity is the most widely accepted name for the new epoch that sociologists and organisation theorists believe society is entering. It brings together a number of social theorists who have attached the 'post' prefix to at least fifteen other terms, the most common being: postFordism, postcapitalism and postindustrialism (Hassard, 1993). In common with postmodernism as epistemology, post-modernism (with a hyphen) as periodisation has led to a proliferation of increasingly vague theoretical perspectives which aspire to capture the alleged increase in diversity of forms of organisation.

Almost as soon as the term postmodern was used in organisation theory (Etzioni, 1968), it was dismissed by Marxists as 'an ideological cover for those who are afraid or unwilling to deal with capitalism as a major sociohistoric formation' (Cook, quoted in Allen, 1975, p. 33). By constantly shifting the ground for debate, in terms of the nature of society and organisations, the postmodernists have largely avoided developing the sort of sophisticated models that might appeal to economists, or the detailed empirical research that might convince historians that the concept of postmodernity has any credibility. There is a parallel between postmodernism, as periodisation, and the managerialist thesis. In the same way that the proponents of the managerialist thesis mistook the neoclassical theory of the firm as an adequate description of organisations in a previous era, the postmodernists make the mistake of characterising modernity as a period of organisational homogeneity, which means that the discovery of apparently ever-increasing diversity in organisations is taken as evidence of a new epoch of widespread organisational change.

The suggestion that organisational diversity is a product of postmodernity implies that models predicated upon organisational homogeneity might have been applicable at one time, in the era of modernity, but that they have been superseded by events. Certainly, as Sydney Winter, one of the more sophisticated evolutionary organisational economists, has conceded: 'the economy is much better at changing itself than economists are at changing their minds' (1993, p. 193). This misses the point that economists need to change their minds, not so much because the economy has changed, but because they need to recognise that their models can never capture the reality of the diversity of human organisation.

The diversity in organisation that has been held up as evidence of post-modernity has probably always existed, as is illustrated by the historical studies of work organisation (highlighted in Chapter 6). Gibson Burrell (1990, 1992) points out that rather than being characteristic of a new epoch, organisational diversity has probably always existed. However, alternative forms of organisation have been 'hidden from history' because they do not fit the evolutionary picture of organisational change as a unilinear progression from lower to higher, or from less efficient to more efficient organisational forms, that are portrayed, typically, by organisational economics and Marxian political economy.

On the one hand, there may good reasons to accept that there is more organisational diversity than is portrayed by overly deterministic evolutionary accounts of organisational change, but on the other hand there are good reasons for believing that organisational change is not, and what is more, *could not* be as rapid as the postmodernists claim. From the concept of bounded rationality, advanced by organisational economics, it can be inferred that human actors are only able to change a limited proportion of their decision-making routines simultaneously. Institutions are likely to persist, even if it cannot be known in advance which institutions will persist and which will be challenged by purposive collective action effected through organisations.

It is unlikely that organisational economics will merge with organisation theory. However, there is the prospect of a fruitful dialogue between the two. This would be facilitated if organisational economists were to become more reflexive about the way their values inform their models. On the other hand, organisation theorists should not dismiss economic models simply because they are deemed to be the expression of a certain set of values. While the diversity of organisations can never be captured by economists' models, any more than it can be by sociologists' typologies, this need not mean that it is pointless to construct models, as is suggested by those organisation theorists who believe that increasing organisational change has rendered virtually all models redundant. Organisational economics as a whole has moved away from the static analysis of neoclassical economics, but most economic models of organisation need a more convincing, more evolutionary, account of organisational change. A more adequate theory of organisational change would not be refuted by evidence of an acceleration of organisational and technological change. Such a theory would only be seriously challenged by evidence of a change in the very nature of change itself.

Guide to further reading

To follow contemporary debates in organisational economics and organisation theory it is necessary to consult the journals, of which there are too many to list. For organisational economics I would recommend the *Journal of Economic Behavior and Organization*. Of more relevance to this book, in terms of airing inter- and intradisciplinary differences, the *Journal of Economic Perspectives* is better. The leading journals in organisation theory have increasingly given attention to organisational economics. The most important are: *Administrative Science Quarterly*; *Academy of Management Review*; *Organization Science*; and *Organization Studies*. In addition, the editors of *Human Relations* are keen on including interdisciplinary work, particularly from sociologists, economists and psychologists.

The main emphasis of this guide is not journal articles but edited collections of readings and introductory books. Starting with game theory, Poundstone, *The Prisoner's Dilemma* (1993), gives a straightforward introduction to, and a history of, the theory. Avoiding the maths again, Dixit and Nalebuff, *Thinking Strategically* (1991), gives an idea of the applications of game theory. Axelrod, *The Evolution of Cooperation* (1990), is not only influential, but highly readable.

Neoclassical, managerial and behavioural theories of the firm are all dealt with clearly in Sawyer's excellent little book, *Theories of the Firm* (1979). For more general overviews and explicit critiques of economics, Galbraith ought to be read at some point, and his book, *A History of Economics* (1987) is better than the many more scholarly histories of economics. Hodgson's *Economics and Institutions* (1988) is a more difficult and sustained critique of contemporary economics, but he gives considerable attention to organisational economics.

For organisational economics in general, Milgrom and Roberts, *Economics, Organization and Management* (1992), seems likely to become the standard textbook for economists looking at organisational issues. This is unfortunate, since they pay almost no attention to the issues raised in this book. Douma and Schreuder's *Economic Approaches to Organization* (1991) is similarly flawed, but it is very accessible and will be appreciated by students. In *The Economics of*

Business Enterprise, Ricketts (1987) takes an openly Austrian line, but this does not detract from the clarity of his book. For an overview of neoinstitutional economics, by far the best introduction is Eggertsson, *Economic Behavior and Institutions* (1990), which is particularly useful for understanding property rights. North is very clear but more concerned with economics history in *Institutions, Institutional Change and Economic Performance* (1990a).

As for edited collections, Putterman's *The Economic Nature of the Firm: A Reader* (1986b) is virtually indispensable as a companion to this book. Barney and Ouchi cover some of the same ground in *Organizational Economics* (1986), but they miss the radical literature, and compared to Putterman their introductions are anodyne. Coase's article, 'The Nature of the Firm', is reproduced in numerous collections, including Putterman (abridged) and Barney and Ouchi, but the best collection of his work is his own: *The Firm, The Market and the Law* (Coase, 1990a). This includes all his other seminal papers. In 1991, Coase received the Nobel Prize for economics. His Nobel Prize lecture is included in *The Nature of the Firm: Origins, Evolution, and Development* (1993), edited by Williamson and Winter. This is a valuable collection of papers discussing Coase's 'The Nature of the Firm'. Coase himself gives an account of how he came to write the article in the first place, which makes fascinating reading. For critiques of Coase and Williamson, Pitelis has collected contributions, largely from British academics, in *Transaction Costs, Markets and Hierarchies* (1993). Pratt and Zeckhauser's *Principals and Agents* (1985) is a useful collection dealing with agency theory, while Singh's collection, *Organizational Evolution: New Directions* (1990) does what its title promises. Both might assume some prior knowledge in places.

The writings of the organisational economists themselves can be daunting for organisation theorists, not least Williamson. He is nothing if not prolific, but the major statement of his version of transaction costs economics remains *The Economic Institutions of Capitalism* (1985). *Economic Organization* (1986b) is a useful collection of his earlier work, and contains an interesting autobiographical sketch. Demsetz gives a similar, but slightly less insightful, sketch in the introduction to a collection of his articles: *Ownership, Control and the Firm* (1988). Hannan and Freeman, *Organizational Ecology* (1989), and Nelson and Winter, *An Evolutionary Theory of Economic Change* (1982), are the major books on evolutionary perspectives. Both are intimidating and time-consuming to read.

There are valuable articles dealing with the relationship between economics and sociology in several collections, mainly from the sociologists' side, it should be said. Probably the best is Zukin and DiMaggio's *Structures of Capital* (1990b), followed by Martinelli and Smelser's *Economy and Society* (1990). Both books contain articles that are relevant to the other issues dealt with in this book. Granovetter and Swedberg have brought together many of the seminal papers in economic sociology in *The Sociology of Economic Life* (1992). For a general insight into the way economists work, the series of books by

McCloskey are useful, starting with *The Rhetoric of Economics* (1986). *If You're so smart* (1990) is probably the most accessible. The *Supplement* to vol. 94 of the *American Journal of Sociology* (1988) contains useful articles on the 'Sociological Analysis of Economic Institutions' and 'Economic Analysis of Social Institutions'.

There is no generally accepted textbook on organisation theory, but Perrow's *Complex Organizations* (1986) gives the best history and overview of the field, albeit from his own radical perspective. *Perspectives on Organization Design and Behavior*, edited by Van de Ven and Joyce (1981), is a little dated but still contains many of the major debates in organisation theory. Thompson and McHugh, *Work Organisations* (1990, now in a second edition) provides a radical critique and overview of contemporary developments in organisational behaviour and organisation theory. They pay particular attention to the treatment of power. *Organization Theory: From Chester Barnard to the Present and Beyond*, edited by Williamson (1995), is idiosyncratic. It does not reflect the diverse concerns of many organisation theorists as well as Reed and Hughes' *Rethinking Organization* (1992). *The Academy of Management Review*, vol. 15, no. 3 (1990) contains a Theory Development Forum devoted to organisational economics, but it is mainly concerned with the relationship with mainstream organisation theory. The 'Symposium' on 'Organizations and Economics' in *The Journal of Economic Perspectives*, vol. 5, no. 2 (1991) is more interesting. For an insight into the divisions within organisation theory, Hassard's *Sociology and Organization Theory* (1993) summarises many contemporary developments, including postmodernism. Powell and DiMaggio, *The New Institutionalism in Organizational Analysis* (1991), contains important empirical and theoretical papers, including their own. Stinchcombe deserves a mention, even though it is difficult to categorise his idiosyncratic synthesis of economic sociology and organisational economics. His *Information and Organizations* (1990) contains several useful chapters. Although they are not aimed at the debate between organisational economics and organisation theory, Lukes' *Power: A Radical View* (1974), and Putterman's *Division of Labor and Welfare* (1990), provide excellent insights into the concepts of power and efficiency respectively.

Abridged versions of the major work on divisions of labour and hierarchy are contained in Putterman (1986b). Nichols' *Capital and Labour* (1980) contains the major Marxist contributions but has been superseded by the labour process debate. Thompson's *The Nature of Work* (1989) remains the best overview of this debate. *Labour Process Theory* (1990), edited by Knights and Willmott, includes some impenetrable pieces, but gives a taste of the labour process debate concerns with power and subjectivity. Child's *Organization* (1984) is possibly outdated as a textbook (the purpose it was intended for), but it remains a clear statement of the strategic choice perspective in organisation theory, especially in relation to work organisation. Braverman's *Labor and Monopoly Capital* (1974) has been criticised endlessly. The critics are probably motivated in part by the power of Braverman's Marxist argument, which they are hard put to match. His book must remain the major starting point for discussions of work organisation in sociology.

It would be almost impossible to summarise the vast literature on the Industrial Revolution in England. Fortunately, it is not necessary since Berg has already virtually done it in *The Age of Manufactures, 1700–1820* (1994). She covers the major debates concerning work organisation during the period. Nelson's *Managers and Workers: Origins of the New Factory System in the United States 1880–1920* (1975) is more concerned with organising original data than addressing broader debates. It could therefore be contrasted with Clawson's Marxist account of the same period in *Bureaucracy and the Labor Process* (1980).

By far the best overview of debates in sociology concerning ownership and control is Scott's *Corporations, Classes and Capitalism* (1985). Bottomore's *Theories of Modern Capitalism* (1985) provides an introduction to the theoretical background to this debate in sociology. Most of the important articles in organisational economics appear in volumes that have already been mentioned. An exception is the second volume of Demsetz' collected articles, *Efficiency, Competition and Policy* (1991), which includes an important polemic against Galbraith's *The New Industrial State* (1967). *The Journal of Law and Economics*, vol. xxvi, no. 2 (1983) is a special issue that contains the articles from a conference commemorating Berle and Means' *The Modern Corporation*. There are important contributions form several major organisational economists.

Chandler remains unrivalled for his account of the development of the modern corporation. Of his major books, *The Visible Hand* (1977) is probably the most important, and it summarises the main points from his earlier *Strategy and Structure* (1962), and more relevant than much of the material in *The Essential Alfred Chandler* (1988), edited by McCraw. There is a separate literature dealing with the multinational corporation, summarised in Pitelis and Sugden's collection, *The Nature of the Transnational Firm* (1991).

References

Abrams, P. (1980) 'History, Sociology, Historical Sociology', *Past and Present*, no. 87, May, pp. 3–16

Ackroyd, S. (1992) 'Paradigms Lost: Paradigms Regained?', in M. Reed and M. Hughes (eds), *Rethinking Organization: New Directions in Organization Theory and Analysis* (London: Sage).

Akerlof, G. A. (1984) *An Economic Theorist's Book of Tales: Essays that Entertain the Consequences of New Assumptions in Economic Theory* (Cambridge University Press).

Alchian, A. A. (1950) 'Uncertainty, Evolution, and Economic Theory', *Journal of Political Economy* vol. LVIII, pp. 211–21.

Alchian, A. A. and H. Demsetz (1986) 'Production, Information Costs, and Economic Organization', in L. Putterman (ed.), *The Economic Nature of the Firm: A Reader* (Cambridge University Press).

Alchian, A. A. and S. Woodward (1988) 'The Firm Is Dead; Long Live the Firm: A Review of Oliver E. Williamson's *The Economic Institutions of Capitalism*', *Journal of Economic Literature*, vol. XXVI, March, pp. 65–79.

Allen, V. L. (1975) *Social Analysis: A Marxist Critique and Alternative* (London: Longman).

Alt, J. E. and K. A. Shepsle (eds) (1990) *Perspectives on Positive Political Economy* (Cambridge University Press).

Alvesson, M. (1987) *Consensus, Control and Critique: Three Paradigms of Work Organization Research* (Aldershot: Avebury).

Alvesson, M. (1993) *Cultural Perspectives on Organizations* (Cambridge University Press).

Anderson, B. L. and A. J. H. Latham (eds) (1986) *The Market in History* (London: Croom Helm).

Aoki, M. (1984) *The Co-operative Game Theory of the Firm* (Oxford: Clarendon Press).

Aoki, M. (1990) 'The Participatory Generation of Information Rents and the Theory of the Firm', in M. Aoki, B. Gustafsson and O. E. Williamson (eds), *The Firm as a Nexus of Treaties* (London: Sage).

Aoki, M., B. Gustafsson and O. E. Williamson (eds) (1990) *The Firm as a Nexus of Treaties* (London: Sage).

Armstrong, P. (1989) 'Management, Labour Process and Agency', *Work, Employment and Society*, vol. 3, pp. 307–22.

Arrow, K. J. (1974) *The Limits of Organization* (New York: W. W. Norton).

Arrow, K. J. (1985) 'The Economics of Agency', in J. W. Pratt and R. J. Zeckhauser (eds), *Principals and Agents: The Structure of Business* (Boston, Mass.: Harvard Business School Press).

Ashton, T. S. (1968) [1948] *The Industrial Revolution 1760–1830* (Oxford University Press).

Axelrod, R. (1990) *The Evolution of Cooperation* (Harmondsworth: Penguin).

Babbage, C. (1832) *On the Economy of Machinery and Manufactures* (London: C. Knight).

Baran, P. A. and P. M. Sweezy (1968) *Monopoly Capital* (Harmondsworth: Penguin)

Baritz, L. (1960) *The Servants of Power: A History of the Use of Social Science in American Industry* (Middletown, Conn.: Wesleyan University Press).

Barnard, C. (1964 [1938] *The Functions of the Executive* (Cambridge, Mass.: Harvard University Press).

Barney, J. B. (1990) 'The Debate Between Traditional Management Theory and Organizational Economics: Substantive Differences or Intergroup Conflict?', *Academy of Management Review*, vol. 15, no. 3, pp. 382–93.

Barney, J. B. and W. G. Ouchi (eds) (1986) *Organizational Economics* (San Francisco: Jossey-Bass).

Baron, J. N. and M. T. Hannan (1994) 'The Impact of Economics on Sociology', *Journal of Economic Literature*, vol. xxxii, September, pp. 1111–46.

Bartlett, R. (1989) *Economics and Power: An Inquiry into Human Relations and Markets* (Cambridge University Press).

Barzel, Y. (1987) 'The Entrepreneur's Reward for Self-Policing', *Economic Inquiry*, vol. xxv, January, pp. 103–16.

Bauer, M. and E. Cohen (1983) 'The Invisibility of Power in Economics: beyond markets and hierarchies', in A. Francis, J. Turk and P. Willman (eds), *Power, Efficiency and Institutions: A Critical Appraisal of the 'Markets and Hierarchies' Paradigm* (London: Heinemann).

Bauman, Z. (1989) *Modernity and the Holocaust* (Cambridge: Polity).

Becker, G. (1976) *The Economic Approach to Human Behavior* (London: University of Chicago Press).

Becker, G. (1979) 'Economic Analysis and Human Behavior', in L. Levy-Garboua (ed.), *Sociological Economics* (London: Sage).

Becker, G. (1981) *A Treatise on the Family* (Cambridge, Mass.: Harvard University Press).

Bell, D. (1974) *The Coming of Post-Industrial Society* (London: Heinemann).

Bellinger, W. K. and G. S. Bergsten (1990) 'The Market for Economic Thought: An Austrian View of Neoclassical Dominance', *History of Political Economy*, vol. 22, no. 4, pp. 697–720.

Bendix, R. (1963) *Work and Authority in Industry: Ideologies of Management in the Course of Industrialization* (New York: Harper & Row).

Benton, T. (1991) 'Biology and Social Science: Why the Return of the Repressed Should be Given a (Cautious) Welcome', *Sociology*, vol. 25, no. 1, pp. 1–29.

Berg, M. (1984) 'The Power of Knowledge: Comments on Marglin's "Knowledge and Power"', in F. H. Stephen (ed.), *Firms, Organization and Labour: Approaches to the Economics of Work Organization* (London: Macmillan).

Berg, M. (1991) 'On the Origins of Capitalist Hierarchy', in B. Gustafsson (ed.), *Power and Economic Institutions: Reinterpretations in Economic History* (Aldershot: Edward Elgar).

Berg, M. (1994) *The Age of Manufactures, 1700–1820: Industry, Innovation and Work in Britain* (2nd edn) (London: Routledge).

Berger, P and T. Luckmann (1971) *The Social Construction of Reality: A Treatise in the Sociology of Knowledge* (Harmondsworth: Penguin).

Berle, A. A. and G. C. Means (1967) [1932] *The Modern Corporation and Private Property* (New York: Macmillan).

Biddle, J. E. (1990) 'Purpose and Evolution in Commons' Institutionalism', *History of Political Economy*, vol. 22, no 1, pp. 19–47.

Block, F. (1990) 'Political Choice and Multiple "logics" of capital', in S. Zukin and P. DiMaggio (eds), *Structures of Capital: The Social Organization of the Economy* (Cambridge University Press).

Bornschier, V. and H. Stamm (1990) 'Transnational Corporations', in A. Martinelli and N. J. Smelser (eds), *Economy and Society: Overviews in Economic Sociology* (London: Sage).

Bottomore, T. (1985) *Theories of Modern Capitalism* (London: George Allen & Unwin).

Bottomore, T. (1991) *A Dictionary of Marxist Thought* (2nd edn) (Oxford: Blackwell).

Bottomore, T. and R. Nisbet (eds) (1979) *A History of Sociological Analysis* (London: Heinemann).

Boulding, K. E. (1981) *Evolutionary Economics* (London: Sage).

Bowles, S. (1986) 'The Production Process in a Competitive Economy: Walrasian, neo-Hobbesian, and Marxian Models', in L. Putterman (ed.), *The Economic Nature of the Firm: A Reader* (Cambridge University Press).

Bowles, S. and H. Gintis (1993) 'The Revenge of Homo Economicus: Contested Exchange and the Revival of Political Economy', *Journal of Economic Perspectives*, vol. 7, no. 1, pp. 83–102.

Bradach, J. L. and R. G. Eccles (1991) 'Price, Authority and Trust: From Ideal Types to Plural Forms', in G. Thompson, J. Frances, R. Levacic and J. Mitchell (eds), *Markets, Hierarchies and Networks: The Coordination of Social Life* (London: Sage).

Bradby, B. (1982) 'The Remystification of Value', *Capital and Class*, no. 17, Summer, pp. 114–33.

Braendgaard, A. (1983) 'Market, Hierarchy and Technology: Some Implications of Economic Internationalism for Labour', in A. Francis, J. Turk and P. Willman (eds), *Power, Efficiency and Institutions: A Critical Appraisal of the 'Markets and Hierarchies' Paradigm* (London: Heinemann).

Braudel, F. (1985) *Civilization and Capitalism: 15th–18th Century*, vol. II, *The Wheels of Commerce* (London: Fontana Press).

Braverman, H. (1974) *Labor and Monopoly Capital: The Degradation of Work in the Twentieth Century* (London: Monthly Review Press).

Braverman, H. (1976) 'Two Comments', *Monthly Review*, vol. 28, part 3, pp. 119–124.

Brubaker, R. (1983) *The Limits of Rationality: An Essay on the Social and Moral Thought of Max Weber* (London: Allen & Unwin).

Bryan, R. (1985) 'Monopoly in Marxist Method', *Capital and Class*, no. 26, Summer, p. 72.

Buchanan, A. (1985) *Ethics, Efficiency, and the Market* (Oxford: Clarendon Press).

Buckley, P. J. and M. Casson (eds) (1992) *Multinational Enterprises in the World Economy: Essays in Honour of John Dunning* (Aldershot: Edward Elgar).

Buckley, P. J. and M. Casson (1993) 'Economics as an Imperialist Social Science', *Human Relations*, vol. 46, no. 9, pp. 1035–52.

Burawoy, M. (1979) *Manufacturing Consent: Changes in the Labor Process under Monopoly Capitalism* (London: University of Chicago Press).

Burawoy, M. (1985) *The Politics of Production* (London: Verso).

Burkett. P. (1991) 'Some Comments on "Capital in General and the Structure of Marx's Capital", *Capital and Class*, no. 44, Summer, pp. 49–72.

Burnham, J. (1962) [1941] *The Managerial Revolution* (Harmondsworth: Penguin).

Burrell, G. (1990) 'Fragmented Labours', in D. Knights, and H. Willmott (eds), *Labour Process Theory* (London: Macmillan).

Burrell, G. (1992) 'Back to the Future: Time and Organization', in M. Reed and M. Hughes (eds), *Rethinking Organization: New Directions in Organization Theory and Analysis* (London: Sage).

Burrell, G. and G. Morgan (1979) *Sociological Paradigms and Organisational Analysis: Elements of the Sociology of Corporate Life* (London: Heinemann).

Burt, R. (1983) *Corporate Profits and Cooptation: Networks of Market Constraints and Directorate Ties in the American Economy* (New York: Academic Press).

Butler, R. (1991) *Designing Organizations: A Decision-Making Perspective* (London: Routledge).

Bythell, D. (1978) *The Sweated Trades: Outwork in 19th-Century Britain* (London: Batsford).

Cable, J. R. (1988) 'Organisational Form and Economic Performance', in S. Thompson and M. Wright (eds), *Internal Organisation, Efficiency and Profit* (Oxford: Philip Allan).

Callinicos, A. (1976) *Althusser's Marxism* (London: Pluto Press).

Callinicos, A. (1989) *Making History* (Cambridge: Polity Press).

Capra, F. (1983) *Turning Point: Science, Society, and the Rising Culture* (London: Fontana).

Carter, J. R. and M. D. Irons (1991) 'Are Economists Different, and If So, Why?', *Journal of Economic Perspectives*, vol. 15, no. 2, Spring, pp. 171–7

Casson, M. (1987) *The Firm and the Market: Studies on Multinational Enterprise and the Scope of the Firm* (Oxford: Basil Blackwell).

Casson, M. (1991) *The Economics of Business Culture: Game Theory, Transaction Costs, and Economic Performance* (Oxford: Clarendon).

Caves, R. E. (1980) 'Corporate Strategy and Structure', *Journal of Economic Literature*, vol. 18, pp. 64–92

Chandler, A. D. (1962) *Strategy and Structure: Chapters in the History of the Industrial Enterprise* (London: MIT Press).

Chandler, A. D. (1977) *The Visible Hand: The Managerial Revolution in American Business*, (London: Belknap Press of Harvard University).

Chandler, A. D. (1981) 'Historical Determinants of Managerial Hierarchies: A Response to Perrow', in A. H. Van De Ven and W. F. Joyce (eds), *Perspectives on Organization Design and Behavior* (New York: John Wiley).

Chandler, A. D. (1984) 'Comparative Business History', in D. C. Coleman and P. Mathias (eds), *Enterprise and History: Essays in Honour of Charles Wilson* (Cambridge University Press).

Chandler, A. D. (1986) in Kantrow, A. M. (ed.), 'Why History Matters to Managers', *Harvard Business Review*, January–February, pp. 81–8.

Chandler, A. D. (1988) in T. K. McCraw (ed.), *the Essential Alfred Chandler: Essays Toward a Historical Theory of Big Business* (Boston, Mass.: Harvard Business School Press).

Chandler, A. D. (1990) *Scale and Scope: The Dynamics of Industrial Capitalism* (London: the Belknap Press of Harvard University Press).

Chandler, A. D. (1992) 'What is a Firm? A historical perspective', *European Economic Review* 36, pp. 483–492.

Chandler, A. D. (1992b) 'Organizational Capabilities and the Economic History of the Industrial Enterprise', *Journal of Economic Perspectives*, vol. 6, no. 3, Summer, pp. 79–100.

Chandler, A. D. and H. Daems (1974) 'Introduction – The Rise of Managerial Capitalism and It's Impact on Investment Strategy in the Western World and Japan', in H. Daems and H. Van der Vee (eds), *The Rise of Managerial Capitalism* (Louvain: Leuven University Press).

Chandler, A. D. Jr and H. Daems (eds) (1980), *Managerial Hierarchies: Comparative Perspectives on the Rise of the Modern Industrial Enterprise* (London: Harvard University Press).

Cheung, S. N. (1974) 'A Theory of Price Control', *Journal of Law and Economics*, vol. 17, pp. 53–71.

Cheung, S. N. (1983) 'The Contractual Nature of the Firm', *Journal of Law and Economics*, vol. xxvi, April, pp. 1–21.

Child, J. (1969) *The Business Enterprise in Modern Industrial Society* (London: Collier Macmillan).

Child, J. (1972) 'Organizational Structure, Environment and Performance: The Role of Strategic Choice', *Sociology*, vol. 6, pp. 1–22.

Child, J. (1984) *Organization: A Guide to Problems and Practice* (London: Harper & Row).

Child, J. (1985) 'Managerial Strategies, New Technology, and the Labour Process', in D. Knights, H. Willmott and D. Collinson (eds), *Job Redesign: Critical Perspectives on the Labour Process* (Aldershot: Gower).

Clapham, J. H. (1922) 'Of Empty Boxes', *Economic Journal*, vol. 32, p. 305.

Clark, P. and N. Staunton (1993) *Innovation in Technology and Organization* (London: Routledge).

Clark, R. C. (1985) 'Agency Costs versus Fiduciary Duties', in J. W. Pratt and R. J. Zeckhauser (eds), *Principals and Agents: The Structure of Business* (Boston, Mass.: Harvard Business School Press).

Clarke, S. (1982) *Marx, Marginalism and Modern Sociology: From Adam Smith to Max Weber* (London: Macmillan).

Clawson, D. (1980) *Bureaucracy and the Labor Process: The Transformation of U.S. Industry, 1860–1920* (London: Monthly Review Press).

Clegg, S. (1990) *Modern Organizations: Organization Studies in the Postmodern World* (London: Sage).

Clegg, S. and D. Dunkerley (1980) *Organization, Class and Control* (London: Routledge & Kegan Paul).

Coase, R. (1984) 'The New Institutional Economics', *Journal of Institutional and Theoretical Economics*, vol. 140, no. 1, pp. 229–31.

Coase, R. H. (1990a) *The Firm, the Market and the Law* (London: University of Chicago Press).

Coase, R. H. (1990b) 'The Nature of the Firm', ch. 2 in R. H. Coase *The Firm, the Market and the Law* (reprinted from *Economica*, vol. 4; (1937) abridged in L. Putterman (ed.), *The Economic Nature of the Firm: A Reader*).

Coase, R. H. (1990c) 'The Firm, the Market and the Law', ch. 1 in R. H. Coase, *The Firm, the Market and the Law*.

Coase, R. H. (1990d) 'The Problem of Social Cost', ch. 5 in R. H. Coase, *The Firm, the Market and the Law* (reprinted from *Journal of Law and Economics*, vol. 3 (1960).

Coase, R. H. (1990e) 'The Lighthouse in Economics', ch. 7 in R. H. Coase, *The Firm, the Market and the Law* (reprinted from *Journal of Law and Economics*, vol. 17, no. 2 (1974).

Coase, R. H. (1990f) 'Notes on the Problem of Social Cost', ch. 6 in R. H. Coase, *The Firm, the Market and the Law*.

Coase, R. H. (1993a) 'The Nature of the Firm: Influence', in O. E. Williamson and S. G. Winter, *The Nature of the Firm: Origins. Evolution, and Development* (Oxford University Press).

Coase, R. H. (1993b) '1991 Nobel Lecture: The Institutional Structure of Production', in O. E. Williamson and S. G. Winter (eds), *The Nature of the Firm: Origins, Evolution, and Development* (Oxford University Press).

Cohen, G. A. (1978) *Karl Marx's Theory of History: A Defence* (Oxford: Clarendon Press).

Coleman, J. S. (1984) 'Introducing Social Structure into Economic Analysis', *The American Economic Review*, vol. 74, no. 2, pp. 84–8.

Coleman, J. S. (1990) *Foundations of Social Theory* (London: Belknap Press of Harvard University).

Coleman, J. S. and T. J. Fararo (1992) 'Introduction', in J. S. Coleman and T. J. Fararo (eds), *Rational Choice Theory: Advocacy and Critique* (London: Sage).

Commons. J. R. (1951) *The Economics of Collective Action* (New York: Macmillan).

Commons, J. R. (1961) *Institutional Economics: Its place in Political Economy*, vol. 1, Madison, Wis.: University of Wisconsin Press).

Coughlin, R. M. (1991) 'Introduction: Toward an Agenda for Socio-Economics', in R. M. Coughlin (ed.), *Morality, Rationality, and Efficiency: New Perspectives on Socio-Economics* (London: M. E. Sharpe).

Cowling, K. and R. Sugden (1993) 'Control, Markets and Firms', in C. Pitelis (ed.), *Transaction Costs, Markets and Hierarchies* (Oxford: Basil Blackwell).

Cyert, R. M. and J. G. March (1963) *A Behavioral Theory of the Firm* (Englewood Cliffs, NJ.: Prentice-Hall).

Daems, H. and H. Van der Vee (eds) (1974) *The Rise of Managerial Capitalism* (Louvain: Louvain University Press).

Daft, R. L. (1992) *Organization Theory and Design* (4th edn) (New York: West).

Daft, R. L. and A. Y. Lewin (1993) 'Where Are the Theories for the "New" Organizational Forms? An Editorial Essay', *Organization Science*, vol. 4, no. 4, pp. i–vi.

Dalton, M. (1992) [1959] 'Men Who Manage', in M. Granovetter and R. Swedberg (eds), *The Sociology of Economic Life* (Oxford: Westview Press).

Davis, G. F. (1991) 'Agents Without Principles? The Spread of the Poison Pill through the Intercorporate Network', *Administrative Science Quarterly*, vol. 36, December, pp. 583–613.

Davis, J. B. (1990) Review of M. A. Lutz and K. Lux (1988) *Humanistic Economics: The New Challenge* in *History of Political Economy*, vol. 22, pp. 751–3.

Dawe, A. (1979) 'Theories of Social Action', in T. Bottomore and R. Nisbet (eds), *A History of Sociological Analysis* (London: Heinemann).

De Alessi, L. (1980) 'The Economics of Property Rights: A Review of the Evidence', *Research in Law and Economics*, vol. 2, pp. 1–47.

Demsetz, H. (1983) 'The Structure of Ownership and the Theory of the Firm', *Journal of Law and Economics*, vol. xxvi, no. 2, pp. 375–89.

Demsetz, H. (1988) *Ownership, Control, and the Firm: The Organization of Economic Activity*, vol. 1, (Oxford: Basil Blackwell).

Demsetz, H. (1991) [1989] *Efficiency, Competition, and Policy: The Organization of Economic Activity*, vol. 2, (Oxford: Basil Blackwell).

Desai, M. (1979) *Marxian Economic Theory* (Oxford: Basil Blackwell).

Desmond, A. and J. Moore (1992) *Darwin* (Harmondsworth: Penguin).

de Vroey, M. (1980) 'A Marxist View of Ownership and Control', in T. Nichols (ed.), *Capital and Labour: Studies in the Capitalist Labour Process* (London: Fontana).

de Vroey, M. (1982) 'On the Obsolescence of the Marxian Theory of Value', *Capital and Class*, no. 17, Summer, pp. 34–59.

Dietrich, M. (1993) 'Transaction Costs . . . and Revenues', in C. Pitelis (ed.), *Transaction Costs, Markets and Hierarchies* (Oxford: Basil Blackwell).

DiMaggio, P. J. and W. W. Powell (1991) 'Introduction', in W. W. Powell and P. J. DiMaggio (eds), *The New Institutionalism in Organizational Analysis* (London: University of Chicago Press).

DiMaggio, P. J. and W. W. Powell (1991) 'The Iron Cage Revisited: Institutional Isomorphism and Collective Rationality in Organizational Fields', in W. W. Powell and P. J. DiMaggio (eds), *The New Institutionalism in Organizational Analysis* (London: University of Chicago Press).

Dixit, A. K. and B. J. Nalebuff (1991) *Thinking Strategically: The Competitive Edge in Business, Politics, and Everyday Life* (London: W. W. Norton).

Doeringer, P. B. and M. J. Piore (1971) *Internal Labor Markets and Manpower Analysis* (Lexington, Mass.: D. C. Heath).

Donaldson, L. (1985) *In Defence of Organization Theory: A Reply to the Critics* (Cambridge University Press).

Donaldson, L. (1990) 'A Rational Basis for Criticisms of Organizational Economics: A Reply to Barney', *Academy of Management Review*, vol. 15, no. 3, pp. 394–401.

Donaldson, L. (1991) 'The Liberal Revolution and Organisation Theory', Paper presented to conference 'Towards a New Theory of Organisations' (1991) University of Keele, England.

Douma, S. and H. Schreuder (1991) *Economic Approaches to Organizations* (London: Prentice Hall).

Du Boff, R. B. and E. S. Herman (1980) 'Alfred Chandler's New Business History: A Review', *Politics and Society*, vol. 10, no. 1, pp. 87–110.

Duesenberry, J. (1960) 'Comment on "An Economic Analysis of Fertility"' in National Bureau committee for Economic Research (ed.), *Demographic and Economic Change in Developed Countries* (Princeton, NJ.: Princeton University Press) pp. 231–4.

Dugger, W. M. (1989) 'Radical Institutionalism: Basic Concepts', in W. M. Dugger (ed.), *Radical Institutionalism: Contemporary Voices* (London: Greenwood Press).

Dunleavy, P. (1991) *Democracy, Bureaucracy and Public Choice: Economic Explanations in Political Science* (London: Harvester Wheatsheaf).

Durkheim, E. (1947) *The Division of Labor in Society* (Glencoe, Ill.: Free Press).

Eatwell, J. (1982) 'Competition', in I. Bradley and M. Howard (eds), *Classical and Marxian Political Economy: Essays in Honour of Ronald L. Meek* (London: Macmillan).

Edwards, R. (1979) *Contested Terrain: The Transformation of the Workplace in the Twentieth Century* (New York: Basic Books) (abridged in L. Putterman (ed.), *The Economic Nature of the Firm: A Reader*).

Eggertsson, T. (1990) *Economic Behavior and Institutions* (Cambridge University Press).

Elbaum, B., W. Lazonick, F. Wilkinson and J. Zeitlin (1979) 'Symposium: The Labour Process, Market Structure and Marxist Theory', *Cambridge Journal of Economics*, vol. 3, pp. 227–30.

Elbaum, B. and W. Lazonick (1982) *The Decline of the British Economy: An Institutional Perspective*, Harvard Institute of Economic Research Discussion Paper, no. 878, January.

Ellerman, D. P. (1991) 'Myth and Metaphor in Orthodox Economics', *Journal of Post Keynesian Economics*, vol. 13, no. 4, pp. 545–64.

Elster, J. (1979) 'Anomalies of Rationality: Some Unresolved Problems in the Theory of Rational Behaviour', in L. Levy-Garboua (ed.), *Sociological Economics* (London: Sage).

Elster, J. (1990) 'Marxism, Functionalism, and Game Theory', in S. Zukin and P. DiMaggio (eds), *Structures of Capital: The Social Organization of the Economy* (Cambridge University Press).

Engels. F. (1969a) [1892] *The Condition of the Working Class in England* (London: Granada Panther).

Engels, F. (1969b) [1873] 'On Authority' in *Karl Marx and Frederick Engels: Selected Works in Three Volumes*, vol. 2 (Moscow: Progress).

Eswaran, M. and A. Kotwal (1989) 'Why are Capitalists the Bosses?', *Economic Journal*, vol. 99, March, pp. 162–76.

Etzioni, A. (1968) *The Active Society: A Theory of Societal and Political Processes* (New York: Free Press).

Etzioni, A. (1988a) *The Moral Dimension: Toward a New Economics* (New York: The Free Press).

Etzioni, A. (1988b) 'Foreword', in M. A. Lutz and K. Lux, *Humanistic Economics: The New Challenge* (New York: Bootstrap Press).

Etzioni, A. and P. R. Lawrence (eds) (1991) *Socio-Economics: Toward a New Synthesis* (London: M. E. Sharpe).

Fama, E. (1986) 'Agency Problems and the Theory of the Firm', in Putterman (ed.), *The Economic Nature of the Firm: A Reader* (Cambridge University Press).

Fama, E. F. and M. Jensen (1983) 'Agency Problems and Residual Claims', *Journal of Law and Economics*, vol. xxvi, no. 2, pp. 327–49.

Fieldhouse, D. K. (1989) 'The Multinational: A Critique of a Concept', in A. M. Teichova, M. Levy-Leboyer, and H. Nussbaum (eds), *Multinational Enterprise in Historical Perspective* (Cambridge University Press).

Fincham, R. (1992) 'Perspectives on Power: Processual, Institutional and "Internal" Forms of Organizational Power', *Journal of Management Studies*, vol. 29, no. 6, pp. 741–60.

Fine, B. and Harris, L. (1979) *Rereading Capital* (London: Macmillan).

Fligstein, N. (1985) 'The Spread of the Multidivisional Form Among Large Firms, 1919–1979', *American Sociological Review*, vol. 50, pp. 377–91.

Fligstein, N. (1990) *The Transformation of Corporate Control* (London: Harvard University Press).

Fligstein, N. and P. Brantley (1992) 'Bank Control, or Organizational Dynamics: Who Controls the Large Modern Corporation?', *American Journal of Sociology*, vol. 98, no. 2, pp. 280–307.

Fogel, R. W. (1964) *Railroads and American Growth: Essays in Econometric History* (Baltimore, Md: Johns Hopkins University Press).

Fourie, F. C. V. N. (1993) 'In the Beginning There Were Markets', in C. Pitelis (ed.), *Transaction Costs, Markets and Hierarchies* (Oxford: Basil Blackwell).

Fox, A. (1974) *Beyond Contract: Work, Power and Trust Relations* (London: Faber).

Frances, J., R. Levacic, J. Mitchell and G. Thompson (1991) 'Introduction', in G. Thompson, J. Frances, R. Levacic and J. Mitchell (eds), *Markets, Hierarchies and Networks: The Coordination of Social Life* (London: Sage).

Francis, A. (1983) 'Markets and Hierarchies: Efficiency or Domination?', in A. Francis, J. Turk and P. Willman (eds), *Power, Efficiency and Institutions: A Critical Appraisal of the "Markets and Hierarchies" Paradigm* (London: Heinemann).

Francis, A., J. Turk and P. Willman (1983) 'Introduction', in A. Francis, J. Turk and P. Willman (eds), *Power, Efficiency and Institutions: A Critical Appraisal of the "Markets and Hierarchies" Paradigm* (London: Heinemann).

Francis, A., J. Turk and P. Willman (eds) (1983) *Power, Efficiency and Institutions: A Critical Appraisal of the "Markets and Hierarchies" Paradigm* (London: Heinemann).

Frank, R. H. (1992) 'Melding Sociology and Economics: James Coleman's *Foundations of Social Theory*', *Journal of Economic Literature*, vol. xxx, pp. 147–70.

Freeman. J. (1990) 'Ecological Analysis of Semiconductor Firm Mortality', in J. V. Singh (ed.), *Organizational Evolution: New Directions* (London: Sage).

Freeman, J. and J. Brittain (1977) 'Union Merger Process and Industrial Environment', *Industrial Relations*, vol. 16, pp. 173–85.

Friedman, A. L. (1977) *Industry and Labour: Class Struggle at Work and Monopoly Capitalism* (London: Macmillan).

Friedman, A. L. (1984) 'Management Strategies, Market Conditions and the Labour Process', in F. H. Stephen (ed.), *Firms, Organization and Labour: Approaches to the Economics of Work Organization* (London: Macmillan).

Friedman, A. (1986) 'Developing the Managerial Strategies Approach to the Labour Process', *Capital and Class*, no. 30, pp. 97–124.

Friedman, A. L. (1990a) 'Strawmania and Beyond: The Development of Labour Process Analysis and Critique', Paper presented to the UMIST Organization and Control of the Labour Process Conference (1990) Aston University.

Friedman, A. L. (1990b) 'Managerial Strategies, Activities, Techniques and Technology: Towards a Complex Theory of the Labour Process', in D. Knights and H. Willmott (eds) *Labour Process Theory* (London: Macmillan).

Friedman, M. (1953) 'The Methodology of Positive Economics' in *Essays in Positive Economics* (University of Chicago Press).

Froebel, F., J. Heinrichs and O. Kreye (1981) *The New International Division of Labour: Structural Unemployment in Industrialized Countries and Industrialization in Developing countries* (Cambridge University Press).

Galbraith, J. K. (1952) *American Capitalism: The Concept of Counterveiling Power* (London: Hamish Hamilton).

Galbraith, J. K. (1958) *The Affluent Society* (London: Hamish Hamilton).

Galbraith, J. K. (1967) *The New Industrial State* (London: Hamish Hamilton).

Galbraith, J. K. (1987) *A History of Economics: The Past as the Present* (London: Hamish Hamilton).

Galbraith, J. K. (1993) *The Culture of Contentment* (Harmondsworth: Penguin).

Gallie, W. B. (1955–6) 'Essentially Contested Concepts', *Proceedings of the Aristotelian Society*, vol. 56, pp. 167–98.

Geertz, C. (1992) 'The Bazaar Economy: Information and Search in Peasant Marketing', in M. Granovetter and R. Swedberg (eds), *The Sociology of Economic Life* (Oxford: Westview Press).

Geras, N. (1983) *Marx and Human Nature: Refutation of a Legend* (London: Verso).

Gerth, H. H. and C. Wright Mills (1991) Introduction to *From Max Weber: Essays in Sociology*, edited by H. H. Gerth and C. Wright Mills (London: Routledge).

Ghoshal, S. and D. E. Westney (1993) 'Introduction and Overview', in S. Ghoshal and D. E. Westney (eds), *Organization Theory and the Multinational Corporation* (London: Macmillan).

Giddens, A. (1979) *Central Problems in Social Theory: Action, Structure and Contradiction in Social Analysis* (London: Macmillan).

Giddens, A. (1986) *The Constitution of Society: Outline of the Theory of Structuration* (Cambridge: Polity Press).

Goldberg, V. P. (1980) 'Bridges Over Contested Terrain: Exploring the Radical Account of the Employment Relationship', *Journal of Economic Behavior and Organization*, vol. 1, pp. 249–74.

Gospel, H. (1992) *Markets, Firms, and the Management of Labour in Modern Britain* (Cambridge University Press).

Gould, S. J. (1991) *Wonderful Life: The Burgess Shale and the Nature of History* (Harmondsworth: Penguin).

Gould, S. J. (1992) *Bully for Brontosaurus: Further Reflections in Natural History* (Harmondsworth: Penguin).

Granovetter, M. (1992a) 'Economic Action and Social Structure: The Problem of Embeddedness', in M. Granovetter and R. Swedberg (eds), *The Sociology of Economic Life*.

Granovetter, M. and R. Swedberg (eds) (1992b) *The Sociology of Economic Life* (Oxford: Westview Press).

Green, F. (1988) 'Neoclassical and Marxian Conceptions of Production', *Cambridge Journal of Economics*, vol. 12, pp. 299–312.

Green, F. (1992) 'Neoclassical and Marxian Models of Production: A Reply to Young', *Cambridge Journal of Economics*, vol. 16, pp. 109–11.

Grossman, S. and O. Hart (1983) 'An Analysis of the Principal–Agent Problem', *Econometrica*, vol. 98, pp. 123–56.

Gustafsson, B. (1991a) 'Introduction', in B. Gustafsson (ed.), *Power and Economic Institutions: Reinterpretations in Economic History*.

Gustafsson, B. (ed.) (1991b) *Power and Economic Institutions: Reinterpretations in Economic History* (Aldershot: Edward Elgar).

Hamilton, D. (1975) [1953] *Newtonian Classicism and Darwinian Institutionalism: A Study of Change in Economic Theory* Westport, Conn.: Greenwood).

Hamilton, G. G. and N. W. Biggart (1988) 'Market, Culture, and Authority: A Comparative Analysis of Management and Organization in the Far East', in C. Winship and S. Rosen (eds), *Organizations and Institutions: Sociological and Economic Approaches to the Analysis of Social Structure* Supplement to *American Journal of Sociology*, vol. 94 (University of Chicago Press).

Hannah, L. (1976) 'Introduction' in *Management Strategy and Business Development: an Historical and Comparative Study* (London: Macmillan).

Hannah, L. (1983) 'New Issues in British Business History', *Business History Review*, vol. LVII, pp. 165–74.

Hannah, L. (1984) 'Entrepreneurs and the Social Sciences', *Economica*, vol. 51, pp. 219–34.

Hannan, M. T. and J. Freeman (1977) 'The Population Ecology of Organizations', *American Journal of Sociology*, vol. 82, pp. 929–64.

Hannan, M. T. and J. Freeman (1989) *Organizational Ecology* (Cambridge, Mass.: Harvard University Press).

Harman, C. (1984) *Explaining the Crisis: A Marxist Re-appraisal* (London: Bookmarks).

Hartman, H. (1979) 'The Unhappy Marriage of Marxism and Feminism: Towards a More Progressive Union'; *Capital & Class*, no. 8, pp. 1–33.

Hassard, J. (1993) *Sociology and Organization Theory: Positivism, Paradigms and Postmodernity* (Cambridge University Press).

Hausman, D. M. (1992) *The Inexact and Separate Science of Economics* (Cambridge University Press).

Hennart, J.-F. (1991) 'The Transaction Cost Theory of the Multinational Enterprise', in C. N. Pitelis, and R. Sugden (eds), *The Nature of the Transnational Firm* (London: Routledge).

Hess, J. D. (1983) *The Economics of Organization* (Oxford: North-Holland).

Hessen, R. (1983) 'The Modern Corporation and Private Property: A Reappraisal', *The Journal of Law and Economics*, vol. XXVI, no. 2, pp. 273–90.

Hesterly, W. M., J. Liebeskind and T. R. Zenger (1990) 'Organizational Economics: An Impending Revolution in Organization Theory?', *Academy of Management Review*, vol. 15, no. 3, pp. 402–20.

Hesterly, W. S. and T. R. Zenger (1993) 'The Myth of a Monolithic Economics: Fundamental Assumptions and the Use of Economic Models in Policy and Strategy Research', *Organization Science*, vol. 4, no. 3, August, pp. 496–510.

Hirsch, P., S. Michaels and R. Friedman (1990) 'Clean Models vs Dirty Hands: Why Economics is Different from Sociology', in S. Zukin and P. DiMaggio (eds), *Structures of Capital: The Social Organization of the Economy* (Cambridge University Press).

Hirschleifer, J. (1977) 'Economics from a Biological Point of View'. *Journal of Law and Economics*, vol. 20, pp. 1–52.

Hirschman, A. O. (1970) *Exit, Voice, and Loyalty: Responses to Decline in Firms, Organizations, and States* (Cambridge, Mass.: Harvard University Press).

Hodgson, G. (1974) 'The Theory of the Falling Rate of Profit', *New Left Review*, no. 84, March/April, pp. 55–82.

Hodgson, G. (1975) *Trotsky and Fatalistic Marxism* (Nottingham: Spokesman Books).

Hodgson, G. (1982a) *Capitalism, Value and Exploitation. A Radical Theory* (Oxford: Martin Robertson).

Hodgson, G. (1982b) 'Marx Without The Labour Theory of Value', *Review of Radical Political Economy*, vol. 14, no. 2, pp. 59–65.

Hodgson, G. M. (1988) *Economics and Institutions: A Manifesto for a Modern Institutional Economics* (Cambridge: Polity Press).

Hodgson, G. M. (1992) 'Thorsten Veblen and Post-Darwinian Economics', *Cambridge Journal of Economics*, vol. 16, pp. 285–301.

Hodgson, G. M. (1993) 'Transaction Costs and the Evolution of the Firm', in C. Pitelis (ed.), *Transaction Costs, Markets and Hierarchies* (Oxford: Basil Blackwell).

Hoksbergen, R. (1994) 'Postmodernism and Institutionalism: Toward a Resolution of the Debate on Relativism', *Journal of Economic Issues*, vol. XXVIII, no. 3, pp. 679–713.

Holton, R. (1992) *Economy and Society* (London: Routledge).

Hoskisson, R. E., C. W. L. Hill and H. Kim (1993) 'The Multidivisional Structure: Organizational Fossil of Source of Value?', *Journal of Management*, vol. 19, no. 2, pp. 269–98.

Hughes, E. C. (1936) 'The Ecological Aspect of Institutions', *American Sociological Review*, vol. 1, pp. 180–9.

Humphrey, R. (1985) 'How Work Roles Influence Perception: Structural–Cognitive Processes and Organizational Behaviour', *American Sociological Review*, vol. 50, pp. 242–52.

Hutchison, T. W. (1981) *The Politics and Philosophy of Economics: Marxians, Keynesians and Austrians* (Oxford: Basil Blackwell).

Jackall, R. (1988) *Moral Mazes: The World of Corporate Managers* (Oxford University Press).

Jensen, M. (1983) 'Organization Theory and Methodology', *Accounting Review*, vol. LVIII, no. 2, April, pp. 319–39.

Jensen, M. and W. Meckling (1986) 'Theory of the Firm: Managerial Behavior, Agency Costs, and Ownership Structure', in L. Putterman (ed.), *The Economic Nature of the Firm: A Reader* (Cambridge University Press).

Kanter, R. M. (1990) *When Giants Learn to Dance* (London: Routledge).

Kantrow, A. M. (ed.) (1986) 'Why History Matters to Managers', *Harvard Business Review*, January–February, pp. 81–8.

Kay, N. M. (1991) 'Multinational Enterprises as Strategic Choice: Some Transaction Cost Perspectives', in C. N. Pitelis, and R. Sugden (eds), *The Nature of the Transnational Firm* (London: Routledge).

Kay, N. M. (1993) 'Markets, False Hierarchies and the Role of Asset Specificity', in C. Pitelis (ed.), *Transaction Costs, Markets and Hierarchies* (Oxford: Blackwell).

Kelly, J. (1988) *Trade Unions and Socialist Politics* (London: Verso).

Knights, D. (1990) 'Subjectivity, Power and the Labour Process', in D. Knights and H. Willmott (eds), *Labour Process Theory* (London: Macmillan).

Knights, D. and H. Willmott (eds) (1990) *Labour Process Theory* (London: Macmillan).

Knights, D., H. Willmott and D. Collinson (eds) (1985) *Job Redesign: Critical Perspectives on the Labour Process* (Aldershot: Gower).

Knights, D. and H. Willmott (1989) 'Power and Subjectivity at Work: From Degradation to Subjugation in Social Relations', *Sociology*, vol. 23, no. 4, pp. 535–58.

Knoke, D. and J. H. Kuklinski (1991) 'Network Analysis: Basic Concepts', in G. Thompson, J. Frances, R. Levacic and J. Mitchell (eds), *Markets, Hierarchies and Networks: The Coordination of Social Life* (London: Sage).

Kreps, D. M. (1990) 'Corporate Culture and Economic Theory', in J. E. Alt and K. A. Shepsle (eds), *Perspectives on Positive Political Economy* (Cambridge University Press).

Kuhn, T. (1970) [1962] *The Structure of Scientific Revolutions* (University of Chicago Press).

Landes. D. (1969) *The Unbound Prometheus: Technological Change and Industrial Development in Europe from 1750 to the Present* (Cambridge University Press).

Landes, D. S. (1986) 'What Do Bosses Really Do?', *The Journal of Economic History*, vol. XLVI, no. 3, pp. 585–623.

Landes, W. M., D. W. Carlton and F. H. Easterbrook (eds) (1983) 'Corporations and Private Property', *Journal of Law and Economics*, vol. XXVI, no. 2, Special issue from the conference commemorating Berle and Means.

Lash, S. and J. Urry (1987) *The End of Organized Capitalism* (Cambridge: Polity in association with Blackwell).

Latsis, S. J. (1972) 'Situational Determinism in Economics', *British Journal of Philosophical Science*, vol. 23, pp. 207–45.

Lazonick, W. (1978) 'The Subjection of Labour to Capital', *Review of Radical Political Economy*, vol. 8, no. 1, pp. 1–31.

Lazonick, W. (1979) 'Industrial Relations and Technical Change: The Case of the Self-acting Mule', *Cambridge Journal of Economics*, vol. 3, pp. 231–62.

Lazonick, W. H. (1983) 'Technological Change and the Control of Work: The Development of Capital–Labour Relations in US Mass Production Industries', in H. F. Gospel and C. R. Littler (eds), *Managerial Strategies and Industrial Relations* (London: Heinemann).

Lazonick, W. (1991) *Business Organization and the Myth of the Market Economy* (Cambridge University Press).

Lazonick, W. (1992) *Organization and Technology in Capitalist Development* (Aldershot: Edward Elgar).

Leibenstein, H. (1986) 'Allocative Efficiency and X-efficiency', in Putterman (ed.), *The Economic Nature of the Firm: A Reader* (Cambridge University Press).

Leibenstein, H. (1986) 'The Prisoners', Dilemma in the Invisible Hand: An Analysis of Intrafirm Productivity', in L. Putterman (ed.), *The Economic Nature of the Firm: A Reader*.

Leibenstein, H. (1987) *Inside the Firm: The Inefficiencies of Hierarchy* (Cambridge, MA: Harvard University Press).

Leinhardt, S. (1977) *Social Networks: A Developing Paradigm* (London: Academic Press).

Lerner, M. (1948) 'Introduction', in M. Lerner (ed.), *The Portable Veblen* (New York: Viking).

Lenski, G. (1976) 'History and Social Change', *American Journal of Sociology*, vol. 82, no. 3, pp. 548–64.

Levy-Garboua, L. (ed.) (1979) *Sociological Economics* (London: Sage).

Levy-Leboyer, M. (1989) 'Introduction', in A. M. Teichova, M. Levy-Leboyer and H. Nussbaum (eds), *Multinational Enterprise in Historical Perspective* (Cambridge University Press).

Libecap, G. D. (1986) 'Property Rights in Economic History: Implications for Research', *Explorations in Economic History*, vol. 23, pp. 227–52.

Littler, C. R. (1990) 'The Labour Process Debate: A Theoretical Review 1974–1988', in D. Knights and H. Willmott (eds), *Labour Process Theory* (London: Macmillan).

Littler, C. and G. Salaman (1982) 'Bravermania and Beyond: Recent Theories of the Labour Process', *Sociology*, vol. 16, pp. 251–69.

Lukes, S. (1974) *Power: A Radical View* (London: Macmillan).

Lupton, T. (1963) *On The Shop Floor: Two Studies of Workshop Organization and Output* (London: Pergamon Press).

Lutz, M. A. and K. Lux (1988) *Humanistic Economics: The New Challenge* (New York: Bootstrap Press).

McCloskey, D. N. (1986) *The Rhetoric of Economics* (Brighton: Wheatsheaf).

McCloskey, D. N. (1987) *Econometric History* (London: Macmillan).

McCloskey, D. N. (1990) *If You're So Smart: The Narrative of Economic Expertise* (London: University of Chicago Press).

McCloskey, D. N. (1991) 'History, Differential Equations, and the Problem of Narration', *History and Theory*, vol. xxx, no. 1, pp. 21–36.

McCraw, T. K. (1988) 'Introduction: The Intellectual Odyssey of Alfred D. Chandler, Jr.', in T. K. McCraw (ed.), *The Essential Alfred Chandler: Essays Toward a Historical theory of Big Business* (Boston, Mass.: Harvard Business School Press).

McDermott, J. (1991) *Corporate Society: Class, Property and Contemporary Capitalism* (Oxford: Westview Press).

McNulty, P. J. (1984) 'On the Nature and Theory of Economic Organization: The Role of the Firm Reconsidered', *History of Political Economy*, vol. 16, no. 2, pp. 233–53.

Macaulay, S. (1992) [1963] 'Non-Contractual Relations in Business: A Preliminary Study', in M. Granovetter and R. Swedberg (eds), *The Sociology of Economic Life* (Oxford: Westview Press).

Machlup, F. (1967) 'Theories of the Firm: Marginalist, Behavioral, and Managerial', *American Economic Review*, vol. LVII, no. 1, pp. 1–33.

Magnusson, L. (1991) 'From *Verlag* to Factory: The Contest for Efficient Property Rights', in B. Gustafsson (ed.), *Power and Economic Institutions: Reinterpretations in Economic History* (Aldershot: Edward Elgar).

Malcomson, J. M. (1984) 'Efficient Labour Organization: Incentives, Power and the Transaction Cost Approach', in F. H. Stephen (ed.), *Firms, Organization and Labour: Approaches to the Economics of Work Organization* (London: Macmillan).

Mandel, E. (1981) 'Introduction', in K. Marx, (1981) *Capital: A Critique of Political Economy*, vol. 3 (Harmondsworth: Penguin).

March, J. G. and H. A. Simon (1961) [1958] *Organizations* (London: John Wiley).

Marginson, P. (1993) 'Power and Efficiency in the Firm: Understanding the Employment Relationship', in C. Pitelis (ed.), *Transaction Costs, Markets and Hierarchies* (Oxford: Basil Blackwell).

Marginson, P., P. K. Edwards, J. Purcell, R. Martin and K. Sisson (1988) *Beyond the Workplace: Managing Industrial Relations in Large Enterprises* (Oxford: Basil Blackwell).

Marglin, S. A. (1976) [1974] 'What Do Bosses Do? The Origins and Functions of Hierarchy in Capitalist Production', in A. Gorz (ed.), *The Division of Labour and Class Struggle in Modern Capitalism* (Brighton: Harvester) (abridged in L. Putterman (ed.), *The Economic Nature of the Firm: A Reader* (Cambridge University Press).

Marglin, S. (1984) 'Knowledge and Power', in F. H. Stephen (ed.), *Firms, Organization and Labour: Approaches to the Economics of Work Organization* (London: Macmillan).

Marglin, S. (1991) 'Understanding Capitalism: Control Versus Efficiency', in B. Gustafsson (ed.), *Power and Economic Institutions: Reinterpretations in Economic History* (Aldershot: Edward Elgar).

Marris, R. and D. C. Mueller (1980) 'The Corporation, Competition, and the Invisible Hand', *Journal of Economic Literature*, vol. 18, pp. 32–63.

Marschak, T. A. (1965) 'Economic Theories of Organization', in J. G. March (ed.), *Handbook of Organization* (Chicago: Rand McNally).

Marsden, R. (1993) 'The Politics of Organizational Analysis', *Organization Studies*, vol. 14, no. 1, pp. 93–124.

Martinelli A. and N. J. Smelser (1990) 'Economic Sociology: Historical Threads and Analytic Issues', in A. Martinelli and N. J. Smelser (eds), *Economy and Society: Overviews in Economic Sociology* (London: Sage).

Marwell, G. and R. E Ames (1981) 'Economists Free Ride, Does Anyone Else?', *Journal of Public Economics*, vol. 15, June, pp. 295–310.

Marx, K. (1969) 'The Eighteenth Brumaire of Louis Bonaparte', in *Karl Marx and Frederick Engels: Selected Works in Three Volumes*, vol. 1 (Moscow: Progress).

Marx, K. (1970) 'Critique of the Gotha Programme' in *Karl Marx and Frederick Engels: Selected Works in Three Volumes*, vol. 3 (Moscow: Progress).

Marx, K. (1976) *Capital: A Critique of Political Economy*, vol. 1 (Harmondsworth: Penguin) (excerpts in L. Putterman (ed.), *The Economic Nature of the Firm: A Reader* (Cambridge University Press).

Marx, K. (1978) *The Poverty of Philosophy: Answer to the 'Philosophy of Poverty', by M. Proudhon* (Peking: Foreign Languages Press).

Marx, K. (1981) *Capital: A Critique of Political Economy*, vol. 3 (Harmondsworth: Penguin).

Masten, S. (1993) 'A Legal Basis for the Firm', in O. E. Williamson and S. G. Winter (eds), *The Nature of the Firm: Origins, Evolution, and Development* (Oxford University Press).

Means, G. C. (1983) 'Hessens's "Reappraisal"', *Journal of Law and Economics*, vol. xxvi, no. 2, pp. 297–300.

Meyer, M. W. (1990a) 'Notes of a Skeptic: From Organizational Ecology to Organizational Evolution', in J. V. Singh (ed.), *Organizational Evolution: New Directions* (London: Sage).

Meyer, M. W. (1990b) 'The Growth of Public and Private Bureaucracies', in S. Zukin and P. DiMaggio (eds), *Structures of Capital: The Social Organization of the Economy*.

Michels, R. (1962) *Political Parties: A Sociological Study of the Oligarchical Tendency of Modern Democracy* (New York: Free Press).

Milgrom, P. and J. Roberts (1988) 'Economic Theories of the Firm: Past, Present, and Future', *Canadian Journal of Economics*, vol. 21, no. 3, pp. 444–58.

Milgrom, P. and J. Roberts (1990) 'Bargaining Costs, Influence Costs, and the Organization of Economic Activity', in J. E. Alt and K. A. Shepsle (eds), *Perspectives on Positive Political Economy* (Cambridge University Press).

Milgrom, P. and J. Roberts (1992) *Economics, Organization and Management* (London: Prentice-Hall.

Miller, W. (ed.) (1979) *Men in Business: Essays on the Historical Role of the Entrepreneur* (Connecticut: Greenwood Press) (reprint of 1962 edn), collection from *Explorations in Entrepreneurial History* (New York: Harper & Row).

Mills, C. W. (1956) *The Power Elite* (New York: Oxford University Press).

Mintzberg, H. (1989) *Mintzberg on Management: Inside Our Strange World of Organizations* (London: Collier Macmillan).

Mirowski, P. (1988) *Against Mechanism: Protecting Economics from Science* (Totawa, New Jersey: Rowman & Littlefield).

Moore, J. I. (1992) *Writers on Strategy and Strategic Management* (Harmondsworth: Penguin).

Moore, T. G. (1983) 'Introduction' in 'Corporations and Private Property', *Journal of Law and Economics*, vol. 26, no. 2, pp. 235–6.

Morgan, G. (1986) *Images of Organization* (London: Sage).

Morgan, G. (1990) *Organizations in Society* (London: Macmillan).

Moss, S. (1984) 'The History of the Theory of the Firm from Marshall to Robinson and Chamberlin: The Source of Positivism in Economics', *Economica*, vol. 51, no. 203, August, pp. 307–18.

Mouzelis, N. (1988) 'Marxism or Post-Marxism?', *New Left Review*, no. 167, January–February, pp. 107–23.

Mouzelis, N. (1993) 'The Poverty of Sociological Theory', *Sociology*, vol. 27, no. 4, pp. 675–95.

Neimark, M. (1990) 'The King is Dead. Long Live the King!', *Critical Perspectives in Accounting*, no. 1, pp. 103–14.

Neimark, M. and T. Tinker (1987) 'Identity and Non-Identity Thinking: A Dialectical Critique of the Transaction Cost Theory of the Modern Corporation', *Journal of Management*, vol. 13, no. 4, pp. 661–73.

Nell, E. (1972) 'Economics: the Revival of Political Economy', in R. Blackburn (ed.), *Ideology in Social Science: Readings in Critical Social Theory* (London: Fontana/Collins).

Nelson, D. (1975) *Managers and Workers: Origins of the New Factory System in the United States 1880–1920* (Madison, Wis.: University of Wisconsin Press).

Nelson, D. (1980) *Frederick Taylor and the Rise of Scientific Management* (Madison, Wis.: University of Wisconsin Press).

Nelson, J. A. and S. M. Sheffrin (1991) 'Economic Literacy or Economic Ideology?, *Journal of Economic Perspectives*, vol. 5, no. 3, Summer, pp. 157–65.

Nelson, R. R. and S. G. Winter (1982) *An Evolutionary Theory of Economic Change* (Cambridge, Mass.: Harvard University Press).

Nichols, T. (1969) *Ownership. Control and Ideology* (London: Allen & Unwin).

Nichols, T. (ed.) (1980) *Capital and Labour: Studies in the Capitalist Labour Process* (London: Fontana).

Nisbet, R. (1969) *Social Change and History: Aspects of the Western Theory of Development* (New York: Oxford University Press).

Nord. W.R. (1985) 'Can Organizational Culture be Managed?', in P.J. Frost, L.F. Moore, M.R. Louis, C.C. Lundberg and J. Martin (eds), *Organizational Culture* (London: Sage).

Nord, W.R. and J.M. Jermier (1992) 'Critical Social Science for Managers? Promising and Perverse Possibilities', in M. Alvesson and H. Willmott (eds), *Critical Management Studies* (London: Sage).

North, D.C. (1983) 'Comment on Stigler and Friedland: "The Literature of Economics: The Case of Berle and Means"', *Journal of Law and Economics*, vol. XXVI, no. 2, pp. 269–71.

North, D.C. (1990a) *Institutions, Institutional Change and Economic Performance* (Cambridge University Press).

North, D.C. (1990b) 'Institutions and a Transaction–Cost Theory of Exchange', in J.E. Alt and K.A. Shepsle (eds), *Perspectives on Positive Political Economy* (Cambridge University Press).

North, D.C. (1991) 'Institutions', *Journal of Economic Perspectives*, vol. 5, no. 1, Winter, pp. 97–112.

Nussbaum, M.C. and A. Sen (eds) (1993) *The Quality of Life* (Oxford: Clarendon Press).

Oberschall, A. and E.M. Leifer (1986) 'Efficiency and social Institutions: Uses and Misuses of Economic Reasoning in Sociology', *Annual Review of Sociology*, vol. 12, pp. 233–53.

O'Brien, D.P. (1984) 'The Evolution of the Theory of the Firm', in F.H. Stephen (ed.), *Firms, Organization and Labour: Approaches to the Economics of Work Organization* (London: Macmillan).

Offe, C. (1985) *Disorganized Capitalism: Contemporary Transformations of Work and Politics*, edited by J. Keane (Cambridge: Polity).

Olson, M. (1971) *The Logic of Collective Action: Public Goods and the Theory of Groups* (London: Harvard University Press).

Ordeshook, P.C. (1990) 'The Emerging Discipline of Political Economy', in J.E. Alt and K.A. Shepsle (eds), *Perspectives on Positive Political Economy* (Cambridge University Press).

Ott, J.S. (1989) *The Organizational Culture Perspective* (Pacific Grove, Calif.: Brooks/Cole).

Ouchi, W.G. (1980) 'Markets, Bureaucracies, and Clans', *Administrative Science Quarterly*, vol. 25, March, pp. 129–41.

Pagano, U. (1985) *Work and Welfare in Economic Theory* (Oxford: Basil Blackwell).

Papandreou, A.G. (1994) *Externality and Institutions* ((Oxford: Clarendon).

Parkin, F. (1982) *Max Weber* (London: Tavistock).

Pejovich, S. (1982) 'Karl Marx, Property Rights School and the Process of Social Change', *Kyklos*, vol. 35, pp. 383–97.

Penrose, E.T. (1952) 'Biological Analogies in the Theory of the Firm', *American Economic Review*, vol. XLII, pp. 804–19.

Penrose, E.T. (1959) *The Theory of the Growth of the Firm* (Oxford: Basil Blackwell).

Perrow, C. (1981) 'Markets, Hierarchies and Hegemony', in A.H. Van De Ven and W.F. Joyce (eds), *Perspectives on Organization Design and Behavior* (New York: John Wiley).

Perrow, C. (1986) *Complex Organizations: A Critical Essay*, (3rd edn) (New York: Random House).

Perrow, C. (1991) 'A Society of Organizations', *Theory and Society*, vol. 20, pp. 725–62.

Perry, N. (1992) 'Putting Theory in its Place: The Social Organization of Organizational Theorizing', ch. 5 in M. Reed and M. Hughes (eds), *Rethinking Organization: New Directions in Organization Theory and Analysis* (London: Sage).

Peters. T. (1992) *Liberation Management* (London: Macmillan).

Peters, T. J. and R. H. Waterman (1982) *In Search of Excellence: Lessons from America's Best Run Companies* (New York: Harper & Row).

Phizacklea, A. and C. Wolkowitz (1995) *Homeworking Women: Gender, Racism and Class at Work* (London: Sage).

Piore, M. J. and C. F. Sabel (1984) *The Second Industrial Divide: Possibilities for Prosperity* (New York: Basic Books).

Pitelis, C. (1987) *Corporate Capital: Control, Ownership, Saving and Crisis* (Cambridge University Press).

Pitelis, C. (1991) 'Beyond the Nation-State? The Transnational Form and the Nation-State', *Capital and Class*, no. 43, Spring, pp. 131–52.

Pitelis, C. (1993) *Market and Non-market Hierarchies: Theory of Institutional Failure* (Oxford: Basil Blackwell).

Pitelis, C. (ed.) (1993) *Transaction Costs, Markets and Hierarchies* (Oxford: Basil Blackwell).

Pitelis, C. N. and R. Sugden (1991) 'On the Theory of the Transnational Firm', in C. N. Pitelis and R. Sugden (eds), *The Nature of the Transnational Firm*.

Pitelis, C. N. and R. Sugden (eds) (1991) *The Nature of the Transnational Firm* (London: Routledge).

Pollak, R. A. (1985) 'A Transaction Cost Approach to Families and Households', *Journal of Economic Literature*, vol. xxiii, June, pp. 581–608.

Pollard, S. (1968) *The Genesis of Modern Management* (Harmondsworth: Penguin).

Pollert, A. (1981) *Girls, Wives, Factory Lives* (London: Macmillan).

Posner, R. (1992) *Sex and Reason* (London: Harvard University Press).

Poundstone, W. (1993) *Prisoner's Dilemma* (Oxford University Press).

Powell, W. W. and P. J. DiMaggio (eds) (1991) *The New Institutionalism Organizational Analysis* (London: University of Chicago).

Power, M. and R. Laughlin (1992) 'Critical Theory and Accounting', in M. Alvesson and H. Willmott (eds), *Critical Management Studies* (London: Sage).

Pratt, J. W. and R. J. Zeckhauser (1985) 'Principals and Agents: An Overview', in J. W. Pratt and R. J. Zeckhauser (eds), *Principals and Agents: The Structure of Business* (Boston, Mass.: Harvard Business School Press).

Prescott, E. C. (1978) 'Papers in Honor of Herbert A. Simon: An Introduction', *Bell Journal of Economics*, vol. 9, no. 2, Autumn, pp. 491–3.

Pringle, R. (1988) *Secretaries Talk: Sexuality, Power and Work* (London: Verso).

Pugh, D. S. (1990a) [1973] 'The Measurement of Organization Structures: Does Context Determine Form?', in D. S. Pugh (ed.), *Organization Theory: Selected Theory*.

Pugh, D. S. (1990b) *Organization Theory: Selected Theory*, introduction to 3rd edn, (Harmondsworth Penguin).

Pugh, D. S., R. Mansfield and M. Warner (1975) *Research in Organizational Behaviour* (London: Heinemann).

Purcell, J. and B. Ahlstrand (1994) *Human Resource Management in the Multidivisional Company* (Oxford University Press).

Putterman, L. (1986a) 'The Economic Nature of the Firm: Overview', in Putterman (ed.), *The Economic Nature of the Firm: A Reader* (Cambridge University Press).

Putterman, L. (ed.) (1986b) *The Economic Nature of the Firm: A Reader* (Cambridge University Press).

Putterman, L. (1990) *Division of Labor and Welfare: An Introduction to Economic Systems* (Oxford University Press).

Ramsay, H. (1985) 'What Is Participation For? A Critical Evaluation of "Labour Process" Analyses of Job Reform', in D. Knights, H. Willmott and D. Collinson (eds), *Job Redesign: Critical Perspectives on the Labour Process* (Aldershot: Gower).

Reed, M. (1989) *The Sociology of Management* (London: Harvester Wheatsheaf).

Reed, M. (1992a) 'Introduction', in M. Reed and M. Hughes (eds), *Rethinking Organization: New Directions in Organization Theory and Analysis* (London: Sage).

Reed, M. (1992b) *The Sociology of Organizations: Themes, Perspectives and Prospects* (London: Harvester Wheatsheaf).

Reve, T. (1990) 'The Firm as a Nexus of Internal and External Contracts', in M. Aoki, B. Gustafsson and O. E. Williamson (eds), *The Firm as Nexus of Treaties* (London: Sage).

Ricketts, M. (1987) *The Economics of Business Enterprise: New Approaches to the Firm* (London: Harvester Wheatsheaf).

Ritzer, G. (1993) *The McDonaldization of Society* (London: Pine Forge Press).

Rosenberg, N. (1982) *Inside the Black Box: Technology and Economics* (Cambridge University Press).

Rowe, G. (1993) 'Playing for High Stakes', Review of Sigmund (1993), *Games of Life, The Times Higher Education Supplement*, 5 November.

Rowlinson, M. (1988) 'The Early Application of Scientific Management by Cadbury', *Business History*, vol. xxx, no. 4, pp. 377–95.

Rowlinson, M. and J. Hassard (1993) 'The Invention of Corporate Culture: A History of the Histories of Cadbury', *Human Relations*, vol. 46, no. 3, pp. 299–326.

Rowlinson, M. and J. Hassard (1994) 'Economics, Politics and Labour Process Theory', *Capital and Class*, no. 53, pp. 65–97.

Roy, D. F. (1973) [1960] 'Banana Time: Job Satisfaction and Informal Interaction', in G. Salaman and K. Thompson (eds), *People and Organizations* (Harlow: Longman for Open University Press).

Ruccio, D. F. (1991) 'Postmodernism and Economics', *Journal of Post Keynesian Economics*, vol. 13, no. 4, pp. 495–510.

Rueschemeyer, D. (1986) *Power and the Division of Labour* (Cambridge: Polity Press).

Rumelt, R. P. (1974) *Strategy, Structure and Economic Performance* (Cambridge Mass.: Harvard University Press).

Rumelt, R. P., D. Schendel and D. J. Teece (1991) 'Strategic Management and Economics', *Strategic Management Journal*, vol. 12, pp. 5–29.

Rumelt, R. P., D. Schendel and DJ. Teece (eds) (1991) 'Strategic Management and Economics', *Strategic Management Journal*, vol. 12, Winter Special Issue.

Samuelson, P. (1957) 'Wages and Interest: A Modern Dissection of Marxian Economic Models', *American Economic Review*, vol. 47, December, pp. 884–912.

Sanderson, S. K. (1990) *Social Evolutionism: A Critical History* (Oxford: Basil Blackwell).

Sappington, D. E. M. (1991) 'Incentives in Principal–Agent Relationships', *Journal of Economic Perspectives*, vol. 5, no. 2, pp. 45–66.

Sawyer, M. (1979) *Theories of the Firm* (London: Weidenfeld and Nicolson).

Sawyer, M. (1993) 'The Nature and Role of the Market', in C. Pitelis (ed.), *Transaction Costs, Markets and Hierarchies* (Oxford: Basil Blackwell).

Schumacher, E. F. (1973) *Small is Beautiful: A Study of Economics as if People Mattered* (London: Blond and Briggs).

Schumpeter, J. A. (1954) *History of Economic Analysis* (New York: Oxford University Press).

Schumpeter, J. A. (1976) *Capitalism, Socialism and Democracy* (London: George Allen & Unwin).

Scott, J. (1985) *Corporations, Classes and Capitalism* (2nd edn) (London: Hutchinson).

Scott, W. R. (1987) 'The Adolescence of Institutional Theory', *Administrative Science Quarterly*, vol. 32, pp. 493–511.

Scott, W. R. (1994) 'Institutions and Organizations: Toward a Theoretical Synthesis', in W. R. Scott and J. W. Meyer and Associates *Institutional Environments and Organizations: Structural Complexity and Individualism* (London: Sage).

Seckler, D. (1975) *Thorstein Veblen and the Insitutionalists: A Study in the Social Philosophy of Economics* (London: Macmillan).

Selznick, P. (1957) *Leadership in Administration: A Sociological Interpretation* (Evanston, Ill.: Row, Peterson).

Semmler, W. (1982) 'Theories of Competition and Monopoly', *Capital and Class*, no. 18, pp. 91–116.

Sen, A. (1982) *Choice, Welfare and Measurement* (Oxford: Basil Blackwell).

Sharrock, W. W. (1987) 'Individual and Society', in R. J. Anderson, J. A. Hughes and W. W. Sharrock (eds), *Classic Disputes in Sociology* (London: George Allen & Unwin).

Shionaya, Y. (1991) 'Schumpeter on Schmoller and Weber: A Methodology of Economic Sociology', *History of Political Economy*, vol. 23, no. 2, pp. 193–219.

Sigmund, K. (1993) *Games of Life: Explorations in Ecology, Evolution, and Behaviour* (Oxford University Press).

Silk, L. (1978) *The Economists* (New York: Avon Books).

Simon, H. (1976) [1945] *Administrative Behavior: A Study of Decision-Making Processes in Administrative Organization* (3rd edn) (London: Free Press, Collier Macmillan).

Simon, H. (1982) 'Introduction' in *Models of Bounded Rationality*, vol. 2, *Behavioral Economics and Business Organization* (London: MIT Press).

Simon, H. (1983) *Reason in Human Affairs* (Stanford: Stanford University Press).

Simon, H. (1986) 'A Formal Theory of the Employment Relationship', in L. Putterman (ed.) *The Economic Nature of the Firm: A Reader* (Cambridge University Press).

Singh, J. V. (1990) 'Introduction', in J. V. Singh (ed.), *Organizational Evolution: New Directions* (London: Sage).

Sklair, L. (1981) 'Sociologies and Marxisms: The Odd Couples', in P. Abrams *et al.* (eds), *Practice and Progress: British Sociology 1950–1980* (London: George Allen & Unwin).

Sloan, A. P. (1986) [1963] *My Years with General Motors* (Harmondsworth: Penguin).

Smircich, L. (1985) 'Is the Concept of Culture a Paradigm for Understanding Organizations and Ourselves?', in P. J. Frost, L. F. Moore, M. R. Louis, C. C. Lundberg and J. Martin (eds), *Organizational Culture* (London: Sage).

Smith, A. (1976) [1776] *An Inquiry into the Nature and Causes of The Wealth of Nations* (University of Chicago Press) (excerpts in L. Putterman (ed.), *The Economic Nature of the Firm: A Reader* (Cambridge University Press).

Sraffa, P. (1960) *The Production of Commodities by Commodities: Prelude to a Critique of Economic Theory* (Cambridge University Press).

Stark, D. (1992) 'Bending the Bars of the Iron Cage: Bureaucratization and Informalization in Capitalism and Socialism', in C. Smith and P. Thompson (eds), *Labour in Transition: The Labour Process in Eastern Europe and China* (London: Routledge).

Stearns, L. B. (1990) 'Capital market effects on external control of corporations', in S. Zukin and P. DiMaggio (eds), *Structures of Capital: The Social Organization of the Economy* (Cambridge University Press).

Steedman, I. (1977) *Marx after Sraffa* (London: NLB).

Steedman, I. (1982) 'Marx on Ricardo' in I. Bradley and M. Howard (eds) *Classical and Marxian Political Economy: Essays in Honour of Ronald L. Meek* (London: Macmillan).

Stephen, F. H. (1984a) 'Economics and Work Organization', in F. H. Stephen (ed.), *Firms, Organization and Labour: Approaches to the Economics of Work Organization.*

Stephen, F. H. (ed.) (1984b) *Firms, Organization and Labour: Approaches to the Economics of Work Organization* (London: Macmillan).

Stephen, F. and S. Thompson (1988) 'Internal Organisation and Investment', in S. Thompson and M. Wright (eds), *Internal Organization, Efficiency and Profit* (Oxford: Philip Allan).

Stewart, R. (1993) 'Listening and Dying with Tom', Review of T. Peters (1992) *Liberation Management* in *The Times Higher Education Supplement*, 26 November.

Stigler, G. J. (1984) 'Economics – The Imperial Science?', *Scandinavian Journal of Economics*, vol. 86, pp. 301–13.

Stigler, G. J. and C. Friedland (1983) 'The Literature of Economics: The Case of Berle and Means', *The Journal of Law and Economics*, vol. xxvi, no. 2, pp. 237–68.

Stiglitz, J. E. (1991) 'Symposium on Organizations and Economics', *Journal of Economic Perspectives*, vol. 5, no. 2, pp. 15–24.

Stinchcombe, A. (1983) *Economic Sociology* (London: Academic Press).

Stinchcombe, A. L. (1990) *Information and Organizations* (Oxford: University of California Press).

Storey, J. (1983) *Managerial Prerogative and the Question of Control* (London: Routledge & Kegan Paul).

Strauss, G. (1992) [1955] 'Group Dynamics and Intergroup Relations', in M. Granovetter and R. Swedberg (eds), *The Sociology of Economic Life* (Oxford: Westview Press).

Swedberg, R. (1991) '"The Battle of Methods": Toward a Paradigm Shift?', in A. Etzioni and P. R. Lawrence (eds) (1991) *Socio-Economics: Toward a New Synthesis* (London: M. E. Sharpe).

Swedberg, R. and M. Granovetter (1992) 'Introduction', in M. Granovetter and R. Swedberg (eds), *The Sociology of Economic Life* (Oxford: Westview Press).

Swedberg, R., U. Himmelstrand and G. Brulin (1990) 'The Paradigm of Economic Sociology', in S. Zukin and P. DiMaggio *Structures of capital: The social organization of the economy* (Cambridge University Press).

Taylor, F. W. (1967) [1911] *The Principles of Scientific Management* (London: W. W. Norton).

Teichova, A., M. Levy-Leboyer, and H. Nussbaum (eds) (1989) *Multinational Enterprise in Historical Perspective* (Cambridge University Press).

Teece, D. and S. Winter (1984) 'The Limits of Neoclassical Theory in Management Education', *The American Economic Review*, vol. 74, no. 2, May, pp. 116–21.

Terkel, S. (1985) [1972] *Working: People Talk About What They Do All Day and How They Feel About What They Do* (New York: Ballantine).

Thomas, P. T. (1985) *Karl Marx and the Anarchists* (London: Routledge & Kegan Paul).

Thompson, E. P. (1978) *The Poverty of Theory and Other Essays* (London: Merlin).

Thompson, E. P. (1993) *Customs in Common* (Harmondsworth: Penguin).

Thompson, G. (1991) 'Introduction' to 'Networks', in G. Thompson, J. Frances, R. Levacic and J. Mitchell (eds), *Markets, Hierarchies and Networks: The Coordination of Social Life*.

Thompson, G., J. Frances, R. Levacic and J. Mitchell (eds) (1991) *Markets, Hierarchies and Networks: The Coordination of Social Life* (London: Sage).

Thompson, P. (1989) *The Nature of Work: An Introduction to Debates on the Labour Process* (London: Macmillan).

Thompson, P. (1990) 'Crawling From the Wreckage: The Labour Process Debate and the Politics of Production', in D. Knights and H. Willmott (eds), *Labour Process Theory* (London: Macmillan).

Thompson, P. (1993) 'Fatal Distraction: Post-Modernism and Organisational Analysis', in J. Hassard and M. Parker (eds), *Postmodernism and Organisation* (London: Sage).

Thompson, P. and D. McHugh (1990) *Work Organisations: A Critical Introduction* (London: Macmillan).

Thompson, S. and M. Wright (eds) (1988) *Internal Organization, Efficiency and Profit* (Oxford: Philip Allan).

Thompson, S. and M. Wright (1993) 'Markets, Hierarchies and Markets Again', in C. Pitelis (ed.), *Transaction Costs, Markets and Hierarchies* (Oxford: Basil Blackwell).

Thorelli, H. B. (1965) 'the Political Economy of the Firm: Basis for a New Theory of Competition?', *Scweiz Zeitschr Volkswirtschaft und Stat*, vol. 101, pp. 248–62.

Trist, E. and K. W. Bamforth (1984) [1951] 'Some Social and Psychological Consequences of the Longwall Method of Coal-getting', in D. S. Pugh (ed.), *Organization Theory: Selected Readings* (3rd edn) (Harmondsworth: Penguin).

Trotsky, L. (1971) *In Defence of Marxism: Against the Petty Bourgeois Opposition* (London: New Park).

Turk, J. (1983) 'Conclusion: Power, Efficiency and Institutions: Some Implications of the Debate for the Scope of Economics', in A. Francis, J. Turk and P. Willman (eds), *Power, Efficiency and Institutions: A Critical Appraisal of the "Markets and Hierarchies" Paradigm* (London: Heinemann).

Van De Ven, A. H. and W. F. Joyce (eds) (1981) 'The Markets and Hierarchies and Visible Hand Perspectives', *Perspectives on Organization Design and Behavior* (New York: John Wiley).

Van Parijs, P. (1980) 'The Falling-Rate-of-Profit Theory of Crisis: A Rational Reconstruction by Way of Obituary', *The Review of Radical Political Economy*, vol. 12, no. 1, Spring, pp. 1–16.

Veblen, T. (1948) *The Portable Veblen*, edited by M. Lerner (New York: Viking).

Weber, M. (1930) *The Protestant Ethic and the Spirit of Capitalism* (London: Unwin University Books).

Weber, M. (1991) *From Max Weber: Essays in Sociology*, edited by H. H. Gerth and C. Wright Mills (London: Routledge).

Weick, K. E. (1979) *The Social Psychology of Organizing* (2nd edn) (New York: Random House).

Wellman, B. and S. D. Berkowitz (eds) (1988) *Social Structures: A Network Approach* (Cambridge University Press).

Wheelock, J. (1983) 'Competition in the Marxist Tradition', *Capital and Class*, no. 21, pp. 18–47.

Wheelock, J. (1986) 'Competition and Monopoly: A Contribution to Debate', *Capital and Class*, no. 30, Winter, p. 184.

Whitaker, A (1992) 'The Transformation in Work: Post-Fordism Revisited', in M. Reed and M. Hughes (eds), *Rethinking Organization: New Directions in Organization Theory and Analysis* (London: Sage).

Whitley, R. (1987) 'Taking Firms Seriously as Economic Actors: Towards a Sociology of Firm Behaviour', *Organization Studies*, vol. 8, no. 2, pp. 125–47.

Whitley, R. (1992) 'The Social Construction of Organizations and Markets: The Comparative Analysis of Business Recipes', in M. Reed and M. Hughes (eds), *Rethinking Organization: New Directions in Organization Theory and Analysis* (London: Sage).

Whyte, W. H. (1960) *The Organization Man* (Harmondsworth: Penguin).

Williams, K., T. Cutler, J. Williams and C. Haslam (1987) 'The End of Mass Production?', Review of M. Piore and C. Sabel (1984) *The Second Industrial Divide*, in *Economy and Society*, vol. 16, no. 3, pp. 405–39.

Williamson, O. E. (1963) 'A Model of Rational Managerial Behavior', in R. M. Cyert and J. G. March *A Behavioral Theory of the Firm* (Englewood Cliffs, NJ.: Prentice-Hall).

Williamson, O. E. (1964) *The Economics of Discretionary Behaviour: Managerial Objectives in a Theory of the Firm* (London: Prentice-Hall).

Williamson, O. E. (1980a) 'The Organization of Work', *Journal of Economic Behavior and Organization*, vol. 1, March, pp. 5–38 (abridged in L. Putterman (ed.), *The Economic Nature of the Firm: A Reader* (Cambridge University Press)).

Williamson, O. E. (1980b) 'Emergence of the Visible Hand: Implications for Industrial Organization', in A. D. Chandler Jr. and H. Daems (eds), *Managerial Hierarchies: Comparative Perspectives on the Rise of the Modern Industrial Enterprise* (London: Harvard University Press).

Williamson, O. E. (1981) 'The Economics of Organization: The Transaction Cost Approach', *American Journal of Sociology*, vol. 87, no. 3, pp. 548–577.

Williamson, O. E. (1983a) [1975] *Markets and Hierarchies: Analysis and Antitrust Implications* (London: Free Press/Collier Macmillan).

Williamson, O. E. (1983) 'Organization Form, Residual Claimants, and Corporate Control', *Journal of Law and Economics*, vol. xxvi, no. 2, pp. 351–66.

Williamson, O. E. (1984) 'Efficient Labour Organization', in F. H. Stephen (ed.), *Firms, Organization and Labour: Approaches to the Economics of Work Organization* (London: Macmillan).

Williamson, O. E. (1985) *The Economic Institutions of Capitalism: Firms, Markets, Relational Contracting* (London: Free Press/Collier Macmillan).

Williamson, O. E. (1986) [1963] 'Managerial Discretion and Business Behaviour', in O. E. Williamson *Economic Organization: Firms, Markets and Policy Control* (London: Harvester Wheatsheaf) (reprinted from 1963 *American Economic Review*, vol. liii, no. 5, pp. 1032–57).

Williamson, O. E. (1986) *Economic Organization: Firms, Markets and Policy Control* (London: Harvester Wheatsheaf).

Williamson, O. E. (1990) 'Introduction', in O. E. Williamson (ed.), *Organization Theory: From Chester Barnard to the Present and Beyond* (Oxford University Press).

Williamson, O. E. (1991) 'Comparative Economic Organization: The Analysis of Discrete Structural Alternatives', *Administrative Science Quarterly*, vol. 36, pp. 269–96.

Williamson, O. E. (1992) 'The Logic of Economic Organization, with Applications to International Business', Address to the European International Business Association 18th Annual Conference, University of Reading.

Williamson, O. E. (1993a) 'The Logic of Economic Organization', in O. E. Williamson and S. G. Winter (eds), *The Nature of the Firm: Origins, Evolution, and Development* (Oxford University Press).

Williamson, O. E. (1993b) 'Contested Exchange Versus the Governance of Contractual Relations', *Journal of Economic Perspectives*, vol. 7, no. 1, pp. 103–8.

Williamson, O. E. (1995) 'Transaction Cost Economics and Organization Theory', in O. E. Williamson (ed.), *Organization Theory: From Chester Barnard to the Present and Beyond*, expanded edition (Oxford University Press).

Williamson, O. E. and W. G. Ouchi (1981) 'The Markets and Hierarchies Program of Research: Origins, Implications, Prospects', in A. H. Van De Ven and W. F. Joyce (eds), *Perspectives on Organization Design and Behavior* (New York: John Wiley).

Williamson, O. E., M. Wachter and J. Harris (1986) 'Understanding the Employment Relation: The Analysis of Idiosyncratic Exchange', in L. Putterman (ed.) *The Economic Nature of the Firm: A Reader* (Cambridge University Press).

Williamson, O. E. and S. G. Winter (eds) (1993) *The Nature of the Firm: Origins, Evolution, and Development* (Oxford University Press).

Willmott, H. (1990) 'Subjectivity and the Dialectics of Praxis: Opening up the Core of Labour Process Analysis', in D. Knights and H. Willmott (eds), *Labour Process Theory* (London: Macmillan).

Wilson, D. C. and R. H. Rosenfeld (1990) *Managing Organizations* (London: McGraw-Hill).

Winship, C and S. Rosen (1988a) 'Introduction: Sociological and Economic Approaches to the Analysis of Social Structure', in C. Winship and S. Rosen (eds), *Organizations and Institutions: Sociological and Economic Approaches to the Analysis of Social Structure*.

Winship, C and S. Rosen (eds) (1988b) *Organizations and Institutions: Sociological and Economic Approaches to the Analysis of Social Structure*, Supplement to *American Journal of Sociology*, vol. 94 (University of Chicago Press).

Winter, S. G. (1990) 'Survival, Selection, and Inheritance in Evolutionary Theories of Organization', in J. V. Singh (ed.), *Organizational Evolution: New Directions* (London: Sage).

Winter, S. G. (1993) 'On Coase, Competence, and the Corporation', in O. E. Williamson and S. G. Winter (eds), *The Nature of the Firm: Origins, Evolution, and Development* (Oxford University Press).

Wood, S. (ed.) (1982) *The Degradation of Work?* (London: Hutchinson).

Woodward, J. (1969) [1968] *Management and Technology*, Excerpt in T. Burns (ed.), *Industrial Man* (Harmondsworth: Penguin).

Wright, E. O. (1981) 'Reconsiderations' in I. Steedman *et al.*, (eds), *The Value Controversy* (London: Verso).

Young, D. (1992) 'Problems in Reconciling Neoclassical and Marxian Models of Production: A Comment on Green', *Cambridge Journal of Economics*, vol. 16, pp. 101–7.

Young, R. C. (1988) 'Is Population Ecology a Useful Paradigm for the Study of Organizations?', *American Journal of Sociology*, vol. 94, no. 1, pp. 1–24.

Zald, M. N. (1987) 'Review Essay: The New Institutional Economics', *American Journal of Sociology*, vol. 93, pp. 701–8.

Zeitlin, M. (1989) *The Large Corporation and Contemporary Classes* (Cambridge: Polity Press).

Zimbalist, A. (ed.) (1979) *Case Studies in the Labour Process* (New York: Monthly Review Press).

Zucker, L. G. (1983) 'Organizations as Institutions', *Research in the Sociology of Organizations*, vol. 2, pp. 1–47.

Zucker, L. G. (1991) 'The Role of Institutionalization in Cultural Persistence', ch. 4 in W. W. Powell and P. J. DiMaggio (eds), *The New Institutionalism in Organizational Analysis* (London: University of Chicago Press).

Zukin, S. and P. DiMaggio (1990) 'Introduction', in S. Zukin and P. DiMaggio (eds), *Structures of Capital: The Social Organization of the Economy* (Cambridge University Press).

Zukin, S. and P. DiMaggio (eds) (1990) *Structures of Capital: The Social Organization of the Economy* (Cambridge University Press).

Name index

Abrams, Philip 60
Ackroyd, S. 221, 222
Akerlof, George A. 55, 56, 223
Alchian, Armen A. 11, 66–67, 73
Alchian, A. and H. Demsetz 71, 78,
    120–2, 126, 132, 136, 139, 160, 170
Alchian, A. and S. Woodward 88
Allen, Vic L. 221, 224
Alvesson, M. 195
Anderson, B. L. and A. J. H. Latham 75
Aoki, M. 129
Armstrong, Peter 106, 187–8
Arrow, Kenneth 30, 31, 74, 91
Ashton, T. S. 147, 155
Axelrod, Robert 8, 10, 11, 12, 13, 19, 68,
    226

Babbage, Charles 118, 123, 139, 158
Baran, P. A. and P. M. Sweezy 77,
    113–14, 161, 189–92
Baritz, L. 113
Barnard, Chester 11, 81, 85
Barney, Jay B. 52, 69, 76, 89
Barney, J. B. and W. G. Ouchi 89
Baron, J. N. and M. T. Hannan 51–2, 62
Bartlett, R. 49, 132, 135–6
Barzel, Yoram 121, 125
Bauer, M. and E. Cohen 124–5
Bauman, Z. 179
Baumol, William 16
Becker, Gary 49, 52–3, 85
Bell, D. 161
Bellinger, W. K. and G. S. Bergsten 141,
    223
Bendix, Reinhard 155, 156, 160
Benton, Ted 42, 65
Berg, Maxine 115, 119, 141, 147, 150,
    151–5, 158, 160, 229

Berger, Peter and Thomas
    Luckmann 83, 87, 97
Berle, Adolfe A. and Gardiner C.
    Means 15, 163–5, 166–7, 169, 181,
    184, 209, 229
Bernstein, Eduard 163
Biddle, J. E. 69
Block, F. 76
Bornschier, V. and H. Stamm 211–14
Bottomore, Tom 112, 161, 163, 229
Boulding, Kenneth E. 39, 40, 42, 64, 65,
    79
Bowles, Samuel 76, 114–15, 119, 132,
    134, 136–7, 139
Bowles, S. and H. Gintis 91, 98–9
Bradach, Jeffrey and Robert Eccles 74–5
Bradby, B. 134
Braendgaard, A. 125
Braudel, Fernand 60
Braverman, Harry 112–14, 139–40, 147,
    157–8, 160, 192, 228
Brubaker, R. 179
Bryan, R. 213
Buchanan, A. 91, 95
Buckley, Peter and M. Casson 55, 211
Burawoy, Michael 115, 140, 156, 192
Burkett, P. 106, 188
Burnham, James 15, 163, 165–7, 173, 181,
    192–3
Burrell, Gibson 112, 225
Burrell, G. and G. Morgan 219–20
Burt, R. 67, 75
Butler, Richard 144
Bythell, Duncan 153, 160

Cable, John R. 204, 215
Callinicos, Alex 42, 60, 63, 64–5, 96–7,
    133, 142

252

Subject index

258

and industrialisation 153, 155, 160
models and 51 (Figure 3.2), **55–61**, 68, 79, 99, 115
narrative 52, 57–8
homeworking 153
holding company (H-form) 202–3, 205 (Table 8.1)
human nature 26–8, 55, 59, 83, 95–7, 123, 142
human needs 54, 101, 102–3, 107
humanism 96–7, 101, 102–3, 106, 151–2
radical 219–20
humanistic economics 54

ideology 50, 53, 65, 76, 151–2, 158, 178
incentives 11
see also monitoring
individual(s) 2, 9, 17
actors 50, 85, 94
choice 61–3, 101
psychology 116
individualism 151–2
Industrial Revolution, the 1, 3, 147, **150–7**, 160, 159, 160, 197, 229
information 18, 19, 20–1, 26, 40, 43, 56, 128
information technology 159
innovation(s) 50, 148–9, 154, 201
efficiency and 100
theory of 98–100
see also organisational innovation *and* technological innovation
inside contracting 148, 157
institution(s) 22, 24, 29, 60, 70, 80, 82–3, 84, 85, 86, 88, 98, 99, 100, 101, 188, 214, 215, 216, 225
capitalist 23, 73, 82, 85, 87, 88, 90, 97–8, 106, 139, 176–7, 217
coercion from 106
firms as 66
markets as 71, 87
optimal 93
organisations and **82–9**, 104
institutional framework 29, 57, 59, 84 (Figure 4.1), 87, 89, 101, 105, 217
institutionalisation 82–3, 85
institutionalism 65, 68, 82, 98, 147, 159
in economic history 38, 68
in economics 22–6, 58, 65, 82, 163
in organisation theory 82, 83, 85–7, 228
in sociology 82, 83, 86

see also neoinstitutional economics *and* new institutional economics
interlocking directorates 75, 187
isomorphism, of organisations 87
invention 141
theory of 198
see also innovation *and* technology
investment 54, 149, 183
asset-specific 27

Japan 88, 210

labour and labour power 131–7, 142–3
labour market 140, 156, 167, 183, 187
core and periphery 212
internal 122
managerial 171
labour movements 214–15
labour process 112, 115–16, 124, 134–5, 139, 140, 147, 157–8, 187–8, 191, 192–3, 209–10, 215, 228
labour theory of value 132–5, 187
laissez-faire 35, 38, 50, 76–7, 174, 176
law and economics 33, 52, 54, 72, 163
leadership
charismatic 177–9
official and unofficial 138
and supervision 143–4
legitimacy 1, 3, 42, 76–7
left wing 76
liberal, behavioural science as 76
lighthouses, in economics 34

Machiavellianism 102
management 3, 14, 15, 16, 25, 32, 41, 58, 72, 78–9, 80, 85, 88, 126, 138, 139, 142, 144, 166, 171–4, 177, 180, 181–3, 188, 189, 195, 197, 198, 209
of labour 157, 187–8, 210
motivation 16, 169
selection and succession 172–3
separation from investment 172
see also hierarchy
management buy-outs and buy-ins 174, 183
managerial discretion 16, 17, 169–72, 174–6, 177, 183, 194, 209
managerial economics 169–70
managerial revolution 3, 15, 165–7, 189, 192–3
managerial theory of the firm 7, **15–16**, 165, 169, 226